全国14家国家特色服务出口基地（语言服务

新文科语言服务学术文库

游戏本地化
面向全球数字娱乐产业的翻译

Game Localization
**Translating for the Global Digital
Entertainment Industry**

Minako O'Hagan　●　著
Carmen Mangiron

王华树　●　导读

上海外语教育出版社

外教社　SHANGHAI FOREIGN LANGUAGE EDUCATION PRESS

图书在版编目（CIP）数据

游戏本地化：面向全球数字娱乐产业的翻译：汉文、英文 /（新西兰）美奈子·奥哈根（Minako O'Hagan），（西）卡门·曼吉龙（Carmen Mangiron）著；王华树导读. —上海：上海外语教育出版社，2024
（新文科语言服务学术文库 / 王立非总主编）
ISBN 978-7-5446-7891-9

Ⅰ.①游…　Ⅱ.①美…②卡…③王…　Ⅲ.①游戏—英语—翻译—研究　Ⅳ.①G898

中国国家版本馆CIP数据核字（2023）第171854号

Original edition *Game Localization: Translating for the global digital entertainment industry* by Minako O'Hagan and Carmen Mangiron.
© 2013 John Benjamins Publishing Company, Amsterdam/Philadelphia
Reprinted by permission for distribution in the People's Republic of China only.
本书由约翰·本杰明出版社授权上海外语教育出版社有限公司出版。
仅供在中华人民共和国境内销售。
图字：09-2022-0943号

出版发行：**上海外语教育出版社**
（上海外国语大学内）　邮编：200083
电　　话：021-65425300 (总机)
电子邮箱：bookinfo@sflep.com.cn
网　　址：http://www.sflep.com
责任编辑：王晓宇

印　　刷：上海宝山译文印刷厂有限公司
开　　本：635×965　1/16　印张 25　字数 492 千字
版　　次：2024 年 1 月第 1 版　2024 年 1 月第 1 次印刷

书　　号：ISBN 978-7-5446-7891-9
定　　价：82.00 元

本版图书如有印装质量问题，可向本社调换
质量服务热线：4008-213-263

"新文科语言服务学术文库" 专家委员会

张天伟（北京外国语大学）

张法连（中国政法大学）

张慧玉（浙江大学）

罗慧芳（当代中国与世界研究院）

屈哨兵（广州大学）

赵蓉晖（上海外国语大学）

胡开宝（上海外国语大学）

俞敬松（北京大学）

祝朝伟（四川外国语大学）

贺永中（美国蒙特雷高等国际研究院）

高明乐（北京语言大学）

高　霄（华北电力大学）

郭英剑（中国人民大学）

黄立波（西安外国语大学）

曹　进（西北师范大学）

崔启亮（对外经济贸易大学）

蒙永业（北京悦尔信息技术有限公司）

蔡基刚（复旦大学）

穆　雷（广东外语外贸大学）

Arle Lommel（美国 CSA 咨询公司）

前　言

　　语言服务兴起于 20 世纪 90 年代的欧美。2010 年，中国翻译协会首次正式在我国提出"语言服务"的概念。语言服务指以语言能力为核心，以促进跨语言、跨文化交流为目标，提供语际信息转化服务和产品，以及相关研究咨询、技术研发、工具应用、资产管理、教育培训等专业化服务的现代服务业。

　　根据统计，尽管全球经济不断受到挑战，但语言服务行业依然保持增长，2022 年，全球语言服务产值突破 600 亿美元。我国对外开放、中外人文交流和"一带一路"建设不断促进我国的语言服务市场增长。2022 年，我国的翻译公司和各类型的语言服务企业总计超过 42 万家，总产值突破 554 亿元人民币。语言服务发展的同时也带来巨大的人才需求。

　　语言服务教育在我国是一个新生事物，目标是培养行业需要的口笔译、语言技术和项目管理人才。2007 年，我国开办翻译硕士专业学位教育，为语言服务行业培养翻译人才。近年来，部分高校通过开设研究方向或独立设置二级学科点等方式，招收本地化管理、技术传播、翻译项目管理、医学语言服务、国际语言服务研究生，培养"语言＋技术""语言＋专业"和"语言＋管理"的复合型和应用型人才。部分高校成立了语言服务研究院所、应急语言服务基地（中心），召开语言服务论坛，编写语言服务研究报告等。2020 年，中国英汉语比较研究会批准成立语言服务研究专业委员会，出版《语言服务研究》集刊。2022 年，商务部、教育部、中国外文局等部委批准成立特色语言服务出口基地，国家发改委和商务部批准语言服务进入鼓励外商投资产业目录。以上举措有力地促进了语言服务的发展。

　　为了帮助广大师生了解国外语言服务领域学术研究和行业发展动态，满足高校语言服务学科建设、人才培养、教学科研的需要，上海外语教育出版社组织专家精心策划了"新文科语言服务学术文库"，从国外原版引进多种语言服务学术著作。本文库涵盖翻译及语言服务的职业技能和企业管理两个方面，包括翻译教学、技术文档写作、本地化技术、质量管理、服务管理、众包翻译管理等，体系完整，内容丰富，值得推荐。同时，为了方便读者理解重点，文库各书还专门配有中文导读和推荐阅读书目。

　　本文库可用作研究生教材，也适合语言服务行业人士和对语言服务感兴趣的广大社会读者作为参考书使用。希望文库的出版能为我国的语言服务发展贡献一份力量。

专家委员会主任

王立非

2023 年 12 月

导　读

一、本领域概述

本地化行业标准协会（Localization Industry Standards Association，LISA）将"本地化"定义为对产品或服务进行加工以满足不同市场需求的过程。中国翻译协会将"本地化"定义为"将一个产品按特定国家/地区或语言市场的需要进行调整，使之满足特定市场上的用户对语言和文化的特殊要求的生产活动"（中国翻译协会，2011）。从处理类型来看，本地化的主要对象是软件、在线帮助文档、网站、多媒体、电子游戏、移动应用等多元化的内容或与之相关的服务；从技术手段来看，本地化可以分解成一系列的工程技术活动（如软件编译、本地化翻译、本地化软件构建、本地化软件测试等），每项活动都需要使用特定的技术工具；从本地化主体来看，本地化需要高度专业化的团队构成，通常设有翻译、质量保证专员、工程师、测试专员、排版专员、项目经理等细分工种，各自需掌握专门的技术，各个工种在本地化实施过程中协同发挥作用。

游戏本地化是本地化行业的一个主要分支，是软件本地化、视听翻译（audiovisual translation，AVT）和多模态翻译（multimodal translation）的交叉领域。Mangiron（2012：3）将"游戏本地化"定义为"在技术、语言和文化层面调整游戏，目的是使本地化游戏在其他地域更好地销售，涉及复杂的技术、语言、文化、法律和营销过程"。游戏本地化是对游戏产品、游戏服务等的文本、程序、用户交互界面、配音等内容在不同国家、不同市场下的翻译、改编或译创，以增强目标市场玩家感知度和沉浸感的过程。

随着游戏全球化的范围与程度不断加深，市场需求更为多元化，跨平台、多语言、短生命周期逐渐成为游戏行业的主流模式。从国内外市场的用户需求来看，游戏消费群体不仅规模在逐年扩大，还呈现更加年轻化、潮流化和个性化的趋势，对游戏本地化提出了更高的要求。

　　在技术驱动之下，游戏开发过程日益敏捷化，游戏的分类越来越细致，本地化工作也越来越复杂。从规模和研发平台来看，目前游戏更多分为端游（PC 或主机游戏）和手游（手机游戏）；从类型特征来看，游戏可以分为动作类游戏、冒险游戏、赛车/竞赛游戏、益智游戏、角色扮演游戏、模拟游戏、运动游戏、战略游戏。从过程来看，游戏本地化项目可以分为启动阶段、计划阶段、执行阶段、监控阶段和收尾阶段；从对象来看，本地化涉及多种文本（菜单、对话框、帮助、消息、道具、技能、剧情、叙事、评论、衍生书籍等）、图片（人物、标识、海报、地图等）、视频（过场动画、广告、衍生动画和电影等）等；从特征来看，本地化整体呈现多语言、多变量、多模态、非线性、标签化、短句化、去语境化、动态化等特点，而且不同类型需要借助不同的工具进行综合处理。

　　游戏本地化是翻译研究中的一个新兴领域，在 20 世纪 90 年代后期开始引起人们的注意。Mangiron（2017）将游戏本地化研究大致分为四个阶段：1999—2005 年属于早期阶段，行业专业人士 Chandler 于2005 年出版了国际上第一本关于游戏本地化的专著，配有大量的案例以及对开发商和发行商的采访，提供了实用的游戏本地化指南；2006年被认为是游戏本地化研究最为重要的转折点，该年有六篇具有代表性的学术论文发表；2007—2012 年被视为发展阶段，其间 *Tradumàtica*期刊 2007 年首次推出了游戏本地化专栏，随后几年研究者日益增多，2010 年举办了首次游戏本地化与游戏无障碍学术会议，几年后翻译研究期刊 *TRANS: Revista de Traductología* 也推出了游戏本地化专栏；2013 年至今被认为是巩固和发展阶段，其间学界出版了四本重要的论著，也出现了更多期刊论文和博士学位论文。

　　近年来，随着融媒体技术和软件技术的突飞猛进，游戏本地化研究受到了更广泛的关注。在游戏本地化领域，一些学者的研究产出较为丰富，这些学者包括 Carmen Mangiron、Miguel Á. Bernal-Merino、Minako O'Hagan、Silvia Pettini、Laura Mejías-Climent、Xiaochun Zhang 等，主要集中在西班牙、英国、爱尔兰、意大利等欧洲国家。这些学者深耕游戏本地化这一领域，不仅有卓越的研究成果，甚至还建立了研究团队，共同推动游戏本地化研究的发展。

　　Minako O'Hagan 和 Carmen Mangiron 是游戏本地化领域中两位极为知名的国际学者。她们合作出版了两部颇具影响力的著作：一本是 *Game Localization: Translating for the Global Digital Entertainment Industry*（即本篇导读所涉著作）；另外一本是 *Fun for All: Translation and Accessibility Practices in Video Games*，该书从多个角度探索了游戏无障碍和游戏本地化的新兴领域。Miguel Á. Bernal-Merino 出版了两本著作：*Translation and Localisation in Video Games: Making Entertainment Software Global* 和 *Media Across Borders: Localizing TV, Film and Video Games*，前者旨在通过跨学科视角研究游戏本地化这一娱乐业的全球现象，详述了当前行业实践的规范以及游戏本地化的整个过程，而后者则对媒体内容如何适应不同市场和跨文化边界的多种方式进行了创新性研究。Silvia Pettini 基于其博士毕业论文出版了一本专著——*The Translation of Realia and Irrealia in Game Localization*，主要探讨了视频游戏的真实性或虚构性程度对其语言维度的影响，研究了翻译现实和非现实所面临的挑战与策略。Laura Mejías-Climent 出版的专著 *Enhancing Video Game Localization Through Dubbing* 从独特的配音视角探讨了在视频游戏本地化中视听翻译的热门话题。Frazer Heritage 出版的一本基于他的博士论文的专著——*Language, Gender and Videogames*，研究了语料库语言技术如何应用于视频游戏文本的分析，尤其是探究语言如何用于构建奇幻视频游戏中的性别表征。Xiaochun Zhang（张晓春）是游戏本地化领域的杰出学者，曾在维也纳大学获得翻译学博士学位，现在在英国的伦敦大学学院工作，长期专注于游戏本地化的研究和教学。她在期刊 The Journal of Internationalization and Localization 合作编辑了一期特刊——《游戏本地化》，收录了六篇文章，这些文章集中探讨了游戏本地化的各个方面。

　　游戏本地化研究涉及翻译学、语言学、人类学、社会学、心理学、叙事学、符号学、美学、计算机科学等多个学科。学者们通常采用跨学科的研究视角，如结合游戏研究、文化研究、多媒体研究等，来探讨游戏本地化的市场、实践操作流程与规范、技术、术语管理、文化、教学培训、性别研究、粉丝本地化、配音等。在最初阶段，学界对游戏本地化的研究侧重于语言、文化和技术等方面。然而，随着研究的深入，主题变得越来越丰富和多元化，从各种视角探讨游戏本地化的策略，如字幕、音轨、文本类型、语料库（翻译记忆库），以及对文字、句法和风格的选择等。展望未来，游戏本地化的研究前景极为广阔。除了已经研究较多的本地化翻译策略、文化复杂性与技术之外，接受性、创译、多模态翻译、众包翻译与协作、项目管理、审查制度、游戏无障碍、培训和教学、敏捷本地化、数据驱动、AI 交互式本地化等，都是未来研究的热门话题。在这些话题中，游戏本地化的培训与教学是连接未来教育和行业的关键环节，它涉及游戏本地化专业教育和人才资源建设，以及语言服务行业人才结构等重大问题，尤其值得深入研究。

二、作者简介

　　本书由两位游戏本地化研究的资深学者 Minako O'Hagan 和 Carmen Mangiron 共同编写。Minako O'Hagan 曾在都柏林城市大学（Dublin City University）工作超过十年，自 2016 年起在新西兰奥克兰大学（University of Auckland）任教，并担任翻译研究学科带头人。本书由她与 Carmen Mangiron 合著，是首部从翻译角度研究视频游戏本地化的专著。自 2016 年以来，她一直致力于探索翻译与技术之间的关系，出版了 *The Routledge Handbook of Translation and Technology*。她曾担任期刊 *Perspectives* 的联合主编（2007—2020 年）和期刊 *Translation Spaces* 的副主编（2010—2020 年），目前是 *The Journal of Internationalization and Localization* 的联合编辑（2020 年至今）。Carmen Mangiron 为巴塞罗那自治大学（Universitat Autònoma de Barcelona，UAB）的讲师，也是视听翻译硕士学位项目的主任。她拥有 UAB 的笔译和口译本科学位、都柏林大学（University College Dublin）的盎格鲁－爱尔兰文学和戏剧硕士学位及 UAB 的哲学博士学位。她在巴塞罗那自治大学和维克大学（Universitat de Vic）等多所大学教授游戏本地化，研究兴趣包括视频翻译、游戏本地化及游戏无障碍。她是将 PlayStation《最终幻想》游戏系列翻译成西班牙语的本地化团队成员之一。她拥有丰富的翻译经验，擅长软件和游戏本地化，在国际期刊上发表了大量的本地化研究成果，并参与过多个研究项目。

三、内容概要

（一）本书概况

视频游戏是不断发展的数字娱乐行业的一部分，游戏本地化已成为服务国际市场的关键。随着游戏本地化的迅速发展，翻译学界对游戏本地化的研究兴趣日益增长。本书较为系统地介绍了这一蓬勃发展的新兴领域，是本地化领域具有重要影响力的代表性著作。本书尝试在当代翻译理论的指导下，将游戏本地化概念化，力图弥合学术理论与游戏本地化商业实践之间存在的鸿沟，满足行业对翻译人员和本地化人员进行系统培训的实际需求，同时激发学界对该领域的研究兴趣。

游戏本地化是一个动态的领域，由现代技术驱动、市场需求引导，并受游戏流行话语的影响。技术进步使本地化和视听翻译的边界不断受到侵蚀，日益模糊并正在慢慢融合。视频游戏本地化的实践就是最好的例证，这种现象值得学界更多关注。在网络时代，读者可以从互联网上找到很多游戏本地化的学习资源，但是网上信息的质量参差不齐，要在浩瀚的互联网中找到可靠的专业资料，并高效地解决本地化培训相关的问题并非易事。而且，长期以来，与游戏本地化相关的话题在学术界通常处在翻译研究的边缘。所以，作者认为有必要撰写一部研究游戏本地化的著作，让更多人了解游戏本地化的全貌，包括游戏本地化发展概况，它如何成为全球视频游戏行业的重要组成部分，以及如何更好地教授学生这种技术和艺术，以期将游戏本地化引入翻译学的主流话语体系之中。

本书借鉴了大量游戏研究和翻译研究领域的文献，以视频游戏本地化为出发点，分析技术发展对本地化翻译的影响，探索翻译研究的新视野。作者使用本地化实践中具有代表性的数十个示例，同时结合大量的图表和插图，共同呈现这个极具发展潜力领域的主要话题，努力在翻译理论和翻译实践层面保持平衡，以便与学界和业界的目标读者建立关联。作者希望促进翻译领域与游戏领域更多的交叉研究，推动游戏本地化最佳实践的发展。本书主要的读者对象是翻译学者、游戏本地化从业者及游戏研究领域对数字娱乐产业的国际化感兴趣的人员。

（二）各章概要

本书内容主体分为引言、七个章节以及结论。

引言明确了游戏本地化研究这一新兴子领域的基本理念，探讨了研究现状，解释了游戏行业在全球市场需求驱动下对翻译的内在需求。除了提供有关该领域的文献综述外，作者还阐释了本书论证的方法论。

第一章　视频游戏和翻译

本章主要介绍了视频游戏本地化的历史发展、视频游戏的定义、关键术语、种类及产业结构等问题，为读者深入理解和研究游戏本地化奠定基础。作者系统梳理了视频游戏本地化的简史，将其划分为五个阶段，分别是早期、成长期、发展期、成熟期和进阶期；详细地介绍了关键概念和术语，讨论现代视频游戏的构成；探讨了游戏本地化产业链上的各方——硬件制造商、游戏开发商、游戏本地化提供商、游戏发行商、游戏分销商、游戏零售商以及消费者——之间的关系。在强调大型游戏公司对本地化施加的控制和操纵时，作者基于Lefevere（1992）的"赞助"（patronage）概念来描述游戏本地化需要理解的背景及游戏本地化实施的条件限制。

第二章　本地化范式：本地化与翻译

本章聚焦实践和理论中的本地化，首先讨论了在翻译研究和本地化行业中与翻译概念相关的本地化的概念，由本地化实践引出国际化概念。其次，作者从语言、技术和文化维度来分析本地化过程，讨论了软件本地化中的文化问题及计算机工具在本地化过程中所发挥的重要作用。再次，作者讲述了本地化在翻译研究中的地位及其发展过程，以游戏本地化为例，讨论了本地化与翻译的关系。最后，强调人的能动性在本地化过程中的重要性。

第三章　游戏本地化中的实践维度

本章详细描述了当前 GILT［即 globalization（全球化）、internationalization（国际化）、localization（本地化）和 translation（翻译）］框架下的本地化实践，重点分析了本地化过程中的不同参与方，包括本地化服务提供商和游戏公司内部的本地化团队。作者详细讨论了两种主要的本地化模式——外包模式和内部模式，以及两种发行模式——市面上同时发布游戏的原始版本和本地化版本（sim-ship）或在原始游戏出版后再发布本地化版本，对本地化的不同影响；然后，根据本地化语言资源的全面性，阐述了不同级别的本地化，即未本地化（零本地化）、包装和手册（box and docs）本地化、部分本地化以及完全本地化。此外，本章还研究了可进行本地化的不同游戏素材，例如游戏内嵌文本、音频和影视素材以及印刷制品，并根据素材类型匹配了适当的本地化策略。最后，作者详细介绍了当前用于游戏本地化的各类工具，并列举了具体的应用实例。

第四章　翻译电子游戏：翻译创作的新视野

本章主要讨论游戏文本引起的翻译问题，着重讨论相关的翻译方法及策略，同时从游戏媒体的维度切入，在分析游戏文本翻译时借鉴了源于目的论的功能主义框架。作者从翻译问题的核心出发，提出现代游戏文本分类，根据文本功能和典型的翻译限制条件，确定翻译的优先级和重点；从语用问题及语际问题两个方面进行案例分析，阐述适宜的游戏本地化翻译策略；通过分析国际知名数字娱乐产品供应商Square Enix 公司的成功案例，分析该公司在游戏本地化方面的创新做法；最后的讨论部分将游戏本地化视为再创造，强调游戏本地化中译者的主体性作用，阐释游戏本地化为翻译研究开拓了新的视野。

第五章　游戏生产的文化语境：数字时代的赞助和改写

本章首先介绍了游戏文化的形成，对比了占主导地位的美、日游戏文化，挖掘了游戏文化差异背后的深层文化原因，并介绍了以此为基础的评级制度和审查制度，分析了游戏本地化过程中必须关注的文化适应问题，强调文化本地化的重要性。最后，作者从翻译即"改写"（rewriting）的角度，对应国家、游戏公司和译者三个主体，分别探讨了游戏本地化中的文化、权力和操控问题。

第六章　培训游戏本地化人员的教学问题

本章主要讨论与游戏本地化领域的专业翻译人员和本地化人员的培训有关的教学问题。尽管社会上对游戏本地化的需求很大，而且世界各地的大学都有大量的游戏本地化翻译培训项目，但教学问题在很大程度上被忽视了。本章首先阐明游戏本地化为一种新兴的专业翻译活动，分析了其发展所面临的市场需求和行业发展状况，重点关注行业的需求。从社会建构主义翻译教学法的视角，详细讨论了游戏本地化人才培养过程中的三个关键环节：翻译能力模型的确定、课程设置和教学质量评估。同时，本章分析了当前教学面临的问题和困境，如真实教学案例材料的匮乏，学术界与行业界在人才培养方面的脱节等。

最后，作者结合职业与学术翻译教育方法的争论，简要讨论了将游戏本地化引入大学课程的问题。本章着眼游戏本地化专业人才的培养，全面分析了目前面临的问题和困境，为改进游戏本地化教学提供了理论依据和实践建议。

第七章　翻译研究中的游戏本地化研究

本章探讨了一些游戏本地化领域出现的关键翻译研究课题。作者从游戏用户的视角出发，探讨了诸如无障碍游戏、粉丝翻译和用户共创等新兴研究路径。本章进一步分析了自然语言处理技术与游戏技术的结合及其对游戏翻译的影响。最后作者简要讨论了研究方法的问题，重点关注基于生物特征的用户研究，如此类研究在游戏接受度分析中的价值，这些研究开始引起学者和业内人士的关注。

结论部分总结了游戏本地化的关键问题及其在翻译研究领域中的地位和贡献。

本书的目标读者是翻译研究人员，旨在提高学界对这一新兴领域的认识，以期将游戏本地化引入翻译学科的主流话语体系中。作者希望能够为培训人员提供一个完整的指南，帮助他们设计游戏本地化课程内容，并根据学习者的水平或兴趣以及课程的总体目标和预期进行调整。作者希望这本书中关于电子游戏翻译研究的观点能够惠及广大读者，促进翻译研究和游戏研究之间的融合研究。

王华树

参考文献

Hevia, C. M. 2007. Video Games Localisation: Posing New Challenges to the Translator. *Perspectives* 14(4): 306–323.

Mangiron, C. 2012. The Localisation of Japanese Video Games: Striking the Right Balance. *The Journal of Internationalization and Localization* 2(1): 1–20.

Mangiron, C. 2017. Research in Game Localisation: An Overview. *The Journal of Internationalization and Localization* 4(2)：74–99.

Lefevere, A. 1992. *Translation, Rewriting and the Manipulation of Literary Frame*. London and New York: Routledge.

LISA. 2007. *The Globalization Industry Primer*. Switzerland: Localizaton Industry Standards Association.

中国翻译协会. 2011. 中国语言服务行业规范：本地化业务基本术语. 北京：中国翻译协会.

推荐阅读

Bernal-Merino, M. Á. 2014. *Translation and Localisation in Video Games: Making Entertainment Software Global*. New York: Routledge.

Chandler, H. 2004. *The Game Localization Handbook*. Boston: Charles River Media.

Chaume, F. 2020. Dubbing. In Ł. Bogucki & M. Deckert (eds.), *The Palgrave Handbook of Audiovisual Translation and Media Accessibility*. Basingstoke: Palgrave Macmillan.

Mangiron, C. 2012. The Localisation of Japanese Video Games: Striking the Right Balance. *The Journal of Internationalization and Localization* 2(1): 1–20.

Mangiron, C. 2017. Research in Game Localisation: An Overview. *The Journal of Internationalization and Localization* 4(2): 74–99.

O'Hagan, M. 2022. Indirect Translation in Game Localization as a Method of Global Circulation of Digital Artefacts: A Socio-Economic Perspective. *Target* 34(3): 441–464.

崔启亮、胡一鸣. 2010. 翻译与本地化工程技术实践. 北京：北京大学出版社.

王华树主编. 2019. 计算机辅助翻译概论. 北京：知识产权出版社.

王华树主编. 2019. 翻译技术 100 问. 北京：科学出版社.

王华树. 2023. 翻译技术研究. 北京：外语教学与研究出版社.

约翰·罗蒂里耶. 2019. 应用程序本地化. 王华树译. 北京：知识产权出版社.

Game Localization

Translating for the global digital
entertainment industry

Minako O'Hagan
Dublin City University

Carmen Mangiron
Universitat Autònoma de Barcelona

Table of contents

Figures and tables

Acknowledgements

We are indebted to many people for being able to complete this book. The project started in 2009 with an ambition to turn in the manuscript the following year, which, of course, was far too optimistic. Accordingly, we are most appreciative of the patience of our publisher John Benjamins in tolerating the long delay. We only hope that the lapsed time is compensated for by more mature conceptualization of the topic. Keeping up with the rapid pace of change occurring in the game industry was admittedly challenging and indeed not possible without the help of a number of informants both in the industry and among our gamer students. Therese Lundin and Brendan Tinnelly, who read the whole manuscript and provided us with extremely useful comments, are our former students and avid gamers with a wealth of industry experience. We are grateful to Therese and Brendan for their suggestions of additional game examples which would have been out of reach of our knowledge alone. Given the book's twin focus on games themselves and their translators, we are most grateful to the veteran Japanese game and literary translator Alexander O. Smith for agreeing to read the manuscript and, above all, for sharing his thoughts behind translation decisions he has made. This provided us with a great insight into the creative process unique to translating games. Our thanks also extend to the other side of the Atlantic to Stephen Mandiberg, a scholar researching game localization, for his detailed comments from the perspective of Communication Studies.

Writing a book in one way or another relies on support from the people who surround the authors and we would like to thank our respective colleagues in Dublin and Barcelona. In particular, we would like to express our gratitude to Prof. Jenny Williams who, at the time we started, was the Director of the Centre for Translation and Textual Studies at Dublin City University (DCU). Without her constant encouragement this book could not have been finished. Jenny also read the manuscript and gave us invaluable comments from a translation scholar's perspective. We are also grateful to Dr. Aphra Kerr and Dr. Colm Caffrey for their comments on our earlier draft and to Ms Magdalena Dombek who gave us assistance with the time-consuming formatting and checking of references. Our thanks are due to Dr. Stephen Doherty whose keen eye spotted highly relevant examples including a customised poster that appeared in Dublin in June 2011 (see

Figure 0.1). Last but not least we wish to express our gratitude to our respective families for their quiet perseverance in letting us get on with writing without too much protest.

The authors wish to acknowledge with gratitude the Publication Assistance Fund provided by DCU, enabling us to engage Dr. John Kearns for his editing and proofreading assistance. Every effort has been made to fulfil requirements with regard to reproducing copyright material. We are most grateful to Nintendo, Sony Computer Entertainment, Square Enix, the DO-IT Program at the University of Washington, Inclusive Technology Ltd., OneOrigin Instruments, and OneSwitch.org.uk for their permission for the use of images and also supplying us with high resolution original images where appropriate. Finally it is our hope, over and above the question of academic merit of our work, that we did not end up taking away the very sense of fun epitomised by games and that this publication will encourage more translators and scholars to start playing and translating games – and theorizing game localization!

Minako O'Hagan and Carmen Mangiron
Dublin and Barcelona, December 2012

About this book

Aim and structure of the book

In response to the growing research interest in game localization within and also outside Translation Studies, this book aims to inform readers about this specialized and dynamic professional area of practice. As well as seeking to stimulate further scholarly interest in this sub-domain, the book attempts to address the practical need of the industry for the systematic training of translators and localizers, informed by contemporary translation theories. The game localization sector will benefit from well-structured resources for the training of new translators who may have competence in areas other than games, and thus need a specific focus on the gaming domain. Game localization is a dynamic field that is driven by technology, led by market demands and influenced by popular discourses on games, and therefore most up-to-date information sources can be found online, as we note in our literature review. However, it is time-consuming to find reliable online resources directly addressing pertinent issues relevant to specific training needs. Similarly, it is still relatively rare to come across the topic analyzed in the context of Translation Studies. In our observation, translation and localization issues have been peripheral in game-related topics addressed in academia, for example in Game Studies, and are often treated casually in an ad hoc rather than a systematic manner. This has led us to conclude that there is a need for a reliable and coherent monograph dedicated to conceptualizing this new sub-domain.

To this end, this book is designed to serve as an introduction to the topic of game localization in Translation Studies. We have endeavoured to keep a balance between theoretical and practical dimensions in order to be relevant to target readers both in academia and in the industry. One of our ultimate goals is to use the subject of game localization as a launch pad from which to explore new horizons of Translation Studies by addressing the impact on translation of technological developments. In particular, localization and audiovisual translation (AVT) face a constant erosion of their mutual boundaries due to technological advances, although they are currently treated as separate domains within Translation Studies. Positioned as intermediaries in the globalization of an increasing range of digital media, these two domains are converging, as exemplified by the practice of game localization. Finally, building on the importance of the links between the industry and academia already stressed by researchers working in other areas of translation, we hope to promote more traffic from research into practice to allow the development of best game localization practices that are informed by solid research and a theoretical basis.

With these objectives in mind, the book is divided into an introduction, seven main chapters and a conclusion.

Following the Prologue, the Introduction establishes the rationale behind studying this new sub-domain and describes the current state of the research. It explains the inherent need for translation in the game industry, which is driven by global market demands. As well as providing a broad literature survey of the field, we explain our main approach in developing the arguments presented in this book.

Chapter 1, "The Video Game and Translation", sets the scene by providing a brief history of video game localization, linking it to the technological evolution of games. We then establish key concepts and terms to discuss what constitutes a modern video game and also the structure of the video game industry. Rather than providing a comprehensive analysis, we have presented this from the perspective of our Translation Studies interests in game localization. In highlighting the control and manipulation by large game companies exerting their influence on localization, we apply the concept of "patronage" based on Lefevere (1992) to depict the context within which game localization needs to be understood and the constraints under which it is carried out.

Chapter 2, "The Localization Paradigm: Localization versus Translation", examines the concept of localization in relation to that of translation as viewed in Translation Studies and in the localization industry. This provides a starting point for our attempt to locate game localization in Translation Studies in theoretical terms, drawing chiefly on the conceptualizations of localization presented by Pym (2004, 2010) and Cronin (2003).

Chapter 3, "Game Localization: A Practical Dimension", homes in on the practical aspects of game localization, explaining the process and the tools which facilitate it, with the aim of giving an overview of the different localization models and approaches used today in the industry. Drawing on Chandler (2005) and Chandler and Deming (2012), this chapter describes the current localization practice, highlighting pertinent issues which characterize localization of games as opposed to other productivity software applications.

Chapter 4, "Translating Video Games: New Vistas for Transcreation", focuses on video games as source texts (STs) for translation, proposing a working taxonomy of game texts. Treating games as narrative as well as ludic objects, we analyze game texts according to the different text types present, with different functions assigned to them, in a single game. This in turn is linked to translation priorities and strategies in relation to translation skopos (purpose) from a functionalist perspective. These allow us to make some observations on translation norms, albeit on the basis of limited examples. Game localization is then conceptualized, with a focus on the translator and the translator's agency, leading to the introduction of the concept of "transcreation".

Chapter 5, "Cultural Contexts of Game Production: Patronage and Rewriting in the Digital Age", addresses broader cultural contexts specific to the video game phenomenon, forming game cultures. In reference to the cultural turn in Translation Studies, we direct our attention to the role of influential game companies in their provision of a modern form of patronage, both embracing and dictating the rewriting of games in the process of localization. As part of the discussion of rewriting we refer to a perspective of video games as transmedia, bringing games and films closer together with implications for translation.

Chapter 6, "Pedagogical Issues in Training Game Localizers", addresses issues pertinent to training needs in game localization in the context of pedagogical concerns in Translation Studies. We discuss game localizer competence with reference to the needs of the industry and also touch on professional issues of working as game translators and localizers.

Chapter 7, "Game Localization Research in Translation Studies", explores a number of key translation research topics that are emerging from the field of game localization. Focusing on users of localized games, we highlight new research avenues such as game accessibility, fan translation and user co-creation. The chapter further considers the growing impact of game technology in conjunction with developments in Natural Language Processing, with implications for the translation of games. We briefly address the question of research methodologies, focusing on biometrics-based user studies which are beginning to attract the attention of scholars and those in the industry as a new direction for reception research.

The "Conclusion" summarizes the key issues which emerged from our conceptualization of game localization and its position in and contribution to the field of Translation Studies.

Target readers

Our core target readership is the translation research community, among whom we wish to raise awareness of this new sub-domain and also to test our conceptualization and applications of translation theories, with a view to introducing game localization into the mainstream discourse in the discipline. The motivation behind writing this book comes from the authors' collective experience over the last ten years in researching and discussing this topic at translation and localization seminars and conferences, as well as teaching the subject across Europe, the US, and Asia. Our overwhelming impression has been that even the least game-literate translation students or scholars can find something intriguing about the subject, while practitioners who have actually been involved in localizing games, as well as those who are enthusiastic gamers, are keen to find out more about the theories behind translation and localization that have a special relevance to their work or pastime activities. Furthermore, we have sensed a strong interest in the topic from trainers of translators and localizers, who wish to integrate it into their teaching. More recently, an increasing number of institutions have introduced this topic as part of their translator or localizer training, though such courses are still few and far between and are delivered to varying degrees of coverage and in different formats. We hope to provide a coherent guide for trainers to help determine what their courses could usefully cover, depending on the level or the interest of the learners and the overall objectives and learning outcomes of the programmes in which game localization would be taught.

Finally, it is also our hope that the Translation Studies perspectives on video games expressed in this book will reach and benefit readers from the dynamic field of Game Studies, whose insights we have found to be essential to explaining some key dimensions in video game localization. In tackling a video game as a relatively new object of translation, we aim to promote increased cross-fertilization between Translation Studies and Game Studies, while also adding to the growing discussion taking place within the Translation Studies community on non-Western perspectives on translation, with regard to STs in a language other than English, particularly involving Asian languages and their cultural contexts.

Conventions used in this book

Introducing this relatively new and specialized subject of game localization in Translation Studies, we have endeavoured to make the content accessible to readers with little knowledge of video games. To this end, terms that are specific to video games and the game industry are marked in bold on their first appearance in each chapter and included in the glossary in the following pages. In addition to a fuller explanation in the glossary, we have made an effort to include a brief explanation in the main text to make specialized concepts more reader-friendly. Regarding the games we mention in the text, we italicize the titles and indicate the year of first release. We also provide a gameography, at the end of the book, listing each game cited in our work with its first year of release and the name of the publisher. Any use of Japanese words is followed by their English translations in square brackets.

Glossary

AAA games: Games with high production budgets, usually referring to flagship titles involving substantial resources.

Advertainment: Portmanteau of the words *advertising* and *entertainment*. In the context of video games, *advertainment* belongs to the category of serious games and refers to video games used for marketing purposes.

Alternate Reality Game (ARG): Designed to be played alternately online and in the real world, a game based on an interactive narrative woven collectively by participants interacting with game characters often in the context of real environments of the participants rather than fictional worlds.

Art assets: Graphics and images, including text, in the original version that must be adapted for the localized versions, such as maps, signs, and notices. Also see **textual graphics** or **graphic text**.

Assets: Different components of a video game.

Audio assets: Components in a game that contains audio files, such as the voiceover files, songs, and audio tutorials.

Avatar: Graphical representation of a player's character on screen in virtual worlds, including games and online communities. The word originates from Sanskrit, where it refers to a Hindu deity represented in physical form.

Beta testing: Testing carried out by volunteer users before the final version of a software program or video game is released. Also known as "public beta testing". See also **Beta version**.

Beta version: Version of a video game that comes before gold, used to obtain users' feedback and put the finishing touches to a game before it goes into production.

Bloodpatch: Unofficial software program that unlocks the blood and violence levels present in the original version of a game that has been censored. Bloodpatches are often used by German players to circumvent the modifications applied to German versions of games to comply with the *Unterhaltungssoftware SelbstKontrolle* (USK) regulations.

Boss: A particularly challenging computer-controlled adversary which the player must defeat, usually at the end of a level, in order to progress and win the game.

Build: A particular version of a game during its production, which typically involves several versions such as the Alpha build and the Beta build, each with significant change before being finalized as the Gold Master. See also **Localization build**, **Beta version** and **Gold master**.

Bug report: Report in which game testers provide notes on errors, faults, or failures they have found in a video game during development.

Casual games: Quick and simple games increasingly played on mobile devices and tablet computers. People who occasionally play games may be called "casual gamers".

Chatbot / chatterbot: A type of computer program known as a "bot" designed to simulate conversations with humans via auditory or textual modes.

Cheat / cheat code: Keyboard or game pad button sequence that gives the player an advantage in the game, such as giving the character infinite health, skipping a level, or becoming invincible.

Cinematic assets / cinematics: Pre-rendered or in-game movies included in a game with multiple functions including providing information about the game story. They are the only non-active gameplay elements in a game.

Compliance testing: Quality assurance (QA) testing that checks for adherence to the technical requirements checklist and the localization standards of each platform hardware manufacturer, as well as legal, ethical, and ratings-related criteria.

Concatenation: Operation consisting of pulling together different strings dynamically at run time to form new strings. This is done according to a pre-set formula on the basis of a particular defined action by the user.

Console games: Games designed to be played in a dedicated computer system specifically designed for playing games. A console can be connected to a TV set or include its own display in the case of handheld consoles.

Console platform holders: Company that manufactures game systems, namely Nintendo, Sony, and Microsoft.

Conversation tree: See Dialogue tree.

Cosmetic testing: QA testing of software that focuses on formal aspects, such as the lack of text spaces, presence of extra spaces, typographical errors, truncations, etc.

Cross-platform games / titles: Games that are released for a range of different consoles and platforms. Also known as "multi-platform games/titles".

Cut-scenes: Cinematic sequence in a video game over which the player usually has no control, used to advance the plot, present character development, and provide background information, clues, etc. Also see **Cinematic assets/cinematics**.

Dating sims: Japanese sub-genre of simulation games, the gameplay of which consists of achieving a romantic relationship after choosing a partner amongst several characters.

Dialogue tree: A gameplay mechanics feature to allow the players to choose their reaction to a given situation usually from a finite list of sentences. It is commonly used in game genres such as adventure games and role-playing games. Also known as a "conversation tree".

Easter egg: Hidden features or alternative narrative paths secretly embedded in a game by the designer as a surprise treat for the players.

Edutainment: Portmanteau of the terms "education" and "entertainment" used to refer to games developed for educational as well as entertainment purposes. More recently referred to as "serious games".

Emergence / emergent gameplay: Game dynamics arising out of unanticipated ways that the player may play the game vis-à-vis the game designer's original intention.

End User Licensing Agreement (EULA): Legal contract between the manufacturer (and / or the author) and the end user of a software application including video games. The EULA details how the software can and cannot be used and any restrictions that the manufacturer imposes.

Exclusive titles: Video games that are only released to be played on a particular platform as opposed to cross- or multi-platform games.

First party developers: Game developing companies that are owned by publishers.

First Person Shooter (FPS): Video game genre designed for the player to shoot the enemy, played in the first-person point of view and set either over-the-shoulder of the player's avatar or through the firing range of the given weapon.

First playable alpha: First functional and usable version of a localized game.

Force-feedback: Type of haptic (or tactile) response given by the game system to the user, such as a jolt on the controller in a racing game. Also see **Haptic feedback.**

Format holders: Hardware manufacturers of consoles. Also konwn as **Platform holders.**

Full localization: Localization that involves translating all assets of a video game, including the audio files and cinematic scenes, which are re-voiced.

Functionality testing: QA testing designed to detect the errors or bugs in any type of software product that may prevent it from working properly, for example, when a game or business application freezes, crashes, or does not respond as it should.

Game accessibility: The playability of a game with regard to different physical conditions of users, including blindness, deafness, or various mobility limitations.

Game developers: Companies that specialise in the creation and development of games.

Game engine: A system designed for the creation of a game world by providing developers with a software framework, allowing game experiences to be divided into discrete chapters.

Game genre: Classification to distinguish between different types of games according to their style of gameplay.

Game metrics: Numerical data obtained from the game software about player behaviour that can be incorporated into game design or used to perform reception and usability research.

Gameplay: Experience of playing a game with reference to the whole host of processes associated with active playing.

Game publishers: Game companies that provide the finance and support for game development and publish games.

Gold master: Final candidate version of a game submitted to the platform holder for its approval. It is also called "**master up**" in Japan.

Graphic text: See under **Textual graphics**.

Grey (market) imports: Source language copies of games unofficially available in the target territories.

Haptic feedback: A force either in the form of resistance or vibrations, relating to or based on the sense of touch, simulated by a device usually through the game controller held by the player. Also see **Force-feedback**.

In-game text: All the text present in the user interface (UI) (menus, help messages, tutorials, system messages, etc.) of a game, as well as narrative and descriptive passages, and all dialogues that are not voiced-over and only appear in written form, such as conversations held with non-playable characters (NPC).

In-house model: Localization model in which the developer/publisher manages the localization process, which takes place in their premises.

Integration: Process by which localized assets are integrated back into the main body of the game (software), generating a playable version of the game, known as a "**build**".

Interactive publishers: Alternative name for video game publishers.

Levelling grind: Effort needed from the player to progress to a higher level in a game.

Linguistic testing: QA testing designed to detect errors or bugs of a linguistic nature in a game or other software applications, such as grammatical or typographic errors.

Locale: In the localization context it refers to a specific combination of geographic region, language, and character encoding. Game localization can be considered as the process of adjusting games to a particular locale.

Localization build: Executable version of a video game that is under development that is compiled for testing purposes. Also known as a "**build**".

Main mission: Primary quest or objective of a game or a level in a game, which must be achieved in order to continue or succeed in the game.

Massively Multiplayer Online Games (MMOGs): Video games that can be played online simultaneously by a large number of players.

Massively Multiplayer Online Role Playing Games (MMORPGs): Role playing games that can be played online simultaneously by a large number of players.

Mini-games: Short video game contained in another video game, the successful completion of which may or may not be required to complete the main mission.

Modding or mods: Shortened form for "modification" in reference to alterations made to commercial games by highly technically-oriented gamers in order to introduce a range of new elements using the existing **game engines**.

MUDs (Multi-User Dungeons): Multi-player real-time virtual world, usually text-based, where players can read or view descriptions of rooms, objects, actions etc. performed in the virtual world. Players interact with each other and the world by typing commands.

Multi-platform games: Games released simultaneously on several platforms. See **Cross-platform games**.

Multi-player games: Games in which more than one person can play in the same game world simultaneously.

Non-playable or non-player characters (NPCs): Minor or secondary characters in a game that cannot be controlled by the player and are controlled by the **game engine**.

One-switch games: Games that can be played by pressing just one single button.

Onscreen text (OST): Synonym of **in-game text**.

Outsourcing: Localization model involving commissioning localization to an external specialised vendor.

Party games: Video game genre involving an offline multi-player mode in which several players are present in the same physical space to play a game together.

Patch: Piece of software designed to fix or update software applications including games.

Partial localization: Localization that involves translating all text-only assets but preserving the original soundtrack of a game, i.e. without re-voicing in the target language.

Placeholder: Symbol used in software applications that will later be replaced by a string, depending on the conditions met.

Platform: Electronic system used to play a video game.

Platform holder: Hardware manufacturer of consoles. Also known as "format holder". See also **Console platform holders**.

Port/porting: Enabling games designed for one system or platform to be playable on another. This process may affect aspects of localization because of technical elements that are platform-dependent. The use of the same **game engine** makes the process of porting easier.

Post-gold localization: Localization process that starts once the original version of a game is completed or quasi-completed.

Pre-master: Final test version of a game prior to the finalisation of the **Release candidate**.

Printed materials: All those elements in print that accompany a game, such as the instruction manual and the packaging.

Readme file: File containing useful information for the user about a PC game or productivity software application, such as the minimum computer specs.

Region lockout: Practice consisting of designing a console or DVD player so that it is only compatible with games or DVDs designed for that particular geographical region.

Region-free: Refers to a DVD or a video game that can be played in any system in any part of the world, without encoding restrictions.

Release candidate (RC): Final version of a console game that is submitted to the platform holder for approval and in order to obtain a license to release the game for that particular platform.

Retro-games: Classic games that were released in the early days of the game industry, which can be played in their original systems or on modern hardware via emulation or more recent compilations.

Role Playing Game (RPG): Video game genre in which players assume the role of a character in a fictional game world setting and embark on a lengthy quest. Characters typically develop as the game progresses.

ROM-hacking: Process of modifying the ROM data (Read-Only Memory therefore not meant to be changed by the user) of a video game to alter various aspects of the game, including the game's language as in the process of fan translation.

Sandbox game: Game designed as a non-linear, open world, where the player can roam freely and has great freedom of action.

Second-party developers: Game companies that are hired by a publisher to work on a particular game concept.

Serious games: Games designed for various educational purposes in contexts other than those of pure entertainment.

Shooter: Game genre in which the player sees the action through the eyes of their avatar with the goal of firing their arsenal.

Side-quests: Tasks and missions included in video games that deviate from the main mission and plot and are often not required to complete the game. Term often used synonymously with "side-missions".

Sim-ship: Abbreviation of "simultaneous shipment": a localization model consisting of releasing an original game and the localized versions at the same time in different territories.

Single-player: Game designed to be played by one person at a time.

Social games: Games usually provided as part of social networking sites such as Facebook and played as a means of social interaction.

Stealth action game: Video game genre which challenges players to avoid alerting the enemy and remain undetected while they perform their mission.

Stock Keeping Unit (SKU): Unique number or code used to identify a product that can be purchased, for data management and for tracking of a product's availability or inventory.

Stitch: Short audio file containing utterances made by game characters such as sports commentators, segmented and recorded separately, so that they can be used at different stages of the game

Stitching: The process of combining different stitches in a game in order to create audio-based sentences.

Submission process: Submitting a copy of the release candidate of a console game to the platform holder in order to obtain their approval and a license to release that game in that given platform.

System messages: Information, questions, warnings, etc. provided by the game system to the users, for example, to ask them if they want to save the game.

Territory: Geographical location for which a game is released.

Textual graphics: Text assets which appear within a graphic, forming part of **art assets**. Also known as "graphic text".

Third party developers: Independent game companies who work on their own game projects and submit them to a platform holder to obtain a license to release their games for a particular platform.

Tooltip: Graphical user interface element that provides information when the cursor is placed over it.

Truncation: Text strings that appear incomplete or cut off on the screen due to space restrictions.

Tutorial: In-game instructions that have the objective of teaching players how to play a game, illustrating the main actions and commands they will have to perform and describing the game rules.

User interface (UI): Set of commands or menus through which a user communicates with a software application.

Variable: Parameter in a software string that can be replaced by different values when certain conditions are met.

Voiceover (VO): In the context of video games, VO refers to the voicing and re-voicing of the dialogues in a game by actors.

Walkthrough: Detailed guide to all the steps to be followed in order to advance in a game, as well as a description of the different levels and actions required to complete it. There are official versions and those created unofficially by fans, both produced to take the player through the game.

Prologue

The posters (Figure 0.1) displayed throughout the city of Dublin during June 2011 were advertising the release of the PlayStation® 3 (PS3) game *inFAMOUS2* (2011), featuring Dublin's O'Connell Street, with its landmark Spire and the historic GPO (General Post Office). Given that the game is set in an imaginary rather than a real place (as is noted by the disclaimer in small print on the top left corner) the poster was clearly aimed at promoting the product in Ireland. This form of targeted customization[1] gives a flavour of the wide range of transformation the game industry routinely applies to marketing games beyond localizing the game itself. Furthermore the poster's somewhat provocative advertising copy *"Save Humanity. If You Feel Like It."* is an apt reminder of the often controversial nature of video games despite their elevation to a massively popular form of entertainment. Similarly, the age rating shown on the top right corner of the poster reflects the general public's guarded attitude towards this contemporary pastime. Such characteristics of modern video games make game localization a divisive topic of interest, yet to be explored in Translation Studies.

Combining technology and entertainment, the video game industry is among the most vibrant high-tech businesses of the 21st century (Chatfield 2010) and one in which translation plays a key role because of the global nature of the industry. The birth of commercial video games some forty years ago led to the emergence of the entirely new field of game translation, arising from the industry's own unique needs. Game localization is intricately intertwined with global business and marketing operations, enabling video games to cross complex socio-cultural and linguistic borders and to reach players in an increasing range of geographical locations which are divided into **territories**. North America (NA) forms the most significant territory for video games, with the US being the single largest market, followed by Japan with estimated game software sales in 2011 of USD 9.25 billion (EUR 7.05 billion) and JPY 318.5 billion (EUR 2.95 billion) respectively (CESA 2012, 183). While the game industry may not always acknowledge the full

---

1. A similar approach is also sometimes used in the film industry for animated films. For example, Pixar produces highly tailored posters for certain regions to promote their film releases.

Figure 0.1 Poster of *inFAMOUS2*[2] © 2011 Sony Computer Entertainment America LLC. Developed by Sucker Punch Productions LLC

significance and implications of translation, the fact remains that the industry needs translation and relies on it for the continuing globalization of the sector.

In order to illustrate the scale of the market and some of the complexities of modern video games, we take the example of the *Call of Duty* game franchise (2003–). Published by Activision Blizzard, these games represent flagship titles with a heavy investment in production, referred to as "**AAA games**" in the industry. The *Modern Warfare* and *Black Ops* series in the *Call of Duty* franchise have World War II and Cold War themes respectively, and belong to the genre of **shooter** games which have become particularly popular in the US and main European markets. *Call of Duty: Modern Warfare 3* (2011) sold 9.3 million copies within 24 hours of the release, exceeding the figures for its previous instalment, *Modern Warfare 2* (2009), at 6 million, and *Black Ops* (2010) at 7 million (Parker 2011). According to Activision Blizzard,[3] the most recent instalment, *Call of Duty:*

---

2.   Original image kindly supplied by Sony Computer Entertainment Inc.

3.   http://investor.activision.com/releasedetail.cfm?ReleaseID=725026.

Black Ops II (2012), has again broken a record, reaching the USD1 billion mark in global retail receipts 15 days after its release in November 2012. The company points out that cumulative sales figures to date of the *Call of Duty* franchise have exceeded the box office receipts of the two most successful movie franchises of all time: *Harry Potter* and *Star Wars*.

Call of Duty games are released on several platforms (and are therefore referred to as "**multi-platform**" or "**cross-platform games**") such as Xbox 360, PS3, PC and Wii. The choice of **platforms** has technical implications for game localization (see Chapter 3), and also relates to power struggles between **platform holders**, i.e. Nintendo, Sony, and Microsoft (see Introduction, Chapters 1 and 5) each trying to dominate the market. The 2011 US game retail chart[4] shows *Modern Warfare 3* twice – in first position for the Xbox 360 version and in fourth for the PS3. This strategy contrasts with **exclusive titles**, such as the *inFAMOUS* series tied to PS3, which link a particular game to a particular platform in order to increase platform loyalty. There are certain market preferences in terms of the choice of consoles and also game genres as well as player mode (see Introduction). While the US and Europe are moving more to consoles such as Xbox 360 the mass audience in the Japanese market is reportedly playing on handhelds such as Nintendo 3DS and PlayStation Portable (Winterhalter 2011). Similarly, while *Modern Warfare 3* topped the 2011 best-selling charts in the US and most major markets in Europe (CESA 2012, 164–179), it did not rate among the top 30 games in the 2011 Japanese ranking[5] despite two editions being released specifically for the Japanese market; a subtitled version and a dubbed version were produced in separate instalments (i.e. two **SKUs**). The 2012 ranking (see Table 1.5) also indicates similar results for *Call of Duty: Black Ops II* (2012) which topped the US and the UK charts but not the Japanese ranking. This suggests that elaborate localization attempts are sometimes still not enough to engage certain markets, as has generally been the case with the *Call of Duty* series in Japan, where American-type shooter games have so far failed to appeal to the majority of gamers (Kohler 2010). These market preferences form a relevant wider context in which to understand the forces behind game localization.

Call of Duty: Modern Warfare 3 was localized from English into seven languages (French, Italian, German, Spanish, Polish, Russian, and Japanese) and released simultaneously in a release model called "simultaneous shipment" (**simship**) to cover as many key territories as possible without delay. The game's target language (TL) selection reflects an increasing trend for the localization of games

---

4.   VGchartz data available at http://www.vgchartz.com/yearly/2011/USA/.

5.   *Famitsu* data available at http://geimin.net/da/db/2011_ne_fa/index.php.

into the languages of emerging markets such as Russian and Polish as well as Asian languages, in addition to the standard localization TLs referred to as FIGS, for French, Italian, German, and Spanish (plus English for Japanese-origin games). For example, *World of Warcraft* (2004–) is released in FIGS, Russian, Polish, and Brazilian Portuguese, as well as Chinese (both simplified and traditional) and Korean. The broadening of the range of the TLs for game localization indicates how gaming and game culture are spreading, although not always in a uniform manner. The Japanese edition of the *Call of Duty* franchise was published by Square Enix, a major Japanese game developer and publisher (see our case study in 4.3), who also undertook localization. Following *Warfare 2*, which was revoiced in Japanese and also with intralingual Japanese subtitles, *Warfare 3* was released as two editions; in November 2011 with subtitles with the original English voice track and in December 2011 as a fully revoiced version in Japanese.

Square Enix's role as third-party publisher of the Japanese editions reflects the company strategy of aiming to promote foreign titles which have historically not been popular in the Japanese market (Ashcraft 2012). The abbreviated Japanese term 洋ゲー [Western games] is often derogatory in connotation and illustrates the general perception of foreign games in Japan as inferior products (Kohler 2010). While efforts to raise the profile of the latter are being made by localizing the latest games for the Japanese market, the Japanese editions of *Call of Duty* have reportedly met with a mixed reception, with frequent criticisms of the quality of translation, including that of the latest Japanese instalment of *Black Ops II* (Ashcraft ibid.). Given the historical limited demand for game localization into Japanese, this could point towards an insufficient pool of translators working into Japanese, and also a lack of competence in the shooter genre in particular, with its military terminology, as war themed games tend to be less popular in Japan.

Major AAA games such as the *Call of Duty* series, developed with a massive budget similar to blockbuster Hollywood films, demonstrate the sophistication of the latest gaming technology and the increasingly cinematic techniques employed as suggested by the term "cinematic games" (Newman 2009). This is resulting in the need for well-crafted scripts in game production, calling for specialized game writers (ibid., xi), and this is also reflected in the creation of a separate editing process that is sometimes incorporated into the translation process to polish the translated game text (see Chapter 4). For example, it is relevant to note that a novelist was appointed specifically to edit the Japanese subtitles of *Warfare 3* in a clear attempt by the publisher to improve the final quality of the Japanese translation text.[6] The cinematic trend is further accentuated by the increasing reliance

---

6. The information was revealed at the 2011 Tokyo Game Show http://game.watch.impress. co.jp/docs/news/20110918_478647.html.

on the use of audio technology in games and the resultant audio localization (see Chapter 3). Game reviews[7] often make special reference to well executed environmental sounds and voice acting, as in the case of *inFAMOUS 2* (2011). This game involved a new voice casting reflecting the altered character design from the first instalment of the series. The change of voice in the new game was immediately picked up on by gamers familiar with the first instalment, highlighting the impact of the role of voice acting on user reception. The significance of the use of audio is further highlighted by the distinction made between **full localization** and **partial localization**, according to whether voiced dialogue is dubbed or only subtitled in the TL. In contrast with the terminology used in Audiovisual Translation (AVT), dubbing is commonly referred to as **voiceover (VO)** in the game industry. VO was initially employed only in AAA titles, but is rapidly becoming a key translation mode of wider application as more developers and publishers seek full localization (Schliem 2012, 8).

Today's games, especially AAA titles, contain within a single game various text types and **assets** and tend to provide extensive scope for the application of different translation techniques. This serves to highlight translator's agency in a new context quite different from the situation in other types of translation. Not only because of their interactivity but owing to the very nature of modern games as affective media (Juul 2005, 7) with technology used to enhance the engagement of the player at a deeper level, game localization is opening up new vistas for translation, with the need to extend the appeal to the end user beyond functionality alone. In reference to the fully localized Spanish version of *inFAMOUS2* (2011) aimed for Latin America, the Senior Director of Product Development at Sony Computer Entertainment America (SCEA) declared:

> Localization is a multi-faceted process that also presents an opportunity to enhance the story and experience for a very particular audience. We will be tailoring the rich, graphic adventure of *inFAMOUS2* just for the Latin America region by creating new elements that will allow gamers to discover this open world in a relevant and unique way.
> (Connie Booth quoted in an SCEA Press Release 29 July 2010[8])

This statement encapsulates what contemporary game localization for major titles seeks to achieve – it is the player "experience" that is to be conveyed to and tailored for the target territory. In this exercise the original game is treated as a malleable base rather than a finished product that is set in stone. Where this is

---

7. See an IGN review of *inFAMOUS2* at http://ie.ps3.ign.com/articles/117/1170808p1.html.

8. See http://ie.ps3.ign.com/articles/110/1109326p1.html.

the goal, the localization task is more akin to recreation than reproduction, which we link to the concepts of "rewriting" (Lefevere 1992) and "transcreation" from Translation Studies perspectives. In this book we argue that game localization is highlighting the translator's creativity, thereby celebrating rather than restraining the variety inherent in human translation.

Intended to provide a glimpse into modern video games and game localization, this brief prologue has introduced a few of the common concepts related to the field to give a taste of what will be discussed in this book. In so doing, we hoped to indicate the specialized nature of video games and in turn the intricacies involved in the work of localizers and translators who bring to life imagined game worlds for gamers from different linguistic and cultural backgrounds. In this book we aim to conceptualize from a Translation Studies perspective the practice of game localization, an industrial process which is rapidly evolving in the growing business of digital entertainment. Game localization adds to the challenge of contemporary translation in the brave new (virtual) world and we believe it will open up new directions for translation research.

Introduction

Rationale

The objective of this book is to introduce the specialized translation sub-domain known as "game localization" (Chandler 2005) within the more established domain of localization. In commercial contexts, game localization refers to all the many and varied processes involved in transforming game software developed in one country into a form suitable for sale in target territories, according to a new set of user environments with specific linguistic, cultural, and technical implications. While sharing some commonality with the existing practice of software localization, developed initially for productivity applications and later extending to include the localization of websites, game localization presents added dimensions arising from the interactive nature of games. Furthermore, unlike business software applications, games are designed as affective media where "the player feels emotionally attached to the outcome" (Juul 2005, 23). The contrast between business applications as productivity software and games as non-productivity software for leisure well defines the different end purposes served by the respective products. While certain games known as **"serious games"** have distinctly didactic intentions, game software in general is first and foremost designed for entertainment, with its main concern being to immerse the user in the game world. Player engagements occur on an electronic platform, thereby creating a cybernetic relationship between the player and the game system (Giddings and Kennedy 2006, 142–143): the player responds to stimuli provided by the game system, which in turn is activated to provide a new set of stimuli. In addition, modern video games take full advantage of multimedia and multimodality to engage the player. In this way, games are highly sophisticated technological products.

Furthermore, games are not only technological artefacts but also cultural products, and these characteristics give rise to new translation issues which we address in this book. Video games are considered to represent symbolic cultural meanings and affect society at large through their production and consumption (Crawford and Rutter 2006, 148). Highlighting the significant impact of game technology on culture, media critic Tom Chatfield (2010, xii) argues that video games exemplify "our culture's increasing augmentation and amplification by technology". Once associated more with cult followings of hardcore gamers, video games have today become pervasive in society at large with their increasingly broad entertainment appeal. According to the 2011 statistics for the US complied by the Entertainment Software Association (ESA 2012, 2), 72% of American households play digital games. This figure may be compared with the 2009 National Gamers Survey conducted by the market research company TNS and gameindustry.com which indicated that 83% and 73% respectively of the US and the UK populations played video games (cited in Chatfield 2010, xiii). While these high figures need to be treated with caution, the latter survey[9] claims that these statistics are based on data representative of the population of those 8 years of age and older in each of the six countries covered. At the very least these results tend to indicate that digital gaming is becoming a widespread pastime in society today.

Modern video games are indeed increasingly enjoyed by all age groups (ESA 2012), and their benefits are also beginning to be recognized in terms of education (Gee 2003) and health (Reinecke 2009). For example, the aforementioned game genre known as "serious games", designed for educational purposes in contexts other than those of pure entertainment, have become the object of intense research interest (see Chapter 1). At the same time, the controversial nature of games can hardly be ignored, with frequent claims highlighting the detrimental impact of games in terms of sociality, creativity, productivity, and literacy, forming the "continued currency of the stereotypes in the popular media" (Newman 2008, 5–7). Furthermore, as Newman (ibid., 7) observes, "the research agenda in this field [video games] is largely set by the popular discourse", indicating the extent to which the wider public view influences the focus of academic studies. For example, issues of game censorship, ratings, and related localization strategies can be swayed by public opinion. The high-profile 1993 public hearings on the impact of video game violence on minors in the US, involving senators Joseph Lieberman and Herb Kohl (Kent 2001, 466–480), serves as an early example to illustrate the public sensitivity to video games. As we discuss in more detail in Chapter 5 in relation to the "cultural turn" in Translation Studies, games as cultural products extend their sphere of influence to wider society with an increasing segment of the population being exposed to games through casual gaming or as pure observers in close proximity to players. This will likely lead to more scrutiny of games on the basis of broader cultural and social values by those who are not necessarily truly familiar with the game medium (Edwards 2012, 22). Localized games will

---

9.   The source indicates that the figures are based on a survey with more than 36,000 respondents in total from the US, the UK, Germany, France, the Netherland and Belgium. In reference to "video games" in this survey, all forms of platforms were included, namely game portals, consoles, mobile phones, MMOs and PCs.

therefore not be immune from social, economic, and ideological views and sometimes even political positions in the receiving country.

While game localization can be considered a sub-area of the better known practice of software localization, there are a number of distinctive differences between translating productivity software and translating video games. For example, games are increasingly becoming movie-like, as evidenced in the term "cinematic games" (Newman 2009). One technological trend is to make certain genres of mainstream **console games** more like movies, where pre-rendered movie sequences (**cut-scenes**) and real-time interactive playing scenes seamlessly merge through the use of high definition graphics and dialogues voiced by professional actors. The cinematic features employed in games have in turn led to the use of subtitling and dubbing of dialogues in game localization, though not necessarily following the more established norms of Audiovisual Translation (AVT). Also notable is the fact that the increasing availability of broadband Internet connections has given rise to an explosion in online games, called **Massively Multiplayer Online Games (MMOGs)** such as *World of Warcraft* (2004–) despite possible security risks. In May 2011, Sony made worldwide headlines with a major security breach when hackers attacked its PlayStation Network for online games, stealing the personal information of more than 100 million customers (Baker 2011). A similar security concern was raised with Microsoft Xbox Live in 2007. Despite such known risks inherent in online gaming, over 9 million players worldwide are still virtually traversing the playground of *World of Warcraft* as of August 2012 although the number has dropped from the previous level of 12 million (Kohler 2012). In fact the fastest growing online games today are the **casual** and **social game** genres (Chatfield 2010, 33), which target a wider audience than hardcore gamers with games playable, for example, on social networks such as Facebook. Unlike mainstream console games, these games cost very little, if anything, and are usually light-weight applications that can be played in short bursts on mobile phones or tablets as well as on desktop PCs. Yet they can be just as engaging and popular as console games. For example, Zynga's *FarmVille* (2009), became the fastest growing game in history, with 83 million monthly active users in 2010 (Takahashi 2011) while *Pet Society* (2008) and *Restaurant City* (2008), developed by PlayFish, had over 200 million active users globally in 2009 (Chatfield 2010, 34). From major console games which may provide over 100 hours of playtime, to casual and social games, the landscape of modern games is complex and is couched in specific industry structures and practices. As the above brief overview indicates, the game industry is technology-driven and dynamic, with a far-reaching impact on culture and society.

In introducing the new domain of game localization to Translation Studies we consider that first and foremost it is the nature of video games that needs to be understood. Following McLuhan's (1967) assertion that "the medium is the message", any study of games, including game localization, calls for a wider understanding of the medium itself before the consideration of specific aspects of localization. Additionally, we also consider an understanding of the surrounding industrial context to be essential. To this end we examine the nature of this modern artefact through multiple lenses, chiefly according to our interest in Translation Studies, but also bringing together insights from the game industry and Game Studies. In so doing, we hope to see game localization enter mainstream Translation Studies discourse, further contributing to the current trend of enlarging the boundaries of the discipline (Tymoczko 2006).

Context

The rapid international development of the digital entertainment industry has often prompted comparison with the film industry in terms of scale (Raessens and Goldstein 2005, xii),[10] indicating their increasing ubiquity in today's society. There is a general consensus today that video games have become a global phenomenon, and indeed, this is the fundamental reason for game localization. It is localization which enables games developed mainly in the USA, Canada, the UK or Japan in English or Japanese, in the case of console games, to be distributed to a wide range of target markets in appropriate versions. Given the complex array of mechanisms of influence and control exercised by the game industry in the production of games and their international distribution, it is pertinent for researchers wishing to address this subject to develop a wider understanding of the industry and the market in which game localization practice is situated. As argued by Egenfeldt-Nielsen et al. (2008, 12) "academic research into games becomes more inclusive – and more valuable – when it shows an understanding of the market". This is particularly relevant to game localization research.

The industry practice commonly known as "software localization" came into existence in response to the need for mainly American-developed computer application software to go global during the 1980s. This meant the source content of localization was mainly written in English, often with American cultural

---

10. Flew and Humphreys (2008, 126) note that measures of game industry size often vary. Similarly, Kerr (2006b, 38) cautions against a superficial comparison between these two industries, since the revenue stream in the game industry can include different sources, ranging from hardware, software, related merchandise, etc.

Table 0.1 The total number of games of Japanese origin in the US top 100 titles vs. games of foreign origin in the Japanese top 100 titles between 2005 and 2011

	Japanese-origin games in the US	Foreign-origin games in Japan
2005	30	1
2006	35	0
2007	34	2
2008	35	1
2009	35	0
2010	26	3
2011	34	4

Source: http://www.vgchartz.com.

assumptions and conventions, as was evident in such references as the currency sign, zip codes or the use of icons familiar in the US culture. Localization norms, as observable mainly in productivity software, can therefore be considered to be generally based on the source language (SL) and cultural contexts of the US. In contrast, the origins of video games are largely divided between the US and Japan, with the main SLs for game localization, especially for console games, being English and Japanese. Relevant to translation issues is the fact that there is a well-recognized trade imbalance in Japan between the export of Japanese games and the import of foreign games, with exports being 80 times greater than imports in 2006 (O'Hagan 2006b, 242). The dominance in Japan of Japanese-made games rather than games of foreign origin can be assumed from the data between 2005 and 2011 in Table 0.1, which contrasts the number of games of Japanese origin in the US top 100 titles as compared with games of foreign origin in the Japanese top 100 titles. This gives an indication of the language directionality of translating games: while Japanese is predominantly a Target Language (TL) for productivity software, for games it is largely an SL. Indeed, the fact that Japanese is one of the major SLs distinguishes game localization from other areas of software localization and other entertainment sectors such as the film and music industries, which are dominated by products with English as the original language (with the exception of Japanese animation – referred to as "anime").

Industry sources indicate that games are localized to cover an increasing number of territories, involving languages beyond the standard FIGS (French, Italian, German, and Spanish) (see Chapter 3). For example, Sony Computer Entertainment Europe (SCEE) notes that with the opening of new territories, its parent company SCE's games are localized into between 10 and 16 different languages (Games Localization Round Table 2008; Ranyard and Wood 2009). While the general economic downturn may have dampened the growth in terms of the number of languages as suggested in the statistics in 2009 (Steussy 2010b),[11] the volume of text and complexity of projects have been climbing. For example, the localization of the Xbox 360 game *Fable II* (2008) entailed the translation of 420,000 words of text, leading to 3,000 hours of translation per language, while the audio files for dialogue exceeded 48,000 per language, involving 54 voice actors per language (Chandler and Deming 2012, 315). Given the increasing quantity of text and the non-linearity of different textual components, these localization jobs call for a well-designed workflow and robust project management, facilitated by the appropriate use of computer-based tools. These aspects, which are well recognized in the localization business (Esselink 2000), are as yet little known in Translation Studies, as game localization has until recently remained relatively unexplored by translation scholars. Indeed, the localization industry itself has only lately begun to embrace game localization: industry bodies such as the Localization Industry Standards Association (LISA)[12] and Localization World only relatively recently started to include game localization topics in their regular fora and conferences (see Table 0.2). A number of factors account for this rather late inclusion.

Firstly, some authors have pointed out that games in general have tended to be perceived as a trivial form of amusement or as not sufficiently respectable to merit serious attention both in the context of academic game research (e.g. Newman 2004) and also in business computing contexts. For example, for a long time game software products were not considered part of the computer software industry and were even excluded from industry statistics (Berry 2008, 66). Secondly, the controversial nature of video games, which were often linked with extreme violence in media reports, may have put them at a further remove from other more "respectable" business-oriented productivity software. For example, in the early 1990s video game manufacturers still did not have their own industry lobbying body. The Software Publishers Association (SPA) was dominated by publishers of business software applications and game publishers were marginalized and left feeling as if they were "the black sheep of the SPA community" (Kent 2001, 469). Because of this background, the game localization sector seems to have followed its own path, independent of the course taken by the mainstream localization industry with its focus mainly on productivity software. Today the situation has changed completely; modern video games form part of "personal lifestyle software" (Berry ibid.) and contribute significantly to this growth sector. Similarly, the 2009 Nielsen report *The State of the Video Gamer* (Nielsen 2009, 2) acknowledges

---

11. In his presentation at the LISA conference in Suzhou, China in June–July 2010, Edwin Steussy showed how the number of localized languages reduced in 2009.

12. Aiming to promote best localization practices through regular forum sessions and publications, LISA was established in 1990 and ended operations in early 2011.

the increased popularity of games as a form of entertainment and the fact that "game consoles have matured into multimedia hubs". Furthermore, as evident in the term "interactive publishing" commonly used in the industry, modern video games are interactive multimedia systems at the "forefront of many of the most significant innovations in new media" (Flew and Humphreys 2008, 126). As well as having strong links with the high-tech sector, the game industry has become closely associated with entertainment sectors such as the film and music industries, increasingly forming formal product tie-ins (see Chapter 1). As we discuss in coming chapters, the combination of technology dimensions and cultural implications makes video game localization a rich area of new translation research as well as practice.

Despite the high profile and the prevailing public discourse on video games, it was not until quite recently that information on the process of game localization began to become available beyond the immediate circles of those directly involved in localizing games. *The Game Localization Handbook* (Chandler 2005) was the first comprehensive publication to focus directly on the practice of game localization, with the second edition (Chandler and Deming 2012) further incorporating areas such as culturalization of game content, translation issues and localization tools. Written from a production-oriented perspective based on the authors' experience in the industry, both editions provide a detailed picture of what is involved in localizing video games from beginning to end from the perspective of producers and project managers. The inclusion of up-to-date relevant interviews with key industry players provides a valuable window into current practices in the game localization business. Whereas *The Game Localization Handbook* brought to light the practical dimension of localizing a video game, we aim to conceptualize game localization essentially as a translation phenomenon, analyzing it according to theoretical frameworks available in Translation Studies while also drawing on Game Studies as appropriate. Our goal is to locate the sub-domain of game localization within Translation Studies so as to reflect the current concerns in the discipline and highlight new research agenda.

With the above objective in mind, this book aims to inform readers about this specialized practice essentially from a Translation Studies perspective. We hope to show the ways in which game localization brings new dimensions to translation practices and concepts, arising from the fresh possibilities afforded by the convergence of computer and media technologies forming the so-called "new media" (Manovich 2001). It is our belief that this sub-domain provides a new direction for the future development of Translation Studies, resonating with Munday's observation that localization and globalization is "the most evident locus of contact between technology, translator identity and the postmodern world" in Translation Studies "causing an exciting re-evaluation of translation practice and theory"

(Munday 2012, 292). We argue that game localization introduces dimensions that challenge some of the current assumptions about translation, thus raising epistemic issues for the discipline. We believe that practitioners will also benefit from a deeper conceptualization of their daily tasks, prompting reflection on current practice as the basis for further improvements in the dynamically changing technological contexts that surround video games.

An overview of translation studies research trajectories in game localization

Despite existing since the 1980s, the practice of game localization went largely ignored in Translation Studies until the surge of interest that occurred in the middle of the first decade of the new millennium (see Chapter 2). For example, according to Translation Studies Abstracts Online, a database specializing in academic papers published in Translation Studies, fewer than 10 articles are to be found on the topic of game localization, all published between 2006 and 2012. As a broad-brush illustration of the locus of game localization research activities, the overview in Table 0.2 shows academic journals, monographs, chapters, and sections in edited volumes as well as translation-related trade magazines[13] and professional association newsletters that have published material on the topic of game localization. While the table also gives information on conferences at which related papers were presented, this data cannot be regarded as exhaustive, since conference proceedings are not always published or searchable online. Given the relative youth of this sub-domain in Translation Studies, we considered it relevant to pay attention to journal names and types of conferences accommodating the topic, which in turn will allow us to locate particular areas within Translation Studies that are associated with game localization. In view of the inherently interdisciplinary nature of game localization research and particularly its close ties with the industry, the table is not limited to purely academic sources and also includes those beyond Translation Studies. There are also increasing numbers of personal accounts and observations as well as official information published by game developers, localizers, reviewers, gamers, and fans (see Chapter 7). These are creating massive online resources in the form of game reviews, blogs, and fan discussion fora which may be linked to official game websites. These sources provide a rich collection of data for researchers, but their comprehensive analysis is beyond the scope of the present book.

---

13. We only include translation and localization trade magazines, mainly indicating special feature issues where several articles on game localization were published within one issue.

Table 0.2 Game localization topic coverage in publications and conferences with a main interest in translation and localization issues

Year	Academic journals (name of author/editor)	Monographs; edited volumes; dissertation[14] (name of author/editor)	Conferences (location)	Trade magazines; association newsletters (issue)
Pre-2001				*American Translators Association (ATA) Chronicle*
2001				*Language International*
2002	*Tradumàtica* (Scholand)			
2003				*Multilingual Computing and Technology*
2004	*Technical Communication* (Thayer and Kolko)		*Languages and the Media* (Berlin) *New Zealand Game Developers Conference (GDC)* (Dunedin)	*LISA Newsletter*
2005		*The Game Localization Handbook* (Chandler) Several sections in テレビゲーム解説論序説 [Towards a General Theory of Video Games] (Yahiro) Several sections in *Power-up* (Kohler) *Traducción y localización. Mercado, gestión y tecnologías* (Reineke [ed.])	*Media for All* (Barcelona) *Multidimensional Translation (MUTRA)* (Saarbrücken)	

14. The search was limited to PhD theses accessible via online databases. We used 'Index to Theses' which covers PhD theses completed at British and Irish universities, 'Dissertation Abstracts' to cover US counterparts, 'Theses Canada Portal' for Canadian theses, as well as 'Dart-Europe E-theses' to cover Central European countries, and 'ADT (Australasian Digital Theses) Program' for Australia and New Zealand. Lin (2006)* was the only doctoral dissertation found closely related to the topic, but this work was not presented in a Translation Studies framework. By comparison, it is difficult to capture Master's dissertations in any systematic and comprehensive manner, and thus they are not included in this table.

Table 0.2 (continued)

Year	Academic journals (name of author/editor)	Monographs; edited volumes; dissertation (name of author/editor)	Conferences (location)	Trade magazines; association newsletters (issue)
2006	*Game Studies* (Ng) *Journal of Specialised Translation (JOSTRANS)* (Bernal-Merino; Mangiron and O'Hagan) *Localization Focus: The International Journal of Localization* (Kehoe and Hickey) *New Media & Society* (Consalvo) *Perspectives: Studies in Translatology* (special issue on Japanese pop culture) (O'Hagan 2006b [ed.])	Two chapters (Dietz; Heimburg) in *Perspectives in Localization* (Dunne [ed.]) *Culture, Technology, Market, and Transnational Circulation of Cultural Products: The Glocalization of EA Digital Games in Chinese Taiwan* (Lin)*	*Languages and the Media* (Berlin) *New Research in Translation and Interpreting Studies Conference* (Tarragona) *Translation Technologies and Culture* (Portsmouth)	*MultiLingual* (December issue: feature articles on game localization)
2007	*Tradumàtica* (special issue on game localization) (Mangiron [ed.])	Sections in *Translation as a Profession* (Gouadec)	*Media for All* (Leiria) *Localization World* (Berlin, Seattle)	*The Linguist*
2008	*JOSTRANS* (Muñoz-Sánchez) *Localization Focus: The International Journal of Localization* (Bernal-Merino 2008b)	One chapter (Bernal-Merino 2008c) in *The Didactics of Audiovisual Translation* (Díaz Cintas [ed.])	GDC (San Francisco) *Languages and the Media* (Berlin) *Localization World* (Berlin, Madison) *Translation and Interpretation Conference of the Japan Association for Interpretation and Translation Studies* (Tokyo)	*ATA Newsletter (the Literary Division)* *MultiLingual* (October/November issue: feature articles on game localization)

Table 0.2 (continued)

Year	Academic journals (name of author/editor)	Monographs; edited volumes; dissertation (name of author/editor)	Conferences (location)	Trade magazines; association newsletters (issue)
2009	*Journal for Computer Game Culture* (Jayemanne) *Journal of Internationalization and Localization* (JIAL) (Muñoz-Sánchez; O'Hagan 2009b) JOSTRANS (Bernal-Merino; O'Hagan 2009a; Ranyard and Wood) *Traduction, Terminologie, Rédaction: Études sur le texte et ses transformations* (TTR) (special issue on translation in Japan) (O'Hagan 2009c)		*Digital Arts and Culture* (Irvine) *eCoLoMedia Workshop* (Brussels) GDC (San Francisco) *LISA Forum Asia* (Taipei) *Localization World* (Berlin, Silicon Valley) *Media for All* (Antwerp)	
2010		One chapter (Mangiron) in *Translation, Humour and the Media* (Chiaro [ed.])	GDC (San Francisco) *5th Latin American International Congress of Translation and Interpreting* (Buenos Aires) *Localization World* (Berlin, Seattle) *LISA Forum Asia* (Suzhou) *Languages and the Media* (Berlin) ScreenIt (Bologna) *Translating Multimodality* (Portsmouth) *Translation Studies in the Japanese Context* (Kyoto) *Translation and Accessibility to Games and Virtual Worlds* (Barcelona)	

Table 0.2 (*continued*)

Year	Academic journals (name of author/editor)	Monographs; edited volumes; dissertation (name of author/editor)	Conferences (location)	Trade magazines; association newsletters (issue)
2011	*Games and Culture* (Carlson and Corliss) *JOSTRANS* (Granell) *TRANS. Revista de Traductología* (Special issue on games localization) (Bernal-Merino [ed.])	One chapter (Mangiron 2011b) in *Japón y la Península Ibérica* (Cid Lucas [ed.]) One chapter (Zhou) in *Translation and Localization Project Management* (Dunne and Dunne [eds.]) One chapter (O'Hagan 2011a) in *Translation Studies* (Sato-Rossberg [ed.])	*ATA Annual Conference* (Boston) *GDC* (San Francisco) *Localization World* (Barcelona) *Media for All* (London) *Points of View in Language and Culture: Audiovisual Translation* (Kraków) *Digital Games Research Association (DiGRA) Conference*	*MultiLingual* (September issue: feature articles on game localization)
2012	*Translation Spaces* (O'Hagan 2012c) *Perspectives Studies in Translatology* (Mangiron) *Monographs in Translation and Interpreting (MONTI)* (Fernández-Costales)	*The Game Localization Handbook 2nd* ed. (Chandler and Deming) One chapter (Mangiron) in *Audiovisual Translation and Media Accessibility at the Crossroads* (Remael et al. [eds.]) One chapter (O'Hagan 2012a) in *Translation and Translation Studies in the Japanese Context* (Sato-Rossberg and Wakabayashi [eds.]) One chapter (Schules) in *Dungeons, Dragons, and Digital Denizens: Digital Role-Playing Game* (Voorhees et al. [eds.])	*GDC* (San Francisco) *Translation and Accessibility to Games and Virtual Worlds* (Barcelona) *Localization World* (Seattle)	*MultiLingual* (June issue: feature articles on game localization)

The following discussion begins with an overview of general research trends with reference to conferences where related papers were presented and to trade magazine contributions, followed by key areas of research interests, mainly based on journal articles as listed in Table 0.2.

General trends in game localization research

The close links between this research area and industry practices is clearly illustrated by the fact that many of the authors who are publishing in this domain are or have been practitioners with first-hand experience in localizing games.[15] In particular, prior to 2005 nearly all articles on game localization appear to be practitioner contributions. For example, Frank Dietz, whose article "Beyond Pac-Man: Translating for the Computer Game Industry" in the *American Translators Association (ATA) Chronicle* appeared in 1999, has been translating games since the mid-1990s for the German market (Dietz 2008); the same is true of Michael Scholand (2002), whose contribution in the Spanish peer-reviewed journal *Tradumàtica*[16] highlighted the main features of game localization on the basis of his experience as a professional in the field. In 2001 the now defunct but once popular translation trade magazine *Language International* featured game localization as a new and different form of translation, which served to raise awareness within the translation community of what was then little known practice. A case-study article by Timiani Grant (2001) from the game developer/publisher Eidos Interactive was novel at the time, focusing on legal issues of age-rating regulations for video games and presenting Germany as a prime example of the imposition of stringent country-specific rules. This dimension still remains barely examined by translation scholars in any depth, despite the fact that censorship is a well explored topic in Translation Studies (e.g. Ní Chuilleanáin et al. [eds.] 2009). Filling the gap left by *Language International*, the magazine *MultiLingual* (formally *Multilingual Computing and Technology*) has been regularly reporting developments in the field of game localization, with special issues on games under "Industry Focus" features (see December 2006; October/November 2008; September 2011 and June 2012). These contributions cover a range of issues such as specific skills required for game translators (Chandler 2008a), issues of terminology (Bernal-Merino 2008a)

---

15. This experiential factor is in line with the reasoning given by Bryce and Rutter (2006, 2) for the recent surge in academic research into digital games as being due to "the entry of researchers who grew up in the Pong, Atari, NES and BBC Micro years into academia".

16. This is an online Spanish journal in Translation Studies which publishes articles in English, Spanish, and Catalan.

and Internet slang (Zhang 2010), cultural issues relating to geopolitical conflicts (Edwards 2008) as well as adapting humour in games (Fernández-Costales 2011). There has been an increasing level of interest in China (e.g. Zhang 2008, 2010, 2011) as a target market for localized games as well as in the Chinese development of online games (Zhang 2009), which raised the issue of Chinese as an SL and the source culture for localization. More recently featured topics include localization issues for games designed for learning (Brink 2012) and the concept of "gamification" (Carter 2012), which refers to the application of game-like mechanics designed to motivate and engage users of a product or service. The contributors are not only industry practitioners but also practitioner-cum-researchers, again illustrating the major pattern of game localization research arising out of significant reflections on practical experience.

Practitioners are clearly in an advantageous position to undertake research in this area thanks to their first-hand experience of the phenomena, especially given the fact that the game industry remains sensitive regarding the disclosure of information, making it difficult for external parties to obtain access to certain localization related data. Similar to the way in which AVT practitioners are bound by confidentiality clauses, game translators and localizers are often required to sign information non-disclosure agreements (NDAs) when they embark on jobs, preventing them from discussing specific projects for a given period of time. That said, an increasing amount of information is becoming available through industry forum sessions, workshops, and seminars devoted to game localization, involving direct industry sources in addition to academic conferences resulting in the dissemination of information including a wide range of online materials. With reference to the conferences listed in Table 0.2, the following can be highlighted as series accommodating the topic on a more regular basis:

- The biannual conference series *Languages and the Media*, Berlin, Germany (2004, 2006, 2008, 2010)
- The biannual conference series *Media for All* (2005, 2007, 2009, 2011)
- *Localization World* series (2007, 2008, 2009, 2010, 2011, 2012)
- Localization Summit at the *International Game Developers Conference* (2008, 2009, 2010, 2011, 2012)
- International Conference in Translation and Accessibility in Games and Virtual Worlds (2010, 2012)

Languages and the Media and *Media for All* are both well established conference series in the field of AVT. The localization industry conference series *Localization World* is well known among localization professionals and has been running the dedicated forum *Game Localization Round Table* since 2007, organized twice yearly in locations in the US and Europe and chaired by Miguel Bernal-Merino.

In turn, one of the key annual game industry events, the *International Game Developers Conference* (GDC) series, hosted a panel on game localization for the first time in San Francisco in February 2008. This officially inaugurated a special interest group (SIG) on game localization chaired by Kate Edwards, which led in 2009 to the annual full-day session called "Game Localization Summit" dedicated to the discussion of game localization at the International GDC. The game localization SIG was established as part of the International Game Developers Association (IGDA)[17] in 2007 to raise awareness among game developers of the need to consider upstreaming localization as part of game development and also to provide fora for networking among game localizers. Since early 2010 the localization SIG mailing list has been running theme-specific online discussions focused on industry practices, gathering insights from practitioners involved in game localization and drafting a best practice document, to which all members had the chance to contribute. The first draft, by Richard Honeywood, was made publicly available in February 2011 and a second version, reviewed by John Fung, was published in 2012 (Honeywood and Fung 2012). The document provides valuable guidelines for localization vendors as well as game companies.[18] Of particular interest among recent developments is a new conference series launched in December 2010 – *Translation and Accessibility in Video Games and Virtual Worlds* – hosted jointly by the TransMedia Catalonia Research Group and the Centre for Accessibility and Ambient Intelligence of Catalonia at the Universitat Autònoma de Barcelona. Spearheaded by Pilar Orero and Carmen Mangiron, this conference series indicates a new interdisciplinary direction in video game localization research, marrying the fields of media accessibility research and intelligent computing and incorporating the interest of Human Computer Interaction (HCI).

While the availability of an increasing amount of insider information from sources such as those listed above is facilitating research based on secondary sources without direct access to companies or individuals, the most common challenge still facing game localization researchers is the difficulty of obtaining permission to use commercial games for research or training purposes (see our discussion in Chapter 6 for training contexts). We will return briefly to this question in Chapter 7 in the context of research, but there is currently no easy way to convince game companies of the need to use materials or of the value of research. Owing to the highly competitive nature of the game industry, where confidentiality is of paramount importance, NDA requirements often jeopardize efficient

---

17. The initial idea for establishing the game localization SIG was initiated by Kate Edwards at the Digital Games Research Association (DIGRA) conference in Tokyo in 2007.

18. The document is available at http://englobe.com/wp-content/uploads/2012/05/Best-Practices-for-Game-Localization-v21.pdf.

internal communication during the localization process (Mandiberg 2012). An ideal way for researchers to gain access to the use of games is through collaborative R&D activities, which can help to establish a mutually beneficial working relationship with industry partners such as game publishers or developers. Game localization research in Translation Studies on the whole is progressing rapidly, being kick-started by contributions by practitioner-researchers. This is reminiscent of the developmental phase of both AVT studies field and interpreting research. As observed by Carlson and Corliss (2011, 65) the reflexive attitudes of some game developers are evident in their interest in the wider impact and implications of localization beyond commercial interests. Game localization research is now at a stage where these insights can be usefully applied in conceptualizing and theorizing this sub-domain. The following section provides a brief commentary on key research areas emerging from the literature.

Key research areas

Since 2005 this sub-domain has seen a surge of interest from translation scholars who have begun to conceptualize this practice. Reflecting the new entry of this sub-domain into Translation Studies, Bernal-Merino (2006) raised the issue of the use of the term "game localization" in introducing the field to Translation Studies and questioned the need for the new term as opposed to "game translation". Taking a critical stance against the unrestricted use of new concepts in this sub-domain, Bernal-Merino cautioned against the introduction of such terms without a clear motivation and definition, and proposed to adhere to "game translation". In the 3rd edition of *Introducing Translation Studies* (Munday 2012, 279–280) and *The Routledge Companion to Translation Studies* (Munday [ed.] 2009, 8), Munday makes brief references to "video game translation", although he does not specifically justify his use of the term except for acknowledging that "localization" is usually used as a superordinate of "translation". While the term "game localization" is commonly understood in the industry to refer to a particular set of practices, the actual definition of the concept is far from settled, as argued by Mandiberg (2009). Taking the specific instance of the Final Mix edition (see Chapter 4 for further discussion on Final Mix) of the transnational Japanese game *Kingdom Hearts* (2002), Mandiberg maintains that contrary to what localization purports to do its goal is in effect to produce "the same game" for different audiences by assuming "a linguistic innocence that rarely, if ever, exists" (ibid, n.p.). He claims that it is "translation" which dwells on issues such as untranslatability between different audiences whereas "localization" is driven by the desire to ensure that "the same game is played" regardless of "the same experience". One of the key concerns arising out of this sub-domain is well illustrated in this argument, where these two core concepts are still somewhat in a state of flux. Taking up this pertinent question, we return to the discussion on the relationship between translation and localization in Chapter 2.

Whereas the boundary between translation and localization remains unclear, game localization can be logically categorized in relation to the established area of practice of software localization. Game localization shares many similarities with software localization, though there are also notable differences. From the perspective of technical communication, Thayer and Kolko (2004) highlighted the key differences between the localization of productivity software and digital game software. While observing the fact that the former has been the mainstay of the field of software localization, they maintain that "localization processes have not kept up with the popularity of entertainment-focused computer applications" (ibid., 477) despite the growth of the game industry. This point is clearly reflected in the scant attention paid to game localization until relatively recently by Translation Studies. Focusing on different models of localization, this relatively early study argued that a "blending" approach is the most time-consuming and complex type of game localization employed when publishers wish to "release a complex game with a culturally-specific narrative in a new country" (ibid., 483). The authors identified the task of "blending domestic and imported cultural elements within a game" as the greatest challenge, and one which forms a distinguishing feature of game localization in comparison with localizing utility applications. The concept of "blending" has since been expressed in different ways by different authors, such as "hybridization" (Consalvo 2006; Di Marco 2007), and indeed characterizes one of the inherent challenges in dealing with modern video games as cultural products of a technological nature (see Chapter 5).

In her article "Console Video Games and Global Corporations: Creating a Hybrid Culture", Mia Consalvo (2006) examined the case of the major Japanese game corporation Square Enix to illustrate how the modern console game industry is creating a hybrid culture between the source (Japanese) and the target (American) cultures through their specific localization strategy. As also highlighted by Di Marco (2007), intricate and specific cultural negotiations are often necessary in order to bring Japanese games to the West, where hybridization of culture and identity is an unavoidable element in the delivery of a commercial localized product. While hurdles posed by cultural issues are nothing new in Translation Studies, video games pose a new kind of challenge in negotiating cultures, with reference to issues often discussed under the umbrella term "culturalization", a process increasingly recognized as essential to game localization. For example, Edwards (2012, 19–33) cites several real-life examples of serious consequences resulting from a lack of culturalization of game content in terms of religious or historical contexts, leading, in the worst case scenario, to games being banned in the target market. What Edwards calls "cultural dissonance" (ibid., 25) is a challenge facing game localization which is now frequently discussed in industry contexts as a dividing line between success and failure highlighting the importance of understanding "localized culture" (Edge Staff 2011). This in turn relates to the issue of censorship and age-ratings (see Chapter 5), which are still under-explored in the study of game localization, as pointed out earlier. Both the academic literature and that coming from the industry itself clearly signal intense interest in the cultural dimensions observed in the practice of game localization today.

The discussion of culturalization has been also tackled in terms of the complex relationship between local and global contexts of the transnational circulation of modern cultural artefacts. Focusing on economic, cultural, and technological factors with the case of American digital games localized for Chinese Taiwan, Lin (2006) examined how the major US game publisher Electronic Arts (EA) is using the discourse of localization in order to operate as a global transnational corporation. Lin emphasizes that localization uses a mixture of universalization and particularization, as well as centralization and decentralization, to address local differences while retaining the company's dominance, controlling the circulation of games as cultural products. The study found that localization in the context of video games does not simply mean domestication, in Venuti's (1995) sense. Given the increasing power of large game corporations, localization is emerging as a less than straightforward transaction between meeting the demands of local customers and keeping corporate identity and power intact in global contexts. This theme also links with the argument of Carlson and Corliss (2011, 78), who view localizers as agents who can never be entirely non-partisan – their activity of filtering cultural differences prevents them from being neutral parties who simply bridge cultures. Carlson and Corliss highlight the complex and nuanced negotiation which takes place between the local target customers on the one hand and the corporate interests and their perceptions of the customer preferences on the other.

These studies allude to the factors behind the situation where the concept of "localization" allegedly caters for the local market along with evidence of savvy strategies at work exercising control over the target territory. Such strategies can have far-reaching consequences in the receiving cultures, as discussed by Ng (2006) in reference to the case of Japanese combat games localized for the market in Hong Kong, China. Writing from the perspective of Asian studies and popular culture studies, Ng notes how these games are selectively domesticated in the process of localization, subsequently making a significant impact on popular culture in Hong Kong. The increasing focus on the cultural dimension of game localization is evident in literature from various fields, including cultural and media studies

(Consalvo 2006), anthropological viewpoints (Carlson and Corliss 2011), global communications (Lin 2006), as well as translation approached from communication studies perspectives (Mandiberg 2009). Without addressing game localization per se, Astrid Ensslin (2012) presents in *The Language of Gaming* a fresh perspective focusing on communication between game developers and their audiences and also communication among stakeholders such as industry professionals and journalists applying discourse analysis. Although this is not directly suggested by Ensslin, research questions on game localization can be developed by focusing on such discourses, and thereby providing a future research avenue for scholars. These examples point to considerable potential scope for the study of game localization and its inherent interdisciplinary nature.

The research activities outlined above illustrate the increasing interest in and recognition of the importance of game localization. In particular, translation and localization conferences now include papers focused on the topic. However, contributions to peer-reviewed translation journals are still limited, with game localization addressed only occasionally in special issues of journals. A 2006 special issue of *Perspectives* featured game localization alongside anime and manga (Japanese comics) translation to explore common threads linking these three genres closely associated with Japan. In the context of game localization research, the editorial (O'Hagan 2006b) pointed out how the relatively new status of Translation Studies in Japan as a standalone academic discipline resulted in a paucity of published research coming from Japan on game localization from a Translation Studies perspective, despite the fact that considerable game localization knowhow had been accumulated by the Japanese game industry (see Kohler 2005). In 2007 the Spanish journal *Tradumàtica* published a special issue solely focusing on game localization (*Localització de videojocs*) with articles written in English, Spanish and Catalan. As explained in the editorial (Mangiron 2007) the aim of the issue was set to reflect a broad range of perspectives on game localization, gathering contributions from industry practitioners, a game journalist, academics, and a gamer/fan translator. For example, the contribution by Pablo Muñoz-Sánchez (2007) on the fan translation of games known as **ROM-hacking** was based on his own personal experience. This particular topic has since become increasingly popular in Translation Studies in relation to the phenomenon variously called collaborative translation (Désilets 2007), community translation (O'Hagan 2011b) or non-professional translation (Pérez-González and Susam-Saraeva 2012), as we discuss in some depth in Chapter 7. Another special issue dedicated to game localization was published in 2011 by the peer-reviewed Spanish journal *TRANS: Revista de Traductología*, with contributions in English and Spanish. In his preface, the editor Miguel Bernal-Merino emphasizes that the special issue aims to fill the gap between academic research and good professional practice by bringing together perspectives of practitioners and academic researchers. The topics covered include culturalization (Edwards 2011), game accessibility (Mangiron 2011a), fan translation (Díaz Montón 2011), game localization management (Bartelt-Krantz 2011) and localizer training in the Spanish context (Vela Valido 2011).

Text types have been one of the key considerations in Translation Studies and are a worthy focus of attention. Bernal-Merino (2008b) investigated the text typologies present in games, characterising the wide range of text-type elements embedded within a single game. This includes associated marketing texts forming a paratext (e.g. the poster in Figure 0.1), which may be consumed online or offline. In a later study (Bernal-Merino 2009) he extended the question of text typology to examine the challenges involved in turning children's literature into video games. Bernal-Merino proposed an initial literary polysystem incorporating interactive and non-interactive media so that they can be studied together for their creative value. Pursuing a similar line of enquiry into game text types, we attempt to develop game text taxonomy and to link them to translation norms and strategies (see Chapter 4). Drawing on Mangiron's first-hand experience involved in the localization of the Japanese game series *Final Fantasy* (*FF*), Mangiron and O'Hagan (2006) in turn analyzed the different factors which influence the translators' approach to translation. The paper found that the tendency towards broad adaptive approaches observed in the localization of the *FF* series was motivated not only by the distance between the source Japanese and target American and European cultures, but also by the games' interactive nature, the space restrictions of the **user interface** (**UI**), and other game specific constraints. In the present book we further develop the "transcreation" concept used in that earlier study, in an attempt to define game localization by focusing on translator's agency. More recent development towards the inclusion of new areas of research such as game localization is the advent of the new translation studies journal *Translation Spaces*, the first issue of which was published in 2012. Described as "A multidisciplinary, multimedia, and multilingual journal of translation", the journal aims to address specifically how globalization and the unparalleled proliferation of technologies are changing the nature and the scope of translation (Folaron and Shreve 2012, 1). Among the identified thematic streams is "Translation and Entertainment", which seeks to incorporate new perspectives concerning entertainment, including video games. With the specific provision of academic publication fora such as this, it is hoped that game localization research will continue to grow, expanding the current disciplinary horizon.

The above brief survey of the literature provides evidence that game localization research is gradually developing in Translation Studies as well as being a topic of potential interest to scholars working outside the discipline. The very early stage of this sub-domain in Translation Studies is nevertheless signalled in the lack of doctoral dissertations on the topic, according to the statistics provided by the searched database (see footnote on Table 0.2) on theses completed in English at the time of writing. Nevertheless given the increasing number of Master's-level postgraduate programmes dedicated to or partially accommodating game localization (see Chapter 6) and our personal experience at our own respective institutions Dublin City University and Universitat Autònoma de Barcelona, we anticipate that doctoral research will be in the pipeline in the next few years. The literature survey indicates that research in the field is paving the way towards a better understanding of game localization, serving to add to the basis of Descriptive Translation Studies (DTS). However, given the dynamic and varied nature of modern digital games, many challenges remain. For example, areas such as online games in general and social and casual games in particular are developing rapidly to become a significant part of the game industry. While acknowledging that some of these new areas have not yet been investigated by translation researchers to any significant extent, we can justifiably argue that initial descriptive work is now beginning to take shape, providing a foundation for in-depth translation research to grow and flourish although research methods and theoretical frameworks need to be addressed. The intention of this book is to consolidate what we consider to be the first stage of game localization research and to provide a theoretical foundation to facilitate future work in this exciting new specialized sub-domain of Translation Studies.

Approach

As demonstrated in the literature survey, game localization is an emerging area of academic study with a relatively small body of work both within and beyond Translation Studies. This goes hand in hand with the relatively recent formation of Game Studies itself. Despite the development of research on games stimulated by the emergence of commercial video games since the 1970s (see Chapter 1 for a brief history), Game Studies was not acknowledged as an independent academic discipline until relatively recently (Aarseth 2001; Wolf and Perron 2003; Newman 2004). However, the rapid development of the field in recent years is now apparent. For example, using ISI Web of Knowledge, Bryce and Rutter (2006, 2) measured the increase in the volume of peer-reviewed journal publications in the field, finding almost twice the number of publications in the period 2000 to 2004 at 535 publications as in the 1995–1999 period (273 publications). Our own search using the same search pattern[19] on the same database puts the total number of publications for the period 2006–2010 at close to 1,600, clearly demonstrating substantial further growth. Given the rapid expansion of the domain and its interdisciplinary nature as has been well acknowledged by Game Studies scholars (Wolf and Perron 2003, 2), we do not claim to provide an exhaustive coverage of all perspectives in the field. Rather, our goal is to start with issues pertinent to game localization practice and to explore a number of potentially productive areas of research from a Translation Studies perspective. We therefore take the early explorer's role in initiating this sub-domain as a new area of translation research.

Having matured into a legitimate area of academic research, Game Studies brings solid and developing insights to this dynamic form of digital entertainment. In *The Handbook of Computer Game Studies* (Raessens and Goldstein [eds.] 2005), designed to serve as a textbook to provide students with an overview of the field, the authors divide the main concerns of the discipline into five thematic areas: (1) design; (2) reception; (3) games as a cultural phenomenon; (4) games as an aesthetic phenomenon, and (5) games as a social phenomenon. These categories demonstrate the multi-faceted nature of modern video games and their far-reaching impact, generating interdisciplinary perspectives from which video games can be studied. In particular, our interest relates to the reception of games, game culture and game design and, to a lesser degree, the social dimensions of games. Given the sheer variety of games, we freely admit that we were only able to focus on a small selective section of contemporary console games subject to game localization. While cognizant of the rapidly growing areas of online and social games which are forming an important part of the 21st-century gaming industry, we opted to focus on console games as a more established and staple diet for game localization. We justify this decision on the basis that at present it is console games that most fully represent the spectrum of characteristics and issues which arise from translating digital interactive games.

Game Studies scholars such as Aarseth (2001), in his attempt to establish this area of academic inquiry as an independent discipline, earlier criticized "colonising attempts" by scholars who treat games as a variation of the existing genres familiar to them, thus overlooking new dimensions pertinent to video games. To this end we take the position that game localization involves dealing with a new medium whose characteristics may not be fully accounted for in the current theoretical framework available in Translation Studies. We therefore endeavour not to be confined within the disciplinary tradition. At the same time, we argue that the addition of viewpoints from Translation Studies facilitates analysis of certain

19. We followed the same keyword search pattern indicated by Bryce and Rutter, searching articles containing the phrase "computer game(s)" or "video game(s)".

aspects of games which may not have been brought to light so far in Game Studies. In this process, Game Studies perspectives and those of Translation Studies which are already informed by many different disciplines will enrich the whole area of study. Such cross-fertilization can be seen as a case of "consilience", which Chesterman (2005) introduced in the context of Translation Studies in reference to progressive unification of knowledge across different fields of science and humanities as advocated by the biologist Edward Wilson (1998). While cautioning against misrepresentation and misinterpretation of borrowed concepts from neighbouring disciplines Chesterman (ibid.) promotes interdisciplinary thinking, pointing out how new disciplines often emerge "at the interface of the existing ones". This is essential in order to address emerging translation phenomena, including game localization, which is a complex new modern translation practice calling for a new perspective. To this end, our study will have an interdisciplinary inclination.

Another approach we chose to take in this book is to focus on Japanese games. This may give some readers the impression that we are biased at the expense of other mainstream American/Western produced games. We firstly justify our focus by the fact that Japan has the longest experience of localising games for radically different cultures. As a major game developing country, Japan's influence on the development of the modern game industry is well noted in the literature (e.g. Kent 2001; Kohler 2005). The reason for this focus also lies in the current trend in Translation Studies to look beyond the West. In recent years a number of key translation theorists, such as Maria Tymoczko (2006) have called for a broadening of the scope of current Western-centric views of translation in Translation Studies. Similarly, in the introduction to the second edition of the *Routledge Encyclopedia of Translation Studies*, editors Mona Baker and Gabriela Saldanha (2009, xx) highlight "engagement with non-Western perspectives at the turn of the century" as a major new trend in Translation Studies which has hitherto been "strongly Euro-centric in orientation". Chief among the publications addressing the same concern are Hung and Wakabayashi (2005), Cheung (2006), and Hermans (2006), presenting perspectives reflecting non-Western views and little known practices and traditions of translation elsewhere. Translation Studies in China is rapidly developing whereas the first international conference on Translation Studies in Japan was held in January 2010 (Sato-Rossberg and Wakabayashi [eds.] 2012, 2), suggesting a somewhat surprising delay as well as solid signs of the field being established. To this end, throughout the book we are mindful of the undercurrent of "Translating Others" (Hermans 2006) in our frequent references to Japanese games as well as translation practices by Japanese game companies. In this context, we hope to make an additional contribution of non-Western translation perspectives to the still vastly Western-oriented discipline of Translation Studies. We also adopt a diachronic approach to understanding the current practice, taking into account the evolution of game localization over time, addressing a gap we have noticed in the way the literature neglects to present the historical context of how the localization practice emerged and matured to its current stage.

There are a number of key theoretical frameworks we attempt to apply to shed light on the practice of game localization. In order to situate game localization within Translation Studies we firstly explore localization as a theoretical construct by building on arguments presented by Pym (2004, 2010), thereby also examining the current tension and ambiguity between translation and localization. Secondly we argue how game localization accentuates broader cultural issues as key considerations, albeit in a new context, given the nature of digital games as a new "text" for translation afforded by new media technologies. We thus focus on the impact of technological elements as one of the key characteristics of this sub-domain. In turn, we argue how this new medium reveals rather than hides the translator's agency, thereby allowing a wide range of interventions by the translator in multimodal and multimedia environments. Our decision to highlight the translator's agency in this way may contrast with one of the key assumptions in the mainstream localization practices so far developed based largely on productivity software applications. Mainstream localization practices today can be seen as treating human agency (i.e. that of the translator) as an undesirable and costly factor inviting variety and heteronomy against more manageable and economical uniformity. In particular, we focus on the creativity arising from human agency in game localization and attempt to further develop the concept of "transcreation" by tracing it to one of its origins, Brazilian post-colonial thinking as initially introduced to Translation Studies by Bassnett and Trivedi (1999) and Vieira (1999) with reference to the Brazilian poet and translator Haraldo de Campos. Furthermore, we also consider the translator's agency in light of the concepts of "patronage" and "rewriting" (Lefevere 1992), focusing on the power exerted by a small group of influential game corporations who can intervene in localization and translation decisions which may provide either constraint or freedom from a translator's point of view. Such industrial settings in turn have an impact on approaches to translator training and pedagogy, which form an increasingly important focus in Translation Studies in responding to new requirements arising from various new forms of translation. Finally, the question of agency is also extended to agency of gamers and fans through user activities which are increasingly facilitated by technological environments such as widespread social networking platforms. The focus on non-translator "user" participation in game localization provides a fresh perspective in considering the issue of user empowerment in the context of video games as "co-creative media" (Morris 2003). This increased visibility of users in the age of Web 2.0 can be framed in terms of agency while also being considered in light of user-generated translation (Perrino 2009; O'Hagan 2009b) or the more commercially-oriented concept of "crowdsourcing" (Howe 2008).

Another key area of research we broach concerns the translation of multimedia products such as games as part of media accessibility, an area of research within Translation Studies that has been gaining the attention of scholars since the early 2000s, particularly in relation to subtitles for the deaf and hard of hearing (SDH) and more recently audio description (AD) for the visually impaired. The perspective of accessibility opens up a broad scope of academic inquiry into the reception and the design of products from a wide ranging user spectrum. Last but not least we maintain that one of the unique characteristics of game localization stems from the fact that modern video games are sophisticated technological artefacts. Presenting a case for "a technological turn" in Translation Studies, we discuss the development of translation practices to deal with artefacts afforded by new technologies.

Before closing this section we wish to make a brief comment on statistical data on games. The importance of capturing accurate market data on this dynamic sector is well recognized by the game industry as well as academic researchers and is demonstrated, for example, by new initiatives by the Interactive Software Federation of Europe (ISFE). Launched in May 2012, a multi-country tracking survey called *GameTrack*[20] seeks to gather game user statistics covering the UK, France, Germany, Spain, and the US. Each month 1,000 surveys are collected in each country from respondents aged 6 and over by a method combining in-home face-to-face interviews and self-completion surveys. This will go some way towards facilitating game localization research by providing statistical information covering a number of regions, if not all territories of interest and relevance to game localization. While an increasing range of sources attempts to cover the data internationally, each region tends to have frequently cited local information sources. For example, in the context of Japanese game market data there are three well-established annual commercial publications: *Famitsu Game Hakusho* is a game industry white paper published in Japanese by the popular Japanese game magazine *Famitsu* and similarly *Game Sangyo Hakusho*, by Media Create, is a game industry report also in Japanese. The Japanese Computer Entertainment Suppliers Association (CESA) publishes the bilingual (English and Japanese) volume *CESA Games White Paper*, which we have used in this book. These reports contain data on regions other than Japan, including some of the less reported Asian markets. For the US market frequently cited sources include *Essential Facts*, published annually by the US-based Entertainment Software Association (ESA).

---

20. See http://www.isfe.eu/industry-facts/statistics.

There are other publications by market research companies such as NPD, GfK, DFC Intelligence and Nielsen, to mention a few examples. However, there is a general lack of dedicated sources specifically designed to address the needs of game localization research, as these call for global and comparative data.

Our aim is to provide a road map introducing this relatively new phenomenon in translation and to open up the field of Translation Studies to the new practices which are already part of the 21st century's key global industry (Chatfield 2010). In doing so, our core approach is descriptive rather than prescriptive, fully acknowledging our own limitation in understanding and explaining this vast and complex topic.

CHAPTER 1

The video game and translation

Introduction

With a view to making explicit the relationship between video games and translation we first set the scene by providing a snapshot of the historical development of game localization, linking it to advances in key gaming technology and the various constraints imposed on game localization due largely to technological limitations especially in the early days. We then identify a number of game-specific concepts and terms and provide definitions which are used throughout this book. Having covered the key concepts, we explain the two main theoretical paradigms in Game Studies to provide a conceptual framework for analyzing games, albeit biased towards our own particular interests in translation. This is followed by a discussion of the structure of the video game industry to show how game localization is couched in specific contexts defined by the roles played by the main stakeholders. This foregrounds power relationships within the industry affecting some of the key game localization decisions. While Game Studies scholars interested in political economy[21] have discussed the game industry structure and its implications (e.g. Williams 2002; Kerr 2006a, 2006b), this dimension has so far not been explored from a perspective focusing on game localization. Touching on the concept of "patronage" forming control and power affecting translation (Lefevere 1992), we focus on game localization as a carefully manipulated operation by powerful high-tech companies who manufacture game hardware and publish as well as develop software. Finally, we examine the growing links developing between the game and film industries and point to the transmediality of modern video games. In doing so, we attempt to paint a holistic picture of the dynamically evolving digital entertainment industry to provide a background against which this relatively new form of translation practice can be understood.

---

21. Kerr (2006b, 37) uses Mosco's (1996, 25) definition of political economy to refer to the study "of the social relations, particularly the power relations, that mutually constitute the production, distribution and consumption of resources".

1.1   A historical sketch of video game localization

The history of video games has been well documented both in academic works (e.g. Wolf 2008) and from popular journalistic perspectives (e.g. Herz 1997; Kent 2001; Donovan 2010). Despite such good coverage and an increasing volume of research on games, there is a distinct paucity of comprehensive sources available on how game localization practices have developed since the early days of the industry. This absence also suggests a general lack of interest in Game Studies in relation to the globalization process of video games through localization. This meant that we had to glean disparate sources of information in an attempt to paint a coherent historical picture, still falling short of depicting a full story. In an attempt to address such deficiencies, we provide a diachronic perspective to illustrate how game localization evolved. In tracing advances in game localization practices, we follow Hasegawa (2009) in dividing the timeline of development phases broadly into: (1) Early phase (prior to the mid-80s); (2) Growth phase (mid-80s to the mid-90s); (3) Development phase (mid-90s to the late-90s); (4) Maturing phase (2000 to 2005), and (5) Advancing phase (2005 to date). We pay special attention to technological dimensions which are closely linked to localization processes. Table 1.1 summarizes milestones noted in the literature on the history of the video games so as to place localization practices in the context of key developments in game as well as related computer technologies. We also note indicative game titles which were popular at the given point in time.

1.1.1   Early days: Before the mid-1980s

The humble beginnings of modern games are usually traced to the prototypes of the electronic games *Tennis for Two* (1958) and *Spacewar!* (1962), which were both developed in the US at public research facilities in a rather incidental context looking for open day attractions. These prototypes, which were freely circulated, gave inspiration to early coin-operated arcade games such as *Computer Space* (1971) and *Pong* (1972), as commercialized by Atari. Atari was the first key US game company to emerge in the 1970s, controlling up to 80% of the American market at its peak (Kerr 2006a, 17). Following these games were the major commercial successes of the Japanese arcade games *Space Invaders* (1978) and *Pac-Man* (1980), which are considered to have set the subsequent course of video games as a cultural phenomenon (Egenfeldt-Nielsen et al. 2008, 52). In the 1970s game technology moved from integrated circuits to microprocessors for smoother and better looking animation (Kohler 2005, 19). Important advances were also made in audio technology in the 1980s. For example, *Manic Miner* (1983) was the first game to use in-game music (McCarthy et al. 2005, 110). Still, by comparison

Table 1.1 Technical milestones of game console evolution

Time	Platform	Sample of milestone games	Technological milestone
1970s	Following the US development of modern video games, Atari dominated the game scene with early arcade games and brought them into the home with game consoles.		
1972	1st generation console Magnavox Odyssey – no sound	1972 *Pong* (US)[22]	Apple II computer supporting a library of games
1976	Channel F – first cartridge home video game system		Use of microprocessors instead of integrated circuits for better quality animation
1977	2nd generation console Atari VCS (Atari 2600) launched	1978 Space Invaders (J) 1979 *Asteroids* (US)	
1980s	This decade saw the dramatic decline of the game industry in the US with the demise of Atari, along with the rise of Japanese console manufacturers such as Nintendo and later Sega, with a shift to 16-bit consoles.		
1982	Commodore 64 (C64); Sinclair ZX Spectrum	1980 *Pac-Man* (J) 1981 *Donkey Kong* (J) 1982 *Microsoft Flight Simulator* (US) 1983 *Mario Bros.* (J)	Use of tape and floppy disks in addition to cartridges for C64; PC sound cards
1983/ 1985	3rd generation console Nintendo Famicom released in Japan in 1983; Nintendo Entertainment System (NES) released elsewhere in 1985	1985 *Tetris* (USSR); *Habitat* (US)	8-bit machine with cartridges
1987/ 1989	Nintendo Game Boy worldwide release in 1989; Sega MegaDrive unveiled in 1987 in Japan (released as Genesis in US in 1989); Atari's handheld Lynx	1987 *The Legend of Zelda* (J) 1988 *Ninja Ryukenden* (J) 1989 *SimCity* (US)	Handheld game consoles with communication cables 16-bit machines with better graphics and sound
1990s	The platform war begins to die down with the release of Sony PlayStation moving to CD-ROM.		
1990/ 1991	4th generation console Nintendo Super Famicom released in Japan in 1990 and as Super Nintendo Entertainment System (SNES) for North America in 1991 (UK in 1992)	1990 *Super Mario Bros. 3* (J) 1991 *Civilization* (US); *Sonic the Hedgehog* (J) 1993 *Mortal Kombat* (US) 1993 *Doom* (US)	SNES still using cartridges 64-bit machines with CPU/GPU; Cartridges replaced by CD-ROM; 2D to 3D; richer soundtracks

22. The brackets after the game title show the country of origin of the game according to the location of the developer of the game.

Table 1.1 (*continued*)

Time	Platform	Sample of milestone games	Technological milestone
1994/1995	5th generation console; Sony PlayStation released in Japan in 1994 and in North America in 1995; Nintendo 64 released in Japan in 1995; Sega Saturn released in Japan in 1994 and in North America in 1995	1994 *Myst* (US); 1996 *Tomb Raider* (UK); *Pocket Monster* (J); 1997 *Grand Theft Auto* (UK); *Final Fantasy VII* (J); *The Legend of Zelda: Ocarina of Time* (J); 1998 *Dance Dance Revolution* (J); *Metal Gear Solid* (J); 1999 *EverQuest* (US)	Inclusion of (unsynthesized) human voice in games becoming more common; Windows 95
Beyond 2000	A move from CD-ROM to DVD, *PlayStation2* further facilitates inclusion of voiced dialogue. Microsoft enters the game scene alongside Japanese console manufacturers Nintendo and Sony, while Sega withdraws from platform manufacturing. With advanced global networking as well as increased computing power, consoles allow online modes and function as multimedia entertainment centres.		
2000	6th generation console; Sony PlayStation 2 launched in Japan, followed by North America	2000 *The Sims* (US)	DVD; integration of games, movies, music; Xbox with internal hard drive
2001	Microsoft Xbox; Nintendo GameCube & Game Boy Advance		Touch-sensitive screen; voice recognition
2004	Nintendo DS	2004 *World of Warcraft* (US); 2004 *Half Life 2* (US)	Radio sensor controller; online networking mode; multimedia storage
2005	7th generation console; Nintendo Wii; Microsoft Xbox360; Sony PSP		Blu-ray and High Definition TV technologies
2007	PlayStation3	2007 *Halo 3* (US); 2009 *Call of Duty: Modern Warfare 2* (US	
2010	PlayStation3 motion controller Move; Xbox360 interface Kinect	2010 *Heavy Rain* (J)	Advanced motion-sensor technologies emerge
2011	Nintendo 3DS; Sony EricssonXperia Play; Sony PlayStationVita	2011 *LA Noire* (AUS); 2011 *Child of Eden* (J); 2011 *Call of Duty: Modern Warfare 3* (US)	Stereoscopic three dimensional effects without requiring additional accessories; PlayStation certified smartphone
2012	Nintendo Wii U	2012 *Assassin's Creed III* (CAN); 2012 *Nintendo Land* (J)	Tablet controller known as "GamePad"; Games can be played offline with GamePad

Sources: Kent (2001); McDougall and O'Brien (2008); Newman and Oram (2006); Egenfeldt-Nielsen et al. (2008).

with today's multimedia and multi-faceted games, *Pong* and *Space Invaders* included few elements which required translation to sell in different markets – they had simple rules and no recognizable characters that were culture-specific, let alone any dialogue to be translated. Furthermore, despite being developed in Japan, games like *Space Invaders*, for example, used English phrases such as "High Score" and "Game Over", requiring no translation for the US market.

While these early Japanese arcade games mostly posed no major language barriers, certain aspects needed to be changed for socio-linguistic reasons. A number of sources (e.g. Kohler 2005, 24 and 212) refer to the change involved in the spelling of *Pac-Man* from its original Japanese transliteration presented as *Puck-Man*. The original naming of the game was derived from the Japanese onomatopoeic expression パクパク [gobble], depicting rapid mouth movements evoking the image of somebody noisily gulping food. The edit was considered necessary because the word "Puck" would likely tempt vandals in the US to slightly alter the first letter. This led to changes in the cabinet art and the title screen of the game in arcade machines. As such, it provided an early taste of what was to come for game localization in the much more complex subsequent development of games. As compared to the earlier games constituting mostly abstract objects, *Pac-Man* also illustrated a meaningful evolution as it featured distinguishable game characters, which gave rise to the need for names and characterization, in turn providing some translatable elements. For example, the original Japanese nicknames of the key characters (four ghosts) were based mainly on colours, plus the demeanour of the last one, i.e. アカベイ ["Reddie"], ピンキー ["Pinky"], アオスケ ["Bluey"] and グズタ ["Slowy"] became *Blinky, Pinky, Inky*, and *Clyde* in the official English translation. These translation choices indicated the importance of pithy and punchy-sounding renditions, even to the point of choosing entirely new names in the target text (TT). This reflected both the pragmatic criterion of space constraints of the game's **user interface** (UI) as well as the product's ultimate goal of providing some amusement to the end player.

Similarly, when Nintendo of America (NOA) decided to print the story of the game on the arcade cabinet for the early popular title *Donkey Kong* (1981), its two main characters, originally referred to as "Jump-Man" and "The Lady" in the Japanese version, called for more specific edgy-sounding names for the American release. Thus the name Mario was born, allegedly inspired by the name of the landlord of the building leased by NOA at the time, while "The Lady" was re-named Polly after the name of an NOA employee's wife (Kohler 2005, 212). Similar anecdotes abound in the game industry, illustrating how arbitrary some translation decisions actually were (see Kent 2001; Chandler 2005; and Kohler 2005). In later PlayStation games such as *ICO* (2001), the Japanese team was happy to leave the main protagonist simply referred to as "a boy", but this was

Figure 1.1 *ICO* box art design for Japanese release (left) versus the North American release (right) © 2011 Sony Computer Entertainment Inc. [Images kindly supplied by Sony Computer Entertainment Inc.]

rejected by the North American market advisors, who demanded the character to be given a specific name (Ueda cited in Sony Computer Entertainment 2002, 82). This difference in preferences for abstract versus concrete in Japan and the US respectively was also reflected in the design of the game's box art for the Japanese and the North American releases (O'Hagan 2009a) as depicted in Figure 1.1. Interestingly the game's European releases followed the Japanese box art and so did the cover of the book for subsequent novelization in Japanese (Miyabe 2004) and its English translation (Smith 2011).

Games gradually moved from arcades to homes with the invention of game consoles. *Magnavox Odyssey,* the earliest home video game console to be connected to a TV screen, was created by Ralph Baer in the US in 1972, followed by *Home-Pong,* a one-game-only console by Atari. After this, in 1976 the *Channel F* console was developed, using plug-in cartridges containing individual games, immediately followed by Atari's similar console *Atari VCS* (Video Computer System, also known as "Atari 2600"). Atari dominated the game market in the US throughout the 1970s by converting popular arcade games, including *Space Invaders* and *Pac-Man,* to be playable on the home console, until the company's spectacular demise in the early 1980s. This is widely understood to have resulted from a loss of consumer confidence following the rushed production of low-quality games sold to the market, stemming partly from Atari's lack of control over game development. The period from 1983 to 1984 is generally known as "the game industry market crash" in the US. Often referred to as the "Atari crash", this created an opportunity for the Japanese companies Nintendo and Sega to enter the scene. By then home computers had also emerged, including the *Commodore 64* (C64) in the US and the *Sinclair Spectrum* in the UK, as well as the earlier *Apple II,* allowing for a range of games to be played on the same machine as opposed to the one-game-only hardwired game consoles. In this period some computer-based American games were localized into Japanese but usually only user manuals were translated whereas text in game software itself was left untranslated, requiring the player to consult dictionaries while playing (Hasegawa 2009, 126). This period is largely considered to be the early days of localization, characterized by trial and error (Hasegawa ibid.), which is further described as "an era in which [game] developers had little control over, or paid little attention to, the quality of translations" (ActiveGaming Media n.d.). Translation was often performed by "friends or other non-professionals", resulting in "many of the now famous mistranslations of the time". This paints the picture of localization as a "fairly amateurish business" with no real localization agencies in existence at the time (ibid.).

1.1.2   Growth phase: The mid-1980s to mid-1990s

Amid the declining image of the game industry, Nintendo's 8-bit *Famicom* was launched in 1983 in Japan with great success. It was subsequently released elsewhere as the *Nintendo Entertainment System* (NES), starting with the North American market in 1985. NES became the most popular console of the time, winning the "platform wars" – the term still used today to describe fierce competition between console hardware manufacturers with their own proprietary systems. However, Ng (2008) reports that in the 1980s the gamer population in the rest of the Asia was not large and the NES console was not considered affordable by many families. This led to an unauthorized NES-compatible machine known as the "red and white machine", manufactured in Hong Kong, China in 1985, which played pirated Nintendo cartridges made mainly in Chinese Taiwan and Thailand (ibid., 213). Many Japanese games were exported to the US market, prompted simply by their domestic success within Japan, with localization efforts often being an afterthought (Corliss 2007). NES used ROM cartridges containing individual games, so players could use the same hardware to play different games. The shift from one-game only, hardwired game consoles to reusable hardware and games on cartridges can be considered a particularly important development in the history of video games. Despite the relative limitations of the technology, there were early signs of cinematic techniques being used in games. For example, one of the Japanese games which appeared during this period was Tecmo's *Ninja Ryukenden* (1988),[23] known for the innovative use of cinematic sequences trademarked as

---

23. This game was initially released as an arcade game that did not contain any cinematic sequences (Kohler 2005, 220). The NES version was released in English in the USA in 1989 as *Ninja Gaiden* following the original Japanese release the year before.

Figure 1.2 Translated texts in a cinematic scene[24] in the 1989 US version *Ninja Gaiden*
© 1988, 1989 Tecmo Ltd. All Rights Reserved

"Tecmo Theatre" with a well-developed storyline (Kohler 2005, 219–222). This Famicom/NES game is an example of nascent attempts at cinematic sequences incorporated into the game narrative. Unlike today's cinematics, these sequences did not have a voice track; rather, narration was given in ticker text, that is, subtitle-like running text (see Figure 1.2 for the US version). This example shows how the emerging connection between game localization and audiovisual translation (AVT) can be traced back over 20 years with clear implications for translation. The cinematic sequences show anime-style pictures occupying the screen in a 3-by-4 aspect ratio, accompanied by the dialogue displayed in English. In this example, the only sound present was computer-generated background music and some sound effects while the texts scrolled from left to right in the lower half of the screen, synchronized with the graphics. As can be discerned from the screenshots, the text does not follow today's subtitling conventions. The first scene shows the text for narration extended to four lines not marked in italics with what seems to be an arbitrary use of ellipsis markers with two dots rather than the typical "triple dots", according to today's AVT typographic norms. Nevertheless, the use of an animation sequence with a textual accompaniment effectively explained the story to the player, as often noted by the game's reviewers (e.g. Feeser 2009).

As far as language issues are concerned, it is relevant to note how the technical limitations of early consoles also affected the representation of the Japanese language. For example, the limited storage capacity of Famicom meant that the console was only equipped to represent the phonetic syllabaries hiragana and

---

24. Screenshots available from http://www.youtube.com/watch?v=_rkaiKYEkDQ.

katakana, consisting of 76 characters each,[25] without kanji characters, which include some 2,000 in customary use. While this did not directly affect localization itself, being unable to use the customary kanji characters must have led to certain constraints in authoring game text in Japanese (see Figure 1.3 for a typical Japanese text using only hiragana). It was not until the era of Super Famicom (known as "SNES" for Super Nintendo Entertainment System elsewhere) in the 1990s that kanji characters could be used in game text. Ironically, since the use of kanji brought an economy of on-screen space for the Japanese text, this sometimes caused a problem when the Japanese was translated into European TLs, requiring more screen space to express the same idea. The production of games for the Nintendo consoles was carefully monitored by Nintendo through the control of ROM cartridges, a lesson learnt from Atari's earlier predicament of being unable to stop the production of low quality games as a result of making the system specifications freely open to game developers. However, while game developers complied with Nintendo, many saw this as "strong-arm tactics" linked to Nintendo's well-known self-censorship policies imposed on developers (Arsenault 2008, 110), which we discuss below. As game machine capacity increased, so too did the translatable content subject to localization. Furthermore, due to the intellectual property (IP) of character design as well as music used in some Japanese games, changes were necessary when they were sold in overseas markets (Hasegawa 2009, 127). In addition, the suitability of the content also needed consideration, particularly regarding the treatment of religious references. This was the period before the establishment of ratings bodies such as the US Entertainment Software Ratings Board (ESRB) and therefore games were checked mainly according to game companies' own internal voluntary guidelines such as Nintendo's "NES Game Standards Policy" (see Chapter 5).

In the late 1980s there was the 16-bit console war between Sega MegaDrive (known as "Genesis" in the US) and SNES. These are considered to be 4th generation consoles, following the earlier *Odyssey*, *Atari 2600* and *NES* classified as 1st, 2nd, and 3rd generation respectively (Flatley and French 2003). In this period there were a number of international mega hit games such as the *Super Mario Bros.* franchise. Relevant to our interest is the fact that the ultimate commercial goal often seemed to justify added playfulness and some of the translations of these high-profile titles were even rather whimsical. A case in point is the liberty taken in the translation of the short closing text in the NES game *Super Mario Bros.3* (1988). In the Japanese original version Princess Peach simply says (back translated from Japanese which is shown in Figure 1.3): "Thank you! Peace has

---

25. The Japanese language uses a combination of three types of scripts: hiragana, katakana and kanji.

Figure 1.3 Ending message in in the Japanese original (left) and in the North American version (right) [26] in *Super Mario Bros.3*™ © Nintendo. All Rights Reserved. Super Mario Bros. is a trademark of Nintendo.

returned to the Mushroom world. The End!". For the American localized version, however, this was rendered as: "Thank you! But our Princess is in another castle! … Just kidding. Ha ha ha! Bye bye" (cited in Kohler 2005, 68) (see Figure 1.3). As is familiar to the players of *Super Mario Bros.* this was in reference to the recurring line in the game ("but our Princess is in another castle" by Mushroom Retainer). With the further addition of the cheeky embellishment the newly created line injects intertextuality and humour into the closing scene of the game. Such examples of translation by invention can be taken as an early sign of what we call "transcreation" (see Chapter 4 for a full discussion), where the extent of the departure from the source text (ST) is such that the creative addition by the translator breathes new life into the TT. However, such liberties were sometimes also taken out of desperation rather than as a creative addition. In the case of the Japanese RPG (J-RPG) *Story of Thor* (1994), re-titled as *Beyond Oasis* in English for Sega Genesis, the poorly translated story and dialogue, which did not make sense to the English editor, were completely re-written, simply using plot points during the editing process without any communication with the original translator (Tony Van cited in Chandler 2005, 56). While this allegedly worked in the above case, such an ad hoc approach could hardly be relied on to result in the creation of a coherent game world in the target version.

---

26. Screenshot sources: http://hakuda2.web.fc2.com/solomon/mari3/u16.html for the Japanese original and http://randomabsurdity.wordpress.com/2010/03/page/2/ for the North American version.

1.1.3   Development phase: The mid- to late 1990s

Tracing the evolution of game consoles, it becomes clear that technological capacities and limitations shaped the games of the time in terms of graphics and sound, affecting the whole game world and **gameplay**[27] design. This also had a follow-on impact on localization. In the late 1990s console games began to become available in versions other than English and Japanese, with European markets finally being served with localized games in their own languages (ActiveGaming Media n.d.). The early 8-bit consoles such as NES severely limited the quantity of text that could be stored, making it necessary to cut down on the amount of translated text. This was also the case even with 16-bit environments. For example, the American translator / localization coordinator Ted Woolsey, who translated the J-RPG *Final Fantasy VI* (1994) for the SNES, recalled how he had to continuously cut and reduce his English translation text to make it fit within the available capacity of the system:

> [I]n spite of some rudimentary compression techniques, I was told it was over by about 50% of the allotted size… When they tested the next set of edited files, I was still over by 15–20%, so it was back to the drawing board, re-editing and rewriting.
> (cited in Kohler 2005, 226)

The need for brevity still remains a hallmark of software localization today to cater to the limited space allocated especially for user interface (UI) elements, yet the above example suggests the text limitation in those days was more fundamentally determined by the storage capacity of the game machine, thus affecting all game texts beyond the UI. In the meantime, with progressive advances in hardware technology, the 16-bit machines started to offer sound sampling options, enhancing the quality of soundtracks. This led to the situation today where many games have licensed music tracks which may be released separately on CD, and some game song lyrics go through an elaborate adaptation phase during the localization process (see Chapter 4). PlayStation® (PS), introduced by Sony Computer Entertainment (SCE) Inc. in Japan in 1994, is a 5th generation 32-bit console which took advantage of the 640MB capacity of the CD-ROM. While this was over 100 times the maximum capacity of a ROM cartridge around that time, the cost was substantially less with this new storage medium. With a 512KB audio RAM and the capacity offered by CD, PS allowed musicians to load a soundtrack and sound

---

27. We use "gameplay" here in the popular sense of "playing the game", highlighting the experiential aspect. In the industry it may be described in terms of interface, speed and strategy (Dovey and Kennedy 2006, 146). Liestrol (2004 cited in Dovey and Kennedy 2006, 7) uses the term to stress the inseparability of games as play objects and as playing action.

effects at the start or stream from CD as required. This technological shift was also significant in that it allowed Sony to enter the game industry directly as a major player after having been approached by Nintendo to help develop a storage facility based on CD-ROM technology (Sheff 1993).

During the 1990s many poor translations were produced which have been un-covered and publicised more recently by widely circulated archives made available by online game fan communities sprouting on the Internet. As part of the revival of **retro-games**, poor translation has become one of the focal points of fan activities (Newman 2008) with fans re-producing and circulating translation errors from earlier games simply for amusement. One of the most frequently cited examples is from the original Japanese **shooter** game *Zero Wing* (1991). The Japanese line uttered by the alien character called CATS "君達の基地はすべて*CATS* がいた だいた。 [CATS has taken over all your base stations.]" translated as "All your base are belong to us" first appeared in the European English version for the Sega console. The translation was reportedly so poor that "it achieved cult status for the terrible word choices throughout the game that often verged on the hilarious" (Langdell 2006, 203). Other examples of blatant translation errors during this era included the major J-RPG titles such as *Final Fantasy VII* (1997), where one char-acter near the beginning says: "That man are sick" and also where a yes / no answer option was phrased as: "Off course! / No, way!" (Kohler 2005, 228). A less obvious issue in this game was the name of the character rendered as "Aeris" in English. It was meant to be derived from "Air" and "Earth", but it was not until later that this connection became more obvious with the corrected spelling "Aerith" (Fenlon 2011). The irony was that this particular game sold even more in the US than on the Japanese market, reaching 1 million units (Honeywood cited in Fenlon ibid.) despite the generally poor translation. Nevertheless, the experience is believed to have prompted its Japanese developer / publisher Square (now Square Enix) to shift subsequent localization work in-house instead of outsourcing (O'Hagan and Mangiron 2004, 58). Another iconic game localized during this period was Hideo Kojima's *Metal Gear Solid* (1998), which established the **stealth** genre of games, whose birth is attributed to the creation of PS (Donovan 2010, 277). The original game consisted of some 150 Japanese messages, of which just over half were trans-lated into English of substandard quality (Tinnelly 2007, 31).

The early period of game localization covering the 1980s and 1990s is in-deed known for having produced an unparalleled quantity of poor translations. Such examples ranged from the unintentionally comical to the wholly nonsensi-cal, with reasons attributed to "technological and financial limitations" as well as "the growing pains of a nascent games industry" (Corliss 2007, n.p.). In reference to the case of the aforementioned *Zero Wing*, the comment by "Walter" in Mike Nowak's blog post (cited in Nornes 2007, 246–247) alludes to the effect of poor translation on the game player behind the seeming delight subsequently taken by some observers:

> I tend to think that crap dialogue is better under a haze of nostalgia. That's why 'All Your Base' got so popular. When that stuff ceases to be the norm, it opens up the possibility of someone recalling it and concentrating the badness in a way that's more pleasurable than being subjected to it over and over.

Given the recursive patterns of certain lines used in games where the same set phrases are triggered repeatedly, annoyance over poor translation could indeed be magnified rather than being perceived as fun. These poor quality translations appear to have resulted from not involving competent translators as well as from a lack of proper localization processes. While the market seemed to have been generally tolerant of translation errors, the quality of translation often adversely affected the gameplay experience itself even if some translation errors may have sometimes created a humorous effect. As a noteworthy example of successful localization of the period, Hasegawa (2009, 129) cites the game *Crash Badicoot* (1996–), initially released on PS. Targeting Japan as a key market, the American developer of this title was prepared to modify many aspects of the game during the localization process (Thayer and Kolko 2004). The changes included the main character's appearance, voice, and the difficulty level of the game. Furthermore, several targeted advertising campaigns including the release of manga were launched (Turner 2002 cited in Thayer and Kolko ibid., 481), leveraging the close ties games have with manga and anime in Japan (O'Hagan 2006b). We will discuss this example further in Chapter 5 as an illustration of culturalization at work.

An early game localization challenge also particularly significant for Japanese games was related to character encoding issues. Unlike modern software localization practices, encoding processes that allowed the correct representation of characters in different languages had not been properly established in the early days. The Japanese text in games used to be stored in picture format and therefore the process of replacing the Japanese with English language files was not a matter of replacing text files (Kohler 2005, 221). This meant that original Japanese games had to be reprogrammed to fit the translated English text. Such cumbersome operations were nevertheless tolerated, given the relative simplicity of the whole game structure and the limited amount of text involved compared with today's major games. In those days the concept of "internationalization", to develop the original games in a localization-friendly manner (see Chapter 2), was virtually unknown, at least in any formalized way, and games were therefore generally not designed on any technical level to accommodate subsequent localization requirements. In this way translation was undermined by technical issues. Furthermore, in the early days the translators of Japanese games had to use the double-byte

Shift-JIS encoding system when typing English, making it impossible to run an English spell-checker (Honeywood cited in Fenlon 2011). This explains some of the blatant spelling errors found in a number of the early games. Honeywood, who worked at Square in this period, reveals how little the game development team at the time understood localization requirements; thus the development and the localization processes were considered to be completely separate (Fenlon ibid.).

In the meantime PS had considerable success in Asian markets in the late 1990s and early 2000s thanks to the availability of pirated games on CDs made in Hong Kong and Taiwan of China, Malaysia, and Thailand (Ng 2008, 214). The success is also attributed to Sony setting up offices in Asian cities and producing 220/240 volt versions of PS (both Japan and the US use 100/110 volt). The manuals were available in English as well as Japanese with a targeted selection of games adapted specifically to Chinese-speaking markets such as in the case of *The Legend of the Condor Heroes* (2000), based on a famous martial arts story by Jinyong (Ng ibid.). Ng highlights the role of piracy in the spread of Japanese games in Asian regions, which echoes the success of other Japanese popular culture genres of anime and manga through similar unofficial channels.

1.1.4   Maturing phase: Early 2000 to 2005

The new century saw the major Japanese game company Sega withdrawing from console manufacturing while Microsoft entered the market, leaving Sony, Nintendo, and Microsoft as the three **console platform holders**. In this period the game consoles moved from CD-ROM to DVD-ROM and text fragments could be stored in ASCII instead of picture format. These advances made the localization process much more efficient while allowing for a much bigger storage capacity for text. However, constraints imposed on the length of textual fragments (strings) embedded in software were not eliminated, as we discuss in Chapters 3 and 4. In the meantime with PS2 the gaming environment was enhanced to embrace 48 channels of sound with audio RAM of 2MB (McCarthy et al. 2005, 111). Audio capacities increased the realism of the gameplay experience and also further widened the scope for smooth implementation of human voiced dialogue, with significant implications for translation. This led to the possibility of re-voicing of the original audio using human voice actors in the form of dubbing in different languages for localized games. *Grand Theft Auto III* (2001), originally released on PS2, hired Hollywood stars for voiceover of game characters, such as Tommy Vercetti, voiced by Ray Liotta (McDougall and O'Brien 2008, 89). Furthermore, one of the great advances of game technology was realized by the use of 3D graphics as well as sounds and movies within games. These **cut-scenes** are cinematic sequences inserted in a game for a number of reasons, including showcasing the technology as well as for functional purposes. *Metal Gear Solid 2: Sons of Liberty* (2001) is a relatively early example containing lengthy cut-scenes lasting up to 40 minutes; these divided gamers, who were either repelled or attracted by the inclusion of such "non-interactive story-telling scenes" (Donovan 2010, 277). From the point of view of translation, cut-scenes gave rise to the explicit use of subtitles and dubbing techniques similar, but not identical, to those used in AVT. Subtitle-like techniques had already been used in games for more rudimentary cinematic sequences as mentioned earlier (see Figure 1.2), and over time these developed into something closer to subtitles used in cinema. In Chapter 4 we look further into how cut-scenes are treated in game localization and discuss them in comparison to norms in AVT. While technology generally improved game play experience, it has had a detrimental impact on deaf and hard-of-hearing gamers in the cases where voiced dialogue replaced previously more prevalent written text. Accessibility in game localization is an under-researched area, as we explore in some depth in Chapter 7.

Advances in technology meant increased complexity of localization work calling for greater attention to detail. Hasegawa (2009, 129) gives an example of the finer attention which became necessary to achieve more accurate lip-synching in the re-voicing of dialogue in the localization process in response to the improved graphic technologies affording details of the facial expressions of game characters. At the major Japanese game developer and publisher Square Enix, cut-scenes in some Japanese games such as *Bouncer* (2000) were voiced in English first to satisfy the demand by North American gamers for accurate lip-synching (Honeywood cited in Fenlon 2011). This led to the engagement of professional voice talent as well as translators specialized in AVT (Hasegawa 2009). This period also saw the increasing availability of programmers experienced in working with texts in different languages and therefore able to efficiently code localization functions (ActiveGaming Media n.d). Another localization trend noted during this period is the entry onto the market of small localization companies enabled by the increased scope for making profits out of localization, in turn increasing competition while reducing the pricing of localization (ibid.). A case study (Tinnelly 2007) on the localization of the internationally acclaimed *Metal Gear* series (1987–) spanning two decades illustrates how advances in game technologies have clearly affected localization in terms of the substantial increase in the volume of in-game text and that of cut-scenes with the use of the human voice. This study also highlights the previously little recognized role played by game translators deeply involved in the creative process of producing games for international consumption (ibid.). This links to our focus on the translator and translators' creativity discussed in Chapter 4.

1.1.5   Advancing phase: 2005 to the present

The most recent consoles such as Xbox 360 and PS3 belong to the latest 7th generation game machines. These consoles are designed to deliver enhanced gameplay experience while also serving as multimedia entertainment centres by offering online connectivity as well as further storage capacity for pictures, music, and communication functions. Also in this group is the Wii, which uses a unique radio-sensor enabled controller to detect the player's hand movements. The more recent motion-sensing controller, called Move and developed by Sony for PS3, allows the player's positional data to be further accurately reflected within the game, combining a webcam and a wand to grant the player a greater freedom of movement in 3-D space. Microsoft's Kinect technology for Xbox 360 in turn attempts to deliver a new experience of controller-free gaming, where the player's kinetic input is captured by a webcam alone. Nintendo's 8th generation console, the Wii U, released in November 2012, features a new controller with an embedded touchscreen, called "GamePad". This controller allows players to continue a gaming session by displaying the game even when the television is switched off. Although the exact implications of these technologies for game localization are not yet clear, dynamic advances in game technologies inevitably feed through to localization, covering linguistic, technological, cultural, and social dimensions of the gameplay experience. From the perspective of accessibility, however, some of these technologies pose new challenges for players with reduced mobility, an issue that developers will be increasingly expected to address (see Chapter 7).

The enhanced hardware capacity of 7th generation consoles also led to an increased volume of game software content needing to be localized, including text, audio, and graphics. Furthermore, as mentioned in the Introduction, the number of TLs for major games now routinely exceeds 10, including European and Asian languages (Hasegawa 2009, 130). In addition many publishers in North America and the UK publish their games using a **sim-ship** (simultaneous shipment) model, where localized games are shipped simultaneously with the original. Contrary to this tendency for global simultaneous release, Japanese **AAA games** – major games with a large budget – have generally been not sim-shipped at least until relatively recently. The most common localization approach by Japanese publishers has been to release games first on the domestic market in Japan, followed by a North American release in English some time later. Their respective European versions are released last, usually based on the North American release. However, this staggered approach is changing. For example, in recent years Nintendo has achieved near-simultaneous releases of localized versions with a reduced time lag after the original game (Gamasutra Podcast 2006) while Square Enix is also following suit. This in turn has significant implications for localization, which has to start before the original game is complete. While sim-ship has become a standard model for most major Western game publishers, the lack of availability of the finished game serving as the stable source at the time of translating makes the task of localization extremely challenging (Dietz 2006, 125–126). Also the more specialized and sophisticated games become, the more difficult it is for translators to fully comprehend the vast and intricate game world without actually seeing and playing the finished product.

Today's AAA games are comparable in a number of ways to big film productions, with the most expensive game at the time of writing being reported to be the MMORPG title *Star Wars: The Old Republic* (2011), costing nearly USD 200 million and taking nearly six years to develop (*Los Angeles Times*, January 20, 2012). These projects may involve several hundred experts, each specializing in different aspects such as sound, programming, animation, graphics, marketing, game design and production (ibid., 15). Not unlike high-profile film directors, some game designers have achieved similar widespread recognition, gaining something of a celebrity status, and their names may appear on game boxes. In this sense, it hints at the emergence of auteurism (Newman 2004, 12), where the names of individual game designers and producers of international repute such as Shigeru Miyamoto (creator of mega hit Nintendo games including *Super Mario*), Hideo Kojima (creator of *Metal Gear* series) or Sir Peter Molyneux (creator of the *Fable* franchise) are exploited for marketing purposes and dominate publicity as well as reviews, fan discussions, and scholarly works. As far as today's game production is concerned, given their technical sophistication and complexity, most big budget modern video games are the result of the game designer's original vision realized through the collaboration of often a large number of multiple specialists. Figure 1.4 illustrates a typical team makeup in today's game development (McCarthy et al. 2005, 26–35). This can be demonstrated by the comparison, for example, between the PC game *SimCity* (1989) released in the late 1980s with the total number of contributors to the production listed as 20, and the later game *Halo 2* (2004), which involved more than 100 personnel (Egenfeldt-Nielsen et al. 2008, 15–16). In the context of localization *Fable II* (2008) reportedly hired a pool of 270 actors and a team of 130 personnel for full localization into five languages and three partial localizations (Chandler and Deming 2012, 317) with the production of the more recent multiplayer online RPG *StarWars: The Old Republic* (2011) further breaking the record. This illustrates the enormity and complexity of the localization task especially with major games and in the case of sim-ship delivering multiple locales.

Figure 1.4 indicates localization undertaken only at the very end, as a handover from the Game Tester to the Localization Manager, although today localization is increasingly being considered more upstream during the game production

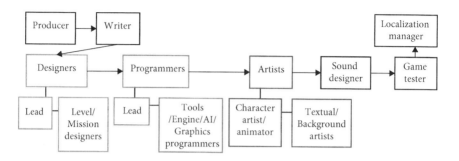

Figure 1.4 A typical modern game development team composition
(adapted from McCarthy et al. 2005, 28–29)

process particularly for major AAA titles (see Chapter 2). The role of the Game Tester in this diagram is not to be confused with that of the game testing of localized versions, which takes place during the localization process, as we describe in detail in Chapter 3. During production a game goes through several versions called **builds**, which may be tested. The first basic playable version is called the "Alpha build", followed by the Beta build before the **gold master** is released. Once reaching the Beta stage, new builds may be created on nearly a daily basis, following new additions of functions, assets, and other elements to the game (Newman 2009, 53). Given that the testing takes time, only those builds which involve significant code changes tend to be tested (ibid.). Unlike the typical testing of productivity software, processes of "real-world testing" (Egenfeldt-Nielsen et al. 2008, 19) are often used to test the beta version of the game (thus known as "**beta testing**"). Usually this is done by invited gamers, called "beta testers", forming part of consumer feedback on the product under development. This is characteristic of the game industry, which has historically developed somewhat more explicit connections to the users of their products compared with other software sectors. For example, the industry's liberal attitude which led to the practices of **modding** or **mods** – modification of games by technically-oriented gamers – is evidence of allowing the active involvement of seasoned users in the game production (Newman 2004, 42). Furthermore, Dovey and Kennedy (2006, 61–62) point out the industry's tendency to absorb "fan-led groups", where fans and gamers subsequently become part of game production teams. As a result the industry is acquiring "an extraordinarily high degree of homogeneity compared to other media" because gamer-cum-developers produce games which they like to play. In Chapter 7 we discuss the role of active users, increasingly significant to the game industry and culture as a future avenue of research in the context of Translation Studies. Among the newly emerging trends is the development of a user-participatory model called "crowdsourcing", introduced to the localization industry in the context of user-volunteer participation in otherwise remunerated professional translation activities. Given the historically close link between gamers and the game industry, the issue of user participation, which has been highlighted with the development of Web 2.0, is also worthy of further research. This little explored characteristic of the game industry in relation to its way of working with fans and gamers will be examined in more detail in Chapter 7.

Further examination of the growing popularity of mobile gaming reveals the significance of added challenges posed by spatial limitations for translated text (Chandler and Deming 2012, 139). The industry is seeing new independent developers of games for mobile phones entering the market while the lack of a proper manufacturer validation system for mobile phones may allow poor quality low-cost localization to undercut the prices of more experienced localization vendors (ActiveGaming Media n.d.). Although we are mainly concerned with console games, these new developments are anticipated to impact on game localization as a whole, with an increasing range of digital devices and platforms becoming available for both **casual games** and **social games**.

1.2   Video games: Domain, terminology and characteristics

Having traced how game localization developed into today's growing specialized field we will now set out to define the key concepts of video games as relevant to our discussion of game localization.

1.2.1   Key terminology: Video game vs. computer game

Despite the increasing visibility of video games in academia and in society at large, those involved in their development and research have yet to agree on a standardized terminology. The use of the term "video games" has not been universally adopted and a variety of other names exist. Espen Aarseth (2001) declared 2001 as Year One of Game Studies in *The International Journal of Computer Game Research*, which is the first peer-reviewed online academic journal dedicated to research on digital games. While the journal chose the term "computer game", a literature survey in the field of Game Studies only confirms a range of terms and variant spellings currently being used to refer to the object of their study. Some authors claim preferences are based on regions. For example, Buckingham (2006, 4–5) points out that the term "computer games" is in common usage in the UK regardless of the platform on which the game is played, be it a PC or a game console. He further claims that this term is more inclusive than the term "video game", which may not include PC games. Yet this does not seem to be consistent among UK-based authors such as James Newman, who uses the orthographic variant "videogame" to encompass PC games in all his publications (Newman 2004, 2008; Newman and Oram 2006) as does the UK author Steven Poole (2000) in his journalistic contribution *Trigger Happy: The Inner Life of Videogames*. When it comes to academic publications, Wolf and Perron (2003, 2 & 21) in their edited volume *The Video Game Theory Reader* claim that the terms "video games" and "computer games" are most commonly used in both popular and scholarly discourse and are often used interchangeably. Nevertheless, they draw certain distinctions, such as that video games do not require any "microprocessor" while computer games do not require any "visuals". However, this argument is becoming less relevant, given the fact that the division between game consoles and computers is increasingly blurred. The game consoles such as PS3 and Xbox 360 function as a computer to some extent as well as a game console, now commonly referred to as "multimedia entertainment hubs". The editors of *The Handbook of Computer Game Studies* (Raessens and Goldstein 2005, xii) in turn define video games as "played on a dedicated console connected to a TV set", whereas computer games are "those played with a personal computer either off-line or online" and both are subsumed in the more generic terms "electronic games" and "digital games". Indeed Kerr (2006a, 2006b) opts to use the term "digital games", arguing that the terms "video games" and "computer games" are, in fact, platform-specific, i.e. the former refers to console games, and the latter to PC games. She concludes that the term "digital games" can be used to cover "the entire field and to embrace arcade, computer, console, and mobile games in all their diversity" (2006a, 3).[28] Similarly, Consalvo (2006, 119) relates the term "video games" closely to the console game industry.

Another source which also illustrates the variation in the usage of terms is the nomenclature provided by game industry associations. In the US, the Entertainment Software Association (ESA) is the body representing game publishers. Initially established in 1994 as the Interactive Digital Software Association, it was renamed in 2003. Their UK counterpart is the Association for UK Interactive Entertainment (UKie) established in 2010, replacing the Entertainment and Leisure Software Publishers Association (ELSPA). An equivalent European-wide organization is called the Interactive Software Federation of Europe (ISFE). The Japanese counterpart is called the Computer Entertainment Suppliers Association (CESA). These associations clearly chose to use broader terms in their titles,

---

28. In using the term "digital games" Kerr (2006a, 3–4) makes reference to a terminological discussion at the inaugural meeting of the Digital Games Research Association (DIGRA) in 2003.

highlighting concepts such as "entertainment", "leisure" or "interactivity". In fact, in their report ESA distinguishes between "computer games" and "video games" to refer to PC games and console games respectively (see ESA 2012). By comparison, ISFE uses in its consumer report the term "video games" as a generic comprehensive term whereas "gaming" in fact is most prevalent throughout the above report (GameVision 2010). Indeed the use of the hypernym "game" is increasingly common, as highlighted by Bernal-Merino (2006). For example, Chandler in her monograph on game localization consistently adheres to the term "game" in referring to all types of games in electronic form subject to localization although at the beginning she makes a distinction as in "the computer and video game industry" (Chandler 2005, 1).

Such terminological heterogeneity can be considered as typical of a relatively young and dynamic discipline driven by technology and further compounded by the fact that the field belongs to a popular culture genre which may be susceptible to journalistic popularization as well as industry and marketing jargon. On the basis of the above observations, we use the term "video game" and the shortened form "game" in this book as it is the most common term both in the game localization sector as well as in academic writing. Also implicit in this choice is our focus on console games which are most commonly called "video games", as argued by various authors mentioned above.

1.2.2 Defining a video game

Having settled on the term, we now move on to its definition, bearing in mind that our main interest is to locate this sub-domain within the framework of Translation Studies. Frasca (2001, 4) defines the video game as "any form of computer-based entertainment software, either textual or image-based, using any electronic platform such as personal computers or consoles and involving one or multiple players in a physical or networked environment". By identifying games as software programs, this pragmatic definition is useful in linking a video game to localization. Most modern video games incorporate written text and graphics as well as audio, often with full motion pictures. Frasca's definition also refers to the **platforms** on which games are played and their mode of play. "Game platforms" refer to devices which are used to play games: dedicated **game consoles**, PCs, or portable game devices which may be called "handhelds". The mode of play can be **single-player** or **multi-player**, where the players may be in the same physical space or linked through electronic networks. The platforms and modes of play also often reveal certain territory-specific preferences. For example, whereas PC games have been more popular in Europe and South East Asia, console games dominate in the US and Japan (Kerr 2006a, 3; McDougall and O'Brien 2008, 45). In terms of player mode, online multi-player games known as **Massively Multiplayer Online Games (MMOGs)** have taken off on a major scale especially in China[29] (see Zhang 2009, 2011) and Korea, whereas they remain less popular in Japan. This is evident in the fact that *World of Warcraft* (2004–) is localized into both simplified and traditional Chinese as well as Korean, but not Japanese. The market preferences affect localization decisions in determining what types of games should be localized for certain territories. Another related dimension to player mode is that of different categories of players. Difference in player engagement levels may be apparent in terms of the player categories often used in the industry, such as casual gamer and hardcore gamer. In addition, "power-gamer" is a term coined by Taylor in her observations of the online game *EverQuest* (1999), describing a particular type of player who is "committed to fully understanding the structure of a game and [who will tend] to focus on efficiency and instrumental play", thus displaying "high levels of technical and skill proficiency" (cited in Kerr 2006a, 116). We will revisit in Chapter 7 the different types of players in reference to the game fan community. As far as our use of terminology in this book is concerned, the terms "player" and "gamer" are treated as synonyms.[30] In the next section we focus on different types of games in terms of game genres, which is an important concept in further understanding what video games are.

1.2.3   Game genres

A wide variety of games are published today and the variation even within the same genre makes a completely standardized approach to game localization difficult, as has frequently been pointed out by industry sources (Darolle 2004; Crosignani et al. 2008). Such diversity granted, **game genre** is one of the key classifications widely used in academia, popular game magazines and websites to differentiate between the huge variety of games. For example, the popular game website

---

29. *World of Warcraft* had more than 3.5 million subscribers in China as of January 2007 (Flew and Humphreys 2008, 131). According to a more recent publication (Chatfield 2010, 93), the total number of global subscribers is quoted as still rising, having exceeded 12 million, of which a significant proportion are assumed to be in China, according to industry sources.

30. Newman (2008, 16–19) provides a discussion of the use of the terms "players", "gamers", "fans" and "otaku". He considers "gamer" to be the most impartial term without added connotations. The term "player" can be seen as stressing the "act of performance and engagements with the game system" (17). "Otaku" in turn is too closely associated with Japanese culture whereas "fans" may often be used in pejorative contexts. We discuss game fandom further in Chapter 7 in the context of fan culture.

Table 1.2 2011 console game genre preference in Japan and the USA

Ranking	Japan	US
1	RPG	Action
2	Action	Shooter
3	Adventure	Sports
4	Shooter	Family
5	Simulation (Nurturing)	Adventure

Source: *CESA Games White Paper* (CESA 2012, 132 & 165).

Gamespot categorizes games into action games, adventure games, driving games, puzzle games, role playing games (RPGs), simulations, sports games and strategy games. These eight categories commonly acknowledged by gamers in the West are in stark contrast with the 26 genres identified by Japanese gamers in a user survey published in the *2012 Games White Paper* by the Japanese Computer Entertainment Suppliers Association (CESA 2012, 132). Among the Japanese-specific genres we find "sound novel" and "study/learning/training" as well as "typing practice". Also, simulation games are divided into "nurturing simulation", "strategic simulation", "romance simulation" (e.g. dating games) and "instrumental simulator" (e.g. pachinko simulator). This shows how game genre classifications may vary, depending on different territories where certain genres seem to be more developed than others (Kerr 2006a, 39). For example, Table 1.2 indicates 2011 popular console games in Japan and the USA according to game genre (CESA 2012).

Although RPGs have their origins in the US (Shintaku and Ikuine 2001), more narrative-driven J-RPGs have become internationally recognized through successful game franchises such as the *Final Fantasy* series, whereas Action and Shooter remain the most popular genres in the US. However, classifications of games in terms of genres are often criticized by game scholars as nebulous and arbitrary (Newman 2004, 12; Egenfeldt-Nielsen et al. 2008, 41). Newman (ibid.) cautions that these genre classifications may straitjacket the game text, thus diverting attention from different contexts of play. There are indeed disagreements among theorists in academia and in popular literature in classifying game genres. For example, Kerr (2006a, 40) highlighted the differences in the genre classifications earlier used by Herz (1997) and Poole (2000), especially with regard to action, simulation, and strategy game genres. Kerr also noted Poole's use of the term "god games"[31] to cover the genres of simulation and strategy. Table 1.3 shows the

---

31. The term is claimed to be created by journalists in reference to games such as *Populous* (1989) in which players assume supernatural powers allowing them to create and change the whole environments, influencing a follower population (Donovan 2010, 195).

Table 1.3 Indicative game genres

Game genre	Explanation	Examples
Action	Any game whose main purpose is the player's action, involving his/her quick reflexes and co-ordination skills. The genre includes "Beat 'em up" games. The latest sub-genre is rhythm action which may be treated as a separate genre.	*Doom* (1993) *Quake* (1996) *Monster Hunter Tri* (2009)
Adventure	The player's perspective is usually fixed just behind her/him. Includes detailed back stories.	*Tomb Raider* (1996) *Resident Evil 5* (2009)
Racing	The player is engaged in driving a vehicle.	*Gran Turismo* (1998) *Mario Kart Wii* (2008)
Shooter	The player sees the action in a first-person (FPS=First Person Shooter) or third-person perspective with the goal of firing the arsenal.	*Half-Life* (1998) *Halo* (2002) *Call of Duty 4: Modern Warfare* (2007)
Massively Multiplayer Online Game (MMOG)	A game is played online with a large number of players.	*EverQuest* (1999) *Lineage II: The Chaotic Chronicle* (2004) *World of Warcraft* (2004–)
Platform	The player needs to overcome various obstacles, while accumulating power (power-up).	*Donkey Kong* (1981) *SuperMario Bros.* series (1985–) *Prince of Persia: The Sands of Time* (2003)
Puzzle	The player's mission is to solve a puzzle, using logic.	*Tetris* (1985)
Role Playing Game (RPG)	The player takes on the role of a character and embarks on a lengthy quest. Includes detailed back stories.	*Final Fantasy* series (1987–) *Baldur's Gate* (1998) *Dragon Quest IX* (2009)
Simulation (sometimes called "God Games")	The player plays God and manages real-world simulated situations.	*Microsoft Flight Simulator* series (1982–) *The Sims* (2000)
Strategy	Games that place the player in a strategic conflict to be resolved.	*Civilization* (1991) *Command and Conquer* (1996) *Age of Empires* (1997)
Sports	Games that emulate sports such as tennis, football, golf, etc.	*FIFA* series (1993–) *Pro Evolution Soccer* series (2001–) *Wii Sports* (2006)
Serious Games	Games designed for specific purposes other than pure entertainment.	*America's Army* (2002) *September 12th* (2003) *Food Force* (2005)
Social Games	Games that are linked to social networking sites such as Facebook.	*Pet Society* (2008) *FarmVille* (2009)

Sources: Newman (2004); McCarthy et al. (2005, 53–55); Kerr (2006a, 38–41); Egenfeldt-Nielsen et al. (2008).

main game genres together with their key characteristics and sample game titles representing different period.

These genres have also evolved over time and continue to develop. For example, the early games such as *Pong* (1972) and *Space Invaders* (1978) in the 1970s are generally categorized as action games, some of which developed into platform games in the 1980s such as *Pac-Man* (1980) and *Mario Bros* (1983). Of particular interest from a translation perspective is the advent of text-based adventure games such as *Adventure* (1976) and later *Zork* (1980), where the player typed commands in a natural language to explore the game world through text. These games marked the beginning of fantasy RPGs, largely drawing on Tolkien-style "Dungeons and Dragons" stories. They subsequently led to so called **MUDs** (**Multi-User Dungeons**), where users who are connected to the game on a network, play against each other through text, forming the basis for today's **Massively Multiplayer Online Role Playing Games** (MMORPGs). Among the early games using text-based interaction is *Habitat* (1985), which further introduced **avatars** as cartoonish graphic representations of the players who were logged in on the game via a modem and who interacted through text input. Although these text-based interfaces had become marginal within the adventure genres and MUDs by the 1990s (Egenfeldt-Nielsen et al. 2008, 79), text-input games are still alive today, despite the advances in graphics and audio technologies. Together with the adventure genre, RPGs tend to be the most text-heavy. The latter typically involve an epic saga with an intricate mission and a complicated back story, featuring many main characters and minor **NPCs** (non-playable characters) with their dialogues, in addition to **mini games, side quests**, and cut-scenes (Mangiron 2004; Newman 2008, 48 & 156). The particular popularity of the RPG genre in Japan sees even very young players accustomed to playing text-heavy games, partly thanks to a high literacy level and also to their persistence in persevering through to the end of a game whose play time may often exceed 100 hours (Yahiro 2005, 116–129).

One of the newer genres includes **serious games**, a term coined by the American sociologist Clark Abt in 1968 (Egenfeldt-Nielsen et al. 2008, 205). These games are used for targeted purposes of training and various initiatives as well as conveying public and private policy messages about such matters as political conflicts, health policies and especially military planning and training (see Kerr 2006a, 137–140 for further details on the use of games by the military). Egenfeldt-Nielsen et al. (2008) also include **advertainment** as well as political and educational games (**edutainment**) in this category, all of which are played for purposes other than pure entertainment. Recent years have seen the rise in popularity of **party games** involving an offline multi-player mode, in which players are present in the same physical space to play the game together. Associated with edutainment and party games is the label "family entertainment" that the ESA uses as a super genre which, for example, includes games developed from popular animation films such as the *Shrek* series as well as dance, quiz, or sports game titles which can be played together by a whole family. According to ESA statistics, this genre accounted for 11% of all video games sold in the US in 2011 (ESA 2012, 8) and its popularity can be linked to the evolution of game hardware initiated by Nintendo Wii, facilitating new group modes of playing games. Another new genre which has emerged is social games, in reference to games played on social networking sites designed for interacting with friends.

The various debates regarding the use of genre classifications notwithstanding, from the perspectives of translation and localization the concept of genre is still relevant and useful, as genre signals text conventions to an extent. As text types are significant in translation, game genres help identify similar characteristics of texts and also often text volume (text-heavy games as opposed to action-heavy), thus indicating the particular translator competence required. Games belonging to a specialized domain such as military, aviation, and various sports genres seek to achieve a great degree of authenticity and realism through accurate visual and verbal representation for the given domain, including the precise use of terminology. A case in point is the early high-profile title *Metal Gear Solid* (1998), which involved terminology in nuclear technology, genetics, international relations, medicine, law enforcement and military affairs, as mentioned by game's translator Jeremy Blaustein (cited in Tinnelly 2007, 31). The authentic use of terminology in games is illustrated by the PC game *688(I) Hunter/Killer* (1997), whose developer had to leave out certain details which were considered by the US Navy to be too sensitive (Dietz 2006, 122). Given the importance of games achieving a level of make-believe, verisimilitude is critical especially in domain-specific games, where incorrect use of terminology in a localized version disengages the player, who may be knowledgeable about the given field (ibid.). Games such as flight simulation, action games taking place in a military context, sports games such as football, golf, or tennis, or RPGs based on courtroom dramas require an accurate use of specialized terminology in a similar way to a technical translation in a specialized field. To this end, the concept of genre has a particular significance from a translation perspective. Chapter 4 makes reference to these issues in analyzing game text in the context of translation. Finally, the concept of game genres is developing dynamically, especially with games with hybrid characteristics crossing over different genres. For example, McDougall and O'Brien (2008, 96–98) argue that the international best seller *Grand Theft Auto (GTA)* series can be considered to belong to at least three genres: RPG, car racing and beat 'em up (Action sub-genre). Further extending the thinking of genre conventions, the next section looks into the characteristics of games which make them amenable to being transferred across different media and platforms, with implications for localization and translation.

1.2.4 Video games as transmedia

Video games are new media characterized by the use of digital technology in the form of software. The fact that software is a malleable entity in the digital landscape (Manovich 2001) gives rise to video games as a new type of transmedial cultural product readily "**ported**" to different platforms (Kerr 2006a, 4). The concept of "transmedia" refers to how games can be integrated into other forms of media, both traditional and new, where games are adapted to present a new form of entertainment. Modern video games are presented and experienced on screen in an interactive manner, forming part of an increasing array of screen products or SPs (Chiaro 2009). A video game version of *Harry Potter* adds an interactive and exploratory dimension to its original written creation which can now be read in ebook as well as in print, while a movie version with special effects can be enjoyed in the cinema as well as on DVD or Blu-ray disk with added bonus materials. In addition to the well demonstrated link between video games and movies, a video game may also appear as a comic or a novel. In novelizing the PS2 Japanese game *ICO* (2001) into *ICO – 霧の城* [*Ico – Castle in the Mist*][32] (Miyabe 2004), the contemporary novelist Miyuki Miyabe (ibid., 537) explains in her afterword to the novel how her fondness of this game led to the novelization for which she was given the liberty of developing her own interpretation of the original game. Her reference to the novel as "a variation of the game" to be enjoyed by the people who liked the original game aptly describes the nature of transmedia. Dovey and Kennedy (2006, 84) in turn use the term "intermedia", which affords users "mediated experiences ... on several related platforms or means of delivery". They define "intermediality" as "the contemporary market-driven form of intertexuality in which texts and activities may refer to the same fictional 'world'" and highlight a tendency of all media texts to "bleed into one another" (ibid., 102). Dovey and Kennedy (ibid.) also emphasize the aspect of video games that enmesh increasingly detailed narratives and play into a single medium. Both transmedia and intermedia seem to refer to the same characteristic of video games that make them transportable across different media and platforms, leading to the creation of interwoven text. For the purposes of this book we treat intermedia and transmedia as synonymous.

---

32. The novel's English translation (*Ico – Castle in the Mist*) appeared in 2011 translated by Alexander O. Smith (Smith 2011), who is an author, a literary and a game translator as introduced in Chapter 4. Many reviews comment on the game's extended longevity by the novelization (e.g. see http://videogamewriters.com/review-ico-castle-in-the-mist-21616).

Through the formal arrangements of product tie-ins, games are officially associated with other media texts such as films, music, or literature. These are known as "character spin-offs" or "licensed games" and aim to target the already existing fan-base (McCarthy et al. 2005, 33). The top selling games derived from Star Wars movies – *Star Wars: Force Unleashed* (2008) and *Star Wars: The Old Republic* (2011) – are such examples. There is a strong link between films and games developed in the form of movie-licensed video games as in the above examples, mostly active in the US through Hollywood connections, where video games are developed based on high profile Hollywood films. Among the best known earlier examples is the Matrix series, whose first game implementation *Enter the Matrix* (2003) was released at the same time as the opening of the movie *Matrix Reloaded*, selling several million units worldwide (Yoshida 2008, 66). Part of the major attraction of such movie games is the original actors rendering their own character's voice in the game. For example, games such as *Batman Begins* (2005) cleared the rights to use all the actors' images in the game and the leading actors of the film participated in voice recording for the game version (Yoshida 2008, 112–113). The process also works in reverse, with games being made into movies; this is rarer, but includes the examples such as *Mortal Kombat* (1995), *Tomb Raider* (2001), the all-CG (computer graphics) films *Final Fantasy: The Spirits Within* (2001), *Final Fantasy VII: Advent Children* (2005), and another CG film *Biohazard: Degeneration* (2008).

Outside Hollywood, the *Pokémon* franchise is frequently cited as one of the most successful cases of video games being turned into a global phenomenon across a range of media. It started as the Nintendo GameBoy RPG *Pocket Monster* (1996) first released in Japan (*Pokémon* is a contraction of the two words *Pocket Monster*). This was quickly followed by transformation into manga (similar to the game *Crash Bandicoot* as mentioned earlier), a TV anime series and then full feature anime movies released in cinemas. In fact, the intrinsic relationship across manga, anime, and video games has long been exploited across these three media in Japan. Already detectable in the early days of Japanese video games, game character design tended to show an undeniable "family resemblance to manga and Japanimation" (Herz 1997, 161). The particular cartoonish drawing style used in early Japanese video game characters such as Mario also suited the lack of technological sophistication where "[s]mall, cute characters had fewer pixels per inch and were easier to use, and so videogames borrowed, for reasons of expediency, what manga had developed as a matter of convention" (Herz 1997, 162). The traditional link between video games and manga and anime was alive and well with *Pokémon*, as the drawing style was that of Japanese cartoons, and its tie-ins with manga and anime media were a natural progression in the Japanese context, where most TV anime are in fact based on bestselling manga. Despite the tremendous success of *Pokémon* in Japan, however, Nintendo of America (NOA) was concerned about whether the RPG game genre, which was not as popular in the US as in Japan at the time, would succeed in the US market and therefore took a further orchestrated transmedia approach to launching *Pokémon* in the US. NOA's strategy was to plan a simultaneous rollout of various *Pokémon* products, taking advantage in particular of the already popular anime form which could draw the audience to the games (Kohler 2005, 245). NOA then adapted the content to suit American children, who were the main target market. The cultural transformation involved careful adaptation in translating the very Japanese-sounding monster names. Also the Japanese content of the TV anime series had to undergo extensive editing as it was deemed unsuitable for American audiences. Religious references, sexual innuendo and particular types of humour were all subject to editing (Kohler 2005, 247). These carefully planned globalization and localization strategies paid off in the end, with the phenomenal success of the *Pokémon* franchise in the US and the rest of the world.

Some media studies scholars use the term "transmedia storytelling" to refer to narratives woven across a range of media, which Jenkins (2007) describes as "integral elements of a fiction…dispersed systematically across multiple delivery channels for the purpose of creating a unified and coordinated entertainment experience". The concept is increasingly applicable with the advent of a broad range of SPs such as mobile phones and tablet computers, often linked to expansive Internet-based virtual communities. For example, the popular TV series *Lost* (2004–2010) generated several spin-offs, including a mobile game *Lost: Via Domus* (2008) and *The Lost Experience* (2006), an Internet-based **Alternate Reality Game** (ARG) where participants drive the story, interacting with game characters in their real environments rather than fictional worlds, to extend the storyline of the original story. As such ARG forms a good example of transmedia storytelling. However, Jenkins (2003a) is critical of the fact that the current state of transmedia storytelling does not always maximize the characteristics of each medium, be it comic books, TV, cinema, or games. In his view, each should display a distinctive flavour, while still providing the consumer with multiple entry points to absorb the media content and to be able to engage fully with the particular content selected as an entry point. In the context of "transmediality", adaptation applied to games can be considered as the process of going beyond a derivative work to a standalone work in its own right, designed specifically for a given platform. And yet there may be reluctance, especially within the game industry, to make a radical departure from the original. The degree of freedom in adaptation clearly depends on the nature of the legal agreements, but is also affected by the typically risk-averse attitude of the game industry, given that the very reason for the use of existing intellectual property (IP) is to leverage the guaranteed audience, even at the expense of stifling innovation (Dovey and Kennedy 2006).

From the viewpoint of translation, approaches based on licensing agreements and marketing strategies can impose a constraint on translation decisions. The above case of transmedia exploitation with *Pokémon* illustrates implications for translation and localization applied across different media. The pre-existing translation usually exerts a certain power over a new translation created to respect the original's authority while fitting into an extended and coherent textual continuum. For example, in the case of the *Harry Potter* series across different media, the retention of the original names was part of the translators' contract so that "Warner Brothers can distribute the films, computer games and other merchandise all around the world with the names everyone recognizes" (Fries-Gedin 2002 cited in Brøndsted and Dollerup 2004, 58). Similarly, *The Simpsons: Hit and Run* (2003) game was only allowed to be translated by the official translator of the Simpsons TV series. In this way, transmedia arrangements are likely to have an impact on the otherwise potentially greater leeway granted to game localization.

A pertinent issue which arises from transmediality is the question of adaptation, a topic well explored in Translation Studies, although still without a clear definition (Bastin 2009, 3). More recently adaptation has been discussed in the context of advertising and localization in addition to translation of children's literature, theatre, and film texts (see Milton 2009). Focusing on the adaptation of theatrical and film media, Zatlin (2005, 161) refers to adaptation as a means of "creative recycling", where transformation is made across media such as TV, stage, and movies. Bastin, in turn, describes adaptation as "a type of creative process which seeks to restore the balance of communication that is often disrupted by the traditional forms of translation" (Bastin 2009, 6). Both authors highlight the creativity involved in the process. Given the extent of manipulation required to mould the product and translation into a shape for each platform which is acceptable also to marketing strategies, we suggest that the concepts of "transmedia" and "intermedia" will provide further scope to explain the uniquely negotiated form of translation, driven by different media forms. Furthermore, we associate the malleable nature of software with the concepts of "transcreation" and "rewriting" as discussed in Chapters 4 and 5 respectively.

Transmedia storytelling can create rich intertextuality across different media if done properly. However, this requires systematic planning for translation and localization strategies beyond simply retaining consistency in translation across media, bearing in mind both the different characteristics of each medium involved and the continuum as a whole. As the media cross their previously distinct boundaries, translators are likely to have to go beyond their own specialist fields. For example, translators who have been working in the field of AVT primarily for cinema may face an increasing need to become familiar with other media such as comics and games, whereas software localization specialists may need to be more specifically versed in audiovisual content requiring AVT techniques. This will have clear implications for future translator training to prepare the profession for a dynamically changing digital entertainment field in which media boundaries are increasingly blurred. The dimension of "transmedia" / "intermedia" adds further complexity to the key goal of localizing entertainment media such as games so as to transfer "user experience" that is specific to the nature of the given medium. These concepts bring home the need to analyze games as stories and also as playable objects in order to understand the intertextuality created across different media texts. The story-focus, seeing games as representation via narratives, may miss out on the performability consideration of the game, whereas the play-focus of a ludic approach concentrating on rules and other gameplay aspects alone will clearly not be sufficient to recognize the intertextuality between the game and other media versions. The following section briefly discusses the two key paradigms of story-focus and play-focus debated by Game Studies scholars.

1.2.5 Video game theory: Narrative theory versus play theory

The defining element of video games is arguably that of interactivity – it is this which sets games apart from other forms of entertainment. As evident in the naming of industry associations such as the UKie and ISFE, the game industry uses terms like "interactive entertainment" ,"interactive software" or "interactive publishing" to stress the importance of interactivity. And yet this term is fraught with misconceptions. Manovich (2001, 55) argues that interactivity is simply a basic feature of computers since "[o]nce an object is represented in a computer, it automatically becomes interactive". So, in order for interactivity to be meaningful, he suggests using more concrete concepts such as "menu-based interactivity", "scalability", or "simulation", and also the concept of "closed" and "open" interactivity (ibid., 56). Similarly, Aarseth (1997) distinguishes between trivial and non-trivial interaction.[33] For example, clicking on web links or selecting from a DVD menu may be considered a trivial level of interactivity, whereas game systems are designed for a deeper level of interaction between the player and the game to elicit both somatic and mental engagement. Manovich (2001) admits a difficulty in addressing interactivity theoretically in relation to user experiences, which would

---

33. Aarseth (1997, 1) introduced the term "ergodicity" to refer to non-trivial interactivity. In defining the "ergodic text" Aarseth explains interactivity as follows: "the user … has to make an effort to traverse the text. This effort is not only directed at understanding the text, but also at constructing it, for example, making decisions … or engaging in some form of contest."

be applicable in the case of games. Games rely on the active participation of the player, involving tangible feedback rather than the more passive spectatorship associated with watching films or TV programmes. To this end, the term "configuration" has emerged deriving from the field of Human Computer Interaction (HCI) to address the specific type of interaction elicited in gameplay of video games. The term is used to describe "the complexity of the active processes of both interpretation and interaction as the player literally constructs the game 'on the fly' through the practices of gameplay" (Dovey and Kennedy 2006, 7). The concept highlights the extent of the impact of the action by the player who makes "significant interventions into a game world that have dynamic effects through its system" (ibid.). Without the player's tangible physical action executed at a prompt through the game's interface, the video game world cannot unfold and thus the player is a necessary actor who sets off the subsequent sequences and drives the game in a certain direction by making deliberate choices within pre-determined parameters. This still allows a degree of openness, as exemplified in what is called "**emergence**" or "**emergent gameplay**", referring to unexpected game dynamics arising out of unanticipated ways that the player may play the game vis-à-vis the game designer's original intention. This stresses the significance of the player's agency and it also has some implications for game localization.

It is relevant at this point to refer to the two main competing paradigms of analyzing games within Game Studies. Arising in reaction to the more traditional approaches by narratologists, based on the view of games as narratives, ludologists focus on the play action dimensions of games and acknowledge games as presenting a highly structured world. It is a world governed by rules according to which the player is able to choose among different paths, leading him/her to different scenarios. Narratologists would apply narrative or dramatic theories in their analysis of games, essentially as texts being decoded by the recipient, whereas ludologists such as Frasca (2001) claim that "games cannot be understood through theories derived from narrative", and focus on the experience of playing a game. The ludologists' views are therefore also referred to as "play theory" (Kerr 2006a). In comparison with narratologists' tendency to treat games as representations, the position adopted by ludologists sees games as a simulation. The ludic approach highlights the fact that not only is interactivity an important defining characteristic of video games, but so too is the fact that it is a regulated interactivity controlled by pre-determined rules. The term "ludology" stems from the Latin term *ludus* as famously used, for example, by the French philosopher Roger Caillois (1958/2001).[34] Many Game Studies scholars refer to Caillois's four categories

---

34. Earlier Johan Huizinga in his *Homo Ludens* (1938/2000) highlighted the otherwise neglected importance of play in cultures, introducing the concept of "magic circle" as a space

of games: competition (*Agōn*), chance (*Alea*), imitation (*Mimicry*), and vertigo (*Ilinx*). He approached each in terms of a spectrum between *paidia* and *ludus*. As opposed to *paidia*, which corresponds to free play, *ludus* is governed by the presence of rules. Caillois's view of *ludus* captures key characteristics applicable to highly systematized modern video games. Although perspectives by ludologists vs. narratologists have created the most divisive paradigm clashes within Game Studies (Egenfeldt-Nielsen et al. 2008), more recently game theorists seem to have struck a middle ground, accommodating the uniqueness of games in terms of their deliberate design and structure as well as their narrative elements (Juul 2005, 16).

These theoretical underpinnings argued by game scholars are relevant in considering game localization, which in turn calls for an understanding of the novel properties of new types of text becoming subject to translation. As we delve into details of localization in theory and practice in the next two chapters we will consider the ludic (simulational) as well as the narrative (representative) dimensions of games. With reference to the theoretical interests of Translation Studies, it is significant to note that players of video games generate meaning not only by reading text, but also by involving play action via physical motor response. In the words of Dovey and Kennedy (2006, 102) "[t]o read is to create meaning cognitively in the encounter with the text. To play is to generate meaning, to express it through play. Play allows us to actively express meaning". It is this change in the relationship between the end users (players) and a text designed to prompt the former to act kinetically in order to generate meaning, which has implications for translating video games. For example, various elements of translated text in a game need to induce players to take an expected action as intended in the original game. When compared to other types of text, this characteristic of game texts highlights not only their representational value but also their affordance property promoting player action. Affordance is a concept initially developed by Gibson (1979) to understand visual perception in the context of depth perception of pilots during the WWII, which has since found wider applications in analysing the relationship between the human user and technology. Technological affordances relate to how a technology facilitates users to do something, such as to make the avatar of the gamer pull the door open by placing a door knob which functions as a specific affordance property. A game's affordance property therefore may impact on translation strategies in some cases, alerting the translator to the significance of the interactive nature of game products. To this end we will take into consideration both play and narrative dimensions in analysing game localization in our

---

delineated from the real world. While frequently quoted by game scholars, Huizinga's concept is considered to be too tied to ideological issues to be usefully applied to modern games (see Egenfeldt-Nielsen et al. 2008, 24–25).

discussion in Chapter 4. Having examined games from a conceptual level, we now turn our attention to the game industry as an essential context which ultimately exerts a significant influence on game localization.

1.3   The structure of the video game industry

In order to understand where game localization is positioned in relation to the whole process of game development and distribution, it is pertinent to understand how the game industry as a whole is structured. In terms of the product chain, the industry actors can be depicted in a linear fashion as in Figure 1.5, starting with the hardware manufacturers (known as **platform** or **format holders**), who provide game platforms, be they for game consoles, PC components or mobile devices. Those which develop and publish games tend to be called **game publishers**, and those focusing only on developing games are called **game developers**, who in turn are often financed by game publishers. According to the *CESA Games White Paper* (CESA 2012, 79), the Japanese situation differs slightly from those in the US and the UK, and the division between companies specialized in either game development or publishing has not always been clear, with varying types of contract formats used. In Japan while hardware manufacturers are simply called "first party", game software publishers may be called "third party". In the common industry structure elsewhere there are three kinds of developers: **first party developers,** who are owned by publishers, **second party developers,** who are hired by a publisher to work on a particular game concept, as well as independent **third party developers,** who work on their own projects (Kerr 2006b, 43). Being the financier of game production, game publishers are often considered to be at the core of the industry's economic system "interfacing developers, consumers and technology manufacturers" (Dovey and Kennedy 2006, 49). At the same time, the role of the current console hardware manufacturers is significant in that they are also all publishers. Second party and third party developers who are developing a game for a specific platform need to "negotiate with the manufacturer, pay a

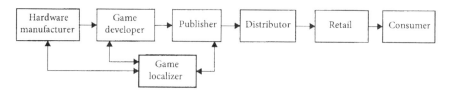

Figure 1.5 The game industry product chain with localization (adapted from Egenfeldt-Nielsen et al. 2008, 16)

licence fee, acquire a specific development kit and follow their quality approval process" (Kerr 2006b, 43).

The concept of "platform" is significant to an understanding of the mechanism of the game industry in a number of ways. Kerr (2006a, 54–61) divides the game market into four segments: Segment 1 consists of console and handheld games; Segment 2 includes PC games; Segment 3 comprises increasingly popular online games (MMOGs), and Segment 4 covers mini games developed for various digital devices such as digital TV, mobile phone, PDAs (Portable Digital Assistants) and the Internet. Of the four segments the first is currently the most significant in terms of market size, where the major game console manufacturers Microsoft, Nintendo, and Sony are also the major game developers and publishers. According to 2011 statistics in the US from the Entertainment Software Association (ESA 2012, 10), the sales figure for console games at USD 8.8 billion is over 19 times that for PC games at USD 0.45 billion, with others such as subscription-based games, mobile and social gaming etc occupying USD 7.3 billion. This indicates the continued significance of the console sector while at the same time games belonging to Segments 3 and 4 are on the increase. The Segment 1 market is described as an oligopoly, as it is controlled by a relatively small number of key companies. The MMOGs market is a relatively recent development and is treated separately from the PC games market in this classification. As we discussed earlier, the competing consoles form mutually exclusive incompatible systems. To gain a competitive edge, certain game titles are, at least initially, published exclusive to one console, while other games are released as **cross-** or **multi-platform titles.** Among the top 10 titles in 2012 in Japan, the US and the UK shown in Table 1.5 are a few exclusive titles such as *Halo 4* (2012) and *Kinect Adventures!* (2010) as well as Nintendo's games on 3DS. The titles *Call of Duty: Black Ops II* (2012), *FIFA Soccer 13* (2012) and *Assassin's Creed III* (2012) appear twice in the charts, ranked for each platform.

In a similar way to the world of book publishing, game publishers play a pivotal role in the game industry, where they finance game development, marketing, and distribution (Egenfeldt-Nielsen et al. 2008, 16) as well as localization. Major game publishers may have their own in-house localization department or may outsource localization to a specialized game localization vendor or translation agency. As shown in Figure 1.4, a localization manager may be appointed by the game developer in some cases. Publishers hold the rights to games, including localized games, and game developers receive royalties from publishers, some of which will be paid as an advance to cover part of the game development costs. All three current console platform holders – Microsoft, Nintendo, and Sony – own their in-house game developing arm (sometimes called a "studio") and also act as publishers and distributors. As such they are able to control the whole process, by accepting or rejecting the game, as well as its distribution, including localization.

In terms of actual operational links, game localization is inherently linked to game development, where games destined for different markets should ideally be designed with localization in mind through the specialized process called "internationalization". This is what is today known as "localization-friendly game development". We will elaborate on the concept of "internationalization" further in Chapter 2. The link between the developer and the localizer may also arise from the process of integration of localized **assets** (elements), as well as the testing of the localized product, depending on the scope of the localization contract with the localization vendor (see Chapter 3). There is a considerable advantage for translators if they have a direct link to the developers as this allows translation-related communication to take place more swiftly and directly. It is also mandatory for third-party developed games to go through an approval process called "**submission**", whereby the games, including localized games, are checked by the platform holders according to a pre-published set of criteria to ensure the game works properly on the given console, does not harm the hardware, and follows the platform holder's terminology and standards (see Chapter 3 for more details). Once approved, console games are manufactured in tightly controlled facilities belonging to the platform holders. In this way, the console game sector has its own uniquely developed hierarchical chain where the platform holders and publishers occupy a powerful position. In the commercially competitive context of the game sector, localization is subject to decisions made by publishers while technically its process is closely linked to game development, which in turn is influenced by the various specifications of the particular platform (or platforms in the case of multi-platform games). Game localization therefore can be seen as influenced by decisions made by publishers, developers, and console holders.

The diachronic view presented earlier showed how the game industry evolved from arcade games to home consoles; it in turn went through hardwired one-game only machines to hardware which is able to play different games supplied as software, the same as the concept of computer hardware and software. With the increased complexity of technology, the cost involved in R&D of consoles has become enormous. For example, the 2012 *CESA Games White Paper* (CESA 2012, 111) provides indicative figures for development costs of regular console game titles according to different platforms shown in Table 1.4. CESA (ibid.) cautions against treating these figures as minimum costs for which one can expect to develop a title for each platform, on the assumption that different interpretations may be made of the exact breakdown of "development costs" according to surveyed companies. Nevertheless they are useful in understanding, even in broad terms, the extent of investment required.

Table 1.4 Indicative development cost per title according to different consoles

Console	Cost per regular title (million JPY)
Wii	391.0
Xbox 360	238.1
PlayStation 3	212.1
Nintendo 3DS	190.5
PlayStation Portable	134.9
PlayStation Vita	96.6
Nintendo DS	72.0

Source: CESA (CESA 2012, 111).

As often pointed out, the business model adopted in the console market is a "loss leader", referred to as "Razor-Razorblade model", where the hardware is sold at a loss to increase market share (e.g. Kerr 2006a, 57). Thus the business relies on subsequent sales of game software, highlighting the crucial importance to the industry of producing mega-hit game titles. This makes game development extremely important for the survival of the industry. In turn, it further stresses the importance to the industry of localization, which is key to generating additional revenues from the world-wide market. Even in the case of Japanese game software, where there is a sufficiently large domestic market, the income generated by the overseas sales of game software is greater than that of the domestic sales (CESA 2012, 107).

At this point we shall turn our attention to the language directionality of game localization in the console sector. It is obvious that currently the Japanese hold the dominant share of console platforms, with two (i.e. Sony and Nintendo) of the three platform holders being Japanese. However, this does not mean that game software is also dominated by products of Japanese origin and the fact that the US is the largest market is a relevant factor to consider in relation to localization issues. Table 1.5 shows the top 10 console and handheld game titles sold in 2012 in Japan, the US and the UK using the sales data at retail provided by VGChartz.[35] This source was chosen due to the availability of the data for these three markets. Other sources such as white papers by CESA (e.g. CESA 2012) also provide similar data, but tend to use different bases in ranking games for different markets. One should bear in mind that there may be discrepancies in such ranking data, depending on the sources, but for our purposes the VGChartz data provide a useful basis for discussion.

A number of observations can be made from this comparison. At first glance it is clear that there is strong overlap of titles in the ranking between the US and

---

35. http://www.vgchartz.com.

Table 1.5 2012 Top 10 console and handheld games sold in Japan, US and UK

Rank	Game title ranking in Japan	Platform/Publisher/ Genre	Game title ranking in US	Platform/Publisher/ Genre	Game title ranking in UK	Platform/Publisher/ Genre
1	Pokémon Black/ White Version 2	DS / Nintendo RPG	Call of Duty: Black Ops II	Xbox360 / Activision Shooter	Call of Duty: Black Ops II	Xbox 360 / Activision Shooter
2	Animal Crossing: New Leaf	3DS / Nintendo Action	Halo 4	Xbox 360 / Microsoft Studio Shooter	FIFA Soccer 13	Xbox 360 / EA Sports
3	New Super Mario Bros. 2	3DS / Nintendo Platform	Call of Duty: Black Ops II	PS3 / Activision Shooter	Call of Duty: Black Ops II	PS3 / Activision Shooter
4	Dragon Quest Monsters: Terry's Wonderland	3DS / Square Enix Action	Kinect Adventures!	Xbox 360 / Microsoft Studio Other	FIFA Soccer 13	PS3 / EA Sports
5	One Piece Pirate Musou	PS3 / Namco Bandai Action	Just Dance 4	Wii / Ubisoft Music	Halo 4	Xbox 360 / Microsoft Studio Shooter
6	Resident Evil 6	PS3 / Capcom Action	Assassin's Creed III	Xbox 360 / Ubisoft Action	Just Dance 4	Wii / Ubisoft Music
7	Mario Kart 7	3DS / Nintendo Racing	Madden NFL 13	Xbox 360 / EA Sports	Assassin's Creed III	Xbox 360 / Ubisoft Action
8	Monster Hunter Tri	3DS / Capcom RPG	Assassin's Creed III	PS3 / Ubisoft Action	Assassin's Creed III	PS3 / Ubisoft Action
9	Super Mario 3D Land	3DS / Nintendo Platform	Pokémon Black/ White Version 2	DS / Nintendo RPG	Far Cry 3	Xbox 360 / Ubisoft Shooter
10	Mario Party 9	Wii / Nintendo Other	New Super Mario Bros. 2	3DS / Nintendo Platform	Kinect Adventures!	Xbox 360 / Microsoft Studio Other

Source: http://www.vgchartz.com/ (yearly/2012/Japan/, yearly/2012/US/, yearly/2012/UK/).

the UK markets while the Japanese market's ranking stands on its own. The fact that the top four games in the Japanese lists are those played on handheld platforms (i.e. DS and 3DS) is also not shared in the US and the UK. In terms of game genres, shooter games (*Call of Duty, Halo, Far Cry*) are prominent in the US and the UK lists and none of them made it in the Japanese list, despite the fact that *Call of Duty* and *Halo* are localized into Japanese. This clearly shows that the gamer preference of the given territory does affect the sales. While the absence of foreign-origin titles in the Japanese list is not new (also see Table 0.1), the fact that there are no Japanese-made games in the UK list with only two Japanese games in the last two games in the ranking in the US list suggests that the previous dominance of Japanese games may no longer be assumed. The reason for the waning popularity of Japanese games in the international market seems self-evident from the ranking showing that the US and the UK markets favour different types of games compared to Japan.

One of the notable changes shown in the Japanese games is that Japanese publishers are moving into a sim-ship model as demonstrated by Nintendo. While the games in the US and the UK lists are all localized for at least one other territory there are three titles in the Japanese list which are shown as not localized at the time (*Animal Crossing, Dragon Quest Monsters* and *Monster Hunter Tri*). This seems specific to the Japanese game sector, where even top selling games in the domestic market are not necessarily destined for international markets. Rather reminiscent of certain Japanese manga and anime titles which never get translated for international markets (O'Hagan 2006b), some Japanese games are not considered suitable for release outside Japan due to various culture-specific content (see 5.1). The suitability issue becomes compounded by the fact that RPG and Action-Adventure genres, which are popular in the Japanese market, are text-rich with a corresponding high volume of translation, thus making them more time-consuming and expensive to localize than purely action-oriented games.

Having dominated the evolution of the game industry for some time, Japanese games are now increasingly seen as falling out of step with the rest of the world, and thus losing international appeal (Kohler 2010; Winterhalter 2011). Some commentators are attributing such trends to Japanese gamers' particular tastes in games and Japanese game developers' consequent focus on satisfying domestic demand. These phenomena are sometimes described as "Galapagos syndrome" (Kohler 2010; Davies 2012) – an expression often used in Japan to describe things that are only popular within Japan, following their own unique patterns of adaptation, an analogy to the Galapagos Islands in Charles Darwin's study on evolution. One interesting factor mentioned by the CESA President Yoichi Wada, who is also the CEO of Square Enix, highlights technical aspects of game development environments in Japan. It is beyond the scope of this book to cover in any detail the technological advances in the area of **game engine**, but it is relevant to mention that the lack of availability until about 2006 of Japanese translations of technical text books on game engines for Japanese game developers was specifically noted by Wada as something that needed to be addressed (CESA 2012, 4). Similar to the way in which productivity software originated in the US in English, game engines were mainly developed in the US in the mid-1990s and have themselves become a product in their own right. In turn, because game engines are closely linked to the evolution of 3-D game genres such as **FPS** (First Person Shooter) (Rehak 2008, 192) it seems no coincidence that these genres are well advanced in the US as compared to Japan. Nevertheless, to the extent that games are cultural artefacts as much as technological products, a cultural idiosyncrasy could set off new global trends with an innovative use of technology. Given these contexts, international collaboration in game development is suggested as a possible future direction for Japanese game developers (Davies 2012) as has already been attempted by companies such as Square Enix (see 4.3). The future course of game localization will depend on the game industry's responses to some of these current challenges, especially those facing game development in Japan, in turn impacting on the location, language, and type of games that may be developed.

As can be discerned from Table 1.5, different market responses result from the global production and distribution of today's technologically sophisticated game products. Accordingly localization is motivated by marketing strategies and is carefully manipulated for maximum commercial gain. This makes it quite clear that localization forms an integral part of the globalization strategy of game publishers, who usually finance game development. Considering these factors which affect overall localization decisions, it becomes apparent that game publishers are in a powerful position to determine issues affecting not only original games, but also localized games. In this way they make a strategic decision as to which game to release in which territories. The role of the publisher in the game industry bears a resemblance to that of the publisher in literary systems. Similar to the arrangements in the book publishing industry, where authors will receive royalties from the sale of the books, game developers receive royalties from the sale of the games which are financed and marketed by publishers. In his analysis of the external factors influencing literary translation, Lefevere (1992) highlighted the concept of patronage as "the powers (persons, institutions) which further or hinder the writing, reading, and rewriting of literature" (ibid., 15). He saw the literary system being affected by professionals within the system, as well as by powerful individuals, publishers, the media, and institutions outside the system. One can draw a certain parallel between interactive publishers and literary publishers and, in turn, between the former and the film industry, which is dominated by "the majors" (Kerr 2006b, 51), who exert considerable power over film production and distribution. In particular, the game industry has come to allow the current platform holders – namely Nintendo, Sony, and Microsoft – to occupy particularly powerful positions in the console game sector. In other words, their influence extends beyond hardware manufacturing, to developing and publishing, as well as distributing game software, thus covering the whole spectrum of console game operations. As such, game localization is significantly affected by their decisions; these range from developing new consoles, to developing games, setting game release schedules, determining the territories and languages for which to localize games, and deciding on the level of localization, as well as responding to ratings and censorship requirements (see Chapter 5). Furthermore, the special power of the platform holders is illustrated by the compliance procedure of the submission process, which is made mandatory by the platform holders for games to be released for their consoles (see Chapter 3). As described in Chandler (2005, 103–109), in most cases approval is needed for the game concept prior to its production and games can be submitted for formal approval during their development for compliance checking, so that they can be manufactured and sold. Although the process is likely to go smoothly for a localized version if the original game is already approved, the submission process still applies to localized games (Chandler ibid.). It is therefore a significant consideration forming an integral part of the game localization process.

In this way, Nintendo, Sony, and Microsoft can be seen as forming powerful modern-day patronage in digital entertainment publishing. Apart from Nintendo, which has always been solely in the toy/game business, Sony and Microsoft started as high tech IT concerns, with Sony in particular already having diversified into other entertainment fields, such as music and films. Further drawing on Lefevere's concept linking translation to "power, ideology, institution and manipulation" (1992, 2), we can see these powerful patrons also as involved in "rewriting" games by means of localization, in one sense, to address the target territory preferences, including ratings requirements and, in another, to pursue their commercial interest and establish a market dominance (Lin 2006). Game publishers, known as "interactive publishers", especially those who hold platforms, exert considerable power over all aspects of the business from content creation to distribution. By comparison, in the modern-day literary scene manipulation may be exerted by publishers but usually in a much more restrained way. However, with the increasing digitization of books, and with mega publishers merging with media and technology conglomerates even producing their own ebook reader platforms, it is not impossible to imagine a future convergence of interactive publishing and the publishing of more traditional genres as print books wholeheartedly shift to ebooks that are interactive. In Chapter 5 we revisit the concept of "translation as rewriting" in an attempt to shed further light on certain deliberate manipulations which take place during the process of game localization. The concept of "patron" also seems useful in the event of the progressive crossover of different entertainment media sectors converging on the basis of digital technologies forming transmedia.

In summary, game localization is a new phenomenon in the context of Translation Studies. Video games challenge a number of assumptions which have governed prior forms of translation practice and theory. The development of localization in the 1980s signalled the beginning of a sea-change in translation, with the introduction of content in an electronic form which needed to be made global-ready. Furthermore, unlike most productivity applications which formed the mainstay of localization, video games are interactive software designed to induce explicit user actions, calling for play as well as narrative dimensions to be taken into consideration. Added to this is the increasing complexity of intertextual links being formed with other media through formal commercial arrangements, where the transmediality of games is exploited. Moreover, the fact that modern console games are mainly developed in two distinct linguistic regions – North America/the UK on the one hand, and Japan, on the other – brings with it significant issues in cultural negotiation in translation. Another major factor in understanding video games is a vibrant layer of global game culture, in addition to a distinctive local layer, made up of territory-specific tastes and preferences for certain game genres, game platforms and even the very manner in which games are played. Similar to the film industry which has a hierarchy of powers ultimately affecting AVT decisions, the translation and localization of games are carefully manipulated by powerful publishers especially those who are platform holders. Localization of video games forms a complex new practice, challenging some of the conventional assumptions and norms of translation practice. In an attempt to locate this new domain in Translation Studies, the next chapter discusses the paradigm of localization, whose somewhat troubled relationship with translation needs to be addressed in order to establish game localization in the context of Translation Studies.

CHAPTER 2

The localization paradigm

Localization versus translation

Introduction

Shifting our focus from the video game in Chapter 1, the present chapter concentrates on localization in practice and theory in order to position game localization in a Translation Studies framework. Localization has today become a well-established practice, having emerged from what was initially a small esoteric sector developed in response to the globalization of the computer industry. Localization has gained recognition in a relatively short period of time as an essential industrial process required by businesses for the efficient globalization of products in electronic form. This in turn has led many university translator training programmes to include localization in their curricula. Despite this, the conceptual relationship between "localization" and "translation" remains ambiguous in Translation Studies mainly due to a lack of theorization of the localization phenomenon. Moving from practice to theory, this chapter sets out to scrutinize the underlying concept of localization and its relationship with translation, relating it to the context of game localization as our central concern.

2.1 Software localization defined by practice: Internationalization

The emergence of the localization sector is associated with the rise of the consumer software industry, prompted by the introduction of personal computers in the 1980s. The term "localization" was coined by software developers in the late 1980s "to reflect the introduction of linguistic-cultural elements considered foreign to the initial source code, content and display in US/American English" (Folaron 2006, 198). The IT industry was primarily developed in the US and therefore centred on American English and the initial awareness of the linguistic requirements of the international market was low. For example, Claude Henri Pesquet (1993, 7), then Engineering Group Manager at Digital Equipment Corporation, observed that the need to consider users of languages other than English when developing office IT products "came as a shock to the application developers who were trained in the late 1960s". While the comment sounds extremely naïve in today's globalized world, it must have been a typical attitude at the time when "the US English speaking market represented more than 70 per cent of the total worldwide information technology market". In the mid-1980s the first multi-language vendors emerged offering localization services, as software publishers began to realize the complexity of localization projects and the need for specialized knowledge in localizing software products (Esselink 2000, 5). The state of the IT industry and its awareness of the needs of the global market have been transformed today, with localization becoming an integral part of globalization strategies and often addressed as part of the development process of the original product. Despite the fact that the localization industry has now become well established, however, the definition of localization still seems to vary, depending on the particular vantage point of the definer. Dunne observes that "localization simply does not lend itself well to being perceived *globally*" (2006, 3, original emphasis), leading to "no consensus as to what precisely constitutes localization" (ibid., 1). Indeed the definition initially given by the Localization Industry Standards Association (LISA) is rather broad and can also apply to translation, as it states that localization means "the process of modifying products or services to account for differences in distinct markets" (Fry 2003, 13). Localization practice evolved with the emergence of electronic products and content, chiefly in the form of software and later incorporating wider spheres such as websites, where the local language and other region-specific conventions such as date and number formats, currency signs and also UI related nonverbal elements needed to be adjusted. Esselink (2000, 1) explains how the term "localization" is derived from the word "**locale**", which signifies a small area or vicinity, but when used in the technical sense it means "a specific combination of region, language and character encoding". The notion of "locale" was also useful in distinguishing, for example, Spanish as spoken in Spain from Spanish as spoken in Argentina, making it possible to associate other information related to the target locality, such as units of currency, number of digits used for telephone numbers, or postal codes specific to the region.

The above explanation shows how the origins of localization are closely tied to electronic platforms on which how to represent and process a given language, including user input, became a critical concern. To give an example of what is subject to localization, when the Microsoft Word application is sold on a non-English speaking market, the user needs to be able to input, edit, and print the text, as well as to navigate the application's menu system in a given TL. To allow this to happen, it is not just the packaging and hardcopy manuals which must be translated, but also the software itself. For example, the **user interface** (**UI**) and online help need to be displayed and accessible in the TL. This requires the use of an appropriate character set which can represent the given language script in an electronic environment. Today most major software programs use the international character encoding system Unicode to support the world's major languages. The practice of localization emerged in order to accommodate the specialized processes required to extract and integrate fragments of text (strings) embedded in the software, in addition to the translation task of converting these strings to a given language. This origin underscores the fundamental link between localization and Information and Communication Technology (ICT) developments, combined with a trend which may be broadly described as "digital globalization" (Folaron 2006, 196) due to the widespread use of digital technology across the world. The localization industry then started to use the term GILT, standing for globalization, internationalization, localization, and translation. The acronym is used to stress how the globalization of modern technological platforms needs to be considered from the beginning with localization in mind, which in turn will be determined by companies' overall globalization strategies.

In particular, internationalization – the pre-localization process – is a concept and a process pioneered by the industry, which in practice boils down to how products are developed with foreign markets in mind. LISA explains it as primarily consisting of:

> abstracting the functionality of a product away from any particular language so that language support can be added back in simply, without worry [sic] that language-specific features will pose a problem when the product is localized.
>
> (Fry 2003, 14)

Although the concept has now become familiar in the globalization cycle in the IT industry, it was a radically new approach when it was first introduced. Based on his experience at Digital Equipment Corporation, Claude Henri Pesquet (1993, 6) explains how the company came to realize the need for internationalization since it first began foreign exports of their office products in the late 1970s. In order to accommodate the need for local language products, the new approach entailed moving away from a method based on the "reengineering of a product after the fact" to developing products that are "designed originally to meet local-language requirements" (ibid.). This involved a major shift in mindset to implement internationalization not just aimed at specific products but as "a pervasive attribute required across systems" (ibid.) as demonstrated in the GILT framework. Pesquet's explanation of the introduction of internationalization illustrates how revolutionary the approach was at the time, involving a major shift in thinking. Today this is increasingly recognized as a necessary prerequisite to ensuring that a product can be localized and made functional and accepted by users in international markets (Esselink 2000, 25). Thus, for example, the internationalization process ensures that the strings which need to be translated are not hardcoded and therefore can be separated from the software code base for the purposes of subsequent translation. Also, as mentioned earlier, it ensures that international language character sets are supported in the product so that an intended TL can be displayed correctly. Internationalization also includes any new functionality or features specific to the target market which may have to be added to a particular locale such as spell-checkers, grammar-checkers or sort functions that are language-specific in a wordprocessing program. Furthermore, the adequacy of internationalization may be tested prior to the localization process. For an English source product, internationalization testing is normally conducted during the development cycle, covering international support such as character sets, localizability tests (e.g. checking hard-coded strings), and text in graphics (bitmap text). During this phase, so-called pseudo-translation may be performed using a specialized tool by inserting a longer string to test any potential problem with **truncations** (where text is cut off due to the allocated space being insufficient to accommodate the translated text) and to check if accented characters will be displayed correctly (Esselink 2000, 149). In the context of game localization, internationalization is synonymous with localization-friendly game development and its importance is clear, as Chandler maintains:

> If the product has been properly internationalized, the game will not need to be redesigned or have additional features added to accommodate the translations. This makes the actual localization process fairly painless.   (2005, 12)

As described above, the need for a specific process of internationalization was gradually recognized and developed empirically in the localization industry on the basis of trial and error. This particular process in turn has been marked by translation scholars (O'Hagan and Ashworth 2002; Pym 2010) as a distinctive characteristic setting localization apart from other forms of translation. The process of internationalization involves technical, socio-cultural and socio-political considerations in preparing the source product. Internationalization in effect pushes the localization process upstream so that localization can be foregrounded within the design of the original source content. GILT was a significant step forward from ad hoc globalization in which translation was commonly treated as an afterthought. Internationalization was developed as a means of heading off at an early stage of product development any major localization challenge and is a logical approach to avoiding costly and time-consuming reengineering. This not only affects technical issues as explained above but also broader cultural questions. However internationalization's tendency towards generalization has provoked some criticism among translation scholars as it could promote "global sameness" and might eventually "spell the death of cultural difference on many levels" (Pym 2004, 37). This raises a relevant question particularly in the context of video games, which are cultural products often imbued with specific cultural traits, even at the level of the conceptualization of game design itself (see Chapter 5). The concept of "internationalization", especially in its extreme form of culling elements considered to be diversions or "culture bumps" (Leppihalme 1997) in the receiving market, is at odds with the creativity (or even idiosyncrasy) which often characterizes the work of game designers, given how certain cultural peculiarities may turn out to be the very attraction of the product even in international markets. For such games, if culture-specific aspects are to be completely removed or neutralized during the internationalization process, it could significantly impact on some unique characteristics of the particular game product and thus the user experience. When games become objects of translation, they come under a complex array of forces: on the one hand pressure for international uniformity for ease of localization, on the other, the obligation to retain the distinctive flavour of the original. Furthermore, there are factors which are game domain-specific such as age ratings and censorship, as well as the degree of control which may be exercised by game publishers and game platform holders over approving localized games. Finally, there is the presence of hardcore fans who are extremely knowledgeable about games and particular franchises and are usually quick to identify any traces of tampering during the localization process, especially if the game is part of a well-established series or by well-known game designers. In view of these considerations, the internationalization process, although intended to generalize a product, actually calls for product-specific approaches when dealing with artefacts such as games that are different in nature from productivity software, so that unique characteristics and factors of the original product may be highlighted rather than eliminated.

2.2   New dimensions of localization

According to LISA (Fry 2003), the localization process can be considered in terms of linguistic, technical, and cultural dimensions. Linguistic conversion allows a given technological platform to be usable in the TL; it is the aspect of localization which is most closely compared to the narrow sense of translation as linguistic transfer and indeed it is often all that is meant by translation in the context of localization. The separation between linguistic and cultural dimensions commonly claimed in the field of localization contrasts with how translators perceive the two to be inseparable in their work, as well recognized in Translation Studies. Such differences may have arisen from new aspects introduced by localization as well as a lack of dialogue between the localization industry and Translation Studies. As regards to the new aspects localization can be considered as a practice of explicit extraction of translatable elements and their reinsersions into the final product. In other words, one of the major characteristics of localization lies in the fact that it deals with texts which are embedded in a technological platform, comprising what Daniel Gouadec (2007, 37) describes as "translation of material embedded in particular media". This makes the whole treatment of linguistic and cultural issues subject to specific technical considerations. For this reason software engineering and text translation need to be seamlessly integrated in software localization. This in turn necessitates the use of specialized tools and quality control procedures (i.e. QA testing) to actually test the localized products for functionality and linguistic errors (see Chapter 3 for functional and linguistic testing in game localization).

As explicit in the original connotation of the term, localization addresses particular target market user parameters, identified collectively as a locale. It therefore follows that localization recognizes the implication of cultural elements in the source content specific to the target user group and the possible need for modifications to make them appropriate and appealing to the end user in the target market. The fact that the localized product is expected to have a similar "look and feel" to an equivalent local product (Fry 2003) generally necessitates broad and specific cultural adjustments which are considered part of the user parameters. To this end, localization often encompasses various kinds of adjustments involving broad nonverbal elements, ranging from the use of colours, icons, graphics, sounds, layout, and product design, to technical aspects related to usability such as navigation mechanisms, including the positioning of the scroll bar in a website. For example, Arabic texts are read bi-directionally from right to left but left to right for foreign words, and it is more ergonomic to have the scroll bar set on the left-hand, rather than the more familiar right hand side on a website. Such cultural considerations are not in themselves new; what is new is that they form specific objects, such as UI on screen, which have to be made meaningful to the end user. For these reasons the localization industry tends to assume that cultural consideration is a new aspect which goes beyond translation, and treats translation as if it does not concern itself with cultural issues, as criticized by Hartley (2009, 107):

> Localization ... entails adapting a product to the linguistic and cultural expectations of the target locale .... In the industry, this is seen as a 'special kind of translation' that takes into account the culture of the location or region where the translated text is expected to be used. However, in the Translation Studies community, this is simply a commonly accepted definition of translation itself.

This state of affairs seems to point to a lack of understanding by the localization industry of the broader concept of translation, on the one hand, and also by translation scholars, on the other, in their failure to recognize the shift which has taken place with new types of content subject to translation.

Bearing in mind this particular gap in conceptualization of localization and translation, the following sections highlight how cultural issues are manifest in a specific way in software localization. This is followed by a focus on the increased role being played by computer tools in the localization process. We consider this intrinsic association with technology to demonstrate the specific nature of localization practice and that of the "software text", thus characterizing new dimensions of software localization. To this end this brief explanation of localization is intended to lead to a more detailed description of the localization process specific to video games in Chapter 3.

2.2.1 Cultural representations and adaptation required in software localization

Cultural differences are manifest in many ways in software products. Various country-specific conventions such as formats in date, time, postal codes, the use of comma as decimal points have been acknowledged as often requiring adaptation in the process of localization. Although it is now largely taken for granted, most fundamentally the very question of being able to represent each language of the world correctly in electronic form can be considered as an issue deeply rooted in culture (Greenwood 1993, 8; O'Hagan and Ashworth 2002, 72). While it is beyond the scope for this book to provide a detailed discussion on the topic, we refer briefly to one example to highlight the point. It concerns a special symbol called a macron which denotes a prolonged vowel as used in, for example, the Māori language (as used above the letter "a"), an official language of New Zealand. One of the authors experienced first-hand how a lack of the symbol in wordprocessing caused a challenge in translation offices in New Zealand in the 1980s. It came to be highlighted in the advent of wordprocessing technology and the subsequent explosion of communication on the Internet before the symbol became available on computer platforms and integrated into common word processing programs. As mentioned in the Introduction of this book implications of technologization of language are acutely reflected in some localization issues which are often considered new dimensions of localization. In our discussion below we give just a few examples of such cultural issues focusing on the UI, usability of software, and broader cultural issues that are specific to software localization.

UI and usability
The UI in software applications is typically menu-driven. As mentioned earlier, certain languages such as Arabic and Hebrew, involving a right-to-left reading direction, need cascading menus to fall from right to left, unlike menus designed

for English and other European language locales. In turn, when Japanese and Chinese scripts are represented in their traditional vertical direction, read from top to bottom and right to left, the horizontal scroll bar is used instead of the typical vertical bar. While these are functional issues, the use of icons in the UI touches on more affective issues. The latter have been discussed extensively for their different cultural implications (e.g. Yunker 2003), such as the image of the letter box with a flag based on the rural mailbox common in the US but not always understood in other cultures. Similarly, even simple symbols can have culture-specific meanings. For example, in Egypt the cross (X) does not have the connotation of prohibition, thus requiring a different symbol to indicate this meaning (Greenwood 1993, 17). Some differences in the cultural interpretations of crosses (X) are illustrated by the keyboard mapping of the PlayStation® 2 controller buttons of (O) and (X) in the Japanese and the US and European versions, where the meaning of each symbol is reversed (see Figure 3.1 and explanations in Chapter 3). Cultural issues may also be manifest in the use of environmental sounds in the software UI, as illustrated by Greenwood (ibid., 17) with the example of the Lotus 1-2-3 application, localized for the Japanese market. Because of the very common open-plan office with workers sitting in close proximity without partitions, the beeps generated by this application to indicate a user error were found to be particularly irritating by users and had to be removed. Today such sounds, as well as certain other features, are typically made user-definable in order for the application to be customizable by the user to the requirement of the specific user context. At the same time, making everything customizable is not necessarily a good solution either. Early user testing in the Japanese market of Lotus 1-2-3 found that the extra customizability especially designed for this market to enable users to change the name of the era to which the given year belongs was not welcome and requests were made for it to be removed (Greenwood ibid., 18). The reason given by the Japanese testers was that the function anticipated the demise of the emperor, since the name of the era is linked to the ascension of the emperor of the time. Software localization has demonstrated how such broad cultural considerations could also affect functionality features of the product.

Other cultural issues
Adaptation in localization also extends to content material in software, as was recognized by an early Microsoft multimedia localization project with its encyclopaedia *Encarta*, delivered on CD-ROM and primarily designed for a US audience. In 1995 Microsoft decided to make the product available in Spanish and German

versions when there was still little awareness of what is involved in localizing multimedia material. This involved lengthy cultural adjustments, including a wide range of socio-political issues relating to the content. For example, geographical names could sometimes cause conflicts due to possible historical territorial disputes between countries, as in the case of the headword "Falkland Islands" which is considered unacceptable in the Spanish version as the islands are referred to as "Islas Malvinas" in Argentina. Similarly, because of the differences in the legal structures of the USA (which follows common law) and Germany (civil law), most law articles for the German version had to be replaced and new headwords added (Kohlmeier 2000, 9–10). These aspects are now commonly understood as localization issues applicable, for instance, to websites. In addition to a focus on linguistic questions the malleable nature of software brings with it the need for broader cultural, social, and political issues to be addressed in such a way as to present the product as if it were originally created for the target market. Software as the object of translation presents, at least theoretically, a tabula rasa on which may be exercised a broad range of manipulations that go beyond linguistic conversions of verbal signs. In particular, such possibilities become even more applicable in video games as they are designed to engage the user often emotionally, in turn calling for careful assessment during the localization process of a wide range of issues including historical events, legends, mythology, and religion, as well as factors affecting age rating considerations specific to different markets, as discussed in Chapters 5.

2.2.2 Localization facilitated by technology

As well as being inextricably rooted in the computer industry, localization has come to be characterized as the most technologized of all translation sectors by its extensive use of translation tools (Lommel 2006, 223). Dedicated applications designed for localization tasks allow translators to work with different types of files, including text-only resource files and binary program files with localization-specific functions, including glossary generation, validation, and pseudo-translation features in some products (Esselink 2000, 383). In the process of software localization, the text that needs to be translated is marked up by various codes and tags which need to be carefully handled, as any accidental tampering could lead to a malfunction in the localized software. The dedicated localization tools achieve this by protecting tags, facilitating the extracting, exporting, and importing back of translatable elements of the software itself. Because of the general lack of contextual information available to the translator, the software strings for error messages, status messages, and tooltips are often the most time-consuming elements to translate (Esselink 2000, 59). The lack of context is inherent in the treatment of text within the localization process, typically presented as separate independent strings, which is something also applicable to game localization. The frequent de-contextualization can be considered a particular feature of localization which makes the translation task extra challenging. Furthermore, parts of software strings may be utilized in different locations with only variable elements called "**variables**" being changed, depending on the user input. In software environments, including video games, a degree of iteration of particular combinations of strings (i.e. a routine re-use of text fragments) is expected, triggered by a certain user action. The technique known as "**concatenation**" makes use of recurring strings, pulling together different strings dynamically at run time to form new strings. This is done according to a pre-set formula on the basis of a particular action defined by the user. As we discuss in more detail in Chapter 3, this technique is common in game localization and often raises linguistic issues. Also common in game localization is the use of the above-mentioned variables, i.e. replaceable parameters normally preceded by a "%" sign in the string to be localized. These **placeholders** are characters to be replaced at application runtime. Without careful prior consideration, the use of variables can lead to non-grammatical construction of strings across different languages (see Chapter 3 for specific examples).

The use of Computer-aided Translation (CAT) tools in localization is justified by certain characteristics of the text that it processes: repetitiveness of text associated with regular updates, as well as constant and last-minute changes which need to be managed especially for **sim-ship** releases of software, where the original software and its localized versions are launched simultaneously. Text recycling has become an essential concept in commercial translation in general, and software localization in particular, to facilitate sim-ship releases, cutting down on the time spent on translating the same or similar text. In addition, it is important to maintain uniformity in the use of terminology and recurring expressions so as to optimize usability and not to affect the functionality of the software or other electronic content. These characteristics make CAT tools such as translation memory (TM), particularly suitable for localization purposes as TM leverages previous translations for repetitions and similarities within and across documents. TM automatically searches and retrieves the same or similar segments (sentence or other stand-alone textual entities) stored in its memory database. TM is designed to allow the translator to recycle previous translations, intended to boost translator productivity by avoiding translating more than once the same or similar segments from scratch. Furthermore, the application of Machine Translation (MT) is becoming increasingly common in the localization sector, where TM and MT are combined in an increasingly automated workflow (Hartley 2009). In technology-based workflows incorporating MT, the source text (ST) may be authored using controlled language (CL) which defines authoring rules to make the text amenable to MT,[36] while post-editing of MT output may also be performed. The use of these technologies is justified on the basis that although publishable quality translation is the aim, the end purpose of localization is largely functionality-driven (i.e. "fit for purpose"), where the user is less likely to be concerned with the literary quality of the text as long as the text's functional goal is met. Because of the highly time-pressured nature of the task, especially in the case of sim-ship releases, localization practices seek to streamline workflow and to maximize standardization in an attempt to achieve consistent optimum quality while retaining productivity. To this end, the localization industry has relied heavily on the use of tools in the workflow which facilitate standardization of the process. This is synonymous in the industry with good localization practice. As we discuss in Chapter 3, however, the use of CAT tools has until recently not been as widespread in game localization as it has in the localization of productivity software. This in turn seems to highlight differences between localizing productivity software and entertainment applications such as video games, which are designed to be affective media more than pure functionality.

While localization indeed involves new dimensions which gave rise to the new name to be used in the industry to distinguish itself from the pre-existing concept "translation", the end function of localization can also be considered within the broad concept of translation: to represent a product in a new linguistic and cultural context. For example, Gouadec (2007, 5) describes the aim of translation as "allowing effective communication – and trade – to take place by overcoming potentially insurmountable obstacles of a linguistic, symbolic, or physical nature". So, while any definition of localization based on its practice highlights a number of unique distinguishing features as discussed above, a marked conceptual difference between localization and translation remains debatable and has so far not been clearly established (Pym 2010, 136). While there may not be a clear-cut answer, we further pursue this point in the next section to locate the source of the quandary.

---

36. There is also human-oriented CL which can be used to increase the readability of the ST for human consumption; this has slightly different parameters to the machine-oriented CL mentioned here.

2.3   Localization in Translation Studies

Since the 1970s Translation Studies has come of age as an academic discipline, after a long history in which the practical dimension of translating received relatively little scholarly attention (Munday 2001, 14). The discipline has gone through several "turns" which have steadily widened in scope and Translation Studies as a whole now has a sophisticated epistemic basis to examine and explain all kinds of translation phenomena. However, the relatively new domain of localization sits somewhat precariously in relation to what is currently considered to be translation proper. The growth of the localization sector in the 1990s led to its professionalization, influencing translator training at universities (Folaron 2006), thus recognizing the fact that localization has become an integral part of the modern translation industry. In this way, localization made inroads into Translation Studies, particularly influencing applied areas such as "translator training" and "translation aids" according to Holmes's map of the field which dates back to 1972 (1988/2000). However, when we consider localization in terms of its epistemic contribution to the discipline of translation as a whole, its impact becomes less certain.

Attempts at the conceptualization of localization at a deeper level have been few and far between in mainstream translation theory. This may be a reflection of a legacy in Translation Studies, with its somewhat ambivalent attitude towards technologization. Even today, research related to MT and CAT tools has made little theoretical impact on the discipline as a whole in contrast with other fields, such as computing and engineering, where language and translation technology research are mainstreamed (O'Hagan 2012b). The lack of interest in technologies as demonstrated by the relative absence of theoretical discussions on technology in Translation Studies is indeed incongruous, with the scholarly interest in technology shown in the context of translator training and pedagogy (e.g. Kenny 2007). As critiqued by Vandepitte (2008), the separation of translation tools (as part of "Applied Translation Studies") and translation process (part of the descriptive branch of "Pure Translation Studies"), which is intrinsic to the conceptualization of the discipline presented in Holmes's taxonomy, has led to a failure on the part of translation theory to consider the ways in which the human translation process is now increasingly facilitated by technology. In the meantime computer-mediated translation has become a matter of routine for most areas of commercial translation and particularly for localization.

This general background explains in part the isolated position currently occupied by localization in Translation Studies. Pym earlier observed that localization has gained acceptance in the discipline mostly "for economic reasons if nothing else" while translation theorists have found "nothing essentially new" behind the "fancy terms" introduced in this domain (Pym 2004, xv). In contrast to its commercial significance within the translation industry, the localization domain is yet to be fully integrated into translation proper. This is often evident at translation conferences, where localization topics tend to be (if included at all) consigned to a special technology track, often divorced from the mainstream translation theory discussion. It is therefore no surprise that a major localization research project (van Genabith 2009) launched in 2008 in Dublin to map the next generation of localization, involving some 120 researchers and industry partners, has attracted hardly any attention in Translation Studies circles. In this way, the position of localization in Translation Studies remains one of separation rather than integration, where it is often seen as a business model rather than as a translation phenomenon worthy of in-depth investigation from a theoretical perspective. The recognition of localization as a significant form of industrial practice in Translation Studies seems to have led to its incorporation into training requirements, but localization research has not yet developed into full theorization (Pym 2010, 120–142).

In the meantime localization practices are in a constant state of flux, exemplified by the way that game localization continuously invents new approaches and procedures to serve its own needs. In this essentially industry-driven sub-domain, Translation Studies could do more to play a critical role to facilitate improved practices and also to gain further insights into new developments in translation by working with the industry, where an increasing amount of experiential data are being accumulated. The dynamic nature of localization makes it even more urgent for the Translation Studies community to pay greater attention to this whole area of practice and to incorporate it into mainstream translation theory. The current conceptual and terminological confusion concerning localization (Mazur 2007) is further evidence that the concept of "localization" has not yet been thoroughly investigated within Translation Studies. The lack of interest by translation theorists can be confirmed by the scarce mention of localization in Gentzler (2001), Hatim (2001) or Munday (2001), as well as in the first edition of *Routledge Encyclopedia of Translation Studies* (Baker 1998) and *Dictionary of Translation Studies* (Shuttleworth and Cowie 1997). It was only recently that key Translation Studies texts started to include a reference to localization. For example, the second edition of the *Routledge Encyclopedia of Translation Studies* (Baker and Saldanha [eds.] 2009) includes an entry on localization (Schäler 2009, 157–161) as does the *Handbook of Translation Studies* (Gambier and Doorslaer [eds.] 2010) by Schäler (2010, 209–214). Munday's revised third edition of *Introducing Translation Studies* has some space allocated to localization, with the recognition that "it is translation practice that has been active in supplying theory with new conceptual terms such as 'localization' and 'locale'" (Munday 2012, 281). Nevertheless Munday provides no further discussion to address the precise nature of the conceptual overlap between translation and localization. Pym (2010, 125) has taken a step towards establishing localization as a paradigm of translation theory, chiefly focusing on the one-to-many relationship set off by "internationalization" as a new and key concept.

Localization came into being owing to the market needs of the computer industry, requiring software applications to be usable in different locales. With this background the domain has developed as an industrial process, so far mostly without the benefit of insights from Translation Studies. This has contributed to certain misconceptions about translation prevailing in the localization industry. Situating the role of translation in the globalized and increasingly networked world, Cronin (2003) is critical of the way in which translation is portrayed in localization discourses as the least problematic operation:

> Translation has a long history of difficulty and approximation which is to its epistemic credit and commercial disadvantage. Localization, on the contrary, implies a wholly new process which engages effortlessly with the 'local', thereby eliminating any unpleasant imperial aftertaste left by agonistic conceptions of translation as conquest .... With its emphasis on target-oriented translation, wholly consonant with the more popular versions of functional and polysystemic theories of translations, 'localization' appears to be the corporate linguistic response to the ecological injunction to think global and act local.   (2003, 63)

Indeed localization has enjoyed success as a commercial practice by ignoring other contextual factors, in effect depoliticizing translation, as Cronin suggests. The relative lack of theorization of localization has so far let certain ramifications inherent in translation be happily overlooked. For example, practice-led approaches dominant in localization seem to have glossed over issues such as the power relationship between the software developer/publisher and the translator and the influence of the former on certain translation decisions which are imposed on the latter. So a localized software product may in fact most strongly resonate with the publisher's (the commissioner's) values despite the fact that it is ostensibly presented as "target-oriented". Such a perspective seems to have remained so far largely unexplored in localization research despite the fact that, as alluded to in Chapter 1, concepts such as "patronage" (Lefevere 1992) have been explored in Translation Studies to acknowledge the influence of patrons (translation clients, publishers, etc.) on translation. Such concerns, well argued in the discipline, have so far not been applied in the domain of localization, which instead has been dominated by the industry's concerns over more immediate practical issues (Schäler 2010, 213) relating, for example, to how to deliver localized products most efficiently on time and within budget. The localization industry has been striving to establish a set of good practices and the main approach to addressing the issue of quality, for example, has been to standardize the localization process by benchmarking and optimizing the use of technology. Such an orientation largely boils down to prescriptive rules. Broader, less immediate questions such as the industry structure and the different stakeholders with their various influences on localization practices and quality have so far attracted little attention within the industry or in Translation Studies. Furthermore, one can argue that implicit in the industry agenda is indifference to human agency in the translation process, which is expected to be carried out uniformly. It assumes and promotes the invisibility of human agency, with localizers expected to engage readily with the prescribed workflow while their inherent inclination towards variety should be regulated by use of tools such as TM.

The restricted role of translators which is commonly assumed in localization may indeed be justified on the basis of the techno-centric workflow adopted in localization. For example, Pym (2004) has noted how the working environment in localization was configured on the basis of CAT tools. Even the very design of earlier TM products seemed to have assumed that the translator did not need to see the wider context beyond the sentence-based segment currently being translated. Such a design forced the translator to work at sentence level rather than according to a more intuitive segmentation at a bigger unit than a sentence. This is a long way from the now more acknowledged vision of translation as taking place on the broader levels of textual units even between cultures. The failure of some CAT tools to factor in many translators' needs has been highlighted in the literature (e.g. Lagoudaki 2008) and indeed has led to various currents of process-oriented research focused on the impact of tools on human translators (Christensen 2011). This deficiency in turn ignores, as Pym points out, the fact that the text is ultimately for human interaction across different cultures, "dehumanizing" the discourse between the sender and the receiver of the message as if it is an exchange of data between machines (Pym 2002). Pym is particularly critical of what sometimes seems like mindless recycling of text via TM. It is true that the repeated use of the same sentence in different documents has become rather common in the practice of "re-purposing", where more or less the same texts are re-used for different purposes, especially in the advent of different media platforms on which text fragments are deployed. Empirical studies investigating the impact of TM on localized websites (e.g., Jiménez-Crespo 2009), provide evidence to show how the quality of translation can sometimes be compromised, rather than enhanced, by the particular nature of the technology mediating the human translation process.

The very restrictive concept of "translation" generally assumed in localization runs counter to contemporary thinking in Translation Studies, which has moved away from analyzing translation on the basis of strictly linguistically motivated equivalence especially at a word or a sentence level. Extending Pym's argument, the scope of translation within the localization paradigm can be illustrated in the core working unit of text, typically referred to in the localization industry as a "string", in contrast to a paragraph, a whole document or even a larger unit of culture. This notion of translation in the localization industry, based mainly on short fragments of decontextualized strings, may be partly responsible for the restricted and reduced scope of translation. In short, in the field of localization, translation has been condemned to be the conversion of these strings from the SL into the TL, allegedly without any cultural implications or other challenging issues, which are treated separately outside "translation". By contrast, Translation Studies research has paid increasing attention to the broader cultural, social, and political contexts in which translation takes place, as well as the reception, function, and historical conditioning of translation in the target culture. Criticisms by Cronin (2003) and Pym (2004) are directed at the fact that the localization-centric view of translation tends to reduce the latter to string replacement, comparable to "changing iPod skins", as explained by a localization expert at localization conferences.[37] In such a view, translation can indeed be reduced to "just a linguistic process" as once remarked by Bill Gates (cited in Brooks 2000, 43) to imply its simplistic nature in contrast to the rest of the technically and culturally complex operation of localization. The localization industry justifies such views from the perspective of procedural efficacy in delivering the product to market on time by maximally standardizing the process, which in turn is closely dictated by the financial bottom line (DePalma 2006).

2.4 Game localization or game translation?

While there has been a lack of interest in theoretical arguments about translation in the localization industry, it is also true that Translation Studies as a whole has not been fully engaged with the localization phenomenon to the extent of integrating it wholeheartedly into the main conceptualization of the discipline. Facing the challenges posed by the emergence of further new areas of localization such as game localization, along with rapid developments in an increasing range of new media facing the need for globalization, the discipline of translation urgently needs to address the current gap between industry and academia in the conceptualization of localization and translation. The topic of game localization

---

37. LISA Forum in Dublin, December 2008 and LISA Asia Forum in Chinese Taipei, April, 2009.

provides a timely reminder and an excellent opportunity to redress the current lack of serious engagement with localization in Translation Studies. Game localization practices call into question these prevailing assumptions about the narrow conceptualization of translation within the localization sector. Modern video games are technically complex cultural artefacts designed to engross the end user, where the nature of engagement is more than merely functional and encroaches into the affective dimensions. Furthermore, as we outlined in Chapter 1, today's games represent a diverse range of titles, which defy easy standardization and the strict benchmarking of translation approaches. Cultural issues both at micro and macro levels loom large, especially for major titles, as the industry seeks finely tuned cultural adaptation to appeal to target users. This delicate negotiation in turn calls for translators' creativity in conveying the right message while they operate under a set of restrictions, further exacerbated by the ever present time pressure. At the same time, the recognition of the need for the final product to have an affective appeal to the end user seems to allow translators a freedom almost unseen with other types of translation (Mangiron and O'Hagan 2006). Here translators' agency is highlighted and celebrated rather than suppressed and disregarded. The question of agency has been well articulated in Translation Studies, including the domestication versus foreignization debate (Venuti 1995). The sociological approach of focussing on translators (Simeoni 1998), which has become popular more recently in the discipline, is also motivated by the need to acknowledge wider factors involved in the translator's role as a visible mediator.

The discussion so far suggests that the possible tension between translation and localization may stem from the somewhat reductionist view of translation prevalent in the localization industry, on the one hand, and the lack of full recognition of localization as a phenomenon of epistemic significance within the Translation Studies community, on the other. This in turn may reflect a fundamental conflict between the goals of localization: advocating conformity as a global product, yet at the same time acknowledging and accepting differences in each locale. The localization industry seeks to develop best practices based on standardization, in turn treating translation as a code-switching exercise between SL and TL. This is done more or less by separating out less clear-cut cultural or wider socio-political implications from translation partly by implementing such processes as internationalization to nip the problem in the bud before translation begins. Perspectives such as one presented by Mandiberg (2009) sees that game localization primarily seeks to move the text (game) from one context to another as "a mechanical or neutral act" whereas translation problematizes the movement as giving rise to issues such as untranslatability. His claims resonate with the views by Cronin (2003) of localization as depoliticization of issues inherent in translation as we discussed earlier. Yet reflections by some game localization practitioners (e.g. see practitioner interviews in Chandler and Deming 2012) and certain examples we discuss in this book imply that the division between translation and localization is not quite as clear-cut as Mandiberg may suggest if one looks at some of the sophisticated localization approaches which are emerging.

As touched on in our literature review in the Introduction, the fledgling status of game localization in Translation Studies is evident in the fact that even the name of the practice itself is not clearly established. As previously noted, Bernal-Merino (2006) made the point that although "game localization" may be commonly used in the industry, it is "too broad a term to be used in TS [Translation Studies]" with the suggestion of using the term "translation" instead of localization. The discussion of the name of the sub-domain is significant in view of our goal to situate this relatively new practice within Translation Studies. In this context we wish to embrace openness to new implications of the emerging phenomenon and adopt a holistic view of game localization, covering the whole spectrum of the practice, encompassing cultural and technical dimensions as well as linguistic operations. As argued above, there is ambiguity in the way the terms "localization" and "translation" are currently used, often interchangeably even within the industry. For example, Chandler (2005, 12) explains game localization as "the process of *translating* the game into other languages" [our emphasis], further obscuring the distinction between the two concepts. Similarly Esselink (2000, 1) defines localization as "the *translation* and adaptation of a software or web product" [our emphasis]. Munday (2008, 191) in turn observes that the distinction between localization and translation is "blurred, but generally localization is seen by industry as a superordinate term that encompasses translation".

From the pragmatic perspective of translation as a profession, Gouadec considers localization within the broad category of "specialised translation" (2007, 37). However, he regards the work performed by translators as a generally narrower component of the whole operation of localization and acknowledges that the use of the term "localization" as a broader term than translation is acceptable insofar as "localization actually involves more than translating text or contents…" (ibid., 38). So again, the distinction is not entirely clear. Our survey of the use of the terminology and the concepts behind translation and localization highlights their ambiguity, but also establishes the widespread usage in the industry of the term "localization" as a superordinate concept of "translation" as claimed by Munday (2008). In this book we adhere to the recognized industry term "game localization", which is defined by industry practice. Also, given the fact that localization is already a well-established field within Translation Studies (even if its conceptualization is still under development), adherence to the term "localization" seems justified. However, we will not subscribe to the narrow concept of translation which seems to be assumed in the localization industry in general, as outlined above.

One way to situate game localization in the context of Translation Studies is to see it as a new translation practice that emerged from a new technological platform, seeking to be adjusted to the different user parameters required by target markets. Gouadec (2007, 38) calls localization "instrumental translation", meaning "translation that literally produces instruments". As noted in Chapter 1, we treat video games as a new media technology constituting a piece of software. In his seminal work *The Language of New Media*, Manovich (2001, 19) argues that as a consequence of the convergence of computing and media technologies, new media are shifting "all culture to computer-mediated forms of production, distribution, and communication". This profound change is affecting "all stages of communication, including acquisition, manipulation, storage, and distribution" as well as "all types of media – texts, still images, moving images, sound, and spatial constructions". Furthermore, among the key characteristics of new media Manovich highlights what he calls "variability":

> A new media object is not something fixed once and for all, but something that can exist in different, potentially infinite versions. This is another consequence of the numerical coding of media ... and the modular structure of a media object.
>
> (2001, 36)

He continues to point out that since new media objects exist as data, they can be scaled to various sizes and levels of detail to users' specifications and can also be regularly updated. This concept is useful in underpinning the fundamentally new translational dimension introduced by software. When translation was conceived as closely linked to physical print media, such variability was not a feature of the media. This has changed with the advent of software, in turn making translation part of the variability, where each locale represents a cloned "version" of the original, albeit with some differences. It is this characteristic of the new media which helps to define software localization and in particular game localization. In the framework of translation, the ST can now be treated as what Manovich calls "base object" (2001, 43), which forms a much more malleable entity with perhaps less prestige attached than that which is normally assumed in Translation Studies by granting primacy to the ST. At the same time, this somewhat changes the relationship between the ST and the TT as entities which are independent of each other yet linked through the same kernel code like DNA shared between siblings. In a sim-ship scenario where the ST and TTs are released together, the concept of "original" attached to the ST becomes even less apparent. The same analogy can be extended to the "transmedia" concept, where a video game may be directly derived from other media such as a film or vice versa, as we discussed in Chapter 1 with reference to the transmedial characteristics of video games. Manovich also considers interactivity as a type of variability as long as "there exists some kernel, some structure, some prototype that remains unchanged throughout the interaction" (ibid., 40). It is therefore this change from more conventional media to new media which can be used to characterize the operation of localization, giving rise to a new dimension to be considered.

Since the late 1990s we have witnessed an expansion of localization, with a move from the early narrow scope of software localization representing mainly productivity applications to encompassing a wider range of digital products and environments such as mobile phones, web applications and audiovisual content delivered on CD-ROM as in the early case of Encarta, extended to DVD, Blu-ray and the streaming techniques commonly used on the Internet. This in turn has made the existing strict boundary between localization and audiovisual translation (AVT) more porous. Such a blurring of borders is also detectable in the emergence of the many different terms used to refer to the field of AVT (Orero 2004, vii–viii). More recently, Chiaro (2009, 141) explains that AVT as an umbrella term includes "'media translation', 'multimedia translation', 'multimodal translation', and 'screen translation'". The emergence of new media resulting from the convergence of technologies is seeing the previously separate domains of localization and AVT come together to cater for the new type of products needing to be prepared to go global. Whether AVT subsumes localization or vice versa remains to be seen, although it is now widely acknowledged that AVT is fast gaining a foothold within Translation Studies (Díaz Cintas and Remael 2007). Regardless of the eventual label the practice may acquire, further convergence of different technologies is under way. As we discussed in Chapter 1, with the evolution of game hardware, game machines have been advancing in the direction of multimedia computers, starting with PlayStation® doubling up as a CD player, followed by PS2 also serving as a DVD player. Both Xbox 360 and PS3 allow the player to go online and also to download and store music and pictures as well as games. Today more and more people are playing games on mobile devices such as smart phones, indicating a platform convergence.

In this way, game localization pre-empts the consequences for translation of a progressive technological convergence driven by digital technology, indicating a broadening range of practices recognizable as at least associated with translation, if not as mainstream types of translation. The fuzzy distinction between localization and translation is a reflection of such ongoing transformation and may be something which needs to be accepted as unresolved for now. Time will settle the debate on the relative conceptual relationship between "game localization" and "game translation", as ongoing pressure from technologization both highlighting and dissolving linguistic and cultural barriers likely reshapes what we today call

translation. In the meantime in this book we will adhere to the label "game localization" as an established practice, but advocate the view that the concept of translation in its broadest sense affords to accommodate the concept of "localization"
if only on an abstract level.

2.5   An absence of agency in localization speak

A concept often used to describe localization is "adaptation" (in addition to translation), as in the definition by Esselink (2000, 1), who maintains that localization
is "the translation and adaptation of a software or web product". In Translation
Studies, adaptation is a polysemous term with various interpretations and connotations expressed by different theorists. It has generated a variety of synonyms
such as "cultural translation" (Nida and Taber 1969) and "oblique translation"
(Vinay and Darbelnet 1958/1995, 39), which aims for "situational equivalence"
as shown in their example of "cricket" in English translated into "Tour de France"
in French. The term "adaptation" usually implies the introduction of considerable changes in translation in order to "make the text more suitable for a specific
audience ... or for the particular purpose behind the translation" (Shuttleworth
and Cowie 1997, 3). Because of the high degree of change involved, adaptation in
some cases approaches the concept of "rewriting" (Lefevere 1992), where translation may only convey selective information in relation to the ST. In Translation
Studies, adaptation has also tended to be discussed in pejorative terms and to be
considered a lesser form of translation. For example, in relation to subtitling Díaz
Cintas and Remael (2007, 9–13) claim that subtitles treated as a form of adaptation have significantly curbed AVT research over a long period of time.

While the concept of "adaptation" encapsulates one of the key characteristics of localization in general and game localization in particular, it remains a
fuzzy concept. For this reason and also in keeping with our own perspectives on
game localization, we will instead use the concept of "transcreation" (Mangiron
and O'Hagan 2006). Owing its origin to both Indian and Brazilian scholars who
coined the term, the concept helps to highlight the unusually extensive freedom
taken by translators working under constraints specific to game text and products.
In particular we focus on the Brazilian post-colonial contexts in which the concept
is largely attributed to Haroldo de Campos (Vieira 1999). The notion of "transcreation" draws attention to the presence of the human agency of the translator
in the process of translation, inviting variable, non-uniform and at times unpredictable solutions. As such, it contrasts with the focus placed on standardization
and uniformity which often characterizes productivity software localization. We
further argue that the concept of "transcreation" can be applied to address the

fundamental tension which currently lies between the concepts of "translation" and "localization". The priority in localization is increasingly being placed on managing complex projects within a tight timeframe and budget by standardizing the processes. In the meantime the translator is given decontextualized strings to translate. This kind of working environment in turn tends to play down or even deliberately disregard the human agency involved in mediating the space between the source and the TL and culture. The benchmarking of translation, which often characterizes productivity software localization, favours a prescriptive approach and rewards uniformity over variety, working from the assumption that homogeneity is generally desirable, measured on the basis of consistency of the end product. Such a notion may be mutually reinforced by the dominant use of certain technologies such as TM, employed to recycle previous translations to ensure the reproduction of the same or similar segments, albeit based on form and not on meaning.

Similarly the use of CL in the authoring of STs could further eliminate variety and thus help to regulate human agency. While CL also often serves to make the text less ambiguous and more readable for humans, it is unlikely that any diegetic elements in the game world would be amenable to an approach based to any great extent on such controlled authoring insofar as games are designed to be affective media, often intended to stir the user's emotions going beyond functionality. It follows that game localization of story-heavy genres is often more analogous to translating literary text, further involving a process more similar to creative writing than to writing intended to be used for purely functional purposes. At the same time games also include technical text typically used for non-diegetic elements designed to serve informative purposes (see Table 4.1). The more successful the localized game is, the more it engages the player, albeit in different ways, depending on game genres and types. Games that are story-driven and pay greater attention to the characterization of game characters, for example, are more likely to highlight the issue of translators' agency in carrying over appeal as affective media across linguistic and cultural boundaries in their localized versions. The very nature of games inherently gives rise to the human agency of translators involved as mediators. This makes human intervention an essential and positive factor rather than the negative one which is often presented in current localization practice. For example, translators are typically not allowed to change 100% TM matches in productivity software localization regardless of different co-texts. Furthermore, for the purposes of efficiency, non-match segments are now often sent to MT and the translator is expected to post-edit rather than translate such segments from scratch. Whereas an affective appeal to the user is usually not a main goal in designing productivity software, it is an integral part of game design because player engagement at a deeper level is a priority. This in turn leaves both more room and greater demand for human intervention during the localization process of games. The application of the concept of "transcreation" thus highlights the role played by a translator or localizer as a creative agent, helping to induce intended affective responses in the end game player so that a similar user gameplay experience could be transferred to the locale.

The reductive view of translation prevalent in localization discourses is reminiscent of the treatment of translation by the MT community in the early days of MT development prior to the mid-1960s. This was when translation was assumed to be largely a mechanical process, involving reference to dictionaries and transcoding between the two language systems and therefore considered as a task perfectly suited to computers. This view eventually proved unworkable when the complexity involved in natural languages and their use, and thus the complexity of the translation task performed by human translators, was recognized (Hutchins and Somers 1992; Melby 1995). As a consequence, understanding the difficulty in formalizing the nature of translation problems finally led to abandoning the initial goal of FAHQT (fully automatic high quality translation), replacing it with a more realistic aim (Hutchins and Somers 1992). More recently, renewed interest in MT has resulted from the need for casual gisting translation services which can be provided by online MT engines, which are considered useful for certain situations ("fit for purpose"). With an increased visibility of online MT applications, a reductive view of translation may be further promoted among some ill-informed lay users, although this is largely no longer the case with the MT research community itself. This in turn can be described as an instrumental view of translation with the issue of human agency of the translator either ignored or considered a hindrance, as criticized by Cronin (2003) and Pym (2004). An irony is that today's data-driven MT systems rely on human translation data, whether or not such contributions are appreciated by their developers (Way 2009).

Localization can be said to be an industrial process primarily opposed to variety, which is often seen in terms of "inconsistencies" introduced by human translators and requiring restraint. From the point of view of industrial processes and procedures, localization clearly encompasses a wider scope of operations than does translation in its narrowest possible sense. However, when the notion of human agency is re-introduced, with its inherent preference for variety over uniformity, there is a significant conceptual overlap between translation and localization. The intense interest shown in culture by localization is further proof of the common ground shared between them. Yet such ostensive attention to culture seems incongruous to its aversion to human agency, given that resolutions of often tricky cultural issues call for nuanced negotiations best performed by the translator, whose creativity is unleashed rather than restrained. For the moment it seems we have to use the term "translation" to highlight human agency, as the term "localization" as it stands in Translation Studies is not endowed with the capacity to accommodate this notion. We continue this theme with our argument on game localization as transcreation in Chapter 4.

Attention to human agency is useful for highlighting some of the new dimensions involved in game localization from the broader perspective of Translation Studies. It is no coincidence that the game localization sector initially distanced itself from the more mainstream productivity software localization sector concentrated on business software applications. The game industry considered itself to belong to the creative cultural sector that includes the film and music industries, given the fact that each game creates its own unique imaginary game world. While games seek to entertain the end user, the development of the productivity software localization sector has been more focused on ensuring that users are able to accomplish pragmatic tasks in an intended uniform manner. In this way, the difference between entertainment software and that intended for pragmatic purposes is apparent. By introducing this new sub-domain of game localization to Translation Studies, we hope to demonstrate the dynamically developing new contexts presented to translation. In our view, the study of game localization provides new vistas and directions which together will form a worthy new research field in Translation Studies. Video games, as a new media technology driving new practices of translation, invite a fresh conceptualization of localization and translation. To begin the journey, we will describe what is involved in the practice of game localization in the next chapter.

CHAPTER 3

Game localization

A practical dimension

Introduction

In Chapter 2 we focused on the general concept of "localization", both in theory and practice, and analyzed its relationship to translation, in order to position game localization within the framework of Translation Studies. This chapter provides a detailed description of what game localization is, reflecting current localization practices within the framework of GILT (Globalization, Internationalization, Localization, and Translation). It also focuses on the localization process and on the different parties involved. The two main localization models – the **outsourcing** and the **in-house model** – will be discussed, as well as the trends in releasing the original and the localized versions of games simultaneously (**sim-ship**) or releasing the localized versions once the original game has been published (**post-gold localization**). The chapter also describes the different levels of localization: full, partial, or "box and docs" localization. In addition, we examine the different components that form a game – "**assets**" – that can be subject to localization, such as the **in-game text**, the **audio and cinematic assets**, and the printed materials. Finally, an overview of the tools currently used in game localization is presented.

3.1   Video games and GILT: Localization-friendly game development

GILT processes have contributed significantly to the worldwide success of the game industry. As mentioned in Chapter 1, most games are currently developed in English and Japanese, but given the high cost of game development, especially for **AAA titles** involving a large team working on the project for a number of years, game companies tend to publish their games in several languages to maximize their return on investment (Dietz 2006, 125). As a result, demand for localization is growing and is expected to continue to do so (Chandler and Deming 2012). Many games are sold in over 30 countries and are translated into more than a dozen languages (Melnick and Kirin 2008), and localization can significantly increase the sales of a game or even a platform in a given territory (Chandler and Deming

2012, 8). For example, sales of the FIFA football game series in Poland experienced a five-fold jump once the localized versions were available (Giné cited in Steussy 2010b). Similarly the US-based global video game publisher Merscom claims that focusing on localization at an early stage has contributed to generating more than 60% of its revenue outside of North America (Melnick and Kirin 2008). Melnick and Kirin (ibid.) state that "strong localization easily can more than double revenue and, more importantly, can mean the difference between creating a hit or just another top-100 game". Chandler and Deming (2012, xiii) cite projections by the Global Industry Analysts (GIA) that approximately 30–50% of the annual revenue for the global video game sector – in excess of USD 90 billion by 2015 – are attributable to the world market reached by means of localization. That said, it should also be stressed that from the point of view of developers and publishers, localization also entails a potential financial risk, as it involves additional investment and if not enough copies of a game are sold or if a key shipment date such as the Christmas period is missed, they may not break even (Chandler and Deming 2012, 8). For this reason it is advisable to "scale the localization process according to the needs and expectations" of each game (ibid.). Localization therefore could entail significant financial rewards as well as a potential loss if it is not planned at the outset from GILT perspectives.

Given its origins, localization is inherently anchored in the globalization of products and services provided on electronic platforms, with video games being a prime example. As promoted by the concept of GILT, companies are constantly advised to approach localization according to their wider global strategies by considering the implications of localizing their products at an early stage of product development through the process of internationalization. Despite the financial significance of localization for many game developers and publishers, in reality it still tends to be an afterthought, often dealt with at a post-production stage (Chandler and Deming 2012). In order to make localization economically efficient, it is critical to implement localization-friendly game development through internationalization at the outset. This means that rather than producing for one market and subsequently localizing as much as possible, developers, and publishers are advised to aim to produce games "for the global market from the start to enable subsequent localization" (Edwards 2008). This will mean that original code will not require modification later on to accommodate the target versions. For complex products such as digital games, systematic fore-thinking is becoming a necessity.

Furthermore, with the advent of the Internet, the meaning of globalization for businesses has changed significantly, especially as regards the sense of time and the manner in which widespread geographical coverage can be achieved through instantaneous communication and information access independent of location. In the process, the Internet has made linguistic barriers more explicit in some ways: online game players may find themselves playing against a group of competitors who are speaking different languages while accessing the same game but from different locations in the world. MMOGs such as *World of Warcraft* (2004–) are connecting millions of players every day from all over the world to combat and collaborate in the virtual world of the online game. While online games are not the focus of this book, they serve to illustrate the reasons for and the scope of internationalization evident in some of today's game developments. A key issue for MMOGs is the compatibility between different localized versions if the game allows players to use different language versions to play together in the same game world. For example, correct displays of special characters typed on different international keyboards need to be checked. Also, a game hosted in a particular country needs to be configured so that server messages appear in appropriate languages. As illustrated by Chandler (2005, 123), if server messages issued by the host computer appear only in the host language and not that of the client, then some of the game-specific messages may not be understood by players accessing the game from different countries. Thus, the decision about whether or not to allow multiplayer combinations across different locales needs to be made prior to localization and followed by actual testing for compatibility of the permitted localized versions.

According to Chandler and Deming (2012) the keys to successful internationalization and localization can be divided into three types: technical criteria, such as the use of localization-friendly code and automation; process-related criteria, such as effective scheduling, asset management and testing; and content-related criteria, such as assessing politically and culturally sensitive issues and meeting the requirements of rating boards (see Chapter 5 for more information about culturally sensitive issues and ratings). In addition to the typical issues that must be taken into account when internationalizing any software product, including different date and time formats and compatibility with special characters as outlined in Chapter 2, below we focus on the technical aspects relating to game consoles which require special attention for the localization of console as well as PC games. The internationalization of cultural content will be explored in detail in Chapters 4 and 5.

Cross-platform portability

Many games are released for more than one platform and are called "**cross-platform games**" or "**multiplatform games**", such as *Grand Theft Auto IV* (2008), released for the PS3, the Xbox 360 and for PC (see Table 1.5 for more examples). Cross-platform portability is an important game trait and a key aspect in game development. Some games are originally designed with one or two platforms in mind, and this may then require major changes to code and data formats for adaptation to the requirements of a different platform. Therefore, it is advisable to include cross-portability in the initial stages of the development of a game if there is a possibility that it will subsequently be ported to other platforms. However, as we described in Chapter 1, it is also quite common to release **exclusive titles**, which are tied to a single platform for a period of time or indefinitely as a marketing strategy of the platform holder to help drive up the sales of their hardware. When consumers are choosing a console, the array of games available for each platform can influence their decision. For example, the *Halo* series, exclusive to the Xbox and the Xbox 360, has helped Microsoft to increase global sales of their consoles and consolidate its global business strategy (Joyce 2007).

NTSC-PAL conversion

Video games are subject to the broadcast television standards applied in different regions of the world. When they are localized for different territories (which are divided according to language groups as well as geographical areas), region-specific technical factors, such as the TV video display standards NTSC (e.g. North America and Japan) and PAL (e.g. Europe and Australasia), need to be considered. This issue has direct implications for the localization of console games, which have to be connected to the user's TV system.[38] For example, the NTSC standard uses 525 lines of image with a refresh rate of 30 (29.97 to be exact) frames per second, whereas the PAL standard is made up of 625 lines and uses a slower speed of 25 frames per second. Thus the conversion between the two systems involves addressing these technical discrepancies. Traditionally the conversion of NTSC games into PAL has been criticised by gamers because the speed of the localized game and the frame rates are inferior to those in the original NTSC versions. As a result, the image flickers and appears with black bars at the top and bottom of the screen because NTSC has 100 fewer lines of resolution (Chandler and Deming 2012, 7). Some of the titles of the best-selling Japanese series *Final Fantasy*, such as *Final Fantasy X* (2001), received harsh criticism from European fans because of this issue, as it reduced the size of the display image and the speed of the game (Darolle 2004). In order to solve this problem, some developers, including Nintendo, release games only supporting a new standard (PAL60), which uses the same colour palette as PAL but shares the same resolution (525 lines) and refresh rate (60Hz) as NTSC (Keller 2004). However, the PAL and NTSC distinction no longer applies to High Definition TV (HDTV) for which Xbox 360 and PS3 are optimized.

---

38. PlayStation® 3 is region-free, but the console is optimized for High Definition TV sets which are not yet common in Europe. As a result, there is an issue with graphics and fonts, which are small and hard to see and read when a standard definition TV set is used.

Keyboard mapping for PC games and controller button mapping for consoles
Keyboard mapping allows different keys to be assigned for different functions, in order to increase usability and accessibility and facilitate the gameplay experience. Left-handed players often need to remap the keyboard of a PC game in order to be able to play it comfortably. Despite the fact that keyboard mapping should be considered from the early stages of the development of any game to be played on a PC, there are games that overlook this feature, such as the online free-to-play Chinese MMORPG game *Ether Saga Online* (2008), which was criticised when it was first released because it did not allow keyboard mapping (Ether Saga Online Forum 2009). In relation to consoles, according to Japanese conventions, a circle "O" is used to indicate that something is correct, while a cross "X" is used for something incorrect. This is reflected in the original Japanese mapping of the PS2 controller, where the O button is used for performing an action, while the X button is used for cancelling it. However, in Western countries, X can be used to tick the appropriate box in forms, indicating an approval. So when Japanese PS games are being localized, these controls are reversed i.e. the cross is used for confirming and the circle is used for cancelling an action. Some of the early Japanese games, such as *Final Fantasy VII* (1997) and *Metal Gear Solid* (1998) maintained their original Japanese mapping when they were localized into English, causing Western players some confusion (Gallant 2008). *Crash Bandicoot* (1996) is an example of a game originally developed in the US and then localized for the Japanese market, so the issue of button mapping for the Japanese PlayStation® had to be addressed. The original North American version used the X button to save

O button: Default button to confirm in Japanese original version

X button: Default button to confirm in NA/EU version

Figure 3.1 Differences in button mapping in PlayStation® 2 Controller
© 1999 Sony Computer Entertainment Inc. [Image kindly supplied by Sony Computer Entertainment Inc.]

the game but the localized Japanese version allowed the player to choose either the X or O button (DeLaHunt 2004, 11). With PS3 the X/O input is controlled at hardware level, but a Japanese model of PS3 always uses O for "confirm" and X for "cancel" as default, even when running an EU localized game.

In the localization of games, broader considerations for specific user parameters affect the whole product design. For example, before launching its Xbox game console in Japan, Microsoft had to modify the game controllers by reducing them in size and moving the buttons closer together so that ergonomically they would better fit Japanese players' hands (*New York Times*, February 18, 2002 cited in Yunker 2003).

3.2   Game localization models

Game localization models can be classified according to two main criteria. The first criterion is that of who performs the localization. With the in-house model it is done under the supervision of the developer or the publisher in their premises whereas in the outsourcing model an external specialized localization vendor or a translator performs the localization. The second criterion is related to the release of the localized version. In the sim-ship localization model, the localization process usually takes place in parallel to the game development process, so that the original game and the localized versions can be released on the same date. This is mainly done for marketing reasons, because of the short shelf-life of games, and to avoid **grey market imports** – source language copies unofficially available in the target territories – and pirate copies from other countries (Chandler 2005, 46–47). In addition, sim-ship releases help to build a sense of community among gamers regardless of their locale, particularly for popular online games, as gamers around the world can start playing on the same day and discussions may take place in specialised fora (Chandler and Deming 2012, 46). It should also be noted that due to the nature of games as transmedia, as discussed in Chapter 1, games that are tied in to movies are often released on the same day as the film or with only a few days' difference. For example, the game *Harry Potter and the Deathly Hallows: Part 2* (2011) was released in North America on July 12th and in Europe on July 14th, before the film was released worldwide on July 15th. The rapid information transmission afforded by the modern communications infrastructure has led to generally higher expectations from users of the availability of various products in their own language without delay, be they books, films, or games.

During the past decade global virtual connectivity has solidified gamer communities irrespective of their physical locations, accelerating the rate of information being disseminated among the community members, where even the mere mention of a forthcoming release of a major new game can lead to an instant global reaction. For example, the announcement in Japan of a release date of popular Japanese AAA franchise titles only available in Japanese frustrates non-Japanese speaking gamers and tends to show up localization as the main cause of delay. Further time-critical factors for games include, as mentioned earlier, a shorter shelf-life than business software applications; a few months after their initial release non-major games may end up in a bargain bin sold at a reduced price (Dietz 2006, 125). According to an industry source (Tinnelly, personal communication, 15 February, 2012), sim-ship localization can be an advantage in the sense that it sometimes provides the translator with an opportunity to give input on the design and implementation of the game which is still undergoing changes. The simultaneous shipment of major game titles is complex and a tiny glitch anywhere in the production chain could cause a major problem and a delay in the release date or affect the quality of the final product. To facilitate the increasing size and the complexity of the process, technological tools and project management have become essential. With its advantages and disadvantages, the sim-ship localization model has been a common business strategy for publishers in the US and Europe for some time, but was still less common until recently for games developed in Japan (see Table 5.1 for staggered release dates of Japanese *Final Fantasy* games for different territories). Nintendo used to be in this category, but has increasingly shifted to a near sim-ship model in recent years while Square Enix has also recently made a move towards simultaneous shipment (see Chapter 4 for a case study on Square Enix).

In contrast, post-gold localization consists of localizing a game once the original version has been completed, which means there is a lag of a few months – sometimes even a year – between the original and the localized version. While this means consumers need to wait for a longer period of time for localized products to become available, there is a certain advantage for translators, who are able to work with finished products where they may even be able to play the original game. While there has usually been a broad alignment between the outsourcing and the sim-ship models, on the one hand, and the in-house and post-gold models, on the other, the arrangement is now more fluid where this correspondence does not always apply according to an industry source (Tinnelly, personal communication, 15 February 2012). For example, game developers who opt for the in-house model may start the localization process concurrently, while the original game is still under development, in order to launch all the versions at the same time. Similarly, post-gold localization may be undertaken by the appointed external localization vendor. In the next sections we will examine in more detail the main features of the outsourcing and the in-house models.

3.2.1 Outsourcing model

This is the game localization model most widely used in the game industry and preferred by most North American and European publishers. According to the Game Developers Conference (GDC) 2012 (Schliem 2012, 8) new trends have been noted in which game companies in emerging markets, notably in Latin America such as Chile, as well as Russia and China, are becoming well-resourced to be major buyers of localization services. Such trends may have an implication for the language directionality of outsourcing of game localization. The outsourcing model usually involves commissioning a specialized vendor, who is put in charge of the whole localization process. For this reason, it tends to be more costly than the in-house model. The vendor selects the translators who will work on the project (usually independently and with no contact with other translators on the team) and is in charge of the integration of the different game assets in order to create the different playable versions. The vendor also arranges the recording of the script for voiceover in a studio, and in some cases even carries out quality assurance on the game, which may otherwise be undertaken by the developer or publisher or be outsourced to a specialized game testing vendor. From a translation point of view, the simultaneous release model has the disadvantage that the translators work with an incomplete and unstable text, subject to changes during the translation process. This often means translating files that will eventually not be used or having to redo the translation or parts of it due to last minute changes to the original. This is where translation memory (TM) tools can be useful in allowing the translator to identify the differences between versions of text and therefore to retain a relevant portion of the translation already performed. Translators are also likely to face the added stress of having to perform their task without being able to play or even see the finished game, often translating strings whose context is not available. They may just receive a spreadsheet with a series of unconnected text strings without any contextual information.

The need to provide translators with contextual information is always important for all types of translation, and yet in software environments de-contextualized text fragments which may belong to different parts of the game are routinely presented. The lack of contextual information can have particularly damaging consequences for the translation of audiovisual texts, such as subtitles and dubbing scripts, as these are synchronized with images and therefore the context in which they appear is vital for the translation to make sense to the player. Furthermore, where both written and aural channels are used simultaneously for the same message, consistency and coherence between them is a clear requirement. For example, the 2009 North American version of the Japanese interactive adventure novel RPG *Lux-Pain* (2008) displays such a marked discrepancy in meaning between the voiced dialogue and its subtitles that it creates dual worlds according to which channel of communication the player follows (Schules 2012). This game was generally reviewed poorly for its translation quality and it seems clear that the translator did not have the full context of the game story and did not know where the translated lines were going to be placed.

Due to the fact that translators often do not have the opportunity to play the very game which they are translating, and are prevented from accessing contextual information, game localization is often described as "blind localization" (Dietz 2006, 2007). Blind localization requires translators to assess the risks associated with the different possible translations and to manage them accordingly, in effect performing what Pym (2005) calls "translation risk management" in order to avoid a negative communicative outcome. Under these circumstances translators have to rely on their own intuition drawing on their game literacy and general understanding of game culture; they must make an educated guess of what the context could be and provide the most flexible translation which is likely to work in different contexts (Chandler 2008a, 35). For example, Chandler (ibid.) gives an example where the translator needs to work out if the phrase "white suits" is slang or a physical description in an isolated text: "The men in white suits are coming". Similarly, when translating from English into Spanish, the pronoun "you" can both refer to a single interlocutor (*tú*) or to a group of people (*vosotros*). Even if there is no contextual information or co-text available, the translator still has to make a decision, carefully calculating which option carries the lower level of risk. For example, if a character meets one single enemy and s/he refers to him/her as *vosotros*, it may puzzle the players, but if he or she addresses a group of people as *tú* it can always be interpreted as if a particular member of the group is being addressed. In order to compensate for a lack of access to the original game and to reduce the number of translation errors, developers and publishers usually provide localization vendors with a localization kit. In reality, the amount and quality of information that developers may pass on to the localization vendor varies, depending on their experience and awareness of the localization process. A localization kit ideally includes the following elements:

1. *General information about the project and the game content*
   Developers may provide information such as specific translation instructions, the list of assets to be translated, internal deadlines for the project (i.e. the start and completion dates for the translation of the different assets; the date when the review process should start; etc.), the name of the contact person in the developer's or publisher's company, and information about the software and tools required to perform the job.

Information about the game may include a general description of the storyline and the characters, as well as the **walkthrough** – a detailed guide to all the steps needed to advance in the game and the different levels required to complete it. It may also include **cheats** containing all the data, codes, and tricks necessary to successfully complete different trials and overcome obstacles in the game.

2. *Reference materials*
   Where possible, publishers also provide localization vendors with glossaries of the terminology used in the game and the terminology and standards specific to the platform or platforms for which the game is going to be published. While Sony and Nintendo's terminology is not publicly available, Microsoft terminology for the Xbox is available on the Microsoft Language Portal, on their terminology database.[39]

3. *Software programs and computer-aided translation (CAT) tools*
   If the translation of the game requires the use of specific tools designed by the developer, these tools will be provided to the localization vendor (for more details, see the last section in this chapter).

4. *Code*
   If the localization vendor is responsible for the **integration** of the game, with localized assets integrated back into the main body of the game, developers will provide the source code necessary to integrate the localized versions of the game and all the setup files necessary to run them.

5. *Assets to translate*
   These assets comprise all the text files, graphics, script, songs, etc. that need to be localized, as will be explained later.

Despite a generally increased awareness among developers of the need to provide contexts in the translation process, smaller and less experienced developers often do not provide much information about the game and simply submit the script and a series of Excel files with text strings and without any contextual information. This makes the translator's task extremely difficult and is likely to lead to a high number of errors in localized versions, especially when different translators are assigned to different parts of a game, do not have access to the other files, and cannot consult with one another. Responding to the question of the main challenges in game localization, the game translator Alexander O. Smith, who is well known for his role as a translator for the North American versions of the J-RPG *Final Fantasy* (*FF*) series, confirms that "insufficient source material, or source material that is

---

39. See http://www.microsoft.com/Language/en-US/Search.aspx.

presented in a confusing way" can create difficulties and "can do much to affect the quality of a localization" (cited in Jayemanne 2009, n.p.).

While blind localization is the most common *modus operandi* in the outsourcing model, more recently some clients also supply a playable debug ROM to localization vendors, owing to increasing awareness by developers and publishers of the importance of context in game localization.

3.2.2 In-house model

This has been the model generally preferred particularly by major Japanese game developers who are also publishers, such as Square Enix (see case study in Chapter 4). In this model, the developer is also responsible for localization into different languages and coordinates the project from start to finish. These companies usually have a localization department and a pool of freelance translators with whom they work regularly. When hiring the services of freelance translators, the developer may bring together translators according to different languages (usually FIGS – French, Italian, German, Spanish – for games published in Europe from English or using English as a pivot language, and FIGS with English for games translated directly from Japanese). Translators work together under the supervision of the localization coordinator, who also liaises between the localizers and the original development team. The localization process usually starts once the original game has been finished or is almost finished. For this reason, there is usually a lag of a few months between the launch of the original game and the localized versions. In the in-house model, localizers not only receive the localization kit, but they usually have full access to the original game as required. They often start the project playing the original game in order to familiarize themselves with the storyline, the characters, and the game mechanics. This makes the localization process longer, but it guarantees better quality in the localized versions, as the translators have access to the game and therefore build up a solid knowledge of it. As a result, they generally make fewer translation errors due to a lack of contextual information and thus the quality assurance process is faster and smoother. However, there is now a general shift towards sim-ship, with the lag between the original and the localized versions becoming shorter where developers opting for the in-house model are also aiming to reduce the lag between versions as much as possible. For example, in the case of Square Enix while there was a seven-month lag between the original Japanese and the North American release of *Final Fantasy XII* (2006), the lag for *Final Fantasy XIII* (2009) was less than three months despite the increased size of the game (see Table 5.1).

3.3 Game assets requiring localization

A video game is made up of different assets that need to be localized, namely in-game text, art assets, audio and cinematic assets, and printed materials (Chandler 2005). All of them have to be translated and integrated harmoniously with the images and the sound files within the code by means of specialised software tools. Occasionally there are other components, such as the **readme file** in PC games, which contain setup information for the user (including the minimum computing specs), press and marketing releases, the official website of the game, online help, and associated official strategy guides (often licensed to third-party publishers by platform holders), which contain written and illustrated information useful to complete the game. Game localization as a whole may also involve broader changes such as to game character designs, animations, as well as game mechanics and difficulty levels. We will cover these issues in Chapters 4 and 5 in the context of scope of adaptation and translation strategies influenced by cultural considerations, while discussing the most commonly localized assets next in more detail.

3.3.1 In-game text

Also known as "**onscreen text**" (OST), in-game text refers to all the text present in the **user interface** (UI) (such as menus, help messages, **tutorials** and **system messages**), narrative and descriptive passages, and all dialogues that are not voiced-over and only appear in written form, such as conversations held with **non-playable characters** (NPCs), who are driven by the game system and cannot be controlled by the player (see Chapter 4). Similarly to productivity software localization, text in the UI is subject to strict space limitations, particularly in menu screens, which usually contain different types of information, such as the statistics for the players, help messages, and lists of items. Thus, game screens can be extremely busy compared to screens for typical productivity software, and this makes space restrictions even more acute when localizing them. However, despite these constraints, the UI of a game should not interfere with the gameplay experience, as it is the gateway to the game world. For this reason it is recommended to use clear language, and to avoid abbreviations when possible. In Dietz's words:

> [A] game interface should not destroy the player's willing suspension of disbelief concerning the 'reality' of the game. Unlike the interface of a normal application, which is integrated into the program, it exists as a quasi-transparent layer between the world of the game and the world of the player. Therefore it must be both unobtrusive and fully functional. (2006, 126)

Texts subject to translation also include system messages from game consoles to the users. They need to adhere to the terminology established by the platform holder; such as Sony for PS and PS Portable or PS Vita, Nintendo for Wii and DS, and Microsoft for Xbox. The terminology used for these different platforms varies considerably, but localizers must be familiar with it and adapt their translations to the terminology used in the platform or platforms for which a game is going to be released. For example, Sony uses the term "analogue stick" in English to define the lever in the controller that allows the player to make selections, scroll screens and control the main characters in a game. However, Microsoft uses "thumb-stick". Adherence to the hardware manufacturer's guidelines is essential, and a game could fail the **submission process** to the platform holder if the wrong terminology is selected. Using "analogue stick" in a game that is going to be published for Microsoft Xbox would mean that the game would be rejected and would have to go back to the developer, who would have to make the necessary changes and resubmit it, paying the required submission fee again. This is an area in which a centralized approach to terminology management will help the game conform to the required set of terminology, avoiding the need for a resubmission.

However, official terminology may sometimes create translation problems as illustrated by the example below relating to the issue of space constraints. The official Swedish term *"den rörelsekänsliga handkontrollen"* [the motion sensitive hand controller], which was imposed by the manufacturer for Sony's PlayStation® 3 controller PS Move, apparently caused considerable problems due to its length (Lundin, personal communication, January 27, 2012). Similarly, when the translation of the phrase "please recalibrate the motion controller" has to fit into a small system pop-up box, the translator has an almost impossible challenge to overcome, as there is no leeway in shortening the official terminology. Furthermore, games are often published simultaneously for different platforms, and it is essential that a thorough check of the platform-related terminology is performed before the submission of the **release candidate** version. This ensures that all the

Table 3.1 Comparison of Sony vs. Microsoft terminology

Sony's terminology for PlayStation	Microsoft terminology for Xbox
analog stick	thumbstick
memory card (8MB) (for PS2)	memory unit
MEMORY CARD slot	memory unit slot
directional buttons	directional pad
L1 Button*	LB Button (Top Left Button)
* placed in the top left part of the back of the controller	
L2 Button*	LT Button (Left Trigger)
* used as trigger	

system messages conform to the terminological and localization standards set by the platform holders. In addition, it helps prevent unnecessary delays at the final stage of localization due to failing the submission process. Table 3.1 contains some examples of the terminology sanctioned by Microsoft and Sony for their Xbox and PlayStation® consoles respectively.

3.3.2   Art assets

Art assets are all those graphics and images, such as maps, signs, and notices that include text in the original version and must be adapted for the localized versions. They are also known as **"textual graphics"** and **"graphic text"**. These assets may have to be modified or redesigned in order to include the text in the TL for the localized versions, similar to productivity software localization. In order to keep the textual world of the game coherent, it is advisable to localize all textual graphics, except when they are originally in a different language and are used simply to create a particular atmosphere, such as graphics containing Russian in a game developed in English about the Cold War. Unfortunately, often developers do not take art assets into account when they are planning the localization process, and in order to save time and resources they may not translate them. As a consequence, some text in the original language is left in the localized version, presenting a heterogeneous textual world that may cause some confusion to the players. In addition, in some cases these textual graphics may include a clue or some information relevant to gameplay, which means that gamers who do not have enough knowledge of the original language are likely to miss out on that information. As this could negatively affect their performance and overall gameplay experience, ideally it is advisable to translate textual graphics and design them so that the textual element may be readily extracted.

3.3.3   Audio and cinematic assets

This includes all those elements with audio and voiceover that need to be translated, such as songs and the script. Nowadays, most AAA titles include **cut-scenes** or cinematics, the only non-interactive element of a game, which gamers cannot usually control. Some games oblige gamers to watch these scenes at least once and repeatedly, if they get stuck at a particular level, but currently many games include the option of skipping these cinematic interludes, depending on the function of such scenes. Cut-scenes turn gamers into spectators for brief periods and have thus proved controversial within the gamer community, as many players resent the lack of interactivity (Newman 2004). This mixed reaction and lukewarm reception from some gamers may have been one of the reasons why the translation of cinematic scenes in games has long been neglected, as gamers generally do not pay much attention to them or to the quality of their translation. However, more recently the trend of "cinematic games" is incorporating many techniques used in the film industry into the game production (Newman 2009, xii). This will likely have implications for game localization. The issue of cut-scenes and dubbing and subtitling for games will be explored in more detail in Chapter 4.

3.3.4 Printed materials

Printed materials include all those elements in print that accompany a game, such as the instruction manual and the packaging. The translation of the printed materials is not always carried out by the same translator(s) who have localized the game, and it can be outsourced to another translator or vendor. This may also apply to press releases, marketing, and legal documents, promotion materials, strategy guides, and online help resources. It is essential that the terminology used for printed materials corresponds exactly to the terminology used in the game to prevent inconsistencies and avoid creating confusion for gamers. Fernández (2007, 25–26), in her case study of the localization into Spanish of the game *Codename: Kids Next Door. Operation: V.I.D.E.O.G.A.M.E.* (2005), highlights some inconsistencies between the manual and the game, such as the name of the character "Stickybeard", translated as *Barbapringosa* in the game, but *Barbapegajosa* in the manual. In addition, some of the objects used in the game appear in Spanish in the manual, while they were left in English in the game itself. This makes it almost impossible for Spanish players with little knowledge of English to identify these items in the game manual. These kinds of inconsistency are likely to project a negative and unprofessional image of the localized version, which could easily be avoided by creating and compiling glossaries and using terminology management technology. It is also important to note that occasionally, when the game manual is translated, the arrangement of information may be re-organized for the localized version in a way that is more in keeping with the target language conventions of text type and market preferences in terms of information presentation, and will thus involve a considerable amount of text editing and re-arranging.

A comparative study (DeLaHunt 2004) of the original and the localized Japanese version of the US-made game *Crash Bandicoot* (1996) highlights such re-arrangements of information and presentation in respective game manuals. While the total number of pages was similar for both booklets, the topic allocation differed between the two. The analysis by DeLaHunt shows that more than 10% of the space in the North American original version was spent on business and legal issues while the Japanese counterpart covered no equivalent topics. The latter de-voted more than 72% of the space to game-related content such as narrative, char-acters, walkthroughs, and gameplay tips, whereas similar content occupied about 57% of the NA version (ibid., 13). According to DeLaHunt, because of the way in which the Japanese manual was presented with detailed game explanations in a more solid and brighter looking booklet, it gave a more user-friendly impression, whereas the NA version came across as "a minimally-filled requirement" (ibid.). In turn, a comparison between the English manual for the localized PAL (Aus-tralia/NZ version) version and the original Japanese manual of the PS2 game *ICO* (2001) reveals a number of differences, including the cover design of the manual and a changed order of information, as well as the use of different sets of illus-trations and layout. Above all, the most striking change is the way certain game actions are explained in both manuals. While the English manual organizes the explanations in bullet points under each heading according to different actions and tools in a manner that is typical of instruction manuals, the Japanese weaves the instructions into narrative prose in a story-like manner (see Figure 3.2).

It is also worth mentioning that in April 2010 French publisher Ubisoft an-nounced that they would eliminate the printed versions of manuals in their games and only provide in-game digital manuals. The move was emulated by Electronic Arts in March 2011 (Gamefreaks 2011) when they announced that EA sports game titles will no longer accompany print manuals, which would be replaced by a version of instructions within the game. Similarly Nintendo has been us-ing e-manuals for some time for their downloadable games. Not only is it more environmentally friendly, but it also helps publishers reduce printing costs con-siderably and therefore this model may become more common in the future. The move may also be justified by the fact that few gamers actually read the manual unless they become stuck in a game, but even then some will opt to search for the relevant information on the Internet rather than look in the manual. In place of manuals, many games now contain tutorial levels within the game itself, often providing a better means to show the user a given set of instruction about the game. However, users express mixed feelings about the decision towards the pa-perless option; some feel they would miss the print manuals while others feel that it does not really make any difference to them (Tinnelly, personal communica-tion, 15 February, 2012). Those who would read the manual first before playing the game are most likely to be a minority today with the majority simply jumping in to play. However, it is also true that some game titles require the player to un-derstand specific instructions conveyed by the print manual before the game can be fully enjoyed. On occasion such requirements in some games led to a situation where pirated Nintendo console games were played in a different way than intend-ed, improvised by players without access to official manuals (Uemura, personal

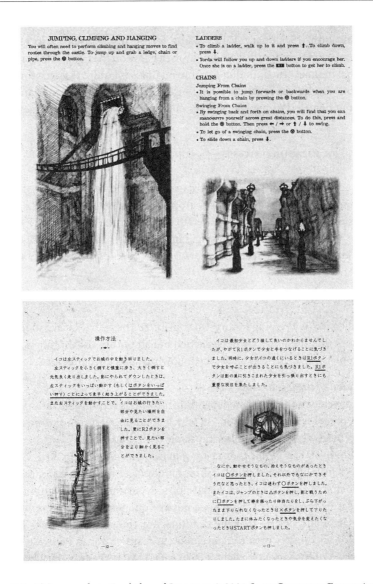

Figure 3.2 *ICO* manuals in English and Japanese © 2001 Sony Computer Entertainment Inc. (with our highlights in the Japanese text to indicate explanations of the functions of different control buttons, woven into the prose of the game story) [Images kindly supplied by Sony Computer Entertainment Inc.]

communication, 19 January 2012). Game forum discussions[40] also reveal that some users seem to judge the authenticity of a game on the basis of the presence of an original manual. The function of game manuals is a valid research topic which is currently under-reported especially in the context of **emergent gameplay** in which unanticipated gameplay emerges due to liberties taken by the gamer.

3.4   The localization process

In this section we describe the main stages of the localization cycle of a typical video game in the best-case scenario, from the moment when its localization is commissioned up to when it is released to the distribution network. The diagram in Figure 3.3 outlines the different stages in the game localization process, each of which is described in the sections below.

3.4.1   Pre-localization

Pre-localization is the preparatory work prior to the actual localization. Its aim is to ensure that the project will be carried out smoothly and on time with minimum problems. During this stage, the following tasks are performed:

1.   *Creation of the localization kit*
     The developer or publisher, depending on who is responsible for the localization, prepares the localization kit, which contains relevant information about the project, as well as the files and assets to be translated.
2.   *Appointment of a localization coordinator and translators*
     In the in-house model, the localization manager appoints a localization co-ordinator (a member of the localization department) who will manage the project in the different languages, answer queries, solve any problems that may arise and ensure that the deadlines for the project are met. The coordinator also liaises with the development team and may be involved in the selection of freelance translators (also called "localizers" or "localization specialists" in the industry). In the outsourcing model, the localization coordinator acts as the link between the game developer or publisher and the vendor. Next, the vendor selects a project manager and the translators to be involved in the project. The project manager supervises the work of the translators throughout the project, collates their queries, sends them to the developer or publisher and liaises between the translation team and the client.

---

40. See, for example, a thread in Nintendolife forum available at: http://www.nintendolife.com/forums/ds/thor_god_of_thunder_ds_pirated_copy.

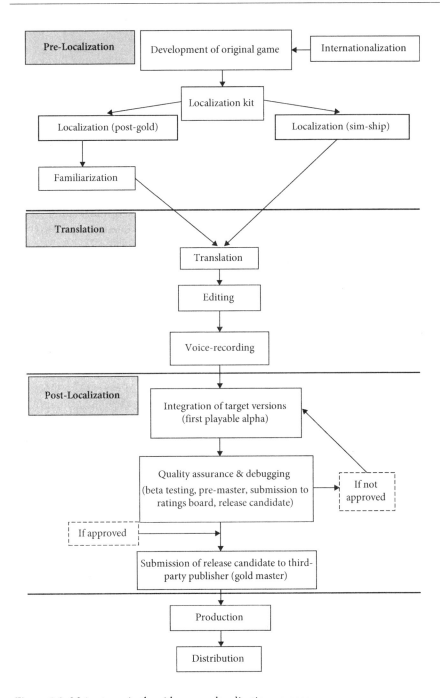

Figure 3.3 Main stages in the video game localization process

3. *Preparatory work*

In the in-house model, translators spend some time familiarizing themselves with the game, playing it, reading information about the plot and the walk-through, compiling glossaries of key terms, and creating style and characterization guides, all to ensure consistency among the different translators working on the project. In the outsourcing model, localizers usually do not have access to the game, but ideally they will familiarize themselves with the information provided in the localization kit. If there is no information available, translators usually try to search for information regarding the game. Even if the original version has not been published, there may be demo versions available, along with press releases or marketing related information which may be useful to the translator. In addition, if translation memories (TMs) are to be used in the project, engineers may pre-process the files contained in the localization kit and check them against existing TMs, in order to standardize and facilitate the translation process (Leary n. d.).

3.4.2 Translation

This is the key stage of the localization process. In a sim-ship model translation is usually carried out in parallel for all target language locales while the original game is still under development. The translator therefore works with a source text (ST) which keeps changing. By comparison, in a post-gold model the original game is published providing the translator with a finished product and a stable text. In the case of Japanese games localized according to this model, they are generally translated first into US English, for the North American market, and then into FIGS as well as UK English, using English as a pivot language. For the UK English version, the original US voiceover is typically kept, but all the non-audio textual assets are adapted to UK English. In the case of Spanish, some games, such as *World of Warcraft* have a Castilian Spanish version, for Spain, and a Latin-American one. The issue of working from a pivot version is further discussed in Chapter 4 as it poses certain challenges to translation. Similar to software localization, game translation is often made more difficult by STs made up of de-contextualized text fragments further complicated by different text types which characterise game translation (see Table 4.1). Furthermore, the non-linearity of game text composition exacerbates the challenge of dealing with the isolated text fragments. This non-linearity is also manifest in the way in which localizers are required to translate certain assets first, not necessarily according to a logical sequence but to fit the particular scheduling of the project, which may be driven by marketing requirements. With the expanding size of game text, the involvement of multiple translators in the same project could lead to inconsistency issues. The

Japanese translation of the popular MMORPG *EverQuest II* (2004), consisting of 1.5 million words, took over a year to complete by a team of 10 Japanese translators working concurrently (Translating EverQuest II 2006, 36–37). In this project different assets and parts of the game were reportedly assigned to the translators, who worked independently, but under the supervision of the localization coordinator. Table 3.5 provides an overview of the typical time-scale involved in a game localization scenario, showing the time allocated to different tasks. Some of these issues are addressed in Chapter 4 in more detail in the context of a Translation Studies theoretical framework.

Below we list a number of common constraints that are pertinent to game localization, specifically affecting translation decisions in terms of space limitations, mainly relating to the UI items, the prescribed use of terminology specified by platform holders, and the application of variables typical in games to allow recycling of recurring phrases which are dynamically linked to the player input.

Space constraints
Space constraints can be extremely severe, particularly when translating from Japanese or Chinese, where one single character can represent a concept that may need to be expressed in more than one word in a Western language. This is particularly true for Romance languages, as well as German, which tend to require more space for in-game text than English. To overcome space constraints, it is advisable to design menus, lists, and text boxes to allow for the need for extra space, similar to what is done in the localization of productivity software. Chandler (2005, 9) recommends leaving at least 30% extra free space when translating from English. Localization from Japanese requires even more space, usually two lines of translated text for one line in the original (Stevens Heath 2010). Another solution to overcoming space limitations consists of using expandable or scrollable text boxes to allow resizing. Occasionally developers and publishers use pseudo-translation, in the same way as the localization of productivity software (see Chapter 2), to get an idea of the space required for the target versions. Other solutions to overcoming space constraints are the use of icons in menus (see Figure 4.1 for an example), the use of tooltips, which provide information on an item when the cursor is placed over it, and the use of page breaks. All these measures help prevent **truncations** of the text on the screen and the use of excessive abbreviations, which the players may find confusing and which can also slow down the pace of gameplay, while making it obvious that the game is not an original. The problem of space constraints is even more acute in games for handheld platforms and in games for mobile phones, due to their smaller screens. The maximum length of text used in games is usually calculated according to the number of pixels, and not characters, because it allows for a more precise calculation of available space.

While some subtitles for cinema now also use pixel counts (Díaz Cintas and Remael 2007, 250), measurement according to number of characters is still common in TV and DVD subtitling.

Platform-specific terminology
Each console platform holder – Sony, Nintendo, and Microsoft – has its own specific technical requirements, as their game standards are different in Asia, Europe, and the United States (Chandler and Deming 2012, 7). All international versions must fulfil these requirements and adhere to the platform-specific terminology. This is particularly important when a game is being released for different platforms, given that the correct technical requirements and terminology must be applied for each platform. This issue will be further discussed in Section 3.4.6.

Use of variables and concatenations
As noted in Chapter 2, **variables** are values that hold the space for different text or numerical strings – such as proper nouns, numerals, and objects – and they change depending on certain conditions specific to the player action. They are also known as "**placeholders**". For example, in the string "MEMORY CARD slot (n)", n is a variable that will be replaced by the value 1 or 2 depending on the slot in which the card is placed in the PS2 console. Translators must be careful not to delete variables and they should understand the type of information that will replace the variable in the game or software program, so that the information that will appear on screen is coherent and will make sense to the users. When translating from Japanese or English into Romance languages, special attention must be paid to possible grammatical agreement issues. The safest option is to use translations that will work in all contexts, regardless of the gender and number of the noun they modify, even if this translation may not be the preferred one stylistically.

Díaz Montón (2007) describes the problems posed by the use of variables in the following example: "%s" gets a "%d". In this case, the variable "%s" stands for the player's name, while variable "%d" represents the item he or she obtains. In her example, the latter variable can be replaced by one of the following three terms: "sword", "hammer" and "shield", equivalent to *espada, martillo,* and *escudo* in Spanish respectively. Due to the need for agreement between articles, adjectives, and nouns in Romance languages, the translation of this variable is likely to pose a problem. For example, if the string "gets a" were translated as "ha conseguido un", this would result in a grammatical problem in the Spanish sentence *Mick ha conseguido un espada,* as *espada* is a feminine noun and *un* is a masculine article. Díaz Montón proposes two solutions at a textual level for the Spanish version:

- The use of a colon, to avoid the use of the indeterminate article: *Mick ha conseguido: espada.*
- Omitting the translation of the indefinite article *a* in the main sentence and including the indefinite article inside the variable in the list of terms that replace the variable, making it agree with the noun it precedes. The string would be translated as "%s" *ha conseguido* "%d" ("%s" gets "%d") in Spanish, including the indefinite article inside the variable translation and the variable "%d" would be replaced by the values *una espada, un martillo* or *un escudo*, as required.

When translating variables all the possible cases where that variable may be used must be considered, and the best possible solution needs to be applied to avoid grammatical errors and inconsistencies that may disrupt the pace of the game by attracting the player's attention for wrong reasons. Due to the increasing importance granted by the game industry to internationalization and localization, developers are becoming more aware of the challenges posed by variables. In order to avoid grammatical errors, some of them use a metalanguage, which is a set of codes embedded in a string that allows the author to incorporate "many grammatical aspects of a language into a given sentence" (Heimburg 2006, 142), such as gender and number. Other developers, like Square Enix, use a system based on grammatical branching macros that allow gender and number to be specified as in Table 3.2 (Honeywood 2007).

As touched on in Chapter 2, **concatenation** is also often used in localization. It consists of combining two or more text strings in order to avoid having to repeat similar strings resulting from a number of alternatives offered by a game or a productivity software application. Occasionally, a game script may be made up by merging two separate strings, resulting in grammatical errors, like in the example by Díaz Montón (2007), "You win a <u>blue</u> car", where the colour of the car the player wins may change depending on the game conditions. Therefore, this is split into three different strings in the game code: (1) "You win" (2) "a blue" and (3) "car". In Spanish, however, the literal translation resulting from the concatenation of the three strings would be ungrammatical – (1) *Has ganado* (2) *un azul* (3) *coche* – because the natural word order is noun + adjective. In this particular case, the problem can be solved by including extra text in the translated string for 1 and eliminating string 3 from the translation: (1) *Has ganado un coche* (2) *azul.*

Table 3.2 Grammatical branching macros

Macro for masculine adjectives	<IF_MALE>...<ELSE_NOT_MALE>...<ENDIF_MALE>
Macro for singular adjectives	<IF_SING xxx>...<ELSE_NOT_SING>...<ENDIF_SING>

Source: After Honeywood (2007).

If the game allowed the possibility of winning other items, another solution would be needed, such as changing the order of the strings in the localized version if possible, or swapping the text content of strings 2 and 3 in the localized version.

3.4.3 Editing

Once the translation is finished, the editing process follows, which consists of the review and the proofreading of the translated assets. In the in-house model if there is a team of translators they usually review each other's work. After that, editors employed by the developer or publisher (or, time and budget permitting, an external vendor) may carry out a thorough review of the translated material to ensure that there are no errors and that the team's translation is coherent and consistent. In the outsourcing model it is usually the vendor who performs the editing. Reviewers may make the appropriate changes to unify the style and the terminology used in the game in order to guarantee the quality of the localized product or they may simply indicate the suggested changes and corrections to the translators, who will then implement them in their files. In Chapter 4 we further discuss the increasing deployment of (re)writers in the TL in order to enhance the level of polish of the final text.

3.4.4 Recording

As mentioned in Chapter 1, the use of human voice for a large volume of text in games is a relatively recent inclusion afforded by improved hardware capacity. Games seek increased realism with the use of voiceover, requiring both voice actors and translators. Translators must be aware that the strings of voiceover dialogue are occasionally presented in a non-linear fashion. For example, all the lines for each character may be grouped together rather than presented in their interactions, and thus translators and voice actors are likely to miss the context of the dialogue exchanges, which makes their job harder. For this reason it is clearly preferable that appropriate contexts and information are provided, although in reality localizers may have to translate the script without any context, thus making them prone to more translation errors.

Once the translation has been edited, it is ready for audio localization. The script and all the voiceover messages are recorded by professional voice actors in a recording studio, with the assistance of an adjuster, a sound engineer, and a dubbing director for major projects. In the in-house model, the localization co-ordinator may be present at the recording sessions to ensure things run smoothly and to deal with any problems that may arise. As happens with other audiovisual products, at this stage the adjuster may modify the final version of the translation for lip-synching or timing purposes. Once the script has been recorded, developers are reluctant to make changes to it, as they are costly. However, if a major error is found after the recording has been finalized (for example, an inconsistency between what is being said and what is seen on the screen), the affected line or lines may be re-recorded. Major projects may schedule "a pick up session" in order to make corrections.

There are five different types of audio recording (Sioli et al. 2007, 19):

1. *Wild*
   There are no characters on screen and the text can be recorded without time constraints, such as a user-initiated audio help file on a fixed screen.

2. *Time-constrained*
   The total duration of the audio file must be identical to the original, usually for technical reasons, and the translated text should not be longer than the original. Despite the fact that no characters appear on screen, there may be times when the audio can be synchronized with events happening on the screen, for example in a tutorial where the player is shown what to do. It is important to identify points of synchronization before the translation begins, to take them into account and not alter the flow of the translated text.

3. *Sound-synch*
   A recording that is synchronized with the audio. The characters appear on screen and their rendering has yet to be completed but sound needs to be synchronized. The translation must not be longer than the original and the text should be adapted so that it matches the pauses in each sentence. This is normally used for characters' interventions when the characters do not appear on screen or their faces and lip movements cannot be seen clearly.

4. *Lip-synch*
   Lip movements are synchronized and therefore the translated text has to be adapted to match them, as in the traditional process for film or television dubbing. Lip-synch is mainly used for character close-ups in dialogues and cut-scenes. The quality of graphics and animations in games is nowadays so advanced and realistic that if a character's intervention is out of synch it is obvious, and players may find it annoying. For this reason, lip-synching can pose a challenge to translators and may even require rewriting the original translation completely. However, the application of advanced lip-synch animation technology to games has helped reduce this problem and has achieved impressive results in some cases, as in the games *Mass Effect 2* (2010) and *Heavenly Sword* (2007). For example, AI-driven facial modelling technology used in *Mass Effect 2* allowed the facial animation to match the audio based on the actor's voice stress and inflection (Lewinski 2010).

Table 3.3 The use of stitches in sports games

Variable element 1	Fixed element	Variable element 2	Fixed element
Player A	just scored the	first goal	of the match!
Player B		second goal	
Player C		third goal	

Source: After Loureiro (2007).

5. *Stitches*

   An important difference between traditional dubbing applied to cinema and voiceover for games lies in the use of variables with audio, named "**stitches**", mainly used in sports games, such as soccer and racing games, in order to save space on the disk (Loureiro 2007). Stitches are short audio files containing utterances made by game characters, segmented and recorded separately, so that they can be used at different stages of the game as appropriate, with variables inserted in run-time. In this type of intervention, there are both fixed and variable elements that the game engine selects when certain conditions are met. As shown in Table 3.3, the first variable element is the name of the player who scores the goal, and the second refers to how many goals the player has scored. In reality, variable elements to be stitched in a sentence are more likely to be limited to one rather than multiple elements. Using stitches allows space to be saved by reducing the amount and size of audio files stored in the game, but localizers should be aware of the pitfalls presented by this technique, similar to those which arise through the use of variables. In addition, when stitching together the different segments, the sentence may sound unnatural even if grammatically correct. Therefore, in order to prevent bugs and unnatural sounding sentences, all the different possible options are considered by the localizers, and the translation most idiomatic and likely to work in all contexts is chosen.

3.4.5 Post-localization

Post-localization includes all the tasks performed after translating and reviewing the target files. It consists mainly of the following two stages:

1. *Integration*

   An engineer or team of engineers integrate the translated files, the audio and art assets, and the image files into the game code and produce a functional and usable version of the localized product, known as the "**first playable alpha**".

2. *Debugging and quality assurance (QA)*

Once the first playable alpha has been integrated, the debugging and QA process begins in order to detect bugs, that is, errors in the game. A team of testers (from the developer's company in the in-house model, the translation vendor or a specialized QA vendor in the outsourcing model) play the **beta version** of the game, exploring all possible options, searching for errors and entering them into a bug database daily. In the in-house model, localizers are usually also involved in the QA or debugging process. As bugs are found and corrected, new versions of the game are integrated and released, known as "**builds**". Once the game is very stable and most of the bugs have been fixed, the **pre-master** version is ready. At this stage only serious bugs are fixed, in order to avoid new complications. Once the pre-master version has been tested and any issues detected have been fixed, the **release candidate (RC)** is made available.

The amount of time devoted to testing varies from title to title, from a few weeks to a few months in the case of AAA titles such as the *Final Fantasy* series. In addition, testing for low-budget or casual games sometimes does not start until the RC is ready. Usually game developers for PC and online games also conduct public **beta testing**. An open call is made for this kind of testing, and game fans happily do it for the thrill of being able to play a new game before it is officially released. This kind of testing usually takes place once the first playable alpha is available. Players can then play the game as they wish and report any detected errors and malfunctions to the developers, so that these bugs can be fixed before releasing the final version; developers may also be provided with more general feedback about the game.

It is important to note that quality assurance in localization usually consists of two stages: the editing and the QA. Most other types of translation only involve a review in the form of a self-check by the translator and/or by a separate editor or the client, but in localization there is another type of check after the editing has been finalized. This is due to the nature of localization, namely that: (a) the TT is embedded in electronic form; (b) the ST is often unstable; (c) sometimes there is no access to the original game and no contextual information, and (d) several translators and reviewers participate in the localization process (although this is not unique to localization). The QA is the stage in the localization process when translators and reviewers can view those isolated strings they translated in context for the first time. This allows them to detect errors caused by the lack of contextual information at the earlier translation stage and improve the quality of the target version. For this reason, the QA process of localized products is given paramount importance by developers and it can be as lengthy as, or lengthier than, the translation process itself. In relation to the type of errors detected in a localized console game, those most commonly found relate to the following three main areas:

- *Functionality*
  These are the most critical type of bugs, and they are related to the game itself and its UI. Functionality bugs mainly relate to stability (e.g. does the game freeze or crash when a certain action is performed?) and game mechanics (e.g. does a particular fighting technique have the effect it is supposed to have?; Do the different commands work?) This type of testing is known as "**functionality testing**".
- *Compliance*
  The localized versions are checked for adherence to the technical requirements checklist, to the localization standards of each platform hardware manufacturer, and to legal, ethical, and ratings-related criteria. This type of testing is known as "**compliance testing**".
- *Linguistic errors*
  These are mainly bugs related to text, such as grammar mistakes, typos, truncations, overlaps, etc. This type of testing is known as "**linguistic testing**". Some software and game companies include cosmetic errors in this category, such as the lack of a blank space between words or the presence of extra blank spaces or extra blank lines. Other companies, however, consider them separately during the **cosmetic testing**. In our experience, however, most game companies have two types of testers: functionality testers and linguistic testers. Functionality testers check the game to make sure there are no technical or gameplay issues and do not necessarily speak the language of the localized versions. By comparison, linguistic testers focus on language, cosmetic, and compliance issues, such as grammar mistakes, the use of unidiomatic language, the use of incorrect platform terminology, truncations, and missing and extra spaces, although they also report any functionality bugs they detect.

Developers and publishers design their own bug report template, although all reports tend to include similar information. When the testing progresses and the bugs are fixed, different versions are released. It is necessary to check that all reported bugs have been fixed in subsequent versions. As long as a bug has not been fixed, it is considered "open"; once it has been fixed it acquires a "closed" status and it is not necessary to check it again in subsequent versions. In addition to the three types of bug mentioned above which are widely recognised and used by the game localization industry, Edwards (2012, 21) recommends introducing a new bug category – "cultural bug" – in order to ensure that any culture-related issues that may have been overlooked during the localization process are also tracked and amended as necessary, although this is not common at present.

The template shown in Table 3.4 illustrates the most common fields found in a bug report and includes a brief explanation of them.

Once the game has been tested and the final version is nearly ready, publishers usually submit a copy of a near final version of the game, together with the appropriate documentation, to the appropriate software ratings board to obtain an age rating (Chandler and Deming 2012, 35).

Table 3.4 Bug report template

Title: *name of game*	Current version: *version of game used for testing*
Platform: *Xbox, DS, Wii, PS3, etc.*	Developer: *name of company who developed the game*
Bug ID: *number assigned to bug*	Reporter: *name of tester who found the bug*
Status: *a bug can have different status:* New, *when it is first detected;* Open, *when it still appears on a later version;* Fixed, *once it has been corrected;* Waived, *when it is not a bug or when it will not be fixed*	Bug type: *this refers to the type of bug, e.g. functionality, compliance, linguistic.*
Severity: *the impact the bug has in the gameplay. This is usually expressed by letters or figures. For example,* A *would mean it is a critical bug, while* D *would mean that correcting this bug would enhance the game, but it actually does not have a negative impact.*	Priority: *this is closely related to the severity of the bug and the urgency to fix it. A critical bug usually has priority 1 (to be fixed immediately), while an enhancement bug usually has priority 4 (fix if time permits)*
Date found: *date when the bug was found*	Version found: *number of the version where the bug was found, which does not necessarily have to be the current version. This is mostly used for checking whether bugs that have been previously reported have been fixed or not.*
Frequency: *how often the bug occurs (i.e. always/sometimes/rarely)*	Language: *language where the problem was found; it could be in several or all languages.*
Assign to: *the person who will be responsible for fixing the bug*	
Summary: *brief and concise description of the problem, explaining what it is and where it can be found.*	
Description: *A more detailed explanation of the bug, which should include the following information:* a. *Reproduce steps: clear explanation of the steps necessary to reproduce the bug* b. *Current problem: description of the bug* c. *Solution/Correction: proposal for fixing the bug*	

3.4.6 Submission of release candidate version

Titles developed for PC or mobile phone platforms currently have no official approval process, except for games for iPhone, while console releases must be submitted to the **platform** or **format holder** for a final and thorough technical compliance check. This is necessary to ensure that the software works properly on the intended platform, that it does not harm the hardware and also as a way of ensuring that the quality of the game meets the standards of the platform holder. Sony publishes a "Technical Requirements Checklist" (TRC), Microsoft issues a "Technical Certification Requirements" (TCR), and Nintendo produces a set of guidelines ("Lot Check") to which developers must strictly adhere. These cover highly technical aspects as well as the terminology, the formatting of standard error messages, the handling of memory card data and the handling of copyrighted material. If the game complies with the technical requirements and localization standards of the format holder, it is approved and the production process can start. If any conflicts are found, the game is rejected and the developer has a limited period of time to fix them and resubmit the game. Once the candidate version has been approved, it is known as the "**gold master**".

3.4.7 Production and distribution

With the gold master ready, the game goes into production. The specific packaged localized copy of the game on disk is called **SKU (Stock Keeping Unit)**. There are usually different SKUs for games localized into different varieties of the same language, such as a UK English SKU and a North American English SKU. Once the production process is finished, the game is distributed to retailers and made available to the public.

3.4.8 Game localization scenario

The following table, based on Chandler (2008c), provides an example of a typical game localization scenario of a multi-platform English title to FIGS for the Xbox 360, the PS3 and PC.

The volume of words in online games is on average much higher than in console games as shown in Table 3.5 and requires a team of translators working simultaneously for long periods of time. From the point of view of project management of game localization projects, Zhou (2011) identifies four areas of management: communications management, scope management, risk management and change management. It is beyond the scope of this book to detail further aspects of project

Table 3.5 A game localization scenario

Task	Volume			Timeframe
Translation	30,000 words in-game text	10,000 in-game words		20 days (single translator)
		20,000 words of dialogue (all dialogue to be subtitled)	12 major characters (100+ lines each) 20 minor characters 400 dubbed lines in cut-scenes	
Casting	32 characters (voice talents)			7 days (including time for approvals)
Voiceover (VO) Recording	2,000 lines, involving 32 characters			14 days (both recording and processing)
Asset Integration	In-game text, audio files (no art assets to be integrated)			1 day
Linguistic Testing	3 rounds testing/fixes			21 days
Ratings Review	Need 100% content			3–4 weeks
Production	1 language / platform			63 days
	1 language / 3 platforms			107 days
	4 languages /3 platforms			428 person days

Source: After Chandler (2008c).

management, but it can be highlighted that a considerable degree of control and monitoring is required for large scale game localization projects to be successfully completed on time and within budget.

3.5   Levels of localization

There are different levels of game localization, determined by marketing strategies and usually prioritized by the size of the market – the bigger the market, the more chance of full localization. Sometimes, however, format holders decide to localize their games into the languages of smaller markets in order to boost hardware sales and increase their presence in those new emerging markets, as in the case of Sony with the Portuguese-speaking market (Ranyard and Wood 2009). Chandler (2005, 12–14) categorizes localization approaches on four main possible levels:

- *No localization*: some budget titles are not localized and are sold in the original language in other countries. This provides the opportunity to sell some extra copies without having to invest in the localization process.
- *Box and docs localization*: this refers to the translation of the packaging and the manual of the game. The game code and language remain in the original language. This is usually done for games that include little text (e.g., platform, sports, and arcade games), games not expected to sell more than a few thousand copies, and games developed in English to be sold in countries where players have a good level of English, such as Scandinavian countries. This was also the common option for games developed in the early days such as *Pong* (1972).
- *Partial localization:* the in-game text is translated, but the voiceover files are not. This helps reduce the time and cost necessary for producing the localized versions, as there is no need to hire voice actors or redesign graphics on account of lip-synching for dubbing. The voiced files containing dialogue are usually subtitled in the TL.
- *Full localization*: this involves translating all assets of a game: in-game text, voiceover assets, manual, and packaging. It is the most expensive type of localization and is usually reserved for AAA titles. This is the maximum level of localization, which provides the players with a game fully tailored to their language needs and facilitates gameplay and immersion in the game.

According to the Game Developers Conference 2012 (Schliem 2012, 8) the trend among game developers and publishers is now towards full localization rather than the basic minimum localization. Most developers opt for either partial or full localization on the basis of the importance of the different target markets and the resources allocated to the project. The biggest game markets in Europe are the UK, France, and Germany (Chandler and Deming 2012, 45) and therefore fully localized versions are usually available in French and German, as well as English for Japanese games. However, Spain and Italy are rapidly growing game markets and full localization is also increasing in those territories (ibid.). For example, *Mass Effect 2* (2010) was fully localized into French, German, Italian, and Polish, but only partially localized to Spanish, Czech, Hungarian, and Russian (Steussy 2010a).

3.6   Tools used in game translation

As mentioned in Chapter 2, the use of technological tools in game localization – particularly CAT tools – is relatively recent, despite the fact that the wider software localization industry has been using various localization tools and translation technologies since the 1990s. This rather late start seems surprising, especially for a high tech sector, yet it relates to the fact that game products are diverse and thus more resistant to a standardized approach that can work well with the localization of productivity applications. The latter tend to generate more consistent and somewhat homogenized texts than those in games, and are thus more suited to the use of such technologies as Translation Memory (TM). Many game designers and developers consider their products to be artistic creations more similar to literature or cinema than productivity software designed for functionality. These perceptions and the diversity of game products seem to have led to a lack of technology applications in the localization process. However, faced with the increasing complexity of the task and the challenge imposed especially by sim-ship requirements involving multiple numbers of languages, the industry has sought technological solutions to help facilitate processes previously carried out manually. As Chandler and Deming claim:

> [T]echnology can be a powerful means of streamlining processes, and using quality tools to increase productivity is essential in the growing market. As the size of games becomes larger and as they reach more territories simultaneously, it is necessary to have the ability to track, modify, and produce changes as development progresses.   (2012, 185)

Project management applications and content management systems are commonly used to share information and files and to create and manage the workflow of the game content. For example, for the localization of the quiz game series *Buzz!* (2005–), in which players have to answer trivia questions relevant to their country, a content management system called Scribe, originally designed for managing websites, was used (Wood et al. 2010). This tool allowed all the information (questions, resources, commentaries) to be stored and was externally available to translators and testers, who had access to all the resources, context and information. In addition localization testers were able to fix bugs directly in the database, reducing the amount of time allocated to bug reporting at the QA stage.

Other companies, such as Canadian developer BioWare, a division of EA specializing in RPGs, use their own proprietary tools for content management and to provide contextual information to the localization team. As we have seen, RPG is one of the most text-intensive of video game genres, often containing a large number of dialogue lines. For example, 80% of the total word count of BioWare's RPG titles *Mass Effect 2* (2010) and *Dragon Age: Origins* (2009) were dialogues (Christou et al. 2011, 48). To illustrate the size of the text of the original English versions, *Mass Effect 2* (2010) contained 440,000 words with 30,000 VO lines while the MMORPG title *Dragon Age: Origins* (2009) had around one million words with 56,000 lines of VO. According to the localization team at BioWare (Christou et al. 2011, 40–41), the total word count reached 2.7 million with 140,000 lines of VO after including the localized versions of *Mass Effect 2* into French, German, Italian, and Polish. In order to facilitate the localization projects of such a scale, BioWare used tools to manage dialogue lines. For example, as in many games, the dialogue in *Mass Effect* (2007) employs **dialogue** or **conversation trees** consisting of a list of all dialogue options which branch off into further options. These account for every single possibility that can arise from selecting a given dialogue option. Their tool allows the conversation strings to be ordered in a tree structure, showing a preceding and following dialogue, to allow the translator to cross-reference an adjacent line (Christou et al. 2011, 48). While content creation tools used by game designers and writers are not used by translators, the BioWare tool "Conversation Previewer" allows dialogues to be seen with all the different answers and possibilities, and can thus be helpful in understanding the context. It also includes other useful information for the translator, such as a description of the way the character is speaking and feeling; the name and gender of the character who is speaking and the one they are addressing, and information about time restrictions for the lines to be translated. This type of tool improves the quality of translation by giving the translator as much contextual information as possible while incorporating the space restriction information.

In addition, BioWare deploys a "character bible" containing information about all characters appearing in their games, such as species, age, general description and importance in the plot (Steussy 2010a). Other developers, such as Lionhead Studios, a subsidiary of Microsoft Game Studios and creators of the RPG series *Fable* (2004–), also use "bibles", that is, databases where all the relevant information about characters, scenarios, plot, and other important aspects of the game is gathered (Sheffield 2011). This type of meta-data is not only useful for maintaining consistency in the development of the game, but also for the localization process, as it provides background and contextual information for the translators, allowing them to provide a more accurate and consistent translation, including VO sessions for appropriate characterization when dealing with games with a large number of characters. BioWare uses a database program to generate a character bible which is exportable to Microsoft Excel for easy sifting and filtering of information (Christou et al. 2011). Such a systematic approach is increasingly essential with the burgeoning complexity and size of games. For example, *Mass Effect 2* (2010) contained 572 distinct game characters (ibid., 42).

There is also a suite of tools, called XLOC, specifically developed for game localization by Stephanie Deming and Mason Deming on the basis of their experience in the game localization sector. XLOC streamlines the localization process by managing game assets and synchronizing them with localized game resources, "generating current and changed assets lists and separating the translated effort from game asset format specifics" (Xloc.com n.d.). In September 2012 memoQ – a popular TM tool – launched the new server-based localization platform Games-Loc which is designed to facilitate the game localization process (kilgray.com 2012). This is a first example among existing TM tools to develop such a specialized application and must reflect an increasing demand for dedicated TM for game localization. In addition, many developers also use proprietary tools, developed in-house to check, for example, the length of in-game text messages and subtitles, in order to avoid truncations and overlapping. Dietz (2006, 132) also emphasizes the need for using source-code tracking software, not only to track revisions of the code, but also to flag any changes in the original for the translators. Microsoft Game Studio also use an in-house tool with TM functionality that allows translators to see screenshots of the game while it is still being developed, in order to provide them with context.

Sony Online Entertainment (SOE), whose games are usually translated into French, German, and Japanese, use a standardization approach to localization based on the following points (Steussy 2010b):

- An integrated translation engine, which allows for improved quality and dynamic grammar
- English strings with persistent and unique IDs, which facilitates tracking changes in the English text
- Standardized translation data exchange format, which simplifies the data import and export processes
- Modern localization workflow with a centralised translation database and tools also providing feedback.

SOE's annual translated word count is related to game updates and comes to 8.5 million words, plus approximately 2.5 million words of new English text (Steussy 2010b). In order to facilitate the localization of updates, the company has a TM system containing more than 60 million words, classified by title (ibid.). As a result of the localization process implemented at SOE, 40% of all translation can be done internally using the above tools, which allows external translation costs to be reduced considerably. In addition, the quality of the translation is claimed to be better, as translators have access to contextual information, which means that the QA process is also faster and more productive (ibid.). Undoubtedly, standardization and the widespread use of tools is the way forward for the game localization industry, as it optimizes the localization process and improves the quality of the localized games.

At the GDC 2012 Game Localization Summit Square Enix unveiled its audio localization tool called "Moomle", developed in-house, which allows the tracking of changes made to the script and the matching audio portion (Parish 2012). According to the presentation given by Square Enix (*Famitsu* 2012), the impetus for the development of the tool came from the need to handle a massive volume of audio scripts in its flagship RPG title *Final Fantasy XIII-2* (2011) (see 4.1.2.3 for further detail). The audio localization task is normally carried out by the company's sound department in conjunction with the localization department, making the process highly complicated. In a typical sim-ship scenario the voice script keeps changing until the last minute, making it extremely difficult to track precisely to ensure synchronization between VO, its translation and the given scene on screen. Moomle ensures centralized management and access to a particular line or scene across all languages aligned with the moving image through the tool's docking view. These features of the tool serve to illustrate the difference between working with AV content for video games and other non-interactive media. This suggests that the standard AVT tools are not sufficient to meet all the requirements specific to audio localization for games. The increasing availability of in-house tools is indicative of such specialized needs and also of the nature of the high-tech industry, which has the capacity to develop its own tools.

Finally, built-in in-game automatic translation software has sometimes been used with MMORPGs such as *Ultima Online* (1997) (Heimburg 2006, 137), addressing real-time translation needs for interlingual communication between gamers in online game environments. In the context of online games, in particular MMORPGs, more recently a computational technique (Arthur et al. 2010) has been tried to overcome the problems we discussed earlier arising from concatenated strings that are prone to grammatical errors in target language generation. Using a set of grammatical rules Arthur et al. (ibid.) developed an automatic text generation tool based on the Rules Engine algorithm in order to generate a grammatically correct target string in a given language version (in this case German, Spanish, and Russian). Such research in technology applications was motivated by the cost implications of using the alternative approach based on full internationalization for localizing MMORPGs, offering a less costly yet effective option. Given the increasing use of translation technology in the online world in general, and the localization industry in particular, game localization practices will be increasingly facilitated by translation tools combining natural language processing (NLP) technologies, as we speculate in Chapter 7.

This chapter has described in some detail how a modern video game is localized, focusing on practical dimensions from a macro perspective and introducing an overview of the localization workflow. Shifting our attention to a micro-perspective and focussing on translation issues, we will next examine games as texts for translation and then the role of the translator.

CHAPTER 4

Translating video games

New vistas for transcreation

Introduction

Building on an overview of today's game localization practices provided in Chapter 3, we now situate game localization in the context of Translation Studies. This chapter focuses on translation issues arising from video games as translation text and homes in on the question of translation strategies and approaches. We draw on a functionalist framework derived from Skopos Theory in our analysis of game text translation, bearing in mind new unique dimensions of game media. We first present a working taxonomy of modern game text viewed from the central interest of translation issues and make observations on the priorities which may be identified according to the function of the text and typical translation constraints. Taking the case of the global game company Square Enix, we then examine some of the innovation and appropriation at work, vis-à-vis translation conventions, in order to characterize translation in the context of digital interactive entertainment. We discuss the translator's agency and translation norms, drawing on Chesterman's (1997) professional and expectancy norms. Finally, the main theoretical discussion is devoted to game localization viewed as transcreation, highlighting the role of the translator as a creative agent.

4.1 Game text taxonomy and text function

As we outlined in Chapter 1, game localization has undergone a transformation since the early days when translation was an error-prone afterthought activity, even when carried out by major game companies (Kohler 2005). Although the complexity of localization is still not fully appreciated by all stakeholders in the game industry today, the level of awareness of major publishers has certainly risen as they at least acknowledge the need for localization, seeing "the international market as a key strategic focus" (Chandler and Deming 2012, xiii). It is also true to say that the increased sophistication of games, especially with major titles, is making ad hoc approaches to localization simply unsustainable, as can be discerned from the description of today's game localization practice in Chapter 3. In addition to the conspicuous increase in the volume of text, the macrostructure of game text has also become more complex and non-linear, often accompanied by embedded components such as **side quests** and **mini games** as well as incorporating **cut-scenes**. For example, the Xbox 360 RPG action game *Fable II* (2008), which on its release was the largest title that Microsoft Game Studio had localized (Chandler and Deming 2012, 315), contained 50 quests with well over 200 hours of gameplay subject to language testing in the localization process (ibid., 316). With projects such as this, a systematic approach is a prerequisite, including the strategic use of purpose-built computer tools (ibid., 315–326) as discussed in the previous chapter.

Behind widely publicized claims of top-selling games making record sales in international markets, the translation process itself remains relatively obscure apart from occasional attention paid typically when errors are picked up by users. In this section we provide a detailed analysis of game texts chiefly from a functionalist perspective, which shifts the focus of translation away from equivalence-based thinking tied to the original source text (ST) to that based on the target text (TT) function. Under the framework of Skopos Theory (Vermeer 1989/2000) we argue that game translation is primarily driven by its purpose (skopos), which is ultimately to entertain the end user of the translated product. In particular, the nature of software, being amenable to radical transformation to create different customized versions of the original, seems to further facilitate widening of the translation capacity to achieve the ultimate goal. With this general approach in mind we set out to analyze games as texts for translation, linking the function of text to translation strategies, mainly drawing on Reiss (1971/2000) in our ST analysis and Nord (1997) and Chesterman (1997) for our discussion of translation strategies. First, we examine dimensions that are specific to game texts.

4.1.1   Game text: Play and narrative dimensions

In examining the characteristics of video games as objects of translation we return briefly to the frameworks introduced in Chapter 1 for analyzing games as play versus narrative. Treating a game as a narrative has been debated by game scholars, who consider "gameness" to come from the ludic dimension of the game as we touched on earlier. However, more recently this adherence to a pure ludic focus has been softened to acknowledge that stories have their place in games (Dovey and Kennedy 2006). The importance of "storytelling" in modern games is recognised by game designers such as Ernest Adams, who includes this particular dimension among 50 key game design innovations in the history of video games (Edge Staff 2007). While admitting that not all games need a story and that "[s]torytelling is the subject of more acrimonious debate than any other design feature", Adams (ibid.) maintains that "without a story a game is just an abstraction". Adams also specifies that "**cut-scenes**" are one of the key innovations closely related to storytelling in modern games. As briefly mentioned in Chapter 3, cut-scenes are among the elements most contested by gamers as well as Game Studies scholars. According to Egenfeldt-Nielsen et al. (2008, 176–177), cut-scenes are used in order to: (1) introduce characters, and set the scene and mood at the beginning; (2) control the narrative in a certain direction during the game; (3) fill the passing of time within the game world; (4) showcase sophisticated cinematic techniques, including dramatic sound and camera work, and (5) provide the player with pertinent information. As such, cut-scenes serve both pragmatic and cosmetic purposes. The multi-functionality of cut-scenes means that they carry a very different type of message from that of a film in cinema. From the point of view of translation, cut-scenes have developed a link between game localization and AVT, while strengthening the connection between games and cinema. However, an important consideration in translating cut-scenes is that they are not the focal point for most gamers, whose interest lies mainly in the interactive gameplay. That said, the increasing trend of the whole game turning into a cinema-like production called a "cinematic game" may yet change the dynamics, with more and more cinematic techniques being used as asserted by Newman (2009, xii): "Why pull the player from the game to watch a cut-scene when you can incorporate good filmmaking techniques throughout the game play and keep the player immersed in the game to experience a deeper emotional impact?"

We shall return to this point later in this chapter. In the meantime we turn our attention to "ludonarrative", which allows us to focus on ludic aspects of games as well as the game narrative, given that story-oriented genres rather than those focused on action are more relevant to our present interests from a translation perspective. Drawing on the accounts of game designers and theorists as well as his own gamer experience, Bissell (2010, 37) points out that "[g]ames with any kind of narrative structure usually employ two kinds of storytelling", one of which is fixed and is conventionally called 'narrative', and the other one fluid and interactive, called "ludonarrative". Describing the latter as "unscripted and gamer-determined", Bissell (ibid.) maintains that they are "the 'fun' portions of the 'played' game" as opposed to the fixed narrative as typically offered in cut-scenes in games as discussed above. The concept of "ludonarrative" attempts to bridge the narrative and the play dimensions as two sides of a coin. Watssman (2012) discusses how a well designed game achieves "ludonarrative resonance", where the reason why the player is allowed to take a certain action is justified according to the game narrative. By comparison, "ludonarrative dissonance" does not provide a

reason for a certain action to be taken or disallows an action which is well justified. In this way ludonarrative links play and narrative, forming a play trajectory
which tells a story in an embodied manner as opposed to the fixed universal story
told in the main narrative. It integrates the play dimension into the basic story
which modern games have to a greater or lesser extent. The concept of "static"
and "dynamic embodied narrative" could further facilitate understanding of the
process in which the game world unfolds once players enter it, driving it in their
own way, albeit within pre-determined parameters. Recognition of this distinction also helps to highlight a certain dissonance between the main narrative and
the "played out" narrative as expressed by Bateman (2006, xxvi), leading to a complexity in classifying game narratives according to game genres:

> Whereas the concept of genre has a clear meaning in the context of a novel or film,
> it is less clear in the context of a game, because they consist of a narrative genre on
> the one hand and a gameplay genre on the other. Games often share a common
> gameplay genre but have different narrative genres (two adventure games may
> share similar gameplay, but one might be fantasy comedy and the other a tale of
> swashbuckling action). Similarly, two games can share the same narrative genre
> but have radically different gameplay (a First Person Shooter (FPS) and an adven-
> ture game may both be rendered in a film noir style, for instance).

The pre-determined narrative may take the form of a *Lord of the Rings*-style epic
saga, whereas the ludonarrative component may be reflected in the game's generic
descriptor such as RPG or FPS. This discussion relates to text genres and text types
which have been considered highly relevant to translation work as the translator
is usually expected to adhere to target language and cultural conventions appropriate for the given text genres or types (Baker 2011, 121) as well as being guided
by the purpose of the translation. While the distinction between text genres and
types is not always clear, both can be understood as the way in which "textual material is packaged by the writer along patterns familiar to the reader" (ibid., 123).
Baker further explains two types of text classification: one more straightforward
such as "journal article" and "science textbook" based on "the contexts in which
texts occur and results in institutionalized labels" and the other "a more subjective, less institutionalized and ... vaguer classification" applicable to parts rather
than the whole of the text such as "narration" and "exposition" (ibid.). At the moment, game genres such as RPG and FPS belong to the first institutionalized label
based on gameplay and can thus be linked to ludonarrative, whereas story genres
used such as Sci-Fi or History are not overtly labelled. For the purposes of translation, a more refined classification is useful in providing a comprehensive coverage
of game text characteristics to reflect games' dual narrative typology as explained
above and also their complex structure made up of different assets, as we have

seen in Chapter 3. This demonstrates that it is important for translators to fully appreciate how the game text is "packaged" so they can still retain the whole picture while they work on unpacked individual assets.

Another useful consideration which can be applied to understanding different elements in game texts is whether they are diegetic or non-diegetic vis-à-vis the game world. For example, for the purposes of translation, promotional posters advertising a new game such as the one mentioned in the Prologue (see Figure 0.1) form part of a paratext, and are non-diegetic, as they are physically located outside the in-game world, whereas dialogue between the player and a **non-playable character** (NPC) taking place within the game is a diegetic element. It is also relevant to point out that not all in-game text is diegetic, such as menu items in UI elements, which facilitate navigation but do not relate directly to the game world. In order to further help examine textual characteristics of a video game for the purposes of translation, we can suggest the initial broad categorization of game text in terms of: (1) official game genre, such as RPG or Sports, to indicate a typology closely relating to gameplay (thus ludonarrative); (2) embedded genre, based on the main game narratives such as Sci-Fi or History, and (3) whether the particular text is considered to be part of the game world or not (i.e. diegetic or non-diegetic). Furthermore, the translator also takes into account the game's intended age ratings which signal the game's main target audience. This allows both the play and narrative dimensions of a game to be borne in mind in game text analysis for the purposes of translation. While it may be debatable where exactly the game world ends in terms of its emotional tie to the player, in the interests of translation the approach of dividing game assets in relation to the game world helps the translator to grasp how each textual component is interlinked and also in what physical environment the text will be used (i.e. displayed on screen or on a physical print poster). This kind of knowledge can then lead to an understanding of the function of the text and thus the priorities for translation, as we attempt to operationalize in the next section.

4.1.2 Game text taxonomy and translation

On the basis of our discussion above, Table 4.1 provides a working taxonomy of a story-oriented console game text which we use to highlight text function, linking it in turn to translation priorities analyzed from a functionalist perspective. In considering each key game asset from the interest of its function, we apply functional characteristics of text types discussed by Katharina Reiss (1971/2000, 24–47): *content-focused* texts, where the informative function is stressed; *form-focused* texts with the expressive function as the main, and *appeal-focused* texts with the persuasive function. Reiss gives examples for each text type, such as commercial correspondence or operating instructions for informative text, literary prose of different kinds as expressive text, and advertising and publicity as persuasive text. She discusses "audio-medial text" as the fourth text type which incorporates technical media and graphic, acoustic, and visual expressions, which in turn can be categorized according to the above three text types but with additional considerations. Although we primarily adopt a TT-oriented perspective in considering translation, Reiss's text categorization based on ST-function is still relevant as game localization is required to largely retain the function of the original game assets. We refer to the labels given to the three main functions of informative, expressive, and persuasive in our text type analysis shown in Table 4.1. Reiss's work has come in for some criticism from theorists (see Munday 2001, 76 for a summary), especially for its rigidity in associating language functions with text types; however, we will not focus on language functions but rather on considering translation priorities and strategies, drawing on Nord's refinement of Reiss's work (Nord 1997, 2005), moving to focus more on the function of the TT from a Skopos Theory perspective (Vermeer 1989/2000). According to Nord (1997) a "translation brief" which constitutes specifications for translation given by the translation commissioner takes precedence and shapes translation priorities and strategies. In the case of game localization, a localization kit (see 3.4.1) is ideally designed to provide such detailed specifications, guiding the ensuing process. Our working game text taxonomy presented in Table 4.1 indicates key assets according to well-established industry categorization of in-game text assets, art, audio, and cinema assets and printed materials. We have further added other online/screen materials which form wider paratext. The first column indicates whether or not the given translation asset is considered to be directly part of the game world (i.e. diegetic or non-diegetic). The remaining columns are arranged in order of translation asset, its text function and description, characteristics of the text when translating and also based on likely instructions given by the commissioner, and finally typical translation priorities and strategies expected of the given asset.

Certain genres such as adventure games and RPGs, which may be either console-based or online, will typically have a high volume of text for translation, with their heavy reliance on "telling a story through character dialogue, in-game cut scenes, and books, notes, or other props found in the game world" (Chandler 2005, 139–140). Furthermore, a wide range of text types, from literary to technical with the use of literary narrative devices, legal text and contemporary dialogue scripts full of street-speak, can be present within one game. Such characteristics of game texts make the streamlined standardization approach common in productivity software localization often unworkable (Darolle 2004). Each title requires a different translation approach in relation to the unique features of the game

Table 4.1 Taxonomy of narrative-oriented game text with text function and translation priorities

Relationship to the game world	Translation assets	Text function and description	Characteristics / translation brief	Translation priorities and strategies
In-game text assets				
Non-diegetic	User Interface (UI)	Informative function for smooth navigation and gameplay. Typically contains short text fragments, such as menu items and also help messages.	Brevity due to space constraints; user-friendliness of text; clarity of text.	Pragmatic and functional choice to address space constraints; creative solutions to overcome space constraints and also to reflect an edgy feel often imbued in game text in terms of expressions and naming of certain items.
Non-diegetic	System messages	Informative function for instructive pragmatic purposes. Messages generated by the system, such as warning messages, instructions, and confirmation messages.	Platform-specific terminology needs to be used.	Prescriptive, conforming to the existing terminology and phraseology of the **platform holder** (see "submission" process in Chapter 3).
Diegetic	Narrative text	Expressive / informative function for imparting certain information in a dramatic manner. Literary passages used to engage the player in the game world or to a new level within the game. They contextualize and provide information about the game story, including a backstory.	Often formal and literary style; natural flowing writing style often asked and separate rewriting may be applied.	Fluency in TL with appropriate register and style.
Non-diegetic	Exposition / tutorial	Informative function with instructive and didactic messages. In-game tutorials may be used to explain game mechanics by way of demonstration and the player practice. Passages describing characters, monsters, animals, geographical locations, etc.	Clarity and informativity are stressed.	Functional while remaining faithful to the instructive intention and the original characterization of main game characters.

Table 4.1 (continued)

Relationship to the game world	Translation assets	Text function and description	Characteristics / translation brief	Translation priorities and strategies
Diegetic	Unvoiced dialogue scripts	Informative / expressive function mainly to provide information and elicit a certain action by the player. Dialogue which appears only in written form, commonly used for Non-Playable Characters (NPCs).	Speech expressed in written text with colloquial style; natural flowing style may be asked.	Fluency in TL typically with casual register to reflect a conversational style.
Art assets (textual graphics)				
Diegetic	Text in images	Informative / expressive function to give the player certain information such as clues in an authentic atmosphere. Any in-game art assets containing text (poster, billboards, maps, etc.).	Varying styles with some space constraints; informativity in case of providing clues is stressed.	Informative function must be prioritized in the case of crucial clues being given; visual / aesthetic dimensions also need to be considered.
Non-diegetic	Text in images	Informative / some persuasive function to provide the player with information not related to the game and to raise brand awareness and loyalty. Game logo art which may need to be translated and re-designed.	Consideration of space constraints and consistency in case of precedence where a certain translation is previously used / officially registered.	Prescriptive approach to conform to official recommendation or prior translation which may be legally binding.
Audio and cinematic assets				
Diegetic	Lip-synch voiceover	Informative / expressive function to provide a clue or a backstory in a dramatized manner.	Oral text with character-specific idiosyncrasies; natural flowing writing style is often called for; dubbing actor/director may suggest changes to the translated script.	Prioritizing lip-synch / space constraints; fluency in TL; characterization may involve the use of linguistic variation and may involve rewriting.
Diegetic	Non lip-synch voiceover			Fluency in TL with correct register, style.

Table 4.1 (*continued*)

Relationship to the game world	Translation assets	Text function and description	Characteristics / translation brief	Translation priorities and strategies
Diegetic/non-diegetic	Songs performed by game characters/ theme songs	Expressive function. Lyrics of songs in the game soundtrack may be translated and re-recorded by a TL singer.	(Cont. from previous page.)	Retaining appropriate thematic feel; may involve rewriting lyrics by involving a TL musician.
Diegetic	Environmental sound	Expressive/informative function for realism and for dramatizing. Various sound effects to enhance the atmosphere.	Socio-culturally appropriate choice must be made for the given sound source in case of cultural differences.	Socio-cultural considerations.
Printed materials				
Non-diegetic	Manual	Informative function for instructions. A hardcopy manual contains information and instructions to get started with the game, whether or not the player actually uses it. This may also include a booklet which may function as a bonus material.	Varying text types, ranging from informative and technical to promotional. When translated by different translators the translation of terms and names must be consistent with the relevant in-game text.	Informativity with pragmatic, functional orientation; may involve re-ordered layout (see Figure 3.2).
	Strategy books	Informative function for instructions. Strategy books functions as a comprehensive walkthrough.		
Non-diegetic	Box	Persuasive/informative function to appeal to the prospective customer while providing product information. Relevant text on packaging. Minimum level of localization, so-called "box and docs", only involving translation of manual and packaging.		Fluent TL, right feel, advertising/ marketing oriented language use prioritized.

Table 4.1 (*continued*)

Relationship to the game world	Translation assets	Text function and description	Characteristics / translation brief	Translation priorities and strategies
Non-diegetic	Other associated paratext, including advertising text (e.g. posters) and strategy books published separately	Persuasive/informative function to appeal to prospective consumers and to provide information such as the game's release date, content and playing guidance. Texts of a varied nature used for legal, marketing, promotional purposes, such as press releases, health and safety precautions, etc.	(Cont. from previous page.)	Free marketing style writing to appeal to users; consistency with similar text used elsewhere within the product; prescriptive with some legal and technical information.
Online/screen materials				
Non-diegetic	Other associated paratext, including the game's official websites and TV ads.	Persuasive / informative function to whet appetite of prospective consumers with some informative content. Texts mainly for marketing and promotional purposes (including TV ads), such as press releases, health and safety precautions, etc.	Natural flowing style to appeal to the audience required; in case of references to names and key terms must correspond to those used in the game.	Free marketing style writing; consistent with similar text used elsewhere within the game; prescriptive with some legal and technical information.

(Chandler 2008a, 37). That said, knowing the most typical taxonomies of game text can facilitate the selection of more appropriate translation strategies which minimize the risk of translation errors, especially when working under time pressure with insufficient context. In the following section we discuss each text-asset shown in Table 4.1 in some detail.

4.1.2.1   *In-game text assets*

In-game text is presented and consumed on screen, usually making up the main text asset to be translated for games. Mainly non-diegetic, and thus not belonging to the game world itself, UI text such as menus, lists, and help messages still affect how the game is played. These texts are typically constrained to fit a pre-allocated space. For example, help messages in the J-RPG *Final Fantasy X* (2001) could only have one line with a restriction of 18 characters for menu items in target European languages. Overall, the translation of in-game text, and especially text associated with the UI, shares certain similarities with productivity software, with the main problem being space constraints resulting in **truncation**, as discussed in Chapter 3. Furthermore, when translating terms such as weapon names in a limited space, it is important to find a translation that not only respects the overt functional meaning of the original, but that also conveys a similar nuance within the strictly enforced space limitations. In addition, many games contain newly created concepts, even those which look like technical terms with real-world referents. For example, in fighting games such as *Street Fighter IV* (2008), a wide array of coined technical terms for fighting techniques are used, such as "Wheel Kick", "Marseilles Roll", "Falling Sky" or "Tornado Throw". This is where a translator's creativity is put to the test, as often the names for items, weapons, commands, and abilities come with the game designer's specific intentions often expressed in an edgy, quirky, or even poetic selection of words. The need to convey such covert meanings has to be balanced against the need for functional translation. The issue of space is something which affects productivity software localization as well as AVT, particularly in the case of subtitling. By comparison, space constraints may be a lesser concern to literary translators, who are even able to create paratext in order to add extra information such as translator's notes, preface, or afterword. Localization prioritizes the overall "look and feel" of the end product, which is expected to be similar to equivalent local products in the target culture, causing translation strategies to be oriented towards domestication in Venuti's (1995) sense.

J-RPGs based on an epic saga tend to include a large array of weaponry with names that are often poetic or with creative twists, along with other names that are sometimes technical and pseudo-technical, such as various kinds of swords, daggers, maces, katanas, and sabres. A few examples can be drawn from *Final Fantasy X* (2001) to demonstrate some of these points. *FFX* featured a sword called 花鳥風月 [beauty of nature], literally meaning "flower, bird, wind and moon" in Japanese. This is a classical expression with a poetic touch. As such, it is a rather curious choice for the name of a sword, unrelated to its function, where its user gains three times the regular ability points. For the North American (NA) version of this game the name of this weapon was translated into English as "Painkiller", which fits the length limitation, in this case 18 characters (note that the original Japanese only contained four kanji characters). According to the explanation given by Alexander O. Smith, one of the translators responsible for the NA version, this solution was chosen in order to provide a user-friendly functional translation (Smith, email message to O'Hagan, February 17, 2009, also see 4.4). The logic used was that this sword gains the user triple points, therefore alleviating the pain usually involved in the "levelling grind" – the effort needed to progress to a higher level in the game. The element of fun was also considered, as explained below by the translator. Another sword, called 雪月花 [beauty of the four seasons], literally meaning "snow, moon, flower", was translated as "Divider" on the basis that the weapon grants the user double ability points, thus halving the user's effort in grinding. The translator's decision allows the translation to serve the desired function of the source term for the target audience while conforming to the space restrictions. The original irony of the poetic naming given to a highly dangerous weapon may be slightly lost, but a sense of fun is restored by the added double-meaning of the chosen word. This point is revisited in section 4.4 with a discussion with the translator as our focus. It illustrates a departure from the source-oriented approach to one that places the importance on the TT function, as advocated by functionalists (Vermeer 1989/2000).

The space constraints for translating UI items for software in general and for game software in particular clearly add to the translator's challenge. The player needs to be able to quickly read the text while in action, and thus a lengthy exposition will not be suitable even if the space is extendable. In pursuing a broader, target-focused functional approach for temporal considerations, text in the menu system may sometimes be replaced by graphic images and icons, as was the case with *Dragon Quest VIII* (2004) (see Figure 4.1). We will explain further this example in the case study of Square Enix in Section 4.3.

Another common in-game asset is the tutorial text which by definition is non-diegetic, although some tutorials are merged with the game world (e.g. *Fallout 3*, 2008). Unique to games are in-game tutorials to teach the player particular game mechanics such as how certain buttons on the controller work or to teach them manoeuvre techniques by offering visual non-verbal demonstrations as well as explanations in written text. Tutorials may provide the player with a training round or show how to make game characters talk to one another. As such, the tutorial style is varied and may be provided in different modes. In comparison with a manual for productivity software, some of the tutorial text in a game may deliberately be left vague, which, according to Thayer and Kolko (2004, 480), creates some degree of "intentional confusion" so as to "preserve the secrets of the game". Such characteristics may be overlooked by translators who are non-gamers, eager to make the message clear. Also common to games is the script for unvoiced dialogue, which is diegetic text. Despite the availability of audio channels, many games still include dialogues that appear only in written form often to conserve the processing capacity of the hardware, as well as to minimise the high cost associated with voiceover. These written dialogue scripts are often used for – but not limited to – the lines of side characters, called NPCs, that are controlled by the game engine and are assigned certain roles in the game. Using the technique known as "**dialogue tree**" (see Chapter 3), which prompts a pre-defined yet still natural sounding response (Edge Staff 2007), text-only dialogue can be considered one of the characteristic elements of game media.

Translation of this type of dialogue can be compared to translating comics, requiring a fluent conversational style in written mode while maintaining an appropriate register to fit the context. These texts in games normally use colloquial and idiomatic language and may include plays on words, rhymes, or humorous remarks. Game dialogues have suffered a long standing reputation of being trite as a result of not giving them enough importance, and thus not engaging a professional writer (Newman 2009, 65). The reason stems from the perceived subordination of the narrative to actual play dimensions of a game. Today more and more game developers are stressing the importance of the storyline and actual dialogues, as evidenced in games such as the *Uncharted* series (2007–) and *Batman: Arkham City* (2011). Stilted language in dialogues may snap players out of the game world, as observed by Jayemanne (2009), who claims that "contemporary titles tend to aspire to the quality of dialogue expected from cinema, television and literature" and this is "indicative of broader trends in localization standards" (n.p.). Certain titles privileging storylines and dialogues are seeing the ST being carefully crafted by a professional writer. Accordingly, an extra rewriting step in the production of the TT may be justified or even considered necessary in the translation process in order to retain the rich diegetic suspension in the target game world.

In addition, there are also certain in-game texts that are platform-specific, such as system messages, which are non-diegetic and require the strict use of approved terminology. Given that non-compliance could lead to a system crash as well as failing the submission process (see Chapter 3), the translator's awareness of the specific requirements of these types of texts is of paramount importance. These are the types of text likely to benefit from the use of CAT tools where TM and terminology management functionality can facilitate consistency of the use of terminology or phraseology as prescribed and used in previously translated texts.

4.1.2.2 *Art assets, printed materials and other online / screen materials*

Texts used in graphics within the game, such as posters, maps, or signs, may be diegetic (fulfilling an informative or cosmetic function) or non-diegetic, or even used for the third-party advertisement of a product. For the purposes of translation, the context in which they appear has paramount importance, given their different relationships to the game world and their ensuing functionality. Similar to the approach discussed earlier, textual graphics also tend to require a pragmatic and function-oriented translation strategy, usually under the imposition of limited space. A case in point is the Japanese localization of the label on crates featured in the US game *Crash Bandicoot* (1996), a game in which considerable effort was spent on localization and which subsequently did well on the Japanese market as a result of its elaborate localization approach (Thayer and Kolko 2004). The letters "TNT" written on the side of the crates were replaced in the Japanese version by the picture of a bomb (DeLaHunt 2004, 9). This can be considered as a functional approach most appropriate for the target user group.

Logo art needs to conform to prior legal or marketing decisions. Printed materials are by definition usually non-diegetic and are designed to help players familiarize themselves with the game system although such sources may be resorted to only after the player becomes stuck in a game or never be consulted. As we illustrated in Figure 3.2, in some cases drastic rearrangement of information and layout changes may be needed to suit the text type conventions for such manuals in the target market or as a requirement for the particular game, which may be markedly different especially between Japanese and their Western counterparts. And such detailed attention being given to the design of the manual may never be appreciated by gamers. However, in some titles game designers rely on the player's understanding of certain specific instructions explained in the manual. A case in point is the early Sci-Fi action adventure game by Nintendo *StarTropics* (1990), which contained a letter in the game's package. Players discover later in the game that they are asked to dip the letter in water to reveal a secret code which they need to progress in the game. This may also be an attempt by the publisher to prevent circulation of illicit copies of the game. From a translation perspective, this type of arrangement requires the intended link to be maintained between a non-diegetic asset and a diegetic one where "a paratextual element becomes part of the game world" (Ensslin 2012, 59). For this reason, functional translation approaches are needed to preserve the intended communicative purpose of instructing the players.

More recent trends to move exclusively to e-manuals and also to embed tutorial sessions in games themselves may see a reduced demand for print manuals in future. Given the need for consonance between the manual and in-game text assets, the streamlining of digital text will further justify an increased use of CAT tools to maintain and manage standardized use of terminology and phraseology across different assets. Finally, major games have other related paratextual materials to be translated, such as websites and other advertising, legal, or health and safety documents. While the consistency of certain key language, including proper names, is essential, marketing texts tend to require the added skill of creative writing to be persuasive to the consumer. The closer links between games and movies through tie-ins will also bring the need to retain key terminology and to have IP-protected names translated in a manner consistent with the pre-existing translation.

4.1.2.3 *Audio and cinematic assets*

In addition to the use of engaging narratives, the sense of realism in modern games has been enhanced by the use of audio, in particular the human voice for in-game dialogues, with more and more console games incorporating lengthy cut-scenes which may be subtitled and also dubbed in full localization. Accordingly, audio localization has become a major issue in game localization, reflecting a general trend of increased numbers of audio projects in translation requests to localization companies over the last five years (Warren 2012). From a translation perspective, the full and regular incorporation of human voices in game systems made game localization more closely associated with AVT. Recordings by celebrities have become common (Chandler and Deming 2012, 170), especially among movie-licensed games. This may add an extra challenge if any re-take is needed at a later stage, both from the point of view of actors' schedules as well as the high costs. While the use of pre-rendered cinematic features began in the 1980s, technological limitations in the early days meant that such cinematic sequences were uncommon and mainly without human voiced dialogue. As mentioned in Chapter 1, *Ninja Ryukenden* (1988) is often credited as a successful early attempt at using cinematics between different levels of a game to tell a story (see Figure 1.2) albeit without the use of audio. While cut-scenes in modern games have become much more sophisticated, their use of AVT modes is generally not well informed by the body of knowledge now available in this field. This is partly due to a lack of awareness but also because of some game-specific contexts.

Re-voicing in the form of dubbing, which is commonly referred to as "voiceover" or VO in the game localization sector, now forms an integral part of game localization. As explained in Chapter 3, subtitling in video games has developed largely independently of AVT. This may be partly due to the specific functionality of cut-scenes and other uses of voice in games not being considered central to the product as a whole or required by the gamer to engage in interactive play. However, this perception is rapidly changing, with audio occupying an increasing part of the game. The immediate difference between subtitles used in games and in other AV materials is the faster speed at which the subtitles in games are displayed (see 7.1.3). Also subtitles in games tend to be longer as the number of characters permitted in game subtitles is mainly dictated by the length of the original script and is independent of the viewer's (player's) estimated reading speed, which is prioritized in AVT. This may also be due to the fact that the subtitles used in a game can be paused and restarted by the player, although this functionality is also available to the viewer watching a film on a DVD. Game localizers are typically given the number of characters calculated from the length of the dialogue and instructed to translate script lines working off an Excel sheet often without visual information. This mode of working also tends to affect segmentation or what are known as "sense blocks" in AVT. It is not unusual to find a character's dialogue in a game segmented into two or even more subtitles in a manner which does not respect semantic units, further hindering smooth comprehension by the recipient. Despite the increasing resources put into the production of cinematic sequences in games and their multiple functionalities including more affective reasons to engage the gamer, the translation of cut-scenes has generally not been treated with sufficient care by game developers and publishers, and AVT norms are clearly not adhered to. However, this may change as more game developers and publishers are aiming for full localization (Schliem 2012, 8).

As is well recognized in practice and in the literature, re-voicing through dubbing is costly if it is to be professionally executed. For this reason, the dubbing mode has normally been available only in fully localized versions for territories which are considered to be of sufficient commercial significance. Translating voice scripts for a game is an extremely time-consuming and challenging process. We have cited several examples to show the increasing scale of the task of audio localization (see Introduction and 3.6). A further illustration of the increasing size and the shrinking timeframe to achieve full localization is the aforementioned *Final Fantasy XIII-2* (2011) involving over 18,000 spoken lines to be translated and voiced (Parish 2012). Furthermore, this game was shipped in English, French, Italian, Spanish, Greek, Chinese, and Korean within seven weeks of the original Japanese release. This contrasts with an earlier title in the same series *FFXII* (2006), which took two translators nine months to translate from Japanese into English, working on the script alone (Smith quoted in Jayemanne 2009, n.p.). Under a sim-ship scenario the schedule is becoming increasingly tight while the number of words to be translated and voiced is expanding. Further challenges are posed by greater numbers of languages.

Full versus partial localization

In the past the general trend was for even top selling **AAA titles** such as the *FF* series to be re-voiced only into English, with the other localized versions being available only with subtitles based on the North American re-voiced version. This in turn gave rise to the issue of using the English language version as a pivot, highlighting the interference factor arising from the use of the intermediate text (rather than the original one) as the source. For example, overseas die-hard fans of Japanese games often resent the typically wide scope of changes frequently incorporated into English-language versions of Japanese games (Mangiron 2004; Mangiron and O'Hagan 2006). Furthermore, players' preferred mode of AVT is not necessarily dubbing, depending on their customary mode of watching foreign films, either subtitled or dubbed. For example, Japanese players are generally accustomed to reading subtitles and may prefer them to dubbing, whereas among American and European players (such as those in FIGS countries) there are some who tend to prefer dubbed versions, as that is the mode of AVT these regions have historically adopted for cinema. The case of the Japanese localized version of the US title *Call of Duty: Modern Warfare 2* (2009) illustrates an example where the target audience did not necessarily prefer full localization, i.e. dubbed mode. Despite the publisher's decision to produce a fully dubbed version in Japanese, Japanese gamers complained that the localized version did not contain the original sound track in English with Japanese subtitles (Square Enix Responds to Modern Warfare 2 English Voice Acting Criticism 2009). While this reaction was also allegedly due to the poor Japanese voice acting highlighted by fans (ibid.) the example demonstrates how additional consideration of market-specific preferences also needs to be given in deciding the most appropriate mode of translation for the target territory.

Use of regional accents in localized games

With these new avenues for presenting voiced dialogue, an earlier study (Mangiron and O'Hagan 2006) commented on the strategic use of regional accents applied to re-voicing certain game characters. The technique is also associated with the use of humour to bring comic relief, which is often a significant and yet under-explored characteristic of video games affecting translation (Mangiron 2010). One important strategy for dealing with linguistic variation in the form of dialect in game translation involves the introduction of a dialect in the TT where there is none in the ST. This may be regarded as a controversial technique and tends to be used only in certain types of translations, such as children's literature, theatre plays, comics, or animation films. While this translation strategy is commonly used in games and international advertising campaigns, other types of translation are likely to be governed by the opposite "homogenizing convention"

(Sternberg 1981, cited in Chiaro 2009, 158), even if various sociolinguistic markers are already present in the original. Chiaro suggests that comedy is an exception to the homogenizing tendency and that "it is not at all unusual for comic or cartoon characters to be dubbed with stereotypical accents" (ibid., 159). This also seems to apply to audio localization for games, where originally unmarked speech is turned into marked speech with the use of regional accents, and this can be recognized as a distinctive translation approach used in game localization, as we discuss in Section 4.2.

Several game reviews, such as one by the popular game site IGN, made special reference to voice acting for *Xenoblade Chronicles* (2011), which was originally released as *Xenoblade* (2010) in Japan. Commending the game for its "generally excellent localized voice acting", the IGN reviewer comments on the use of a variety of British accents:

> [B]ecause *Xenoblade Chronicles* has been localised for Europe, the voice acting is all charmingly British-accented. Shulk sounds like he's just come out of finishing school, his best mate Reyn sounds like a plucky Londoner, and other characters contribute accents from Yorkshire man to Welsh. Only the Especially Evil Robot Bad Guys miss the mark with their way-over-the-top Cockney guffawing...
>
> (MacDonald, 2012)

This Nintendo Wii game was first localized in 2011 for PAL regions in Europe, including the UK before its North American release in 2012 with the justified use of British rather than American accent. The way in which particular regional accents are chosen in game localization is significant, as in the case of this game, which targets a British audience. However, the English language version of the J-RPG *Dragon Quest VIII* (2004) used mostly British English, not linked to the target market as the game was first released for the North American territory. The game's Japanese publisher Square Enix normally prioritizes the NA region and tends to make American English their first choice. In this case, the use of British English was positively received by players, as stated by a reviewer who considered that it fit "the somewhat regal nature of the setting" of the game (Dunham 2005), and conveyed the "feel" of the game, achieving a critical objective of game localization.

The availability of an audio track for human voices afforded video games new scope to improve localization, and indeed localized games leverage various sociolinguistic devices through the use of human voices. For example, this particular game's liberal use of regional dialect is commented on by the above reviewer: "[J]ust about every character sports an accent of some kind (mostly British, but there are Italian and Irish ones thrown in there too)" (Dunham ibid.). One supporting character, Yangus, a former thief and a friend of the protagonist, speaks with a Cockney accent and occasionally even uses Cockney rhyming slang. Interestingly, the original Japanese game did not include voice acting, but the publisher decided to voice the script for the localized versions, a decision that proved popular among target players. According to another reviewer who comments on the overall localization quality, the reception of accented voiced dialogue in the localized version was extremely positive:

> ...even if the story is pedestrian, the characters and especially the localization make the run-of-the-mill plot shine .... Some aspects of the translation (which has voice acting not present in the original Japanese release) are so good, they may actually bring you out of the game for a moment to marvel at how deftly and naturally the humor comes through. (Maragos 2005)

Recording process for VO

While audio localization has provided a new avenue towards superior localized games maintaining high quality in VO is costly and time-consuming. For example, Alexander O. Smith describes the handling of VO based on his experience in translating VO scripts from Japanese into English for *FFXII* (2006) (quoted in Jayemanne 2009, n.p.):

> Voice scripts pose an additional challenge in the form of timings, and sometimes, matching an actor's take on a character. A single line can take hours of work to get right. Ultimately, practically every line in the FF12 voice script reflects the work of the original writer and editor, one translator's initial take on the line, another translator's crosscheck, the editor's check, the voice director's opinion and the actor's interpretation ....

This description illustrates how input from different specialists has to come together, hence the time-consuming nature of re-voicing. However, VO is a relatively new process in game localization, with poor treatment of voice scripts frequently discussed by gamers, such as problems ranging from the quality of voice acting to lack of synchronization with the image. This is also due to certain work procedures imposed upon translators, such as translating files where all the interventions of one particular character are listed, without indicating who s/he is talking about or at what stage s/he is in the game. Apart from the cases where video captures are made available to voice actors, an added difficulty in re-voicing for games is the need for actors to record isolated strings or even words on their own, sometimes in the absence of sufficient contextual information. Nevertheless, the increasing importance placed on characterization in games seems to be recognizing re-voicing as an effective technique to leverage the narrative power of the game in engaging the gamer, drawing more attention to audio localization.

How dubbing takes place for VO scripts in a game can be further illustrated with the Japanese game *Catherine* (2011), which develops in psycho-drama sequences, featuring conversations between characters. An interview (Ishaan 2011) with the voice director of the North American version of the game shows the extra challenges posed by the way in which voice recording is typically conducted for games. Each voice actor's recording is made individually and according to lines or scenes which are not always in sequence, even though the situational context is clearly the key to providing an appropriate take for each line. Furthermore, in this particular game the voice recording was reportedly conducted concurrently for the original Japanese and the English version, even though the game was not sim-shipped (the Japanese version was released in February 2011, followed by the US version in July 2011). This meant that the common practice of having original takes available at the time of the recording of the English track to provide the feel for a particular scene, was not followed (ibid.). If games include specialized terms with difficult pronunciations particular to the game titles, reference materials such as a pronunciation guide for a VO recording session become necessary. For example, the localization project for *Mass Effect 2* (2010) created such a guide to be used across all localized versions, containing a recording of esoteric terms by its original English VO team (Christou et al. 2011, 41). Above all, these examples highlight the way in which in-game VO assets are primarily handled as information objects rather than as a coherent narrative stream in sequence from start to end, unlike in most AVT scenarios.

Modifying the original visuals
Another distinctive feature of translating AV content for games is the fact that it is not unusual to change the visuals, depending on the target market, as part of the localization process. In the J-RPG *Final Fantasy X-2* (2003) there is a cut-scene where a Japanese-specific nonverbal cue could have confused those who are not familiar with Japanese conventions regarding responses to negative questions. In the relevant scene, Yuna, the protagonist, has found a sphere belonging to a rival gang, and she intends to keep it. One of her enemies accuses her by saying 「返し てくれないの？」 [Aren't you gonna give it back?], to which Yuna simply nods. According to the Japanese convention, this gesture accompanying the negative question means "You're right. I am not going to give it back". However, a Western audience would interpret this nod as "Yes, I will give it back", the opposite of the intended meaning. Faced with this situation, the most common AVT solution would be to change the question around in translation and ask something like "So you're gonna keep it?", so that the character's nonverbal cue (in this case nodding) does not contradict the verbal message. This would be a cost-effective option, but

in this particular instance Square Enix decided to redesign the graphics, so that Yuna would shake her head in negation in the NA and European versions.

This suggests how the skopos of localization is prioritized with a view to serving the target players' interests, ensuring their understanding of all elements of the game. Driven by this goal, game companies seem to take advantage of the malleability of digital media to incorporate changes to cater for the target audience in the best possible way. This also illustrates that the "original" can be subject to major alterations in the process of localization. Furthermore, localization approaches taken by some game publishers indicate that the localization process is used as part of a game ecosystem to improve the original product rather than simply producing copies of the original game in different locales. Such flexibility and malleability assumed with respect to the original product can be considered a unique aspect of video game localization. In other AVT contexts, particularly subtitling, text has traditionally been subordinated to the image. However, today some animation films are incorporating subsequent changes in visuals for their "international versions" as is demonstrated by Pixar animation films. For example, the US flag in the home version of *Toy Story 2* (1999) was replaced by a spinning globe in international versions, and there are many more elaborate examples[41] for specific local releases with their other subsequent movies where a local flavour of the target culture is carefully injected or the original culture-specific element deliberately substituted by using some other strategies.

Stitching

Another interesting aspect characteristic of video game localization is the use of the audio technique called "**stitching**" (see 3.4.4 in Chapter 3). As mentioned earlier it is common in games for the voice actor to record isolated words or phrases, unlike the way re-voicing is usually done for cinema. As well as being difficult at times for the voice actors, this leads to the technical challenge of making the artificially joined sentences link seamlessly with the rest of the spoken sentence. For example, the commentary often used in sports games needs to reflect the way the game is played and be able to announce the winning team's name in real-time. These techniques rely not only on professional voice talents, but also on well-trained sound engineers and voice directors who understand the TL and can detect takes which are not natural and therefore jarring to the target player. This may be an area where technological advances are likely to provide improved techniques in the future.

---

41. http://www.stitchkingdom.com/disney-cars-2-clips-international-versions-16464/.

Music and songs

The important role played by audio is increasingly acknowledged also with the inclusion of music in games; indeed research has found that players can attribute up to 30% of their overall enjoyment of a game to the quality of the soundtrack (McCarthy et al. 2005, 113). For example, *Grand Theft Auto: Vice City* (2002) incorporated an in-car radio with music entirely from the 1980s. The use of audio in games has reached the stage where the major US game developer / publisher Electronic Arts (EA) has a significant collection of licensed music tracks (ibid., 110). EA developed the delivery format called "EA Trax" (ibid., 111), working with up-and-coming artists as well as established musicians to include their songs in EA titles. Songs are an integral part of the overall gameplay experience – many Japanese AAA games have specially composed music scores that are released on CD as game music, and some of them have become bestsellers. Theme songs are typically non-diegetic while other songs performed by game characters within the game form a diegetic element. Despite being outside the game world in the strict sense of their link to gameplay, theme songs nevertheless form an important part of the game creating an emotional tie for many fans, thus acting as a means of player engagement.

Translating song lyrics to be sung in the TL, as is sometimes done for the key theme songs for the game, calls for special skills akin to those required for translating poetry and can involve complete rewriting. Rather than translating the original song, which often does not work well in the rhythmic conventions of the TL, a new song may replace the original (O'Hagan 2005). Nevertheless if such a replacement is not a specifically composed score for the game, fans who consider the theme song to be an extension of the game world may question the decision. For example, the original theme song 君がいるから [Because You are Here] in *Final Fantasy XIII* (2009) sung by Sayuri Sugawara was replaced in the game's North American and European releases with the song "My Hands" by the British pop singer Leona Lewis from her hit album. However, the relevance of this choice was questioned by fans writing in blog posts regarding the preference of special compositions over the use of a previously recorded song by an artist who may be popular but whose song bore no relation to the game.[42] As with the use of "adaptive music" techniques, which allow specific music to be prompted in relation to a particular event in a game, music has long been linked to affecting the player's emotional state and also raises cultural implications in game localization. With the availability of high fidelity sound on PCs and consoles, a new genre of music games such as *SingStar* (2004–) and *Guitar Hero* (2005–) has emerged, in

---

42. For example, see http://techland.time.com/2010/01/20/ffxiii/.

turn affecting localization approaches. The *SingStar* series by Sony Computer Entertainment provides a karaoke-style singing competition based on the contestant's pitch and timing. The localization process for this series involves including a certain percentage of local content by local artists relevant to the given locale. These are more similar to an approach based on re-makes often used in the film industry, as we discuss further in Chapter 5.

While the use of audio and audio localization generally increased the scope for localized games to transfer the original gameplay experience, the replacement of written text with audio in games has led to reduced accessibility for deaf and hard-of-hearing players. In contrast to the increasing awareness of accessibility issues by governments and AV producers today, this is something which remains largely unaddressed and neglected in the game industry (Mangiron 2011a, 2012). Given the significance of the issue in view of the wider media usability agenda, we shall examine the topic in some detail in Chapter 7 as one of the important areas of future research in game localization. This current problem and the gap in knowledge about AVT conventions in the game industry in general provide an opportunity for game localizer training as well as focused translation research. In particular, with the advent of cinematic games developing with a wholesale uptake of cinematic techniques (Newman 2009), audio related issues will form a highly relevant area of research.

4.2   Translation strategies applied in game localization

The previous section examined different text types typically found in a console game with their functions, constraints, and translation priorities, followed by a discussion citing a number of actual examples under each key asset type. Translation needs to respond to different functions assigned to these different assets as well as accommodating specific constraints which arise from the nature of the medium as well as work practices. Compared to productivity software localization, translating game texts has a greater number of specific restrictions inherent in the medium both technically and also for socio-cultural reasons such as age rating issues, as we covered in Chapter 3. In order to further systematize our observations on game translation, we draw on a broadly functionalist perspective based on Nord, making particular reference to her approach to translation problems (1997, 64–68) before linking it to a discussion on translation strategies. Her hierarchy of translation problems developed for didactic purposes takes a top-down approach, moving from pragmatic, intercultural, and interlingual kinds, to text-specific problems in contrast to an ST-oriented bottom-up approach. According to Nord (ibid.), the pragmatic problems refer to culture-bound phenomena which need to be adjusted depending on the TT contexts based on the translation brief. The intercultural issues in turn refer to different norms and conventions associated with text types. Interlingual problems arise from structural differences between SL and TL. Finally, the text-specific issues refer to challenges such as figures of speech, puns, etc. specific to the given text.

Following Nord, a functional translation process starts with deciding whether the ST should be reproduced as such ("documentary translation" in which the recipient is well aware it is a translation) or whether the ST should be adapted to a new communicative situation in the TT ("instrumental translation" in which the function of the ST is preserved in the TT). This distinction in turn leads the translation style to either conform to source-culture or target-culture conventions (Nord ibid., 68). Finally, text-specific issues are tackled. Game localization, in our view, mainly fits what Nord terms "instrumental translation", which calls for preserving the function of the ST but is produced as an independent text adjusted to the new communicative situation of the TT. However, as shown in game text taxonomy, different game genres and text types present within a single game serving different functions mean that certain assets may be translated in a way which is oriented towards documentary translation. For example, some of the non-diegetic elements such as system messages, legal information or certain UI items will fall into this category.

In an attempt to highlight some of the main translation strategies used to deal with different types of translation problems of game text, we refer to Nord's translation problems mentioned above but only focus on the most relevant "pragmatic translation problems" and also some examples of "interlingual translation problems". In the discussion below, we link these categorizations of problems by Nord to Chesterman's pragmatic translation strategies (1997, 107) (see Schäffner 2001). They are essentially macro strategies formulated as a result of "a translator's global decisions concerning the appropriate way to translate the text as a whole", and thus are concerned with "the selection of information in the TT" by the translator, in view of the TT readership (ibid.). There are different types of strategies used depending on the context, but the most common in game localization is what Chesterman (1997, 108) calls "cultural filtering", which is analogous to adaptation. We use Chesterman's term given that the definition of adaptation remains unclear in Translation Studies. However, it has to be acknowledged that among the more recent observations on adaptation as a translation strategy is its advocacy in the wider translation community, including some Asian traditions (Baker 2011, 50; O'Hagan 2012a). As far as poetry and drama translation are concerned, translations that deviate considerably from the original text to include target culture references are often considered adaptations. Giving the example of classical Greek plays that develop their plot but are not based on the translation of the original dialogue, Munday (2009, 166) suggests that adaptation denotes "a TT that draws on an ST but which has extensively modified it for a new cultural context". Such extensive modifications may also be found in other types of translation (e.g. the translation of children's literature, dramatic production, comics, and advertising) albeit to a lesser extent. However, adaptation remains a nebulous concept in Translation Studies, often loosely linked to localization where "some see localization as an unconstrained form of adaptation" despite "quite extreme constraints" (Pym 2010, 120). This raises questions of whether the concept of "adaptation" is too general, especially for characterizing game localization in the context of Translation Studies. For now, cultural filtering provides a pragmatic label for the frequently applied manipulation in game localization, which also influences lower level operations concerning interlingual issues. Moving from macro- to more micro-strategies concerned with the difference between the specific SL and TL pair, we then focus on interlingual issues likely to arise in the process of game localization.

4.2.1 Translation strategies for pragmatic translation problems

We first discuss macro strategies taken by translators concerned with the overall "look and feel" of the TT appropriate for the target users.

4.2.1.1 *Culture-bound phenomena*

There are numerous instances of cultural filtering applied in game translation, as might be evident in our examples cited so far. A particularly interesting example (Mangiron 2004; O'Hagan and Mangiron 2004) can be found in the translation of the North American (NA) version of *Final Fantasy X* (2001). This occurs in a scene in which the key female protagonist Yuna bids farewell to Tidus, another key character who is her love interest, realizing she will never see him again. In this highly dramatic moment, Yuna slightly bows to Tidus while saying ありがとう [thank you] to him. In the Japanese cultural context this seemingly common and simple word is perfectly appropriate and able to convey multiple layers of meaning behind the word's familiar surface. However, US translators considered that a literal translation would not work for NA culture; to the NA audience it would seem out of place that Yuna's last words to Tidus were a simple "thank you". In addition, the scene was a close-up of Yuna, so the translation had the additional requirement of lip-synch for voiceover, thus justifying the rendition "I love you" as the most appropriate choice. This decision was controversial amongst some followers of the series, because they believed it was too explicit and did not fit in with Yuna's characterization (Mangiron ibid.; O'Hagan and Mangiron ibid.). However, from a functionalist perspective this strategy can be justified as it focuses on the TT function expected of the translation. The only difficulty is the varied target group made up both of die-hard fans of the *FF* franchise and less devoted gamers who simply wish to have fun playing the game. Alexander O. Smith (2001), who was one of the translators making this decision, argues that this solution served both the necessary cultural and technical (lip-synch) requirements. This example shows that translation challenges may not always readily be resolved by a translation brief or even the translator's understanding of the desired TT function. We will return to this topic in Section 4.4, when we further analyze translation decisions made by translators and the motivations behind them.

As one might expect, not all culture-specific phenomena need adaptation as cultural filtering of the source content may antagonize the end players of a game who may be seeking an exotic feel by choosing to play foreign-made games. For example, the game *Ōkami* (2006) set in ancient Japan, which tells the story of a Shinto goddess who takes the form of a white wolf trying to save the land from darkness, contains numerous Japanese cultural references. Such references were largely kept in the US version of the game and this title was a success in Western countries, winning several awards and selling 200,000 copies in North America in 2006 (Edge Online 2007). This example shows that games overtly referencing foreign cultural elements can also be successful internationally if their theme and gameplay experience are appealing and engaging for players from other cultures. The strategy required then is preservation of such cultural factors.

Occasionally, games set in imaginary scenarios also present implicit cultural references, either in the script or in the visuals. They may also allude to customs and traditions of the original culture that are not common in the target culture. If these references do not pose any serious issue in terms of game reception and ratings, they can be maintained, such as bathing in a public bath in *Final Fantasy VII* (1997), based on the common Japanese practice. However, if the reference interferes with the understanding or the enjoyment of the game, the more common strategy will be to omit it completely from the target version. In order to achieve understanding by the target receiver, what seems an extreme yet common translation strategy often used in games is omission or what Chesterman (1997, 107) refers to broadly as "information change". Although this strategy may sound like "an easy way out", it is a legitimate procedure used by professional translators under certain justifiable circumstances (Baker

2011, 42–43). The fact that games are interactive audiovisual products means that if a cultural allusion is obscure it could not only puzzle the user but could actively hinder the gameplay. The fast pace of most games and their interactive nature also call for brevity and user-friendliness, so long explanations about unknown source-culture elements are generally not appropriate. If there are opaque or offensive cultural references in a game, they are likely to have a negative impact on the player's engagement and the primary entertainment function of video games may fail. Cultural allusions to religion, customs and habits, and historical and political events are therefore likely to require a degree of manipulation. The decision to remove cultural references is also often linked to ratings and censorship issues (see Chapter 5).

Other than the strategies mentioned above, which are commonly used to deal with culture-specific phenomena in games, there are further radical transformations commonly undertaken during localization (O'Hagan 2012a). Game localizers sometimes use the strategy of adding new references to the TT, with the aim of giving the localized version a more local flavour. In order to bring the game closer to target players and compensate for the loss of the original cultural allusions, game localizers may sometimes opt to rewrite and recreate to differing degrees, based on the original. Game localizers tend to have greater freedom in applying the strategy of cultural filtering and information change, than most other translators. Extreme cases of such operations are akin to re-makes, as mentioned earlier. Chandler (2008a, 34–35) cites the localization of *Seaman* (1999), a Japanese game about a pet fish that asks the player questions and tailors the conversation according to the player's preferences. The original content was heavily addressed to a Japanese audience and contained numerous cultural references, so the localization team had to significantly adapt all the Japanese cultural content for the first half of the game. Then the company decided to work with writers for the second half, and create original content aimed at a US audience. Similarly, the Nintendo simulation game *Animal Crossing* (2001) was full of references specific to Japanese culture, as it was originally intended only for the Japanese market. When the game was subsequently localized into English for the North American market, all the cultural elements were fully adapted and rewritten in order to make them fit North American culture. Even the visuals were redesigned in order to depict the American way of life (Nutt 2008). The localized version of this game was so successful that it was subsequently retranslated into Japanese and marketed in Japan with the American content as *Animal Crossing E-Plus* (2003), which also became a hit title in Japan (ibid.). Such an extreme case of adaptation is considered as worthy of being treated as a new product in some cases as illustrated by certain Japanese publishers that systematically capitalize on them, as mentioned in our case study on Square Enix (see 4.3). The quiz game *Buzz!* (2005–) in turn provides an apt example in which some of the content of the game needed to be rewritten to be relevant to the target territory. It therefore involved a substantial amount of recreation, as detailed by Crosignani and Ravetto (2011), who attribute the international success of the series to the application of "transcreation". There are currently no particular agreed-upon labels given to these forms of radical manipulation as types of translation strategy. We revisit this particular approach in Section 4.4 and Chapter 5 as transcreation in the context of the broad cultural implications for game localization.

4.2.1.2   *Proper names*

Games are full of names and labels not only for people, but a wide array of things. The strategy of substitution is often used, where the original name is replaced with a reference analogous in the target culture, with the aim of achieving a similar effect on the target user. Furthermore, this may result in a type of "explicitness change" (Chesterman 1997, 107) in terms of shifting cultural markedness. For example, in *Final Fantasy X-2* (2003), US translators turned the culturally unmarked original Japanese name for a concert 雷平原ライブ ("live concert at Thunder Plains") into the culturally marked term *Yunapalooza*, with a reference to *Lollapalooza*, in which *Lolla* is replaced with *Yuna*, the name of the main character (Mangiron and O'Hagan 2006). *Lollapalooza* is a rock festival held in different locations every year in the US and the resultant translation thus added a local flavour to the target culture. Interestingly there was an episode in *The Simpsons* called "Homerpalooza" (aired 19th of May 1996), indicating how widely this concert series is known in the US culture, as well as the need for the translator to be familiar with such broader cultural events and their allusions which may be made across different media.

Similarly, games often make intertextual references by naming well-known people and stories in the source culture. Even if the whole game is set in a fantasy world, latent references to the original culture often need to be substituted. For example, in *Chocobo Racing* (1999), the Japanese folktale character references Momotaro (a boy's name) and Kiji [a pheasant] would be familiar to Japanese children but unlikely to be understood elsewhere. They were therefore replaced by Hansel and Gretel in the NA version (Parish 2007) in order to make them understandable to target players and bring the game closer to them by using a comparable intertextual reference in the target culture. These strategies considered as translation by cultural substitution are widely practiced by translators both through their own decisions and largely supported by translation commissioners who seek to maximize the entertainment value of the game for the target players.

4.2.2 Translation strategies for interlingual translation problems

In this section, based on a functionalist approach, we focus on the appropriateness of the TT for the given purpose by highlighting the question of linguistic variation in reference to the use of regional accents and taboo words. Linguistic variation present in the ST often causes problems when translating games from English whereas it manifests in the TT as innovative solutions when Japanese games containing no linguistic variation are the source.

4.2.2.1 *Linguistic variation*

As discussed earlier, games are increasingly exploiting the scope of the audio channel, leading to audio localization which we can consider to be a translation strategy partly motivated by a new technological avenue. It also fits the specific use of humour often found in games designed to alleviate the intense level of concentration demanded of the gamer (Mangiron 2010). In association with the injection of a touch of humour, the practice of adding accents in audio localization of a game character has become an increasingly common translation strategy even in cases where it was linguistically unmarked in the original dialogue, as discussed in Section 4.1.2.3. Given the cost implications and the risk of alienating part of the target audience, the addition of accents entails a serious translation decision. To this end, such decisions will require prudent analysis of the given game character and are thus likely to be made by game producers rather than translators, unless they are part of the in-house localization team working alongside the game development team. There is also the opposite technique of neutralization. For example, a character in the original game speaking with a specific accent may be neutralized if it is considered that no local accents would reflect the same connotations as the original. The merchant O'aka, who speaks in Cockney in the NA version of *Final Fantasy X* (2001), for example, did not speak with any particular accent in the Spanish version, so the reference to the working-class Londoner was neutralized because no Spanish dialect would reflect the same nuances. However, in this case, Spanish translators were translating from the NA version, in which the Cockney accent had been introduced, rather than the original Japanese version. To avoid the interference arising from the use of a pivot version, major game companies are now attempting to translate directly from the original game where appropriate resources are available.

4.2.2.2 *Taboo/discriminatory words*

The next two examples concern the inadvertent use of a taboo/discriminatory word especially when the term was not present in the original version but introduced in the localized versions. While the case of neutralising or omitting such words is more common in most other types of translation, the opposite may happen in game localization. The PAL English version of the brain training game *MindQuiz* (2007) released for Nintendo DS and Sony PSP contained the phrase "super spastic" whenever the player's performance failed to reach a certain level. Following a complaint on BBC talkback radio by a user of the game who had a disabled child, the issue was brought under public scrutiny and led to the product's recall by the game's publisher Ubisoft (Richards 2007). Shortly after this incident, Wii *Mario Party 8* (2007) was also recalled due to its use of the same word "spastic" as part of the blue wizard's incantation in the game, primarily intended for rhyming effect rather than its meaning. These incidents illustrate a number of game-specific translation issues. First, the original Japanese games did not contain an equivalent discriminatory word. However, given the nature of the product, translators often take a broad adaptive approach in their translation, including the use of less formal language. Second, in this particular case, the word in question in the TL turned out to be one of the most offensive expressions in the UK's list of discriminatory words against disabled people whereas it was not the case in the US; Wii *Mario Party 8* (2007) had been published in the US earlier in the same year without causing any issue and the game had sold well. Nintendo usually adapts US English to UK English during the process of NTSC to PAL conversion, but this particular case clearly had fallen through their check. That may have been partly due to the way in which the word was used in the game; it appeared in the wizard's spell: "*Magikoopa magic! Turn the train spastic! Make this ticket tragic!*" Its usage therefore clearly differs from the case with *MindQuiz*. Nevertheless, these examples point to the potential risk of translation strategies which take extensive liberty, inadvertently introducing in the target product a negative factor which was not present in the original. This example also underscores the fact that in certain cases the difference between being creative and offensive may not be as clear-cut as one may expect when the product crosses different varieties of the same language.

A functionalist perspective applied to game translation strategies highlights the main challenge involved in game localization to be a difficulty in catering to the needs of all target users, who are often part of a heterogeneous group. Nevertheless, thinking about translation strategies typically used in game localization helps to point to translation norms which translators gradually come to understand in negotiating a complex combination of factors. The next section presents a mini case study to further portray contemporary game translation operations by focusing on the game localization process undertaken by a major game company with a substantial experience in localizing AAA titles which often sell millions of units in international markets.

4.3   A brief case study of Square Enix

Having provided a componential analysis of game translation according to game assets and translation strategies, we now provide a brief case study of a major game company heavily involved in game localization. In an attempt to paint an authentic picture we focus on the overall localization process used and how macro-level product decisions are made to accommodate and affect translation. In choosing Square Enix we were motivated by several factors in addition to the fact that one of the authors of this book worked for the company for a number of years. Square Enix has been heavily involved in game localization for well over a decade and is widely known for its awareness of intercultural communication in developing games (Consalvo 2006), with a track-record of producing internationally successful game titles through localization. Also the company's role as a publisher as well as a developer of games was a key factor for our purposes, as we hoped to demonstrate the GILT concept at work where localization is closely tied to product development. As mentioned in the Prologue, the company's involvement as third-party publisher and localizer for foreign AAA titles such as the *Call of Duty* series (2003–) in Japan indicates its attitudes towards introducing previously less popular non-Japanese games to the Japanese market. While gaining insider information from high profile game companies is notoriously difficult, as we mentioned in the Introduction, more recently some companies including Square Enix have been generous in sharing information through game industry events as well as published interviews by staff members. For example, the presentation entitled "The Square Enix Approach to Localization" by the then Localization Director Richard Honeywood at the International Game Developers Conference (GDC) in 2007 (Honeywood 2007) provided a glimpse into the philosophy behind game localization as well as into specific localization approaches taken at the firm. More recently the company again presented at the Localization Summit at GDC 2012. The session entitled "Audio Localization Done Right: Simultaneous Scripting and Recording" was delivered by the sound engineer, Hikaru Taniyama and the translator, Masaharu Shibayama, discussing their new tools to increase the quality of audio localization (*Famitsu* 2012). Furthermore, we were also fortunate to be able to have personal contact with Alexander O. Smith, a former Square Enix translator well known for his English translations of some of the major titles, including the *FF* series. Other published interviews with Square Enix staff from online and print sources were also used.

4.3.1   Overview

The Japanese game developer and publisher Square Enix was created in 2003 as a result of the merger between the two separate game companies, Square and Enix. The company's full and formal involvement in localization goes back to 1997, when the former Square established its own localization department in its head-quarters in Tokyo. Despite the company's status today, its history indicates that it has climbed a learning curve over time, even with its flagship titles. For example, localization of *Final Fantasy VII* (*FFVII*) (1997) published by the then Square was "full of grammatical errors and weird turns of phrases that have become an integral part of the game's legacy" (Fenlon 2011). Widespread criticism from fans about the poor quality led the company to shift localization in-house from that time on (O'Hagan and Mangiron 2004). Nevertheless *FFVII* was a commercial success internationally and led the company to realise the significance of the North American market and, consequently, of localization (Fenlon ibid.).

Square Enix is today known as a global game corporation adept at produc-ing games which sell internationally through high quality localization (Consalvo 2006; Fenlon 2011). Consalvo's study of the company suggests that their products "designed for global consumption are carefully localized, to ensure that their in-ternational flavour is not *too* foreign for non-Japanese tastes" (Consalvo 2006, 120 [emphasis in the original]). An earlier example of their vision to create a game to be played by both Japanese and English speaking players was its MMORPG title *Final Fantasy XI* (2002). *FFXI* allowed the players using the Japanese and the English versions to play together simultaneously on the same servers, which also incorporated a phrase-book-based automatic translation functionality be-tween English and Japanese (see 7.3.2 for further discussion on Natural Language Processing technology applied in games). Another relevant case in point is their *FFXIII* (2009), which was reportedly developed using feedback from focus groups from both the US and Japanese regions, geared to understand the appeal of the product to international audiences beyond the home turf.[43] The company is also known for its involvement in transnational video game development, more re-cently in association with Microsoft, in creating games to be played on Xbox 360, which appeal to Japanese gamers (Picard 2009, 99–100).

According to Honeywood (2007) Square Enix's in-house localization depart-ment consists of localization coordinators and translators (who are called "locali-zation specialists"), editors, and localization engineers. While it has subsidiaries in

---

43. See http://en.wikipedia.org/wiki/Final_Fantasy_XIII.

North America and Europe that look after marketing, sales, and QA,[44] the localization is mainly undertaken within the company's Tokyo headquarters, where the localization team can work closely with the development team. The former Square Enix employee Tom Slattery confirms in a recent interview (Cunningham 2012) that translators, editors, and localization producers work alongside the development team in the Tokyo office for the most part. Such an arrangement reflects recognition by the company of the critical link between game development and game localization, conducive to the creation of culturally appropriate target-language versions that respect the original intention of the game designer. This is also a privilege of a company being the developer as well as publisher, and would not be readily manageable in the common outsourcing model, where localization is typically cut off from game development. According to Richard Honeywood (quoted in Fenlon 2011), in the early days his localization team had to convince the development team that it was inevitable that some things would be lost in translation when, for example, the latter would insist on retaining Japanese names across different language versions. The aforementioned *FFXI*, which was designed at the outset to let Japanese and English-speaking gamers play in the same game world, provides an apt example regarding decisions about names in games. In another interview Honeywood[45] explained how all the names used in *FFXI* such as characters, spells, place names etc. were set in English from the start, although the game was first published only in Japanese with the intention of making the Japanese players accustomed to English names in anticipation of the interlingual play environments to come once the English version was released the following year.

Honeywood (2007) maintains that in order to best address cultural differences and target users, no aspect of the original game specifications should be immune from changes during the localization process at Square Enix. Such a privileging of localization would be considered radical by most other game companies even today. It is only conceivable in a context where the company treats localization as a fundamental rather than skin-deep operation and where there is a trusting and close working relationship between the game's development and localization teams. In previous chapters we observed that even in the early days of localization, games often underwent changes beyond the language itself, affecting symbols, graphics, and sometimes game mechanics, including the level of challenge (Kohler 2005, 206). However, these changes tended to be largely motivated by a fear of the wider public reaction rather than as a means to fine-tune the game

---

44. QA is carried out in Tokyo, even for FIGS. This assessment mainly addresses functional issues, but also consistency with glossaries, terms, etc. Then the linguistic testing for FIGS is done in the UK office, although it also checks for functional bugs.

45. http://www.ffcompendium.com/h/interview2.shtml.

to match target player expectations. Today the importance of trust between the developer of the game and the localization team is gradually being recognized, even if not to an extent that allows all game specifications to be open to changes during localization.

According to Honeywood (2007) the five-step approach to game localization used at Square Enix consists of: (1) preparation and familiarization; (2) glossary creation; (3) translation and editing; (4) integration and QA, and (5) gold master and after-sales care. The creation of a glossary was considered particularly significant, involving making a list of all characters, monsters, items, place names, events, etc. that feature in the game. Although time-consuming, the company believes that the development of such a glossary contributes to better understanding by translators of the traits of the game characters and, accordingly, determines the style of writing. This may also be a reflection of the fact that Square Enix is known for story-heavy RPG titles making the narrative dimension and the portrayal of game characters particularly important. As stressed by Honeywood, the creation of a glossary is considered indispensable in ensuring consistency, especially in the case of long-running game series with certain recurring legacy properties. According to terminology management principles widely adopted in the localization industry, this would be an obvious requirement in handling products in multilingual versions, yet such an approach is relatively new in game localization. A principled approach to terminology is further stressed by the fact that the first things that need to be translated in game localization are usually place names and character names for promotional purposes (Alexander O. Smith quoted in Jayemanne 2009, n.p.). To be able to do so requires more than terminology management and calls for a sufficient degree of familiarity by the translators with the game world so that they can "start making decisions about word choice and tone" (Chandler and Deming 2012, 147–148). Their approach is characterized by a heavy emphasis on providing translators with contextual details, including a familiarization with the game. However, more recently the company has been moving towards a sim-ship model, with a potentially detrimental impact on their ideal approach to thoroughly familiarize translators with the game world before the translation work starts. Given Japan's shrinking domestic market, the post-gold model, in which there may be a gap of over a year between the original release and a localized version, is no longer sustainable (see Table 5.1 for the release date gaps of *Final Fantasy* series). Such new requirements are reflected in the changing workflow and the need for tools to facilitate simultaneous releases, as indicated in the company's presentation at GDC 2012 (*Famitsu* 2012).

As explained in Chapter 1, in the early days of game localization a multistage translation process was commonly used, where the initial translation was followed by a separate step often referred to in the industry as "rewriting"[46] in the sense of extensive edits applied to a translation. This method was originally often used as a stopgap, rather than a well-planned part of the workflow, to compensate for the lack of involvement of professional translators. While much of the ad hoc translation approach has been discarded today, multi-stage translation, albeit in a much more refined way, continues to be used at both Square Enix and other major Japanese game publishers. For example, Nate Bihldorff and Bill Trinen of Nintendo of America (NOA), at the time in charge of editing and translation respectively, maintain that this approach is conducive to good quality translation when the translator and the rewriter work closely together during the process (Gamasutra Podcast 2006). Such efforts are considered essential by these game publishers, given that game texts are exposed to a large number of consumers who may reach several million, with bestselling AAA games; therefore game texts have to be presented as being professionally written in the TL in their own right. Similarly Alexander O. Smith advocates the merits of the multi-tier model with a co-translator and/or a separate editor, where "one person gets to play fast-and-loose with the text, pushing it to the borderline and frequently beyond" and the other can "choose where to draw the line" (quoted in Jayemanne 2009, n.p.). Another translator Joseph Reeder, who formerly worked at Square Enix with Smith on the North American version of *FFXII* (2006), refers to the value of the additional TL editing process applied by an editor in the company's London Office (FF Archives & FF 20th Anniversary DVD 2007). Smith notes that the way in which the multi-tier model is used by Square Enix ensures that it is the translator who is in charge of final decisions even when an independent editor is involved in the process as he explains:

> [B]oth primary translators are fully aware of the ST, and are therefore making decisions to honor or change the text in light of the original meaning at all times. Furthermore, though a third-party editor also reviews the text, the primary translator is given final say on the translation, so at no point are decisions concerning the final product being made without knowledge of the original.
>
> (Smith, e-mail message to O'Hagan, 10 December, 2012)

The same point is made by the aforementioned Square Enix translator Slattery (quoted in Cunningham 2012), who confirms that the translator makes the call on "how (or even whether) to implement any feedback or suggestions they receive from editors and game testers." As apparent in these explanations of the translator's role at Square Enix, there is a clear sign of "loyalty" (Nord 2005) to

---

46. This term is here used in a generic sense, as compared to the specific concept used by Lefevere (1992) in a Translation Studies context (see Chapter 5).

the ST as opposed to free-for-all changes being implemented irrespective of the ST. This is a demonstration of a functionalist approach at work in a nuanced way, enabling a focus on the function of the TT, yet done in a controlled manner to guard the original message. In this way, greater freedom to manipulate the text is accepted, but closely guided by the original message and how the text fits with the feel of the gameplay in the eyes of the target players, often making the translation process more akin to creative writing. It is also interesting to note how a multi-stage translation process has been widely used in the other popular culture genre of manga translation (Schodt 1996), where a separate editing process typically follows the initial faithful translation often conducted by a native speaker of Japanese. However, it is unclear to what extent the "loyalty" to ST is respected in the application of a multi-stage translation approach in the commercial manga translation process.

According to observations made by Chandler (Gamasutra Podcast 2006) and Alexander O. Smith (quoted in Jayemanne 2009, n.p.), Japanese publishers tend to have a better appreciation of the requirements of localization and are generally better prepared than their counterparts in North America or Europe. However, such a perception may need to be further qualified by saying that while Japanese companies are more aware of and adept at localizing Japanese games into English, their awareness of the differences among FIGS markets, for example, may not be any greater than or even as good as that of US or UK publishers. Nevertheless the cultural gap between the East and the West extends beyond game cultures and is also to some extent manifest in localization approaches themselves (see Chapter 5). For example, while sim-ship is already a standard model for publishers in the West, Japanese counterparts have only relatively recently begun to move towards this model. Perhaps related to this, we found that Japanese companies seem to have lagged behind in their use of CAT tools in the game translation process. Although Square Enix's new tool discussed at GDC 2012 shows the changing landscape, many localization practices at Japanese game companies seem to be reliant on more generic tools, such as Excel spreadsheets, than specialized CAT applications. The use of dedicated terminology management systems, for example, integrated with a TM system still seems to be relatively rare.

4.3.2 Examples of innovation and appropriation of translation

Following this overview of the approach to game localization undertaken at Square Enix, this section cites a number of specific examples which we consider to demonstrate the company's wholesale readiness to transform their products through the localization process, involving innovation and appropriation, in terms of translation norms established by other forms of translation.

4.3.2.1 *Use of icon and voice replacing original written text*

The English localized versions of Square Enix's flagship series *Dragon Quest VIII* (2004) (see Figure 4.1) introduced the use of icons, which replaced the original text-based menu system and aimed to make the localized version user-friendly. A game reviewer's comment indicates that the solution served the purpose as he remarks: "Square Enix has taken great care in going back into the Japanese code and has streamlined the menu system to be cleaner and more accessible for US gamers" (Dunham 2005).

This illustrates the approach to localization by Square Enix as unreservedly target-oriented, which also alleviates problems of space constraints. The same game also shows an innovative localization approach, using voiced dialogue to replace the original written dialogue. In localized versions of this game, the original written Japanese dialogues were voiced into English. Yuji Horii, the game's creator, explains that this was considered a better way of conveying characters' emotions in localized versions, whereas written text was sufficient for Japanese gamers to fully appreciate the nuances of the intended effect (cited in Onyett 2005). This suggests that isosemiotic translation (Gottlieb 2004, 86) – i.e. translation using the same communication channel, in this case from written to written form – was not considered to be sufficient to create an equivalent affective result between the original game and the source language player, and the localized game and the target player. This case demonstrates the extended scope of localization affording the

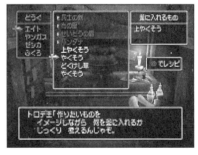

Figure 4.1 User Interface for *Dragon Quest VIII*: a menu based on image icons from the English localized version (left) versus the Japanese original based on text (right)[47]

---

47. The screenshots are not the exact corresponding part between the original Japanese version and the English version. However, the images serve to give a flavour of the extent to which the original game's UI is mainly text based in comparison with the localized version. Images kindly supplied by Square Enix.

use of a new communication channel to better achieve the intended communicative effect. This kind of practice is rare under current AVT norms, where diasemiotic translation (Gottlieb ibid.) – i.e. translation across different communication channels – is generally limited to the transfer from speech to writing, as in the case of subtitles, but normally not the other way around. The mode of audio description (AD) could be considered an exception, although its intended purpose is primarily different as it is designed to cater to the blind and visually impaired. AD is discussed in Chapter 7 in the context of game accessibility.

4.3.2.2   *Changed character relationships and designs in the localized version*

The next example is one of the few cases of a sim-shipped action RPG published by Square Enix. This game serves as a case in which the scope of game localization has been stretched in a number of areas. Released exclusively in Japan for PS3, *NierReplicant* (2010) presents a story based on a sibling relationship, where the protagonist, Nier, tries to save his sister, Yonah. However, in the North American and European versions, *NierGestalt* (2010) released for Xbox 360 and PS3, the brother character was replaced with a much older adult figure as Yonah's father, with a completely re-designed character image, transformed from the somewhat androgynous depiction of the adolescent Nier to the more masculine father character Nier. Furthermore, *NierReplicant* was made Japanese-market exclusive, meaning only on the Japanese market were *NierReplicant* (on PS3) and *NierGestalt* (on Xbox 360) both made available (see Figure 4.2). This departed from the standard approach to **multi-platform games**, where the same game is offered on different platforms, with Square Enix turning the formula into an opportunity to introduce a region-specific version. This new approach led to some pre-release confusion and debate, with some fan forum discussions extending to the issue of cultural specificity of Japanese games and international fans' desire to experience the original through an unadulterated version (Bailey 2009).

    With the project intended for global sim-ship release, an interview (Game Watch 2010) with the producer, Yosuke Saito of Square Enix, and the director, Taro Yokoo of the game developer Cavia, reveals, first of all, the international make-up of the production team consisting of Japanese, American, and European members and also how from an early stage in the development their feedback was reflected in the game. This was intended to break the post-gold model which Square Enix had routinely been using and was an attempt to incorporate international viewpoints of game development from the outset. Such an approach is also reflected in the way the game addresses different regions by featuring a different landmark according to the locale, such as the Empire State Building, Big Ben and the Eiffel Tower in place of the original Tokyo Tower. Regarding the character design, while the Japanese side were in favour of having an adolescent Nier as the

Figure 4.2 Nier in *NierGestalt* versus Nier in *NierReplicant* © 2010 SQUARE ENIX CO., LTD. All Rights Reserved. Developed by Cavia Inc.[48]

main protagonist, the American side opposed having the feeble looking adolescent as the hero by insisting that such a character would not be convincing when handling heavy-duty weapons, and thus would not be treated seriously by the NA audience. Despite such opposition, the original Nier character design was strongly supported by the Japanese team and eventually it was decided it would be retained, but only for the version to be released in Japan. This decision involved changes in parts of the scripts, voice, and the camera positions due to different heights between the adolescent and the adult Nier. This example alone demonstrates how seriously the localization process is treated for different market receptions. It also illustrates the way in which the scope of localization when applied to entertainment products is dynamically changing whereby providing a mechanism to serve specific regions with specific versions of a product with changes that are not essential in terms of functionality.

In addition to such a significant macro adjustment in the game's character design, another relevant aspect from a micro perspective relates to more subtle changes made during localization regarding the image of Kaine. Introduced as a hermaphrodite with an apparent female look, this character's signs of masculinity – visible in cut-scenes in the Japanese version – were toned down in the US release (Cooke 2010, 24). The depiction of different sexual phenomena such as transvestism is fairly common across many Japanese games, and is therefore familiar to the Japanese gamers. However, it is often an element subject to changes in localized versions and also affects age ratings (see Chapter 5). Characterizing of Kaine by highlighting the way s/he speaks also provides a relevant

---

48. Box art images kindly supplied by Square Enix.

Figure 4.3 Subtitles with vulgarities masked by pseudo-censorship symbols
© 2010 SQUARE ENIX CO., LTD. All Rights Reserved. Developed by Cavia Inc.[49]
(with our emphasis)

example in relation to localization. Kaine is cursed by a male demon and speaks with a foul mouth, and Kaine's line subtitled in Japanese is often marked with pseudo-censorship symbols, masking certain offensive words as in Figure 4.3 (「テメエの汚ねえ※△☆をギタギタに刻んでやる。」 [I'll chop your filthy XXXX into pieces]). The voiced Japanese dialogue deliberately used a censorship-like technique and bleeped out the profanity. However, the English voiced version got away with the use of vulgarities while its intralingual subtitles used a similar technique to the Japanese subtitles by masking what are considered to be offensive words.

The original intention had been for voices in the Japanese version to be in English, but subsequently it was decided to use Japanese voices, and the Japanese actors had to fill in the gaps (that is, the words which were originally masked in the subtitles), which were to be replaced by bleeps. This was necessary in order to measure the length of the line of the dialogue to fit in the allocated space. The mimicked use of the bleep censor in any major games had not been seen before and was the producer's attempt to try a new approach. However, the US team opposed the idea of the use of bleeps as they argued that they would sound farcical to US audiences.

The above examples demonstrate how cultural differences which arise in the making of the original and its localized version are accommodated in the localization process and how the game company exploits the variability of the software medium to explore experimental approaches in the process of localization.

---

49. Source: http://game.watch.impress.co.jp/img/gmw/docs/370/231/html/nier08.jpg.html.

Despite the high stakes involved, the greater degree of freedom to experiment seems to come from the nature of the game business as a dynamic young industry not bound by a particular tradition and, most of all, because of its purpose as a creator of mass entertainment, and this has clearly seeped into innovative new translation approaches.

4.3.2.3 *Reverse localization model: International and Final Mix editions*

The last category of our examples refers to particular editions of games, specifically prepared for the domestic Japanese market, of certain popular series such as the *Final Fantasy* (1987–) and *Kingdom Hearts* (2002). They are known as "International" and "Final Mix" respectively for each series and constitute a reverse localization model (O'Hagan 2012a), where localized NA versions are reintroduced to the Japanese home market by retaining voiced dialogue in English with newly added Japanese subtitles. These editions are intended only for Japanese speakers, with all UI turned back into Japanese. As further explanations are provided in Chapter 5, we only briefly introduce this model here as an example to characterize a new approach to localization regularly used by Square Enix. Figure 4.4 illustrates the flow of the product development, taking the example of *FFXIII* (2009) and its International edition *FFXIII Ultimate Hits International* (2010) which is based on the NA version of *FFXIII*. This means the International edition can be taken as

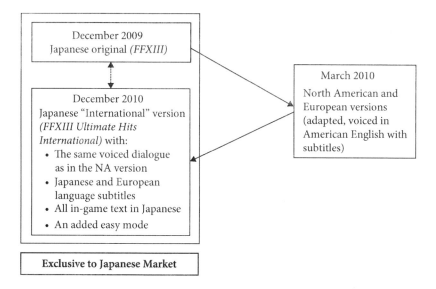

Figure 4.4 Original *Final Fantasy XIII* vs. the re-localized version *Final Fantasy XIII Ultimate Hits International*

a version to show to Japanese players the changes made in the NA version. The key added-value of these editions seems to be the English voiced dialogue, which is preferred to Japanese voice by certain Japanese gamers (O'Hagan 2009c), and any other added features and changes incorporated into the NA locale. While other major Japanese publishers such as Nintendo, Sega, Konami and Capcom also use this model (albeit somewhat more sporadically), Square Enix seems to be the developer/publisher employing it most systematically, thus suggesting the company's exploratory approach to localization.

We acknowledge that the above brief case study based on the example of a global game developer/publisher who undertakes game localization as part of game development cannot be taken as representative of contemporary game localization as a whole. However, we argue that Square Enix's approaches and their underlying philosophy serve to illustrate some of the unique characteristics of translating games and the new perspectives that have emerged in shaping new translation practices. The purpose of the case study was therefore to grapple with new dimensions of translation practice in action as well as to get a sense of direction of where game localization is heading. Insights highlighted by Square Enix's approach to localization might be characterized as: (1) providing an international outlook in developing games and a close link between game development and game localization; (2) recognizing the importance of providing contextual information to translators; (3) assigning a pair of translators to work on the same game and/or use of a third-party editing and rewriting process, and (4) continuous experimentation through localization as part of game development. These observations highlight the company's approach as not treating localized games as lesser derivative products but as new creations which can stand on their own with new added value. What is striking is their liberal leveraging of the localization process in transforming the original product. In their approach the nature of the malleable medium is exploited, which is likely to stem from their expertise as an established game developer and publisher in understanding games as new media entertainment. With these key findings in mind, the next section attempts to identify game localization in terms of translation norms with a focus on translators.

4.4   The translator as a creative agent: Game localization as transcreation

While localizing games has come a long way from its haphazard origins, at the same time technological advances are leading to more challenging work environments for translators. In this section we cast a spotlight on translators, progressing from our analysis focused on games as translation texts and as products.

In order to define the dynamic practice of game localization from a translator-centric perspective, we now focus on the translator's agency and the concept of transcreation.

4.4.1 Internal knowledge versus external knowledge as professional norms versus expectancy norms

The examples at Square Enix demonstrate how new translation practices are being invented as part of the whole innovative process of video game production designed to entertain gamers the world over. This complex and dynamic process in turn is made possible by translators constantly readjusting to meet the changing demands of highly challenging tasks. To introduce a focus on translators our discussion begins with our interview with Alexander O. Smith, a former Square Enix translator now operating as an independent translator in his own right. This provides an insight into how translation decisions are made by game translators. In response to our question regarding the particularly curious translation choice of the name of a particular weapon in the game *FFX* (2001) which we touched on in Section 4.1.2.1, Smith gave an explanation of his team's approach as follows:

> As for why no attempt was made to 'translate' the Japanese terms, it basically comes down to a decision about the feel of the finished product. Games in the Final Fantasy series often feature weapons from classic Japanese sources, like Murasame, and since these are part of the lore of the game, we transliterate those item names directly for the English version. However, names like 花鳥風月, which first appeared in FFX, are not part of the game lore, and the description arguably has nothing to do with the item itself. Thus we made the decision that the gamer was better served by a name that, though unrelated to the original item name, had some relevance to the item's function in the game. The name has further merit in that it's a bit of a pun on the word 'painkiller' in that it both removes the pain of levelling your abilities, and kills enemies painfully.
>
> (Smith, e-mail message to O'Hagan, February 17, 2009)

The above explanations illustrate how the decision-making process is informed by an understanding by the translator of the game world specific to the *FF* series and the required function of the TT for the end users. This is in marked contrast to the approach based on the literal meaning of ST, irrespective of the diachronic dimension of the game, which prevailed for game translation in the early days and still exists to a degree. Going from "花鳥風月 [beauty of nature]" to "painkiller" demonstrates an active contribution to meaning-making by the translators (as Smith explained, a pair of them as a team were working on the same translation) to facilitate the final localized product taking on a life of its own to serve its new audience as distinct from that of the ST. Such a process is also afforded by sufficient contextual information, including the game's history, made available to the translators as opposed to a "blind-fold" approach not uncommon in localization projects.

In reference to the same game, Smith was also responsible for the script "I love you" in the game's North American version, translated from the original "ありがとう [thank you]" as we discussed in Section 4.2.1.1. Smith's explanation of this translation decision is published in the Japanese literary magazine *Subaru*. Smith (2001, 36–37) demonstrates how translation is ultimately about communicating the key message across cultures, in this case privileging the target culture convention. He maintains that there was no acceptable translation available in this case other than "I love you" in English for the intended American audience. He cites the well-known scene from the film *Titanic* where Rose says "I love you, Jack" in the dwindling hope of survival, to which Jack responds to her by pleading "No, don't you say your good-byes, Rose. Don't you give up. Don't do it!", interpreting her words to mean her final good-bye. Smith illustrates how, just like ありがとう in the original Japanese, "I love you" in English can have multitudes of meaning. He adds that the lip-synch between this chosen translation in English and the original Japanese line was an accidental bonus. This example indicates how translation decisions are carefully considered with reference to the intended audience in a given situation. Furthermore, regardless of whether all users appreciated the particular strategy, the translator is prepared to commit to his/her decision and be accountable to the extent that he or she can explain how the decision is taken. Such a conviction can only be based on the translator's deep familiarity with the particular game world and the given context, which is not always granted to game translators as we have discussed elsewhere.

Approaches in Translation Studies derived from Sociology have focussed on the translator's active role and agency, with a view to shedding light on translation as product and process (Milton and Bandia 2008). In the field of game translation, there are a number of individual translators who have become well-known to gamers due to their translation work, especially those who are behind international best sellers. In this sense, the game industry and gamers in particular seem to pay great attention to translators' roles in delivering the products in their language. Accordingly an increasing range of published interviews is becoming available which will provide a valuable source for further research into how translation decisions are made and what influences them, including cases where a considerable compromise had to be made. It is beyond the scope of this book to delve into this particular dimension in any depth, but our first attempt at bringing translators into the equation is to consider them in terms of "professional norms" as compared to "expectancy norms" (Chesterman 1997, 68). Building on Toury's earlier introduction of the concept of "norms" with the shift in focus to the TT, Chesterman proposed adding professional norms which "regulate translation process itself" and expectancy norms which are "established by readers' expectations on a translation". The main motivation in applying the concepts of norms here is to further elicit the complex forces under which the translation decisions are being made by the translator in the particular context of game localization.

Chesterman's professional norms and expectancy norms can be linked to what Pym (2004, 28) calls "internal knowledge" and "external knowledge" in the context of localization. According to Pym, internal knowledge means "localization as known from the perspective of the localizer, from the person within the actual process", whereas external knowledge refers to "localization as known by someone outside the process, most prominently the end-user" (ibid.). These concepts can be useful in underpinning one of the unique characteristics of video game culture and the industry in terms of its localization goals and its end users. Compared to other types of localization mainly applied to productivity tools, the game industry has a much closer relationship to its users, as discussed at the beginning of the book. Certain users act as product testers and can be extremely knowledgeable about game products. In such cases the distinction between the internal knowledge by the translator and the external knowledge by hard-core gamers may blur, especially when the translator is not game-literate or is given very little context to work with. While some translators possess genre knowledge of video games in addition to their translation expertise, not all have such domain-specific knowledge. If localization is taking place in an outsourcing sim-ship model, with little contact between the game developer and the translator, the gap in the translator's knowledge of the game can be further widened. This potential lack of domain knowledge on the part of the translator, compounded by the lack of context for texts being translated, can easily be detected by some end users with an in-depth knowledge of games. Thus translators need to meet at least some of the expectancy norms in order to be able to deliver an "acceptable" translation to the market, to use Toury's term. Expectancy norms are also something which may be "validated by a norm-authority" (Chesterman 1997, 66), thus involving not only the user side such as gamers and third parties such as game reviewers, but also the production side, including developers and publishers as well as platform holders. Given the historical link between the game industry and its users, user feedback indeed often impacts on game production. The problem arises when professional norms shared by game translators are in conflict with the expectancy norms of the developer or the publisher of the game, or indeed those of the end users. Furthermore there may also be a conflict in the expectations of the end users and the interests of a developer or publisher. There is currently no research available to answer the question of how different norms are operating in the context of game localization.

In the meantime the game industry's concern over how the end product will be received by the final target players is now leading to their pursuit of concrete and direct user data. More recently some game companies have started to collect game player statistics, called "game metrics", to gain further concrete evidence of player behaviour, so that such data can be incorporated into game design (Nacke and Drachen 2011, n.p.). For example, Microsoft's TRUE system tracks real-time player experience as the game is played (Kim et al. 2008), illustrating new avenues of data collection from direct user response to the game system (see Chapter 7). The increasing interest in user responses further stresses the ultimate concern of game companies regarding the player experience in the target market. This in turn reconfirms the strong tendency for game localization to prioritize translation focused on the entertainment value of the TT in the eyes of the target users (Mangiron and O'Hagan 2006). For this reason, game development itself is sometimes conducted involving an international team in an attempt to address at the onset of the product design, some of the potential issues likely raised by the end user in a specific locale as we have shown in our case study. Beyond long-standing methods of play testing and beta testing of the original products by players in the domestic market alone, such testing should ideally be extended to an international group of players even on a case-by-case basis (O'Hagan 2009a). Given the tight schedule for sim-ship localization and also the need to keep new games under wraps until their official release, formalizing such an arrangement will admittedly be extremely challenging. This makes game metrics extremely attractive in providing certain types of quantitative data aimed at understanding user behaviour even after the product is launched. The challenge is to extend the data collection to localized games as we discuss further in Chapter 7.

Game translation operates under a complex array of forces: on the one hand, the obligation to cater to cultural specificities in each target territory and, on the other, the pressure to retain the original flavour. Furthermore, there are factors which are specific to the game domain, such as age ratings and the degree of control wielded by game publishers and game platform holders over approving localized games and deciding on the localization approach and which language versions to release. Finally, there is the presence of hardcore fans and super users[50] who are extremely knowledgeable about games and particular franchises. These factors all contribute to the formation of expectancy norms, in turn affecting

---

50. We use the term in analogy to "superplay", which is a generic term to refer to game playing practices which seek to "demonstrate mastery of the game through performance" (Newman 2008, 123).

professional norms by translators. More recently, the game industry has developed a unique relationship with users as creators, where user input is actively solicited by encouraging users to add new value to the game by making tools available to users for adapting the original product. User-generated content is becoming part of the draw for players, who are offered a chance to co-create or simply to enjoy sharing their own creations with fellow gamers. In a practice known as "modding", well-established in the game sector, technologically savvy gamers have been attempting varying degrees of modifications of a commercial game. These various types of legitimate user participation promote user co-creation, which is regarded positively by game companies as adding value to the original product.

Fan activities are part and parcel of modern video game culture, contributing to wider industry contexts. With the changing role of consumers in the Web 2.0 era to more active participants in the co-creation of products, the position of some game fans can be re-evaluated. Non-gamer translators who may be engaged in a particular game localization project on an ad hoc basis are not likely to have the same level of extensive knowledge of games or particular game series as hardcore fans. In this way, the question of internal knowledge and external knowledge also relates to the current debate on the rise of the amateur invading previously sacred professional areas of work versus "the crisis of the experts" failing to provide sufficient expert knowledge in the face of complex systems (Gee and Hayes 2011, 44). This suggests a means of enabling professional localizers to tap into the skills of devoted gamers would address user perspectives and expectancy norms. While the former may lack a full understanding of the game domain, the latter are unlikely to possess full translation competence (including the ability to deliver under pressure and under less than optimal conditions), even though their game knowledge may be superior. The historical background of the game industry vis-à-vis game localization makes it well-positioned to exploit the current climate of user empowerment in relation to user co-creation. The concept of "user-professional collaboration" will be a challenging, yet potentially rewarding game translation model. In such collaboration, professional norms and expectancy norms will come in closer contact and likely re-shape one another, possibly leading to a new set of norms arising out of the convergence of internal and external knowledge. A research avenue to investigate the relationship between professional norms and expectancy norms by users may open up in the increasingly visible user translation activities of fan translation and translation hacking of games (see Chapter 7). This in turn has significant implications for translator training and also for translation strategies, which form our next topic.

In our attempt to highlight the unique dimension of game translation we have begun to focus on translator's agency in reference to particular examples of their decision-making process. We further consider professional norms under the concept of "transcreation" in the next section.

4.4.2 Translator's agency and transcreation

In order to convey how game localization involves a broad range of sometimes radical adaptive strategies, we previously borrowed the concept of "transcreation" "to explain the freedom granted to the translator, albeit within severe space limitations" in earlier studies (Mangiron and O'Hagan 2006, 11). In them we stressed the creativity and freedom that game translators exercise. We observed that such creativity indeed seemed to be promoted rather than diminished, at least in some cases, even by the very constraints of various kinds imposed on the translators. However, the use of the term "transcreation" in the context of game localization calls for clarification, especially given its historical origins and more recent revival mainly in the context of translation for advertising (Ortiz-Sotomayor 2007). In particular, Bernal-Merino (2006, 32-33) observes how the term "transcreation" has come to be used by "a new wave of companies seeking to distance themselves from traditional translation firms".

The original concept of "transcreation" as discussed in Translation Studies can be traced to India and Brazil. While our main focus is Brazilian contexts, a brief reference to the concept's dual origin in India is warranted. It was *Post-colonial Translation: Theory and Practice* (1999) edited by Susan Bassnett and Harish Trivedi, that first brought to light in the Anglophone academic community the Brazilian conceptualization of translation as a "cannibalistic undertaking" (ibid., 15), including transcreation, and its coincidental dual sources. The Indian tradition of transcreation was described as "symbiotic intermingling of the original with the translation", for example, in reference to the reformation of the scriptural epic *Ramayanada* originally in Sanskrit brought to vernacular consumption by the Hindi poet Tulsi Das (1532-1623) (Bassnett and Trivedi 1999, 10). Subsequently the concept was revisited by the Indian poet and translator P. Lal (1996), and was further extended by Indian scholars in postcolonial contexts. In this way, the Indian context seems to link transcreation with a didactic goal in one sense. The prevalence and significance of this concept in contemporary India seem evident in the fact that the term "transcreation" was included in a supplement to the *Oxford Advanced Learners' Dictionary of Contemporary English* (1996) as part of an "Indian English" list of words (cited in Bassnett and Trivedi 1999, 10).

In contrast to the Indian developments of transcreation which are likened to the lifecycle of a banyan tree as "a natural process of organic, ramifying, vegetative growth and renewal", the Brazilian take is linked more to bloodthirsty cannibalism[51] (Bassnett and Trivedi 1999, 10). In the 1960s, the Brazilian poet and translator Haroldo de Campos used the term "transcreation" (transcriação in Portuguese). This emerged in the Brazilian context of constructing "cultural identity through translation and self-translation" (Guldin 2008, 110) in opposition to Western colonial hegemony. According to de Campos, conveyed via Vieira, transcreation is a "radical translation praxis", where translation "visualizes the notion of mimesis not as a theory of copy but as the production of difference in sameness" (de Campos 1981, 183 cited in Vieira 1999, 110). Transcreation was used as a means of advocating a renewal of the concept of "translation" as an act of appropriation, recreation and even as a blood transfusion "that moves translation beyond the dichotomy source/target and cites original and translation in a third dimension, where each is both a donor and a receiver" (Vieira 1999, 97). In this sense, transcreation challenges the concept of "translation" rather than being subsumed by it. As explained by Vieira (ibid., 98), the digestive analogy to the concept of "cannibalism" seems fit, even if de Campos had actually not referred to the concept explicitly, in that "foreign input, far from being denied, is absorbed and transformed, which brings cannibalism and the dialogical principle close together". In other words, the act of translation is seen as a two-way transaction in which, rather than the translator being totally subservient to the ST, his or her agency is privileged, enriching the original text in the process of translation. Transcreation is presented as a mode of translation that "unsettles the single reference, the logocentric tyranny of the original" (de Campos 1997 cited in Vieira 1999, 111) where "translation can be "servitude" and also "freedom" in Vieira's words (ibid.). As we argued in this chapter, game localization, at least in the best case scenario, strives to re-create the player experience in the target version and has emerged as a negotiation between constraints and freedom in a specific manner shaped by the nature of the medium i.e. the software. With the possibility of infinite variability through changes in its software code (Manovich 2001), a game can be transformed in a multitude of ways and different versions created. Furthermore, this involves not only verbal but also nonverbal signs, widening the scope of transcreation beyond words. The application of the concept "transcreation" by Di Giovanni (2008) in highlighting the treatment of visual and verbal elements in contemporary audiovisual texts across distant cultures is therefore relevant here. Her case study addressing Indian films and commercials broadcast in Italy illus-

---

51. Oswald de Andrade coined the term cannibalism in reference to a practice once common among Brazilian Indians (Milton and Bandia 2008, 12). In Translation Studies the concept's circulation owes much to Else Vieira and Susan Bassnet in the context of "cannibalistic translation" in relation to Haroldo de Campos, although Milton and Bandia (ibid.) note that de Campos never used the term "cannibal".

trates the limitations of the concept "translation" in representing distant cultures in audiovisual texts. Di Giovanni's concluding remark provides a useful insight for the current discussion of game localization as transcreation, as she suggests:

> ...the term 'translation' has proven inadequate to account for processes of transfer where verbal and visual language cannot come apart, as images always determine the semantic content and, ultimately, the perception of words. Shifting from translation to transcreation, verbal language has definitely lost its prominence and words have come together with visual references to form broader cultural units.   (Di Giovanni 2008, 40)

In the case of video games, the game world is constructed in the highly structured use of multimedia and multimodality, involving the verbal and the non-verbal. Furthermore, some games may also involve an additional tactile sensory channel via the game interface. The player's action may prompt the game system to give **haptic** (tactile) responses, such as a jolt on the controller (technically called "**force-feedback**") to physically convey the consequence of the action taken by the player in the game, forming part of each individual player's own ludonarrative. More recent game-player interface design concepts such as Kinect even allow the player to use his/her own body to interact with the game, going beyond motion-sensitive controllers such as Wii remote and Move. All of these elements come together to make up the gameplay experience of the player and, as a package, they ideally need to be transferred across to a new locale through game localization. In order to recreate a gameplay experience that is equivalent to that provided by the original, game localization operates at all levels from linguistic manipulations at the micro level to the macro level of the product as a whole, retaining not only functionality but also the intended affective appeal to the end users. In this way, game localization needs to work in a broad framework so as to recreate and relocate the original game experience in the target culture and in a given target player setting in both a technical and a socio-cultural context. In the localization industry this is simply described as retaining a similar "look and feel" of equivalent, locally available products (Fry 2003). To achieve this goal some major game companies such as Square Enix are pushing the boundaries of translation by constantly defying conventions and developing innovative forms of linguistic and cultural mediation most suitable for and afforded by modern games as cultural and technological artefacts.

A broad localization framework entails a transformation involving explicit multi-faceted changes beyond the verbal textual manipulations which have been well discussed in Translation Studies. Game localization introduces manipulations that are not fully explored by mainstream translation theories today other than those generally considered under the concept of "adaptation". As discussed earlier in the context of Translation Studies, the notion of adaptation leaves room for clarification, despite its recent recognition in a more positive light. By comparison, transcreation is less encumbered and is, rather, imbued with a sense of defiance and, most of all, translator's agency, given its historical heritage. As such, it removes the preconceived authority of the original and allows room for another original to be created. As we have seen, some of the extreme cases of game localization could involve all kinds of transformative operations, such as changes to the visual imagery, recreating game properties, including names of weapons and designs of characters, as well as adjustments to elements of the game design, gameplay difficulty levels or other game mechanics. Primarily "video games are changed in any number of ways for distribution in different regional markets" (Corliss 2007). The scope of transformation which game localization allows is such that the practice can even fit the extreme metaphor of a blood transfusion, as in de Campos's conceptualization of transcreation, where "the anthropophagic, transcreative use of the original in order to 'nourish' new work in the TL breaks the notion of faithfulness to the original text as a necessary criterion of translation" (Munday 2009, 8). Some of the examples we discuss in this book can therefore arguably be better represented as transcreation, which still expresses the concept of translation and yet gives way to the fresh avenue of the creation of a new entity. Given the rather broad and vague meaning attached to adaptation, we believe that the concept of "transcreation" better represents the deliberate transformative approaches which are present in game localization, operating at multiple levels and in multimodality to recreate the whole gameplay experience in a new target-user setting.

Turning the argument around, we insist that video games must sometimes be transcreated to retain the same affective appeal of the original game to the end player through multiple sensory channels, incorporating verbal and non-verbal stimuli while taking into consideration several imposed constraints. The overall skopos of translation of the product geared to entertain the end user permits varying degrees of customization which may affect: (1) nonverbal visual signs (character design, background scene, lighting, costume, props, etc.); (2) verbal visual signs (text in graphics, dialogue in written form; UI items, etc.); (3) non-verbal acoustic signs (music, sound effects, etc.); (4) verbal acoustic signs (voiced dialogues, song lyrics, etc.), and (5) kinetic feedback loops with the system responding to the player's input. In an effort to depict the increasing blurring of the borders of AVT, Zabalbeascoa (2008, 29) provides a detailed schema to map AVT texts according to a cline between verbal and nonverbal codes on the one hand, and visual and audio channels, on the other, allowing new AVT products to be accommodated in relation to these double axes. The scope for transcreation applied in game localization can further involve the kinetic dimension gradually extending to the whole human body as system interface. In this way, games as something constructed on a technological platform as software and designed for entertainment, seem to present the most malleable of texts and a type of content that permits almost limitless customization, in turn calling for new concepts required to accommodate such transformations.

These considerations support the characteristic of the medium of digital games as providing an unprecedented breadth of scope for the translator's creativity to be exercised, as is reflected in the term "transcreation". Modern digital interactive entertainment generates a narrative space which provides an exploratory and kinetic play area accommodating individual ludonarrative, where each player is prompted to use sensory channels other than those most traditionally linked to the function of translation as in verbal visual and verbal acoustic signs. It is in the context of these expanded spheres that the concept of "transcreation" can be placed. Here indeed, something so fundamental yet often forgotten about translation which is articulated by Robinson (2003, 142) applies most aptly: "translators don't translate words; they translate what people do with words". Translators need to unpack the play experience potential in the game for a new set of players with different linguistic and socio-cultural backgrounds. Transcreation at times poses a greater risk, as we have seen, because of its extended scope of modification, while the other side of the coin is that translation that is too timid and ST-driven is more likely to fail to convey the excitement and the sense of fun packed in the source/original content. These new dimensions of translating games, which we now call "transcreation", are gradually seeping into game translators' consciousness and are contributing to the formation of professional norms. In order to provide further evidence of the unique characteristics of game localization and to explore its position in Translation Studies, we next examine the broader cultural context surrounding games and its impact on translation practice in Chapter 5.

Cultural contexts of game production
Patronage and rewriting in the digital age

Introduction

In Chapter 4 we analyzed game localization from the point of view of the textual characteristics of games and observed translation strategies and norms, highlighting the translator's agency, which we consider can be explained by the post-colonial concept of "transcreation", albeit in new contexts. Building further on transcreation, this chapter examines macro-cultural contexts as a key factor in shaping game localization. Acknowledging that the production and consumption of video games are deeply embedded in cultural contexts (Rutter and Bryce 2006), we turn our attention to wider cultural issues prevailing in the game industry. We begin our discussion with video games as cultural objects, tracing the development of different game cultures, and we examine the various types of cultural adjustments called for during the localization process. In an attempt to further conceptualize game localization, we draw on the concept of "rewriting" (Bassnett and Lefevere 1990; Lefevere 1992), highlighting the power and control exerted by game companies in the production and distribution of games, forming a new type of patronage in the digital age, following on from our discussion in Chapter 1. In doing so, we illustrate the changing practice of translation, whose boundaries are increasingly being pushed as a result of new technological and cultural artefacts exemplified by video games.

5.1 Video games as cultural products

Examining the evolution of Translation Studies, Jeremy Munday (2012, 297) cautions against approaching the translation phenomena by treating linguistic and cultural dimensions as discrete, creating a "simplistic linguistics-cultural studies divide". It is indeed not our intention to diminish the linguistic aspects, yet the cultural dimensions are manifest in game localization in a distinct way and therefore merit special attention. The cultural turn in Translation Studies (Bassnett and Lefevere 1990; Snell-Hornby 1990) instigated a shift in the focus on translation of text from a linguistic orientation to one that embraced the broader influence of cultural factors. This emphasis of culture in translation theories considered to be an integral part of the dominant descriptive paradigm in Translation Studies (Pym 2010, 149) is particularly relevant in understanding the localization practices of games since their production and use are ingrained in broader cultural contexts. The translator's choices are not only determined by the textual features of games, but are also affected by the way games are produced and decisions made by powerful game companies. Furthermore, to the extent that video games are subject to public scrutiny due to their perceived controversial nature, game localization calls for a consideration of the wider socio-cultural contexts which affect games' reception.

As touched on in Chapter 1, cultural acceptance is something for which video games have had to battle due to their association with "lowbrow catalogues of geek and adolescent male culture" (Juul 2005, 20). Egenfeldt-Nielsen et al. (2008, 132) describe such a status as "a contested cultural niche" in reference to the somewhat precarious position occupied by games in the cultural sphere. All these factors tended to conspire against video games being considered culturally significant. Furthermore, the view held by some sectors of society that video games are addictive and promote violence has continued to undermine the social perception of games. However, with the emergence of social gaming and the growth of casual games, video games are winning over an increasingly diverse range of audiences (Chatfield 2010), beating more established entertainment industries in some countries. The Interactive Software Federation of Europe (ISFE) states on its website[52] under *Industry Facts* that games generate more revenue than the cinema box office or video rental as far as the major markets are concerned. For example, in the UK video games sales surpassed sales of movies, both in cinema tickets and DVD sales, in 2009, with £1.73 billion being spent on games as compared to £1.19 billion spent at the box office and on DVD and Blu-ray sales (Wallop 2009). In 2011 game sales surpassed the combined sales of DVDs and other video formats, as well as music sales (BBC News Technology 2012).

As early as 1982, game designer and scholar Chris Crawford defined the video game as a rudimentary cultural form and today video games are widely considered to be cultural artefacts by critics (see, for example, Greenfield 1996; Jenkins 2003b, 2006; McAllister 2004; Bogost 2006; Steinkuehler 2006). Similarly, several governments officially consider them in cultural terms and provide funding and tax incentives to encourage the local video game industry – this is the case in France, Germany, Scandinavia, South Korea, Japan, and Canada (TIGA 2011),

---

52. See http://www.isfe.eu/industry-facts.

and in Spain (Nae 2009). The European Commission also acknowledged the cultural dimension of video games in 2007 (Behrmann 2010) and UNESCO includes video games on their list of cultural goods among the global cultural and creative industries (UNESCO Institute for Statistics 2005). According to the European Commission, "video games can act as a vehicle for images, values and themes that reflect the cultural environment in which they are created and may act on the ways of thinking and the cultural references of users, especially among young people" (Kroes 2008, 23). In the UK, the British Academy of Film and Television Arts (BAFTA) has been holding a Video Games Awards ceremony since 2003. For TIGA (The Independent Game Developers' Association), the trade association representing the UK video game industry, "[v]ideo games development can be a cultural industry, using creativity, cultural knowledge and intellectual property to develop products and services with social and cultural meaning" (2011, 7). Similarly, the German Computer/Video Game Award (*Deutsche Computerspielpreis*) was established in 2009 by the Federal Government Commissioner for Culture and Media to "to promote Germany's standing as an economic and cultural centre for the young, innovative computer games industry".[53] This initiative is largely attributed to the efforts of the German Cultural Council (Ensslin 2012, 2).

In this way video games have become an integral part of global popular culture. As well as generating iconic characters, such as Mario, Sonic, and Lara Croft, some games have developed a cult following, ranging from well-known series in the 1980s such as *The Legend of Zelda* (1986–) and *Final Fantasy* (1987–), to later titles including the series *Grand Theft Auto* (1997–), *Halo* (2002–), and *Call of Duty* (2003–) in the 1990s and the 2000s. Given the explosive diversity of games in the 21st century it is no longer possible to name a few representative titles. The narrative themes present in these games, and particularly in RPGs and action and adventure games, are in many ways comparable to those found in literary works, and the advanced and photo-realistic graphics used in some modern games make them more akin to films as evident in the term cinematic games. Some critics also consider video games to be an art form because their expressive goals are similar to those of other recognized art forms (see, for example, Jenkins 2005; Smuts 2005; Gee 2006). While this remains a moot point, and many detractors of games may yet be opposed to the idea, there now seems to be enough evidence to support the argument that video games are indeed cultural products (see TIGA ibid.). As video games have become more mainstream, video game culture has also developed.

---

53. See http://www.game-bundesverband.de/index.php/en/topics/financial-assistance-and-awards/the-german-computer-games-award-deutscher-computerspielpreis.

5.1.1 Game culture: Japan versus the US

The term "game culture" is often used by game scholars, journalists, and critics, albeit without a clear definition. It is typically "framed by descriptions of who plays, what they play, and how they play" (Behrmann 2010, 414). Thus, the term is mainly used to refer to the discourse surrounding the consumption of games, such as the way specific groups of players play depending on their age, gender, whether they are hardcore or casual gamers, the game genres they play, the amount of time spent playing, whether they play in a group or alone, etc. "Game culture" is also often used in a broad sense to refer to how games are played in different countries, an issue which is often covered in journalistic discourse but deserves further attention from academia (Mäyrä 2006, 4). From a journalistic perspective, discourse on game culture often revolves around the main differences between Japan's game culture and its counterpart in the West, with the latter often mainly referring to US game culture. The focus on these two main game cultures is due to the importance of both countries in the game industry since its origins, as the main producers and consumers of video games. It should be stressed, however, that these discourses can be rather over-generalized and do not always take into account the different game subcultures existing in a given country, but rather present them somewhat misleadingly as unified wholes. It should also not be forgotten that game localization and internationalization strategies are closely tied to marketing initiatives and therefore they "often reveal more about distributors' motives or preconceptions than the tastes of international game audiences" (Carlson and Corliss 2011, 67). That said, some of these general comments serve to draw attention to a number of relevant trends and differences between Japan and the US in terms of video game consumption and player preferences. In this way, they still shed light on the significant impact of cultural issues in determining the success or failure of games in international markets.

Despite the more recent criticism against the Japanese game industry being perceived in the West as suffering from the Galapagos syndrome (Winterhalter 2011), the degree of success achieved historically by Japanese games in international markets makes them still highly relevant to the study of game localization, especially given their reliance on localization to succeed globally. Furthermore, in order to illustrate the need for adjustments during game localization, a comparison between Japanese and US/Western games can be useful. At the risk of generalizing, the following summary of the literature aims to outline some of the main perceived differences between Japanese and Western game cultures, particularly in the US, as they relate to the cultural adaptation of games.

Preferences for game genres and types

Western players tend to prefer games involving action, such genres as sports, crime, and shooting games, particularly **first-person shooters** (FPS), and they favour depth of graphics and interactivity in a game. On the other hand, Japanese players prefer simulation and narrative-driven games, such as fantasy, adventure and RPGs (Kent 2004; also see Tables 1.2 and 1.5). Certain genres such as **dating sims**, which allow the player to experience the simulated development of a romantic relationship as the main goal of the game, are popular in Japan, but not in the West, where Japanese attempts to introduce the genre have yet to succeed (O'Hagan 2007). Western developers and players tend to favour games tied to licenses and franchises, such as games related to blockbuster movies, e.g. the *James Bond* series or *Ice Age*, or professional sportsmen or teams, such as Tiger Woods. By comparison, Japanese players are generally not as interested in licensed games (Kent 2004). Western players are found to prefer games with a first-person perspective, while Japanese players prefer games played from a third-person perspective, as this makes it easier for them to relate to the game character (Ashcraft 2008a). In addition, Japanese players prefer a linear style of play with more restricted spaces and rules, while Western players like more open, non-linear games, known as **sandbox** games, where they can have freedom to explore with less rigid game mechanics (Kent ibid.; O'Hagan 2009a).

Preferences for game character design and characterization

Japanese video game designers often deploy anime and manga for character design and prefer stylized, cute characters such as Sonic, Link, and Mario. North American and European players prefer more masculine and realistic character design (Pruett 2005; Ashcraft 2008a). Female characters are also portrayed in a less cartoonish manner in Western games, such as Lara Croft of *Tomb Raider* (1996–). Often considered as the first rare example of a non-native game to succeed on the Japanese market, *Crash Bandicoot* (1996) went through discernible changes to the design of the main character Crash to make him slightly softer and more tame-looking, as we detail in a later section. The localized version of the Japanese survival horror game 零 *[zero]* (2001) in turn presents an illustrative example of subtle cultural adaptation of character design to take into consideration the different preferences of the US and European market from that of Japan.

The main character of the Japanese original, Miku, is a seventeen year-old girl wearing a school uniform, but her character was redesigned for the Western versions.[54] She became older, taller, spoke in a more adult manner and did not wear

---

54. For screenshot, see: http://www.fti.uab.es/tradumatica/revista/num5/articles/06/06art.htm.

a school uniform (Di Marco 2007, 2). According to Di Marco, this adaptation of the visuals of the game is an "explicit example of cultural deterritorialization" in which "the 'native' culture of the video game has been deprived of its signs and logos and globalized in order to be more palatable for the American and European audience" (ibid., 3). The game's Japanese developer/publisher Tecmo (Tecmo Koei as of 2009) believed this change would help Western players identify more with the character, which would likely increase sales of the localized version (ibid.). In an interview (Nintendo President Interview Series 2013) the game's director Makoto Shibata explained that the key design focus of Miku's character in the original version was the portrayal of someone in fear. This led to the design of a young female protagonist whose vulnerable psychological state is exploited in the familiar backdrop of the J-horror genre, which has been globalized by the success of Japanese horror cinema (see Picard 2009).

In the context of cultural issues pertaining to game characters, the design of the Asian-looking female protagonist Faith in the Swedish-made game by DICE (EA Digital Illusions CE) *Mirror's Edge* (2008) triggered yet another complicating factor. The original character image had deliberately aimed for "inclusive character design" to defy the hypersexualization of female protagonists in video games and to appeal to both men and women (Owen O'Brien, DICE Senior Producer, cited in blogpost by Brinster December 15, 2009). However, this attempt was somewhat undermined by a fan posting of a modified image initially sent to a Korean message board. It represented an Asian player's perspective, depicting an image of a preferred Asian female character design with bigger eyes and enlarged breasts (see Tang 2009, 35). This image created a surge of responses by gamers the world over, leading to a debate on the portrayal of women in games and the practice of designers from one culture depicting what they consider to be a "more real" character in another culture. In an interview with the MTV game channel, the character's creator Tom Farrer responded:

> I remember when I first had that image sent to me. To be honest, I found it kind of sad. We've spent time in developing Faith. And the important thing for us was that she was human, that she was more real... We really wanted to get away from the typical portrayal of women in games... We wanted her to look athletic and fit and strong [enough] that she could do the things that she's doing.
>
> (cited in blogpost by Stephen Totilo, November 25 2008)

In the meantime the modified image was reportedly well received by most Asian gamers (Tang 2009, 34). In fact, it was speculated that the poor sales of the game in the Chinese market were partly attributable to "the unpopular, original Faith created by Western designers" that was "unappealing to Asians" (Tang ibid.). While it is obvious that some degree of cultural adaptation in localized versions contributes to their success in target markets (Chandler 2005; Edwards 2008b, 2012; Tang 2009), in reality, how culturalization of a game may affect its market reception is not always predictable.

With the cost of game development and localization continuing to rise, the industry can benefit hugely from further research providing more specific insights into how to operationalize the handling of such cultural issues. Gender stereotyping is a well-recognized area of research in Game Studies, with broad social and economic implications for modern video games (Kafai et al. 2008). It is relevant to note that on the box art for all regions[55] of the 2013 edition of *Tomb Raider* (2013) the image of Lara Croft is depicted as a forlorn fighter figure rather than a sexual object, suggesting a deliberate attempt to go against hypersexualization. As we discuss in the following sections, issues such as transgenderism in game characters further complicate the approach to localization as they may also affect age ratings and even lead to censorship. Given the broadening appeal of games to a diverse player population and the increasing number of female gamers, gender-related questions in games will continue to pose significant challenges. This in turn can logically link to the established field investigating gender issues in Translation Studies (e.g. Simon 1996). These cultural questions relating to the characterization of game protagonists in terms of both verbal and nonverbal visual dimensions could form a productive area of localization research for addressing concerns in the game industry.

Cultural tolerance of sexual and violent content
While Western games tend to depict more graphic violence and gore than their Japanese counterparts, Japanese games tend to contain more overt and covert sexual references. As illustrated in a comparative study between the Japanese originals and North American versions of earlier Nintendo RPGs published between 1989 and 1996 (Yahiro 2005, 10–36), Japanese games tend to present a more nonchalant attitude towards issues related to religion and social minorities and in reference to nudity, alcohol, and sexuality. Relatively common references to homosexuality, cross-dressing or transgenderism in Japanese games often have an impact on the ratings of the localized versions, as we will explore later. Adult content games are also well-established in Japan, following the tradition of sexually explicit manga and anime. For example, adult genres commonly known in Japan as エロゲー [erotic games] or 変態ゲーム [pervert games] target mature audiences and are intended for sale on the Japanese market only. Despite their wide circulation in Japan and also elsewhere through fan translations on the Internet

---

55. For screenshot, see: http://kotaku.com/5954369/tomb-raiders-box-art-resists-the-obvious-temptation.

Yahiro's (2005, 374) earlier study indicated a paucity of academic literature in Japan on such Japanese adult games. However, certain rape games have caused great controversy in the West, with games such as *RapeLay* (2006) triggering a UN petition to Japanese authorities for such games to be banned. Western pressure led the Ethics Organization of Computer Software (EOCS), a self-regulated body that rates PC games in Japan, to ban these games, although it was not legally binding (Ashcraft 2009). As far as violence is concerned, Western games tend to be more explicit and sanguinary, while Japanese games usually portray little blood (Kent 2004). It should be noted, however, that Japanese games designed with a Western audience in mind, like the *Resident Evil* series (1996–), contain a considerable amount of gore and violence, although occasionally the violence is toned down in the Japanese original. This is the case in the game *No More Heroes* (2007), where enemies spout ash instead of blood after they sustain sword wounds in the original Japanese release, while the uncensored version was published for the North American market (Plunkett 2007a). Interestingly, the European version was also censored, possibly to overcome a potential German ban by the Unterhaltungssoftware SelbstKontrolle (USK), the ratings body in Germany (Plunkett 2007b).

Cross-cultural game design
Our brief survey of examples illustrates how cultural issues and preferences affect game localization, in some cases posing significant issues which must be addressed in game development. In Kalata's words "[e]very area of a game is heavily influenced by the culture that produced it" (2007, 1), in turn pointing to the benefit of cross-cultural game design. In order to maximize their return on investment, developers strive through the internationalization process to design games with an international appeal that do not require much modification for different territories. For this reason, cross-cultural game design is gaining importance in game development, as its benefit in boosting international sales is apparent. Chandler advises developers to design games that contain UI, characters, and gameplay mechanics that are accessible and enjoyable to players all over the world (Chandler 2005, 26). She also recommends keeping cultural references to a minimum and developing games in as culturally neutral a way as possible, so that it is not obvious for international gamers that the game was primarily developed for an English-speaking audience (ibid., 299). However, academic studies on games have so far failed to "identify a set of universally accepted design guidelines that are useful to developers in designing games for a cross cultural audience" (Chakraborty and Norcio 2009, 13).

In order to explore how cultural influences in game design are perceived by target players, O'Hagan (2009a) carried out a preliminary study using a player interview, a player log and the play trajectory of the localized English version of the

Japanese game *ICO* (2001). Her pilot study identified three main areas where cultural assumptions embedded within game design may have hindered the gameplay experience of the target player, who highlighted the following issues: (1) a limitation in freedom of play; (2) some ambiguity in cut-scenes providing the back story, and (3) unfamiliar narrative techniques. The first point related to the fact that Japanese players generally shy away from sandbox games, and thus Japanese game design may tend to cater to such a gamer preference. The second and the third points were concerned with the narrative structure, which was not familiar to the non-Japanese audience, and was not made clear even when translation was provided. The study focused on how the interpersonal relationship between the two main characters in the game was successfully developed through symbolic means (such as hand holding gestures) rather than verbal means, as intended by game's design, thus eliminating the need for text and translation in localized versions. The study found the use of rich nonverbal communication promising and "one direction of future cross-cultural game design strategy" (ibid., 218). As suggested by this study, involving test players from different target territories in a focused testing setup at the initial stage of the design of a game could provide valuable feedback about the features of game design that work internationally and would allow developers to design games with a universal appeal. This will require willingness in the industry to address cultural differences as a key factor influencing the successful globalization of their game. However, the other side of the coin is that it is cultural specificity that often gives a game its edge and unique appeal. By comparison, games which do not reveal any trace of the cultural specificities (if this kind of total de-culturalization is possible) may risk being received by players as rather bland. The way in which culture is expressed in a game is complex, and no formulaic approach is likely to guarantee an international best seller.

5.1.2   Cultural content in games and cultural localization

While many games are set in fantasy scenarios, and thus typically do not belong to any specific existing culture they are still inevitably embedded in the culture in which they were produced. Game designers belong to specific cultures and reflect certain values and beliefs, to a greater or lesser extent, in their work. For Di Marco, the text of a video game does not consist primarily of language, but of culture with "verbal and non-verbal representation being, in effect, a vehicle of the social and moral background from which a video game is produced" (2007, 2). Zhang also emphasizes the impossibility of dissociating games from the values governing the societies in which they are produced:

> Culture, ideology and even philosophy are embedded in games through sto-
> rylines, rules and interfaces. The features in a game are conceived by the develop-
> ing team (game designers, script writers, graphic artists and others), and their set
> of values and beliefs is in the products they create. All cultures have the concept
> of "entertainment", but what it means to different people around the world or
> what is regarded as funny and exciting is not necessarily universal.   (2008, 47)

It would be difficult to find a completely acultural game, devoid of any overt or
covert references to the culture in which it was produced. For example, culture-
bound humour and intertextual allusions are often found in games across a wide
range of genres other than narrative-oriented RPGs or adventure games. With
the use of motion-capture and the recent motion scan technology in computer
graphics applied in some games, the body language of the game characters may
also reflect the gestures and facial expressions characteristic of the original culture, rendering them in a way which is not always familiar to players from a different cultural background. In particular, given the pronounced cultural distance
between Japan and Asia, on the one side, and, on the other, North America and
Europe, there are usually abundant culture-specific references that may require
attention, especially when localising Japanese or other Asian produced games.
For example, in the Japanese original version of *Final Fantasy VIII* (1999), one of
the villains, Seifer Almassy, wears an overcoat with a left-facing swastika symbol,
which represents good luck in Buddhism. However, this could have been miscon-
strued as a Nazi symbol in Europe, so the localization team advised the localization coordinator to change it. The development team agreed and they designed
a new symbol similar to a fleur-de-lis for the international versions (Di Marco
2006). Another example of a covert culture-specific reference included in the
visuals of a game is found in *Final Fantasy XI* (2002). There is a cut-scene where
an Elvaan prince sneezes while his men are gossiping about him. This is based on
the Japanese folk belief that when one sneezes somebody is talking about them
behind their back. As such, the meaning is immediately clear to those who are
familiar with the local context and the scene has a somewhat comical function in
the original. In an attempt to make the reference understandable and funny to the
US audience, the localized version made it a particular habit of Elvaan people to
sneeze when somebody is talking about them (Edge Online 2006).

   While cultural issues have been identified as also creating localization problems in productivity software (see Chapter 2), they are far more pronounced with
game localization, given the more visual, affective, and occasionally even deliberately controversial nature of video games. The process of cultural adaptation in
games is a particularly significant dimension of the localization process, and it is
referred to by some authors as "cultural localization" (Di Marco 2007; Mangiron

2008), and "culturalization" (Chandler 2005; Dietz 2006; Edwards 2008, 2012). Di Marco (2007, 2) defines cultural localization as:

> [A]daptation of visuals, sound and scripts conceived in one language by members of one culture to another language and another culture, in such a way that they seem at once fully consistent with the assumptions, values and other boundaries and outlooks of the second culture, and internally consistent within the semiotic strategies of the original video game text, visuals and sound.

Mangiron (2008) in turn defines cultural localization as the "adaptation of the cultural content of a game to be able to market it successfully internationally". Chandler (2005) uses the term "culturalization" to describe any cultural issues that require attention, and usually adaptation, for the internationalization of the game. Citing Trainor (2003), Dietz (2006, 9) defines "culturalization" as the adaptation of games "to account for certain cultural conventions and preferences", mainly related to the areas of sex, violence, and religion. For Edwards (2008, 26) culturalization "helps gamers to potentially engage with the game's content at a much deeper, more meaningful level". Expanding this definition she also adds that culturalization is "the ability to discern and resolve potentially problematic issues before the game title goes out the door" (ibid., 27).

Culturalization is also often essential to maintaining the affective appeal of a game in the localized versions and to preserving the player's suspension of disbelief, defined in a video game context as the "tolerance of implausible media content…and the willingness of the public to accept the limitations of the medium and to prevent these limitations from interfering in any way with acceptance of the content offered by authors" (Crosignani et al. 2008, 39). According to Crosignani et al., suspension of disbelief is one of the keys to successful game design, as it allows the measurement of "the cohesion of plot, characters, setting and all the other elements created to fine-tune a winning game experience" (ibid.). Poor localization risks breaking the suspension of disbelief, as they explain:

> One out-of-context expression in a script of half-a-million words can make a crucial difference…That is why localizers must never lose sight of the entire scene, paying particular attention to context, the rhythm of narration, shades of meaning in dialogue and every other minuscule, seemingly insignificant element that might break the spell.   (Crosignani et al. 2008, 39–40)

Undoubtedly, cultural references that are opaque or offensive for players are likely to break their willing suspension of disbelief and prevent them from enjoying the game. In addition, poor localization serves as a constant reminder to players of the fact that the game has not been originally intended for them. In Chandler's words "[i]f end users are convinced that the international versions were planned for them from the beginning, they will be satisfied that they are getting the same game experience as the [originally intended] English-speaking player" (2005, 12). For this reason, Japanese developers of **AAA titles**, such as Square Enix and Nintendo, devote considerable attention to the adaptation of the cultural content of their games. This ensures there are no sensitive issues, oddities, or "culture bumps" (Leppihalme 1997) that may break the suspension of disbelief and affect negatively the reception of the localized game in the target markets.

Edwards (2008) highlights the need to include the culturalization of the original content of a game from the early stages of development in order to avoid damaging the commercial interests and the public image of the companies involved. She cites several examples of games heavily criticized or even banned because they overlooked geocultural issues, such as *Resistance: Fall of Man* (2006), which contained an exact reproduction of Manchester Cathedral without having asked for permission. This angered the Church of England, who strongly oppose violent games, and they demanded an apology from the developer. To address potentially sensitive cultural issues in a game, Edwards (ibid.) suggests trying to identify overt geocultural issues by examining theme, locale, and content type, and looking at issues such as the use of religion, beliefs, ethnicity, gender, historical events, political systems and cultural practices. Once these issues are identified, their severity should be established, distinguishing between overt offence, likely to cause local problems, and reasonable risk, which could cause some minor negative feedback. Game companies are becoming aware of, and are increasingly paying more attention to, cultural, and ideological issues in games. For example, Peter Fitzpatrick, Senior Project Manager in Microsoft Game Studios, confirms that Microsoft spends "considerable time and effort during the development cycle to ensure that insensitive or offensive content is addressed so that the game will appeal to a global audience" (cited in Chandler 2005, 101).

In addition to changes derived from geopolitical issues, culturalization is also triggered by marketing and promotional issues. Game titles, similar to movie titles, are often changed when localizing a game for other territories. For example, the Japanese game 零 [zero] (2001) was renamed *Fatal Frame* for North America and *Project Zero* in Europe and Australia. The original Japanese title reportedly refers to "a void" in reference to the ephemeral presence of a spirit and suggests a play on words, as the original title 零, when pronounced as "rei", is the homophone of the Japanese word 霊 for "spirit" or "ghost". Due to the impossibility of translating this pun, the NA title became *Fatal Frame*, a more transparent and concrete title in reference to the camera that Miku, the main protagonist, uses to fight and capture ghosts. On the other hand, the Australian and European title, *Project Zero*, is closer to the literal meaning of the original Japanese title, retaining the original cynical intent. In reference to previously discussed games, the two Japanese releases *NierReplicant* (2010) and *NierGestalt* (2010), with practically identical content other than some altered character design, are somewhat anomalous cases in which the differences in the titles are mainly motivated by the need to signify a different platform for which each version is released (see Chapter 4). Additionally, the naming of *NierReplicant* derives from the rebel androids called "replicants" in the classic sci-fi film *Blade Runner* (1982) and is an example of intertextuality alluded to in the game title by the developer.

Another element of games that is often adapted for releases in different regions is the box art, as we illustrated with the marked differences for *ICO* (2001) between Japanese / European and NA versions in Chapter 1 (see Figure 1.1). Game fan communities are usually well aware of different packaging and titles used in different regional releases as evident on numerous fan sites.[56] Japanese releases of foreign-origin games may often employ anime and manga style drawings. For example, the original box art for the EA boxing game *Facebreaker* (2008) was replaced with characteristic Japanese anime style drawings for release in Japan. While the original US design, also using a cartoon-like style, focuses on action by a character, the Japanese version with a noir style anime conveys ominous characterization of game characters.[57] Another example of box art localized for Japan which brings noticeable differences to light can be found in the cover for the shooter game *Crackdown* (2007). In the localized Japanese version, retitled as *Riot Act* (2008), all game characters are re-drawn in a Japanese manga-anime style. Furthermore, the main protagonist, a black character, is shown with much paler skin, creating an inaccurate representation that conflicts with the depiction in the actual game. This sort of incongruity gives the impression that the approach to globalization and localization was not entirely streamlined. Even though localization of a game's software may have been undertaken in a well co-ordinated manner, the product's wider collateral such as paratext assets, if showing a major inconsistency, could lead to poor publicity and reception. While the exact reasons for changes made to game box art are not always revealed, the difference in art design used for Japan versus the NA regions points to certain cultural preferences even if they are largely based on the perception of a given game's marketing departments:

–   For the NA market the focus tends to be on actions by game characters while for the Japanese market their characterization is more likely to be the main focus.

---

56. For example, see http://hardcoregaming101.net/japanboxes/japanboxes5.htm from which we drew some of our examples as indicated for the sources of screenshots.

57. For screenshot, see: http://hardcoregaming101.net/japanboxes/japanboxes5.htm.

- Overt anime/manga style in original Japanese artwork may be replaced by more realistic drawing style for the NA market.
- An emphasis on cuteness in original Japanese design may be replaced by some other features stressed for the NA market.
- An abstract image tends to be preferred for the Japanese market whereas the NA market is likely to choose a more concrete image with a specific game character.

Box art for European releases of Japanese games seems to be determined by the localization arrangement and usually follows either the NA or the Japanese design although there are exceptions. Some games such as 零 [zero] (2001) have three different designs released for the PS2, reflecting different titles under which the game is marketed for Japan, the NA, and separately for the European and Australian regions. An example of a different kind of change made especially for the Australian region is the Xbox 360 version of FarCry 3 (2012) in which the art work had to be printed in mirror image in order to avoid the original image being obscured by the relatively large age classification label placed on the left-hand lower corner of the box.[58] As we discuss later in this chapter, such a change is associated with Australia's strict ratings system applied to video games. This is yet further proof that game localization is affected by a broad spectrum of cultural conditioning, manifesting as market-specific issues.

In the context of the many levels of cultural operation applied to game localization, the role of translation is one of cultural mediation, matching the gameplay experience between the original and its localized versions appropriate to the cultural background of the player. To achieve such a goal, the localization team will be required to have a broad understanding of the source culture and be able to detect any covert cultural references in the original, assess them and translate them appropriately for the target audience (Dietz 2006). This includes the recognition of any potentially sensitive cultural issues that may have escaped the developer's attention which could lead to serious consequences such as a product recall in the worst case scenario. As Richard Honeywood, a former localization director at Square Enix (2007), insists, "You don't just need good translators – you need cultural experts". The broad evidence we have presented above of games as cultural products with their cultural implications further supports our claim that game localization underscores the translator's role as an active agent making sense of a diverse range of cultural elements unique to the game's source culture and to the game world and transferring them to a new cultural context.

---

58. For screenshot, see: http://kotaku.com/5907934/see-video-game-covers-in-the-us-are-like-this-and-in-australia-theyre-like-it.

5.2   Cultural adjustments

As we have shown, terms such as "cultural localization", "culturalization" and "cultural adaptation" are used more or less synonymously both in the game industry and in the literature on game localization. They all tend to refer to the process of modifying any elements, verbal and nonverbal, of an original video game that are deemed obscure, offensive, difficult to grasp by the target audience, or perceived as not tailored to them because of some cultural incongruity. These aspects can therefore be considered as being operationalized as cultural adjustments during the localization process. All elements of a game can be subject to such adjustments, which can take place at a macro or micro level. Macro-level culturalization can affect the whole game design; the visuals (graphics and character design), the game mechanics, and the storylines. In particular, the decision to opt for full as opposed to partial localization, thus involving audio localization, will provide further scope for finely-tuned culturalization of the game, with the possible use of regional accents or voicing of text which may have appeared only in written form in the original, for example, as discussed in Chapters 3 and 4. However, given its significant financial and operational implications, audio localization is something which should not be decided on as an afterthought. In the meantime, micro-level culturalization of varying degrees takes place at a textual level, involving changes to the in-game text, the script, the **art assets** (text in graphics), and the printed materials. As indicated in the case study (see Chapter 4) with Square Enix, where the developer and the localization team work closely together in a trusting relationship, the in-house translators are likely to be given more freedom to make changes in the treatment of cultural factors. While culturalization is motivated by an attempt to increase enjoyment of the game in a given market, it can be seen as a primarily commercially-driven operation, including factors such as retaining a brand image. Culturalization of games indeed involves a wider sphere of consideration, most of all legal issues. In reality, the marketing departments of publishers are typically involved in decisions affecting changes at macro level, such as the title, the box art, or some of the visuals of a game. The localization department is usually behind cultural adaptation at micro level, although it may also be able to influence decisions about macro-level modifications, as in the case of Square Enix.

Successful localization strives to transcend technical and linguistic localization and to encompass the customization of the cultural content of a game when this is required to facilitate the gameplay experience of target players, and ultimately the success of a product in a target territory. Langdell (2006, 206) stresses the fact that good localization is "far more than just selecting the best words to replace the language of the original game design", especially in view of the fact that games are increasingly being "adapted to entertain completely different cultures". Bernal-Merino (2008d, 64) further insists that game localization must be "completely geared towards the user":

> Game publishers need to bring not only the language, but also the characters and the whole game experience closer to the player. The place of origin or the language of development is not relevant to video game fans. The game has to be not only linguistically, but also culturally tailored since it is not going to tell just any story, but the player's story.

The interactive nature of the game, with the player ideally becoming fully immersed and creating his or her own ludonarrative, makes cultural elements even more important. Furthermore, compared with other cultural products, freedom of expression in games is subject to various rules, as we will examine next. Cultural adjustments in game localization therefore encompass a range of operations which may be mandatory or optional, or rather subject to ideological or pragmatic considerations.

5.2.1   Mandatory requirements for change

In addition to including territory-specific content for target versions, developers and publishers must ensure that the game and its content conform to mandatory territory-specific requirements and regulations. Legal teams in publishers always perform a thorough check of the content of a game before it is released, to make sure it complies with all local regulations regarding violence, explicit sexual content, references to drugs, etc. In some countries, such as Germany, Australia, and China, government bodies perform a comprehensive check of games to confirm that they comply with their legislation, as we will explain in more detail in the following sections. In addition, legal teams devote a lot of time to checking the content of games for potential copyright or trademark infringements, as law suits are both common and costly in this industry. When translating games developed in other territories, the possibility of overlooking a potentially problematic issue increases, such as when a particular name or trademark may not be registered in the target country. For example, the Californian company Buzz Entertainment, developer of a line of electronic trivia games found in bars and restaurants, filed a law suit against Sony Computer Entertainment Europe (SCEE) for trademark violation because of their use of the name *Buzz!* as the title of a quiz and trivia game series developed by Relentless Software and published by SCEE (Sinclair 2008). It is essential that localizers remain alert to potentially contentious issues in the original game and report anything which arouses suspicion, so that the legal team can check it. Another example concerns the name of a main character in the original Japanese version of *Final Fantasy IX* (2000) called ジタン (Jitan), which was transliterated as Zidane in the US version. This posed a potentially contentious issue for the FIGS versions, as it is also the name of a famous French football player, so translators requested permission to change it for some of the European versions to avoid a potential problem (Mangiron and O'Hagan 2006, 17–18). Similarly, in the remake of the 1987 NES fighting game *Punch-Out!!* (1987) for the Wii platform, released in 2009, the name of one of the characters, the Japanese-born Piston Honda, was changed to Piston Hondo, probably to avoid any trademark issues with the Japanese car manufacturer, despite the fact that 'Honda' is also a common Japanese surname (Giantbomb n.d.). Interestingly, Capcom's *Street Fighter* (2008–) series has a character called Honda which is retained in this game, while the Mike Tyson inspired character M. Bison had its name changed to Balrog for all Western versions for fear of potential legal issues (Lundin, personal communication, January 27, 2012). It is also interesting to note that the North American version of *Punch-Out!!* was released as *Mike Tyson's Punch-Out!!* (1987).

Other territory-specific requirements are related to sensitive geopolitical issues, such as naming or territorial disputes (Edwards 2007). For example, the sea between Japan and Korea is known as the "East Sea" in Korea rather than the "Sea of Japan". In order to be able to publish a game that contains a reference to this sea, it should be named according to the naming tradition in the target country (ibid.). Another territory-specific adjustment consists of using different varieties of the same language for different territories, an established practice in software localization. In the case of the English language, some games have separate North American and UK versions. For example, the *Final Fantasy* series, when localized in a post-gold model, is first localized into US English, and subsequently all written assets (UI, subtitles, textual graphics, etc.) are adapted to UK English usage and spelling. The different usage in English words in NA and the UK could lead to a serious issue if a particularly negative connotation attached to a certain word or expression in one territory goes unnoticed for a release in the other (see 4.2.2.2). The only assets that remain in US English in the case of this series are the audio files of the voiceover dialogue, due to the high cost of audio localization. Furthermore, the division between the NA and the UK versions also occurs at a technical level due to different regional coding of software / hardware and because of different TV standards (see under 'Region lockout' in Section 5.3).

5.2.1.1 *Rating systems*
The wide variety of games available on the market addressed to different audiences, as well as the public demand to control the distribution of games to protect young players, led developers, publishers, and distributors to form associations to rate the content of games. Their main objective is to protect children and ensure

that games with graphic depictions of sex, violence, drug use, or bad language clearly indicate this on their packaging to ensure they do not reach an under-age audience. In general, most countries reject games which contain very graphic violence or explicit nudity, racism, and drug-abuse (Chandler 2005, 26–27). Games with a high level of graphic violence are controversial, and are occasionally banned by governments or withdrawn from the shelves by retailers, such as *Manhunt 2* (2007). The main goal of this third-person **stealth action game** is to kill as many people as gruesomely as possible. This game was banned in Australia, New Zealand, and Ireland, and received an 18+ rating in the US, while in the UK it received an 18+ rating only after the original game was refused classification and an edited version was resubmitted.

Due to the well-known strict German regulations regarding video game content, many companies release a toned down version of their games for Germany. For example, the German version of the online multiplayer game *Team Fortress 2* (2007) contains no blood and no body parts scattered on the floor after an assault; these are replaced by hamburgers, metal springs, etc. (Lundin 2009). Interestingly this puts German players at a disadvantage because they are unable to tell whether they have hit an enemy because nothing has replaced the removal of blood to confirm the strike. In order to overcome this problem, German fans started to reverse the changes to the original versions by using **bloodpatches**, which are "small programs that unlock the blood and violence levels present in the US version of the game" (Dietz 2006, 131). By doing this, gamers manage to bypass the censorship applied to games in Germany and play the same games their counterparts in other European countries play. It is also relevant to note that in June 2009, all 16 German interior ministers requested in the Bundestag that the production and distribution of all violent games be banned in Germany. The call was made shortly after a 17 year-old committed mass murder in the German locality of Winnenden in March 2009. However, German gamers came out in force against this ban and managed to collect almost 70,000 signatures for an online petition (Gadget Boy 2009). According to German legislation, any online petition with 50,000 or more signatures must be reviewed by the Bundestag, so the ban was finally not implemented. This example highlights the volatile nature of games which, from time to time, leads to moral panic from the general public and in turn a backlash from the fan community.

Below we provide a brief introduction to some of the main rating bodies; further details of their classification systems can be found in Chandler and Deming (2012, 35–42). These systems serve an important purpose in the game industry and they are often closely associated with the cultural values prevalent in specific territories.

Pan-European Game Information (PEGI)

PEGI provides a single common age-rating system in Europe. According to their official website,[59] PEGI "was established to help European parents make informed decisions on buying computer games". It is a self-regulatory body launched in 2003 and supported by console manufactures, publishers, and most developers in Europe. Game developers and publishers are not legally obliged to submit their games to be rated, but in practice they all do (Chandler 2005). PEGI replaced several national rating systems in order to provide a single and unified rating system for Europe. The age rating system it uses was developed by the ISFE (Interactive Software Federation of Europe).[60]

PEGI provides access to their database online, where parents can check the age ratings for a game or all games classified for a particular age. The site also includes statistics about ratings. Interestingly, of all the games rated by PEGI from its establishment in 2003 up to the end of July 2011, 49% of the games sold in Europe were rated 3+ [3-year-olds and over], 22% were rated 12+, 13% were rated 16+, 11% were rated 7+, and 5% were rated 18+. These figures illustrate developers' and publishers' desire to try to reach the widest possible market: only 5% of games were rated for mature audiences, as well as the fact that the majority of published games are actually not as offensive as many people may think. In addition to the ratings for console and PC games, PEGI also rates online games (Chandler and Deming 2012, 39) and some game applications for mobile phones, such as iPhone.

Unterhaltungssoftware SelbstKontrolle (USK)

In place of PEGI, German law states that all video games must be submitted to the USK,[61] a government body which assigns ratings. The ratings are very similar to those used by PEGI, with the exception of the "No age restriction" rating, which corresponds to 3+ in PEGI, and the "Age 6" rating, which corresponds to 7+ in the PEGI system. The rating system in Germany is very strict and, according to Chandler (2005, 33), developers planning to release a game in Germany should adhere to the following guidelines to prevent their game from being banned or rated 18+:

---

59. For more information about PEGI, see http://www.pegi.info/en/index/.

60. For more information about ISFE, see http://www.isfe-eu.org/.

61. For more information about the USK, see http://www.usk.de/.

- Remove blood and gore: blood should be removed or changed to a different colour, the most frequent being green, and parts of dead bodies and full corpses cannot be shown on the screen.
- Avoid use of profanity: profane language should be omitted.
- Avoid use of symbols associated with racial hatred: this is particularly strict in relation to the use of Nazi symbols, except in the case of a game set during World War II.

The USK check is very thorough and includes game code, packaging, manual, **cheat codes** (tips that allow players to succeed in different tasks and missions), and **walkthroughs** (step by step guides of all the actions that need to be taken in order to complete the game). If any offensive content is found, the game is sent back to the developers for modification and resubmission to the USK. If the USK is not satisfied with the changes, the game could be banned (Chandler ibid.).

Entertainment Software Rating Board (ESRB)
In the US, Canada, and Mexico, the ratings board is the ESRB, a self-regulatory body established in 1994. The ESRB also offers the facility to search for the ratings of games online. Of the 1,638 ratings assigned by the ESRB in 2010, 1% received an EC (Early Childhood),[62] 55% an E (Everyone) rating, 18% received a T (Teen) rating, 21% received an E10+ (Everyone 10+) rating and 5% received an M (Mature) rating. This shows a similar trend to the ratings applied in Europe by PEGI. The ESRB also rates games for Android, iPhone, and Windows Mobile 7 mobile operating systems.

The Computer Entertainment Rating Organization (CERO)
Drawing on the ESRB as a model, Japan's CERO[63] was established in 2002 as a non-profit organization with the aim of informing cunsumers of the nature of games and their suitability for different ages (Watanabe 2010, 5). CERO uses a letter- and colour-based classification, with five ratings: A (black): suitable for all ages; B (green): suitable for ages 12+; C (blue): suitable for ages 15+; D (orange): suitable for ages 17+, and Z (red): suitable for ages 18+. The classification for younger audiences is the widest one compared to other rating boards, as it comprises ages from 0 to 11, as opposed to the PEGI and ESRB systems, both of which subdivide this group into three categories. In addition, CERO uses the following nine content descriptors: romance, sexual content, violence, horror, alcohol/tobacco, gambling, crime, drugs, language/other.

---

62. The EC category is for content intended for young children as compared to the E category.

63. For more information about CERO, see http://www.cero.gr.jp/.

The Australian Classification Board (ACB)
The ACB[64] is the rating body in Australia, replacing the former Office of Literature and Film Classification (OLFC) which dissolved in 2006. Like USK in Germany, the ACB is a government body and its decisions are legally binding. If a game is refused classification, it cannot be sold in Australia. The ACB classifies video games into four categories, colour-coded according to the impact level of their content: G (green): General, the content is very mild; PG (yellow): Parental guidance, the content is mild; M (blue): Mature, the content is moderate in impact; and MA 15+ (red): Mature Accompanied, the content is not suitable for people under 15, who must be accompanied by a parent or adult guardian. It is interesting to note that the highest rating allowable for a game in Australia has been 15+ until 2012, while the other rating boards include an 18+ classification. The game industry in Australia has reportedly[65] been lobbying to introduce the 18+ category (R), given that the average gamer age in Australia is around 28. An R18+ rating came into effect as of January 2013 as indicated by ACB on its website.[66] Decisions such as this by the State highlight a dilemma between moral issues and commercial interests.

The Entertainment Software Rating Association (ESRA)
The newest ratings system is the ESRA[67] launched in November 2010 and established to be applied to games distributed in Islamic countries as of January 2011. The unique characteristic of the ESRA is that it is not based on one particular national classification law but rather on the Islamic faith (Plunkett 2010). It uses the ratings criteria developed by Iran's National Foundation of Computer Games in terms of violence, nudity, substance use, and sexuality (including sexual deviancy). The launch of the ESRA can be seen as demonstrating the seriousness of the impact that digital games are having on religion.

5.2.1.2   *Differences in ratings*
In order to be able to publish their games in different territories, developers must ensure their games conform to the specific ratings system applied in the countries where the localized game is to be released. Based on their cultural values,

---

64. For more information about the OCB, see http://www.classification.gov.au/Pages/Home.

65. See the interview with Chris Hanlong, CEO of the Interactive Entertainment Association of Australia (IEAA) at http://ie.xbox360.ign.com/articles/809/809043p1.html.

66. See http://www.classification.gov.au/Pages/News/1January2013R18classificationfor-computergamesstarts1January2013.aspx.

67. For more information about ESRA, see http://www.ircg.ir/sn/pages/id/23/pt/full/lang/en.

different countries have different levels of tolerance and acceptance of violent or sexual content, and each country tends to have its own ideas about what is acceptable for a particular age group. All these factors need to be taken into account when planning the international release of a game. Germany and Australia are two countries with particularly strict rules and censorship of video games, while Japan has a more permissive attitude towards references to sex and the consumption of alcohol and tobacco. References to all of the above may sometimes be found in Japanese games rated as suitable for all ages, but they often need to be removed or toned down in the localized versions for other countries if the same age rating is to be obtained.

However, a somewhat liberal attitude regarding ratings is observed in some target markets. Di Marco (2007) takes the case of the game *Paper Mario: The Thousand Year Door* (2004), showing the way in which cultural transformations are applied when Japanese games are localized into English. In this game, Vivian, one of the Shadow Sirens (Mario's enemies), is transgender. This information is revealed in an argument between Vivian and her older sister, Marilyn, who clearly says that Vivian is a man, and therefore cannot be one of the sisters. This game received an A rating in Japan, which means it was suitable for all ages. However, European localizers noted that a game with a reference to transgenderism was unlikely to receive a 3+ rating by PEGI. Nintendo decided to modify the dialogue by replacing the reference to transgenderism with one to a sex-change operation, which still allowed the original flavour to be maintained. In the Italian version Vivian states that she has turned into a woman, and this small change was deemed enough to obtain a 3+ rating for this particular game from PEGI (ibid.).

By comparison, despite publishers' efforts to obtain the same ratings across different countries, occasionally this is not possible due to the varying territory-specific requirements. For example, *Final Fantasy XII* (2006) was rated A (suitable for all ages) in Japan; T (13+) in the US, as the ESRB considered that it contained alcohol references, fantasy violence, mild use of offensive language, partial nudity, and suggestive themes; 16+ by PEGI, which considered that the game contained realistic-looking violence, and M (mature) in Australia because it includes moderate violence. The fact that different territories have different attitudes towards certain issues as illustrated above makes it crucial that game localizers have an acute cultural awareness and that they are able to detect the elements in the original games that may be controversial in the target territory from a ratings point of view. Once localizers have identified the potential issues, they should alert the publisher, who can assess the best way to proceed, editing the game as required or releasing it for a different, older audience in the target market.

It is also important to note that sometimes the same title may be awarded different ratings in a given territory, depending on the platforms for which the game is published. For example, the game *Ghostbusters* (2009), developed by three different US-based companies for different platforms, has different content depending on the target audience of the given platform, and consequently it was awarded different ratings; it obtained a rating of 12+ for the PS3 and the Xbox 360, and a 7+ for the Nintendo Wii, the DS and the PS2. According to Lovell (2009), this is due to the fact that the different platforms have different target audiences. While the Wii, the DS and the PS2 tend to appeal to a younger audience and are more family-oriented, the PS3 and the Xbox 360 have a much older user demographic. For this reason, the game platform on which a game is released becomes another factor to be taken into account when localizing a game, especially if the same rating is sought for all platforms and localized versions.

Another example is the American action game *Saints Row: The Third* (2011), which made the headlines because of its graphic sex toy depicting genitals.[68] This led to issues with the Japanese ratings body CERO on the grounds that the object in question violated the CERO guidelines on the depiction of genitalia. Compared to the CERO's rating of the game as Z (Ages 18 and up), its US counterpart ESRB gave it M (Mature 17+), subtly lower than its highest Adults Only (AO) category for audiences of 18+ (equivalent to the CERO Z rating). Furthermore, while this particular element reportedly caused a stir in Japan, it was not controversial in the US. Given that there are many adult-themed games developed and published in Japan, the Japanese reaction to this particular game seems somewhat incongruous. At the same time, Nintendo's strict internal criteria applied to their games for release in North America and Europe are implemented through their local companies, i.e. Nintendo of America and Nintendo of Europe. These examples serve to demonstrate that the notion of age criteria is company-specific as well as country-specific. Standardized universal criteria are something of a misnomer, particularly given the inherent cultural bias in assessing foreign-made content based on different cultural systems.

5.2.1.3 *Censorship in games*

The relationship between translation and censorship has attracted much attention in Translation Studies. It has been explored by scholars from different angles, such as self-censorship (e.g., Brownlie 2007; Tymoczko 2009) and institutional censorship (e.g., see Rundle 2000 for censorship in Fascist Italy, or Merino and Rabadán 2002 for censorship in Franco's Spain). There are also studies focused on the application of censorship to different types of translation, such as literary translation (see the volume edited by Jones 2001), the translation of children's literature

---

68. For example, see http://www.technologytell.com/gaming/80212/saints-row-the-thirds-sex-toy-weapon-is-making-headlines/.

(e.g., Thomson-Wohlgemuth 2007) and audiovisual translation (e.g., Díaz-Cintas 2003; Vandaele 2007). Billiani (2009, 28) defines censorship as:

> [A] coercive and forceful act that blocks, manipulates, and controls cross-cultural interaction in various ways. It must be understood as one of the discourses, and often the dominant one, articulated by a given society at a given time and expressed through repressive cultural, aesthetic, linguistic, and economic practices. Censorship operates largely according to a set of specific values and criteria established by a dominant body and exercised over a dominated one; the former can often be identified with either the State or the Church, or with those social conventions which regulate one's freedom of choice at both public and personal levels.

In the case of video games, censorship is mainly applied by regulatory and government bodies who refuse classification to a game, making its sale and distribution illegal in a particular country. When this situation arises, developers and publishers have two options: (1) to withdraw the game and not release it in that particular country, or (2) to edit the objectionable content or remove it from the game and resubmit it, in the hope of obtaining a classification and being able to publish the game. For example, the game *Ghost Recon 2* (2004) was banned in South Korea by the Korean Media Rating Board (KMRB) since it considered the story to be too "extreme and sensitive for the Korean market" as it involves a North Korean general trying to consolidate his power (Chandler and Deming 2012, 41). For the same reason more recently the shooter game *Homefront* (2011), depicting a fictional military occupation of the US by newly united Korea set in 2027, was banned in South Korea.

Certain countries have strict regulations about content prohibited in video games. Germany's strict law against the use of the swastika led to a recall of the German localized version of the World War II shooter game *Wolfenstein* (2009), which inadvertently left one swastika faintly visible in the game. Comparisons[69] between the original version, which was rated as M by the ESRB in the US, and its German version, rated as 18 by USK, illustrate a large number of changes having been made in order to conform to the USK standards. Nevertheless, the game's publisher, Activision, decided not to take a chance, given the severe penalty for violating German law. In turn, in China any content "endangering the unity, sovereignty and territorial integrity of the state" is forbidden (Zhang 2008, 48). Games that do not follow these regulations are banned in China. For example, *Hearts of Iron* (2002) was prohibited because Tibet and Taiwan were not shown as Chinese

---

69. Among the websites showing comparative screenshots is: http://www.schnittberichte.com/schnittbericht.php?ID=5982811.

territory (Edwards 2008). *Football Manager* (2005) was also banned because it included Tibet, Taiwan, and Hong Kong as available teams, thus granting them a status equal to that of China (Zhang 2008). Australia is another country known for its strict regulations. The Australian game *Escape from Woomera* (2004), developed as a "mod" of *Half-Life* (1998), provides a relevant example where the game was used as a vehicle to address a political agenda by activists protesting against the conditions of the immigration centre in Woomera (Apperley 2008, 227). In this case a particular controversy erupted especially due to government funding which had been provided to support this game development project as an artistic expression by the New Media Arts Board through the Australian Council of the Arts. The subsequent criticism by the Federal Minister of Immigration for funding such a project resulted in a highly publicised case. Apperley (ibid., 227) suggests the heavy handed approach by the government to what seemed to be a small local project is "appreciable", considering Australia's stringent policy applied to all video games imported into Australia and given this particular project involved modding of a foreign game. However, Apperley is critical of the attitude of the Australian government in extending its restrictions to video games not only for the original purpose of protecting children but also for controlling certain anti-establishment views, leading to the effect that "video games must also be detached from any suggestion or possibility of artistic or political critique" (ibid., 227).

Aside from being state imposed, censorship can be self-imposed by the developer or the publisher of a game for commercial and marketing reasons. They may self-censor some of the content of a game to avoid sensitive issues that could cause a backlash and damage their public image. During the mid-1980s and the early 1990s prior to the establishment of the ESRB Nintendo of America (NOA) was well-known for its strict voluntary censoring practices (Nintendo's Censorship n.d.). Japanese games released for the North American market used to undergo a thorough check by NOA for sexual references and nudity, discriminatory references, gratuitous violence, the illustration of death, domestic violence, and abuse, the use of excessive force in sports, ethnic, religious, nationalist, or sexual stereotypes, profanity, and obscenity, use of drugs, tobacco, and alcohol, and overt political messages (ibid.). NOA used to heavily adapt Japanese games for their release in North America, removing any elements they deemed problematic. For example, they covered a nude statue in *Super Castlevania 4* (1991) and removed red crosses from hospital signs and nurses' caps in *Earthbound* (1994) and crosses from tombstones in *Ducktales* (1990) (ibid.). NOA's rather paternalistic attitude was probably due to the fact that their target audience were primarily children, although it might also be attributed to the prevailing negative view of games by the general public at the time. Once the ESRB was established in the US in 1994, game companies were for the first time able to target their games to different age groups, which led to the relaxation and almost disappearance of in-house censorship practices such as those of NOA (ibid.). Still, both NOA and Nintendo of Europe are known to apply a certain level of internal censorship especially regarding religious issues (Tinnelly, personal communication, 15 February 2012). Similar approaches are taken by other publishers who decide not to release a game in a given country or recall it in order to prevent further damage to their reputation and presence in that territory. For example, *Kakuto Chojin* (2002) was banned in Saudi Arabia and other Muslim countries because of an audio track that contained the vocal chanting of a verse from the Qur'an. The heavy criticism the game received, together with its lack of commercial success, led Microsoft to eventually recall the game globally and discontinue the production (Edwards 2008). Similarly, two references to Qur'an verse in the licensed background music used in *LittleBigPlanet* (2008) led to a recall and a delay in releasing the game in Europe (Bramwell 2008).

As in other types of translation, self-censorship can also be applied by the translators themselves. In these cases, translators intervene in the text and remove the contentious element or tone it down for ideological reasons or the fear that the target audience may find a particular reference offensive or unacceptable. Sometimes translators manipulate or remove the element perceived as problematic if they feel that it portrays the original culture in a negative light to the target audience. For example, in the Japanese original version of *Final Fantasy XII* (2006) one of the **non-playable characters** (NPCs) is introduced as a transgender member of the imaginary Seeq race. As mentioned earlier, such game characters frequently appear in Japanese games and are received as unproblematic in Japan. However, they are usually considered politically incorrect elsewhere. For this reason, in the North American and the FIGS versions this character was turned into a woman in translation, with the approval of the development team.

In practice censorship is applied to video games not only by the state authorities but also by several agents, such as the translator, the localization coordinator, the reviewer, and the legal and marketing departments of the publisher. For console games, the **platform holder** also has the authority not to license a game, which effectively means banning it. In addition, government ratings bodies, where they exist, have the final say about the type of content that is permitted and the content that is censored in a game. Different countries are sensitive to different issues, depending on their historical, political, religious, and ideological backgrounds, as well as their cultural values and expectations. For example, the US-origin game *Fallout 3* (2008), a sci-fi action RPG set in a devastated post-nuclear world, was subject to censorship for different reasons in different territories. In Australia, the game was originally refused classification by the ACB because of the realistic representations of real-life drug use portrayed in the game. An edited version of the game was subsequently resubmitted and obtained a classification of 15+. The developer, Bethesda, decided to release this edited version worldwide, so that players from English-speaking territories would be able to play exactly the same game (Ellison 2009). For the Japanese market, however, the censorship was self-imposed by the developer because of sensitive contexts related to the portrayal of nuclear warfare. The **side quest** "Power of the Atom", in which the player has the option of destroying an inhabited area with a nuclear bomb, was removed from the game. In addition, they changed the name of a weapon, "Fat-Man", a mini-nuke launcher, because of the real-life referent i.e. the nuclear bomb detonated over Nagasaki during World War II (Snow 2008). They also reduced the amount of blood and corpses displayed in the game (ibid.), in consideration of Japanese gamers' sensitivity.

While many gamers were not happy about the edits made to *Fallout 3* (Ashcraft 2008b; Prakash 2008), the game would have undoubtedly aroused a major controversy in Japan if it had been released unedited. For the Indian market, the censorship was applied by Microsoft, the Xbox 360 platform holder, who decided not to release the game there "in light of cultural sensitivities" (Prakash 2008). The specific reasons for not releasing this game were not revealed, although the widespread speculation is that the game features two-headed mutant cows called "brahmin", the name of a revered cast of Hindu scholars and preachers. In addition, the portrayal of cows, which are sacred animals in India, could also have been considered offensive. Rather than releasing a game that could offend the religious beliefs in the target culture and damage Microsoft's image, they opted not to release the game in that market. Another technique sometimes used by game companies is to include a filter as a user option within the game in a manner akin to parental censorship. For example, *Call of Duty: Modern Warfare 3* (2011) is rated as M (Mature) in the NA region, but the game also offers the option on the menu to filter bad language and gore marked as "explicit content". When this option is selected the game is free of swearing, blood, etc.

Interestingly, however, as observed by Edwards (2012, 22), it is in fact often non-gamers rather than gamers who generate cultural controversy. While stressing the importance of the cultural awareness of game developers, Edwards (ibid.) is critical of a certain "unintended audience" with "a negative predisposition towards games" who are prone to stir up a cultural backlash, even though these are typically people "who don't play games, who don't understand the content-context relationship between the game world and real world". This point can be linked to a case discussed by Apperley (2008, 226–227) in reference to the game *Marc Eckō's Getting Up: Contents Under Pressure* (2006) set in a dystopian world with graffiti as the main means of mobilizing the masses against the authoritarian police state. The game had been initially granted an MA15+ rating in Australia, against which the Queensland Local Government Association successfully appealed to have the game banned. Part of the context of this argument relates to the authority's fear of promoting graffiti and other anti-social behaviour in the tourist region. Citing the review board record, Apperley (ibid., 227) compares the reasons given by those saw the game as serving to "glamorize and normalize the crime of graffiti" with the dissenting opinion in support of the initial classification, pointing out that the game is "escapist and has been designed as entertainment".

This case relevantly portrays divisive perceptions surrounding video games. Nevertheless, if public opinion condemns a game, it can cause considerable damage to the reputation of the developer, publisher, and platform holder. It can also lead to major retailers withdrawing the offending products from their shelves in order to appease the general public. However, unlike censorship applied to other media and types of translation, censorship in video games can sometimes be relatively easily circumvented by end users purchasing **grey imports** with uncensored versions from other regions or downloading illegal copies from the Internet. In the case of PC games, fans can also create mods or **patches** that reveal the edited or cut elements. The nature of digital technologies and the widespread availability of various tools on the Internet have empowered users of new digital media and provided them with ways of reversing the censorship applied to games by the State, the platform holders, or the developers themselves.

As regards the question of why games are subject to a much stricter control and censorship than other media such as films (which can also include extremely violent content), it is probably because of games' interactive nature, involving the player's active decision-making and participation. A player is seen as an active agent in the game, as opposed to a passive spectator even in fictional scenarios. In the above Australian case, Apperley (ibid., 226–227) adds how the game's interactivity was perceived by the review board as "training simulations" to train "a person in crime". Furthermore, the fact that children often have access to games not suitable for their age because of loose parental control has also raised controversy and has possibly resulted in stricter control and increased censorship being applied to games in some countries. Finally, the fact that games still do not enjoy unreserved endorsement from the general public as an art form, on a par with cinema or literature, might make them more susceptible to limitations imposed in terms of freedom of expression. Interestingly, the Japanese ratings body CERO's charter states that its goal is to "judge games in light of the ethical standards of society … *while paying the utmost respect to freedom of expression, for the sake of the sound development of computer entertainment culture* [our emphasis]" (Watanabe 2010, 9). As such, it unambiguously indicates CERO's dual role of safeguarding the interests of the general public, on the one hand, and the freedom of expression of the game industry, on the other. Yet, as was the case in Australia cited above, the higher government authority could overturn the stance represented by the ratings boards.

5.2.2 Market-driven adjustments: Market relevance and preferences

Adjustments in view of cultural contexts are not always initiated by official regulations. In order to publish and sell their products internationally some developers may deliberately seek universal themes and then customize the games for the target markets by including territory-specific content for each market to increase the relevance of the game to the market. For example, the *SingStar* series (2004–), a sing-off video game where players compete by singing along with the music to score points, is culturally localized at a macro level for different territory releases. Each game contains approximately thirty tracks, and some of the European localized versions such as the Spanish, the Italian and the German versions include popular hits from the target country so that players are generally familiar with them. There is also some degree of customization in the versions for English-speaking territories. For example, the version of *SingStar Rocks* (2006) released in Australia includes hit songs from Australian bands such as Men at Work. Another example of a series of games whose content was adjusted to be relevant to particular target territories is the *Buzz!* series (2005–) of quiz video games. In particular, the game *Buzz! Brain of the UK* (2009) has 21 regional varieties, including the original UK version, with different titles and content, but based on the same concept: a quiz about how well the players know their own country and culture (Relentless Software 2009). Car racing games are also subject to territory-specific adjustments. Games designed in Japan, with right-hand drive vehicle handling settings often need to be modified for North American and European markets (except the UK and Ireland). For the game *Tokyo Xtreme Racer* (1999), developers also included popular US-import car parts in the version for North America, and arranged a promotional deal with an import car magazine (Pitts cited in Chandler 2005).

As one of the few early examples of a foreign game successfully breaking into the Japanese market, the *Crash Bandicoot* (1996-) series illustrates the benefit of taking cultural considerations seriously. The game became the first foreign console title to break the sales record in Japan by exceeding 500,000 units by May 1997 following its launch in December 1996 (Thayer and Kolko 2004, 481). Spurred by media speculation in Japan that this game, with its strong American flavour, would not succeed in the Japanese market, the game's American development team redesigned it based on feedback from Japan, especially from the game's publisher Sony (Carless 2004). The changes involved making the main character's appearance less threatening, as well as lowering the game's overall difficulty level by adding hints (Thayer and Kolko 2004, 481). The change in the design of the main character also included a modification from three claws and a thumb in the original US version, the style set by Disney and most Western cartoons, to four claws and a thumb in the Japanese version typical of Japanese *anime* characters (Kehoe and Hickey 2006). Edwards (2007, 29) believes the modification is mainly due to various negative connotations associated with four fingers in Japanese cultural contexts. Another interesting modification that Sony requested for the Japanese version of *Crash Bandicoot* was the replacement of the music for the battles against **bosses** with less nostalgic and more "video-game like" music according to Japanese expectations (Crash Mania 2008). Thayer and Kolko (2004, 481) attributed the title's record breaking success in Japan to "a significant localization effort that combines original cultural elements with country-specific elements" while the exact process of modification was driven by the nature of this particular game. They concluded:

> Clearly, for that game to succeed in the Japanese market, the localization effort had to produce a new game, one that hundreds of thousands of Japanese people would purchase and play repeatedly. But their choices and design processes did not follow any particular prescribed industry standard for localization.   (ibid.)

The situation remains much the same today as regards the difficulty of non-Japanese games breaking into the Japanese market. It is indeed difficult to work out any precise formula for adjustments of cultural content, while the formula for failure would be to totally ignore cultural contexts. Localized games have to be entertaining without being offensive and yet need to retain unique characteristics which are present in the original game, making the game appeal to the player. Precisely because of the difficulty in establishing exact prescriptions for a successful approach, developers and publishers generally pay considerable attention to the feedback they receive from players, either directly, via focus groups or beta testing, or indirectly, through the comments that are made on fan forums and game review sites. For example, after receiving feedback from a focus group, developer, and publisher, Square adapted the game mechanics of the North American version of *Chocobo Racing* (1999) and reduced the level of difficulty of the final race by placing guard rails in strategic locations in order to prevent falls (Edge Online 2006). Similarly, Nintendo decided to make changes to the design and the storyline of the localized version of *Advance Wars: Days of Ruin* (2008)[70] based

---

70. Interestingly, the original Japanese version was never released after several cancellations (see http://en.wikipedia.org/wiki/Advance_wars_days_of_ruin), which might be explained by the fact that war games tend to be more popular in the US and Europe than in Japan.

on feedback from Japanese players of previous titles in the series, feedback on previous North American versions, and feedback from the localization team. As a result the North American version became darker and more sombre, in order to meet US players' expectations of a war game (Nutt 2008).

In the age of viral marketing, where virtual word of mouth spreads instantaneously online, the influence of users and the value of their feedback should not be underestimated. Game production and game consumption are at the heart of game culture, where the two sides are intrinsically connected. In comparison with other types of translation the feedback loop in game localization between the translator and the translation user can be potentially much more immediate and tangible. In particular, cultural issues are something which could affect the player in a significant and lasting manner and they justify the investment of time and effort by the production side. In such endeavours users become a central focus, in some cases, over and above other commercial considerations. Chapter 7 further discusses the metaculture of gamers and their direct interest in localization and translation issues, sometimes to the point of voluntarily undertaking game localization projects themselves when they deem that the official versions are not delivering what the gamers want. We next discuss the issue of the control and power applied by major game corporations under whose direction game localization needs to operate and their impact on translators' transcreative contributions.

5.3   Culture of game production: Power game

The wider cultural contexts surrounding the production of games make it clear that the game industry operates in a complex web of relationships which involve players as actively engaged users of games at one end, and the general public at the other, who may act as watchful commentators on any cultural or moral issues present in games which are perceived to be problematic. From the perspective of the game industry the general public can be considered often ill-informed about games due to their lack of actual playing experience, in contrast to seasoned gamers as "informed" outsiders. Nevertheless the opinion of the wider public can influence certain internal decisions by game companies on the production side, which may subsequently affect localization in a significant manner.

On the basis of our earlier discussions of the practice of game localization, this section further highlights the influence on translation of various controls exerted by dominant global game corporations. As we discussed in Chapter 1, the way in which the console sector in the game industry is structured creates particular spheres of influence by a relatively small number of organizations. Similar to the book publishing world, game publishers play a critical role in the game industry, financing and marketing games and, furthermore, developing games, as the majority of game developers are either fully or partially owned by publishers (Kerr 2006b, 43). Unlike the relationship between the original and its translation in literary publishing, the technical nature of a video game inherently links localization to game development, creating a triadic relationship between the game localizer, the developer, and the publisher (see Figure 1.5). This in turn only confirms the extent of the control wielded by the current three main platform holders – Nintendo, Sony, and Microsoft – who are also game developers and publishers with in-house localization divisions. These three corporations can be seen to be in an extremely powerful position to manipulate and control games and their localization decisions, particularly through the added means of technology. For example, certain game hardware and software are region-coded, restricting their use outside the assigned regions. These companies control not only the content of a locale, but also the release dates of different language versions and the platform on which the game is to be played. In their game publishers' role they decide which region will be prioritized in terms of the release timing and also the level of localization (see Chapter 3). In this way the extent of the control applied by major game organizations, especially the current three platform holders, in interactive publishing seem to far surpass that of literary publishers. We revisit below some of the main localization practices (described in Chapter 3) from the point of view of the specific types of control exerted, both implicitly and explicitly, by game companies in relation to their impact on localization.

Region lockout

Due to the different TV standards used in different parts of the world, one way in which the main console game markets are broadly divided is in terms of PAL (Europe/UK/Australia) and NTSC (North America/Japan) regions.[71] As a result the difference between the NA version and the UK version of a Japanese game – although both in English – relates not only to the spelling and the variety of English used, but can also be discussed in terms of NTSC and PAL versions respectively. In addition to the technical significance of the different region codes for the localization process, these versions enable control of consumption of different localized versions of games. Some consoles have what is known as **region lockout**, as opposed to being region free. For example, PS2 consoles designed for Japan will not work in Europe when connecting to the local PAL-standard TV. This also

---

71. More precisely, the main regions are: (a) Asia (NTSC-J); (b) North America (NTSC U/C); (c) Europe and Oceania (PAL, PAL/E) and (d) China (NTSC-C). For more information see, for example, http://reviews.ebay.com.au/What-is-Region-Coding-on-Video-Games_W0QQugid Z10000000011951829.

applies to game software that can only be used with the specified regional version of the console. Whereas PS3 Blu-ray disks are region free, PS2 disks are region locked. Region locking therefore controls the distribution of region-specific versions of games. For the same reasons, online stores such as Amazon will not deliver games with region lockout beyond the designated region. The same policy is used for distribution of films on DVD, where the same films may be released at different times in different regions and region lockout will prevent them from being viewed in other regions.

Exclusive versus multi-platform titles
Another form of control can be seen in exclusive titles, where games are made exclusive to a particular game platform to ensure platform loyalty, although some initially exclusive titles may subsequently be made available to other platforms. The case of the International Edition of *FFXIII, Final Fantasy XIII Ultimate Hits International* (2010) suggests that these decisions are made according to a particular commercial strategy between the publisher and the platform holder. According to the game's developer/publisher Square Enix this title, only available in Japan, was made exclusive to the Xbox 360 platform (see Table 5.1), allegedly taking into account Japanese players who only own an Xbox 360 (cited in Kietzmann 2010). However, at the time Japanese gamers who owned Xbox 360 seemed to be a relative minority (CESA 2010, 124). The Xbox 360 exclusive release therefore indicates a deliberate strategic decision by the platform holder and the publisher

Table 5.1 *Final Fantasy* series release timeline

Title	Initial platform	Japanese original	North American version	European version	International edition (JP market only)
FFVII	PS	Jan. 1997	Sep. 1997	Nov. 1997	Oct. 1997
FFVIII	PS	Feb. 1999	Sep. 1999	Oct. 1999	N/A
FFIX	PS	Jul. 2000	Nov. 2000	Feb. 2001	N/A
FFX	PS2	Jul. 2001	Dec. 2001	May 2002	Jan. 2002
FFXI	PS2, Xbox 360, Windows (MMORPG)	May 2002	Oct. 2003	Sep. 2004	N/A
FFX-2	PS2	Mar. 2003	Nov. 2003	Feb. 2004	Feb. 2004
FFXII	PS2	Mar. 2006	Oct. 2006	Feb. 2007	Aug. 2007
FFXIII	PS3, Xbox 360	Dec. 2009	Mar. 2010	Mar. 2010	Dec. 2010 (Xbox 360 only)
FFXIV	PS3, Windows (MMORPG)	Sep. 2010	Sep. 2010	Sep. 2010	N/A
FFXIII-2	PS3, Xbox 360	Dec. 2011	Jan. 2012	Feb. 2012	N/A

Source: Updated from O'Hagan (2009c, 156).

to increase the platform loyalty in Japan. The publisher Square Enix used to be closely linked to Sony in developing and publishing games for PlayStation® but the changing nature of the relationship is evident. As previously mentioned (see 4.3.2.2) a similar strategy may be noted with the Japanese release of *NierGestalt* (2010), as an exclusive title for Xbox 360, in addition to *NierReplicant* (2010) intended for the Japanese market on PS3. These decisions clearly affect the gamers as the consumers of the product, by making certain games not available to them unless new hardware is purchased. The gamers' concerns and dissatisfaction are often aired in game discussion forums, indicating their awareness of the control applied by game companies.

Sim-ship versus post-gold model
The different release timing derived from the sim-ship and post-gold localization models can also be considered as a type of control. As explained earlier, most major Western-produced games tend to be sim-shipped, whereas Japanese AAA titles have tended to be released in a post-gold model, although more recently near sim-ship is increasingly being practised. Aside from the relative lack of translator resources to translate directly from Japanese into European languages, part of the reason for opting for post-gold releases against the sim-ship model possibly relates to the degree of perceived cultural distance between Asian markets and North American/European markets. Perhaps for the same reason Western publishers do not always sim-ship Asian versions of games while releasing FIGS versions, for example, simultaneously. In the context of video game products North American game culture is considered far more similar to its European counterpart than to game culture in Japan, as we discussed at the beginning of this chapter. Other likely reasons for the delayed uptake of sim-ship by Japanese publishers are the size of the Japanese domestic consumer-base being traditionally relatively large, creating a self-sufficient market. However, these market conditions are changing, with the Japanese market shrinking and the global market growing in significance (Parish 2012). As a result, the general global trend now is to sim-ship games (Schliem 2012).

In order to illustrate such trends towards sim-ship among Japanese publishers, Table 5.1 shows in chronological order the time-delay between release dates of consecutive versions of J-RPG *Final Fantasy* series with the lag clearly becoming shorter with more recent titles. Overall, the gap between the NA and the European versions is shorter than that between the original Japanese and the NA releases with the exception of the MMORPG titles (*FFXI, FFXIV*). As explained earlier, this approach based on the post-gold model will become less common in future with both platform holders and publishers aiming to release all versions with a minimum time lag. Such decisions will be made by these powerful stakeholders, with translators having to adapt to the new reality of their changing working environment and conditions.

Full versus partial localization
The decision made by game companies on the extent of localization to be applied to a given game is another type of control. While the recent trend as reported from GDC 2012 (Schliem 2012, 8) seems to suggest a shift towards full localization, publishers will determine the approach based on economic factors especially with text-heavy titles. In the case of major Japanese games, the large North American market is usually served not only first but also by full localization including voiceover, whereas European versions are often only subtitled, as in the case of the *FF* series so far. When the NA or UK version of a Japanese game is used as the basis for subsequent European versions, the pivot locale can be considered to have a greater influence than the original in terms of the number of subsequent locales directly derived from it. In this way, it may serve to mask the Japanese origin whether or not this is the publisher's intention, although most seasoned gamers tend to be aware of how the mode of translation bas been applied (Newman 2008, 61).

Release of special editions in a particular market
The *Final Fantasy* series' developer/publisher Square Enix release what they call an "International Edition" or "Final Mix Edition" for some of their popular game titles exclusively for the Japanese market, as touched on in our case study in Chapter 4 (see Figure 4.4). As shown in the last column in Table 5.1, this further illustrates another type of control applied by certain game companies. This "reverse localization model" (O'Hagan 2009c) or "recursive import",[72] is used by a number of Japanese game companies other than Square Enix, albeit not on a regular basis. These editions exploit the different "look and feel" resulting from a localized version of the original Japanese game in order to re-release it back to the Japanese market as a separate new product. In the case of Square Enix, these editions are usually based directly on the games' North American versions and are designed for the benefit of Japanese players who enjoy discovering the differences made in the NA version (Square Enix 2004, 40), seeking the "feel of a foreign movie" (ibid., 598). While these games' UI elements are all in Japanese, the English voice track of the NA version is retained with additional Japanese subtitles. This means that apart from a few differences, the game is practically identical to the original release. And yet, the International Editions are presented as separate, even enhanced products in some ways (O'Hagan 2009c, 2012a). These

---

72. For more information and a list of recursive import examples see: http://tvtropes.org/pmwiki/pmwiki.php/Main/RecursiveImport.

particular editions serve to demonstrate the nature and the use of digital technology, opening up new avenues for product development, which allows "continuous content upgrades" and improvements made "through a different language version" (O'Hagan 2009c, 160). A reverse localization model shows how technology-savvy game companies are quick to exploit software's malleable characteristics in direct manipulation of the localization process.

This section revisited some of the globalization/localization approaches which are widely used in the game industry in order to demonstrate how they can be traced to specific controls applied by game companies who commission translations. These controls are facilitated by the nature of modern video games as technological and cultural artefacts to manipulate the distribution and production of differentiated versions. By extending the discussion on a range of controls exerted by game companies to define game localization, the next section applies the concept of translation as "rewriting", chiefly based on Lefevere (1992). This allows us to shed further light on how translation is influenced by different power factors, and also on the reception of translated games, shaping the landscape of the new digital-age translation ecosystem. We will build on this discussion to further support our view of the translator being at the heart of game localization as a creative agent.

5.4   Game localization as rewriting

In their influential volume *Translation, History and Culture* Susan Bassnett and André Lefevere (1990) made it plain that translation is best considered against a complex backdrop of "power and manipulation" (ibid., 12). In introducing a major shift in approaching translation from the earlier linguistic-orientation to one which stresses culture, they used the concept of translation as "rewriting" in reference to the literary system:

> 'Translation' ... is one of the many forms in which works of literature are 'rewritten', one of many 'rewritings'. In our day and age, these 'rewritings' are at least as influential in ensuring the survival of a work of literature as the originals ... One might even take the next step and say that if a work is not 'rewritten' in one way or another, it is not likely to survive its publication date by all that many years, or even months. Needless to say, this state of affairs invests a non-negligible power in the rewriters: translators...   (Bassnett and Lefevere 1990, 10)

The above statement made over two decades ago is still applicable to today's technologized and globalized world, where we can replace the word "rewriting" with "localization" and "literature" with "digital entertainment media". The concept of "rewriting" can be useful to shed light on game localization by highlighting the significance of culture, power, and manipulation. Lefevere (1992, 2) discussed how those who are in a position of power can influence the literary system and can therefore "rewrite" literature. In particular, he acknowledged translation as a significant type of rewriting with considerable influence on readers. In proposing the concept, Lefevere's main concern was about the "general reception and survival of works of literature among non-professional readers" (ibid., 1), by which he meant "the majority of readers in contemporary societies" (ibid., 6). Modern video games and their localized versions may today reach tens of millions of recipients, as demonstrated by recent examples such as the *Call of Duty* franchise (see Prologue) or the success of the casual game *Angry Birds* (2009). The impact of games is indeed spreading among heterogeneous groups of players worldwide, supporting the view that game localization is a significant and influential contemporary mode of rewriting, exposed to a sizable and wide ranging global audience.

Furthermore, just as rewritings are considered to be "produced in the service, or under the constraints, of certain ideological and/or poetological currents" (Lefevere 1992, 5), game localization is indeed subject to various constraints, including ideological issues sometimes coming from the public and sometimes from the game industry, while the current "poetology" can be seen to exert an influence on the basis of game genre and type of narrative. Even though the "popular" nature of the game products may mask the concern of poetology (loosely defined by Lefevere [ibid.] as "dominant concept of what literature should be"), the fact that narrative-oriented AAA games tell a complex story sometimes in excess of 100 hours of playtime exposed to tens of millions of players suggests that it is not trivial. This in turn has raised awareness among some game companies of the need for professional writing standards, not only in the original games but also in their localized versions (Gamasutra Podcast 2006). This has led to an additional specific editing process often carried out by professional writers, over and above the translation process itself, as we discussed in Chapters 3 and 4. This seems to suggest that such writers are applying and expected to apply the "poetics dominant in the receiving literature" (Lefevere 1992, 41) relevant to the particular game, as well as the narrative genre conventions. In Chapter 4 we further considered ludonarratives, where players interactively contribute to the unfolding of a story on a technological platform, inducing their own story. While the fact that games are also technological objects adds further new twists and challenges to the concept of "rewriting" as elaborated by Lefevere (1992), we argue that the concept is still highly relevant to this relatively recent translation practice serving the contemporary interactive digital entertainment industry.

Rewriting acknowledges and advocates manipulation (Lefevere 1992, 9) and it also highlights the presence of different forces which affect translation. We have observed the various types of control used by game companies under which the translator needs to operate. The game industry is indeed controlled by powerful game (interactive) publishers, who also develop games under their own labels as in the case of Square Enix and Electronic Arts (EA) among others. Furthermore, as we discussed, the control exerted by Sony, Nintendo, and Microsoft over console manufacturing as well as game development, along with publishing and game marketing and distribution can be seen as constituting a kind of "patronage" as discussed by Lefevere (1992). Lefevere includes publishers as an example of patronage, and therefore we argue that interactive publishers – especially the three platform holders – can be considered as part of the game industry patronage system. We can consider the concept of "rewriting" as operating at both macro and micro levels in game localization. On a macro level, interactive publishers in control of the regions, forms, and timing of releases of games can be seen to be governing the distribution of localized games with region-specific adjustments. For example, a US game company may release a more or less unmodified version of a game in the UK market while it prepares a version for Germany with a reduced blood and gore level. In this process, the German localization team is likely to be directed to systematically tone down verbal expressions of profanity or racial hatred in translation, while accompanying graphics will also be suitably adjusted. In the meantime, Australian and Chinese versions may also have specific dimensions of the game adjusted in respect of censorship considerations. Thus, the game will exist not only in different language versions, but in versions reflecting certain different ideological stances, even if these differences may result more directly from the force of regulations than from the interactive publisher's own philosophy. At other times some publishers may decide not to make changes to meet the German or Australian regulations on the basis of their own belief in publishing a certain game, at the risk of having the game banned in those countries.

In other cases some of the changes made in a locale can be considered as driven by a given publisher's corporate stance, such as Nintendo exercising a strict in-house censorship system according to its own company values. Some such changes may be motivated by a desire to retain a certain company "image". Lefevere (1992, 4) refers to the significance of "creating images" through rewriting and explains how translation can arguably be the most influential type of rewriting "because it is able to project the image of an author and/or a (series of) work(s) in another culture" (ibid., 9). In the context of games, an interactive publisher may indeed demand, for example, the deletion of sexual or violent content or the use of discriminating words in the original work as well as in localized versions in an attempt to portray the image of a more family-oriented company. The concern about the reception of their products in different markets and the subsequent image which may be created of the company can be illustrated by their swift action in withdrawing certain products from the market. Game companies are most wary of repercussions among the wider public as well as gamers, and this sometimes leads to a costly yet voluntary recall of games, as was the case with Microsoft with *Kakuto Chojin* (2002), Nintendo's Wii *Mario Party 8* (2007) and *MindQuiz* (2007) by Ubisoft as mentioned earlier. In today's electronically connected world any negative publicity could go viral. The issue with *MindQuiz* was raised on a talkback radio by a Belfast woman with a disabled child who happened to discover the offending word when she was playing the DS game (Richards 2007) (see 4.2.2.2). This kind of publicity is extremely damaging to a company's reputation and image, thus to be avoided at all cost.

As we stress throughout this book, game localization was chiefly a game industry invention for globalizing highly technological cultural products, generally uninformed by any existing norms of translation. The process used today resulted from a long period of trial and error, with a number of distinctive approaches shaped by specific characteristics of the medium and also industry requirements. One such example is game localization itself providing an opportunity to incorporate improvements in the order of sequential releases, as in the case of the post-gold model, so as to capitalize on the nature of software which can be upgradable by a changing of the code. These manipulations are in part based on the reception of the previous release of the product in a preceding target market. Such a practice seems to fit the concept of "rewriting" proposed by Lefevere (1992) as a means of accommodating the updates resulting from the different major forces and dominant literary style of the time, although here it is being applied to games produced within a relatively condensed time span.

Perhaps one area where the passage of time can be detected in Bassnett and Lefevere's discussion of rewriting (1990, 10) is their focus on "rewritings in the written medium" with the concept's extension to the film genre being presented as "one pole of a future 'translation/rewriting studies'". This is indeed the case with game localization as the production of a multimedia and multimodal product. In particular, in the context of video games as transmedia (see Chapter 1), for which game localization provides further evidence of a form of "rewriting" in order to create a re-entry point for users to savour a previously known work in a new way in a new media format. Games as transmedia, with an explicit link made between games, literature, cinema, music, or comics, also provides the opportunity for rewriting sometimes canonical works. For example, Tolkien's *The Lord of the Rings* has been made into several versions of video games, especially following the success of the film trilogy (2001–2003) by Peter Jackson. Apart from the fact that Tolkien's work has always been considered as forming the prototypical basis of RPGs, video games as transmedia are providing game companies with new opportunities for rewriting the canon across different genres and media. However, freedom of adaptation is conditioned by the type of license the game company may obtain. For example, while the game publisher Sierra obtained the book rights to *The Lord of the Rings* without the rights to the films, EA gained the film rights but missed out initially on the book rights (Deaf Gamers 2011). This situation affected their respective transmedial creations of the games, conditioned by the nature of the rights. Another film tie-in example is the game *Watchmen: The End is Nigh* (2009). This title was released as a prequel to its film version, which in turn is based on the original graphic novel series. The game's link to comics was made apparent by the use of comic-strip sequences within the game while two playable characters – Rorschach and Nite Owl – were voiced by the same actors who played these protagonists in the film version.

The link between games and films is clearly intensifying, blurring the boundaries between the previously separate entertainment genres. *Peter Jackson's King Kong* (2005) published by Ubisoft was developed based on Jackson's film version in collaboration with Jackson, who is also a gamer. His creative contribution to the game design is reported to have further brought the gameplay experience closer to that of cinema, for example, by replacing the health bar typically used in games to display a character's health, with the screen changing to blood-red when a player is attacked (Holson 2005). Considering the ever increasing capacity of video games to immerse players using stories and enhanced game mechanics, facilitated by high-definition graphics and sounds, it can be argued that the avenues for rewriting in the context of transmedia are widening. At the same time, given the already established readership of aficionados with their expectations from the book or film, rewriting in transmedial transactions is always constrained. These examples demonstrate how game companies can be seen as contributing to a contemporary system of patronage to propagate a new form of entertainment through localization as rewriting, exerting more influence on the distribution of rewritten products. The view of the controlled distribution of games as rewritten artefacts for which translators exercise their agency by way of transcreation facilitates an understanding of the game localization paradigm far more clearly than the ill-defined term "adaptation" can signify.

In summary, we have applied the concept of "rewriting" to game localization while also drawing on the notion of "patronage" to understand the location and the nature of power which influence the localization practice. When treated as a form of rewriting, game localization can be seen as a series of iterations in response to various constraints and forces. The role of powerful game corporations that both protect and dictate game localization practice was considered to effect something akin to the idea of patronage. Above all, our goal was ultimately to further explain and solidify our claim that game localization is a mode of transcreation. Lefevere's (1992, 8) view of the role of rewriters clearly highlights the fact that they rewrite "to make [the originals] fit in with the dominant, or one of the dominant ideological and poetological currents of their time" and ultimately rewriting "manipulates, and it is effective" (ibid., 9). Given the complex nature of game products themselves, which are in turn positioned within the specific structure of a dynamic game industry, transcreation cannot be fully understood without acknowledging the wider environment within which games are localized by teams of specialists working under specific constraints. In the end, it is their collective creation which makes it possible to deliver a sophisticated modern technological and cultural artefact which meets the internal approval of the patron and also the external approval of gamers. In this process, professional norms and expectancy norms may constantly collide and be negotiated before eventually being reshaped. Despite less than ideal conditions imposed by different parties, translators' contributions are an essential factor behind internationally successful games that engage gamers in diverse geographical locations. Game localization as rewriting highlights the translator's active role in finding innovative ways to transmit the essence of game play experience from one culture to another. In the next chapter we focus on the issue of the training required for this specialized area of work, catering for the needs of this dynamic and creative industry.

Pedagogical issues in training game localizers

Introduction

This chapter focuses on pedagogical issues concerned with the training of specialist translators and localizers who will work in the field of game localization. In
particular, it approaches the subject of training on the basis of a social constructivist approach to translator education (Kiraly 2000). We first provide information on game localization as an emergent professional activity, focusing on the
industry's needs. We then discuss translation competence, course design, and assessment practices in some detail, drawing on limited existing literature on game
localization pedagogy. The issue of teaching resources and the difficulty of gaining access to authentic materials for teaching are also considered, as they form
one of the major challenges in creating game localization training content. Finally,
we briefly address the introduction of game localization into a university curriculum with reference to the debate on vocational versus academic approaches
to translator education.

6.1 Game localization as an emerging professional translation activity

The increasing success of the game industry is reflected in the high demand for
localizers, who until now mainly had to learn game localization skills on the job
in an ad hoc manner, due to the lack of formal training available (Bernal-Merino
2008c). Despite the rapid expansion of the game localization industry and the existence of numerous translator training programmes offered by universities around
the world, most undergraduate programmes do not include game localization in
their curriculum as a fully-fledged subject. At postgraduate level, however, there
are a number of institutions in Europe offering game localization courses (see the
Appendix for relevant courses in Spain). It should also be noted that, due to the
relative youth of the industry and of localization as a professional practice, there is
some terminological variation relating to the job titles game translators are given
by the industry, similar to the terminological variation we explained in Chapter 1 in relation to the term "video game". In particular, this relates to the blurred

distinction between translation and localization as discussed in Chapter 2. For example, the terms "game localizer", "game translator", "localization translator", and "localization specialist" are all commonly used in the industry and this is reflected in the terminology used in job ads for this field. We therefore use the terms "localizer" and "translator" interchangeably.

There are currently no professional associations of game localizers, but the International Game Developers Association (IGDA) has a Localization Special Interest Group (SIG) (see Introduction and Chapter 1) to bring together the game localization community. Their goal is:

> to provide a focal point and nexus for the growing number of game localization professionals in order to build community, ... draw together best practices and processes, as well as emphasize the requisite international dimension of game content development towards the goal of improving global game development processes and local end user experiences.　　　(IGDA Localization SIG n.d.)

Joining the Game Localization SIG[73] is a good way of meeting other professionals and people working in the game industry, as well as of keeping up to date with the latest developments in the field. In relation to the form of employment, most game localizers are freelancers working for localization agencies or directly for their client. Some of the major developers and publishers such as Blizzard, Square Enix and Nintendo, have a localization department with some permanent staff, and also a portfolio of freelancers who work on site when there is more than one project running at the same time. They may also outsource some small-scale projects to game localization vendors. In terms of working conditions, salaries for freelancers on a contract tend to be higher, but in-house employees have the security of a permanent job as well as various benefits. Freelancers working directly for major developers and publishers who localize their products using the in-house model usually have to work on-site for the duration of the project, which could be anything from a month to a year. From our experience in the industry, many of the freelance localizers working on-site tend to be relatively young early to mid-career translators. Other developers, like Sony Computer Entertainment Europe (SCEE), have a localization department which oversees and coordinates localization into different languages, but the actual translation of the game assets is outsourced to seven or eight specialized vendors (Ranyard and Wood 2009).

While some companies do not require previous professional experience in the field they emphasize that applicants must be avid gamers, and they consider a solid knowledge of game culture to be more important than translation expertise in the area. This has clear implications for training, as it is important to include in

---

73. For more information, see http://www.igda.org/wiki/Localization_SIG.

the design of courses some degree of familiarization with the game industry and the history of games, as well as making students play different games, in order to introduce some gaming experience. Gameplay experience is particularly necessary when translating "blind-folded" without any contextual information, as a gamer is more likely to be able to guess the right context for a given string than somebody who has never played a video game.

Game localizers can get started in the field in several different ways. One involves applying for work directly through specialized game industry employment websites.[74] Similarly, the vacancies sections on developers' and publishers' websites often feature localization jobs. Candidates are likely to have to do some kind of test to demonstrate their aptitude and skills for the position. Usually tests include the translation of different text types related to games, together with some proof-reading and a review of a translated text. In our experience, if a test contains two or three mistakes, such as an extra blank space between two words, a punctuation error, an orthographic or a typographic mistake, the candidate is likely to fail the process, even if the translation is good. In addition, good writing ability in one's mother tongue is considered of paramount importance in this industry. Another way of getting started in game localization is to begin as a linguistic tester (see Chapter 3 for a description of the role). This allows future game translators to become familiar with the game industry, different game genres, and the terminology used in different platforms, and provides a solid foundation to start working as a localizer in this sector. Vacancy advertisements for linguistic testers can usually be found on developers' and publishers' websites, as well as on the game industry websites mentioned above.

Finally, university-industry partnerships in the form of internships can be very beneficial for both future translators and game localization companies and should be fostered when possible. For example, the M.A. in Audiovisual Translation at the Universitat Autònoma de Barcelona provides students with the possibility of internships with game localization vendors. This is a relatively easy way for students to gain a foothold in the game localization industry, hone their translation skills, and specialize in this field. Localization vendors can also benefit from the work of trainees who have specialized knowledge on translation and interest in the game industry and who usually become accustomed to the company's work practices quickly and efficiently. Once the internship finishes the students often continue working for the company, either at in-house or outsourcing level.

---

74. Such websites include http://www.gamejobs.com/, http://www.gamesjobnews.com/, or http://www.gamesindustry.biz. The site http://www.toplanguagejobs.co.uk/ also has a section on translation and interpreting jobs that features ads for game translators occasionally.

6.2   Training future game localizers

Translator training is largely a 20th century phenomenon, with a wide array of university training programmes having been developed worldwide since the late 1980s and early 1990s (Pym 2009).[75] In addition, the topic of translator training has attracted the attention of translation scholars[76] who have debated the best approaches to education in the field. The debate usually centres on the competences to be developed in translation programmes, so that training matches the needs of the industry and students are well equipped to embark on a professional career when they graduate.

Among the scholars who have addressed this topic, one of the most influential has been Don Kiraly (2000) with his social constructivist approach to translator education. Kiraly advocates a student-centred approach based on active learning, whereby students are empowered to reflect and construct knowledge and the teacher adopts the role of the facilitator. Kiraly's approach attempts to provide an alternative to the teacher-centred, content-based transmissionist approach which has traditionally predominated in translator training, in which the teacher conveys the knowledge to students, who adopt a more passive role and are not encouraged to develop critical thinking or learner autonomy. For Kiraly, traditional translation classes not based on authentic texts and real world situations are unmotivating and disempowering. He stresses the need to use authentic materials and reproduce real-world tasks and also emphasises the benefits of group work and collaboration to reflect professional translation practice in the classroom. Like many others who advocate this approach, we also use a constructivist framework based on Kiraly and refer back to his work when discussing game translators' competences, course design and assessment practices.

The issue of training localizers for the software industry has attracted scholars' attention since the late 1990s.[77] However, to our knowledge, there is practically no

---

75. For a detailed account of the history of translator training as well as an overview of the different types of courses available, see Pym (2009).

76. For more information on translation pedagogy and training, see, for example, the following dedicated volumes: Dollerup and Loddegaard (1992), Dollerup and Lindegaard (1994), Kussmaul (1995), Dollerup and Appel (1996), Malmkjær (1998, 2004), Hurtado Albir (1999), Kiraly (2000), Schäffner and Adab (2000), Hung (2002), Baer and Koby (2003), González Davies (2004), Kelly (2005), Tennent (2005), Kearns (2006, 2008), and Pym (2009).

77. See, for example, Pym (1999, 2006), Freigang (2001), Zervaki (2002), Altanero (2002, 2006), Kosaka and Itagaki (2003), Mata (2004), Marazzato (2005), Muzii (2005), Bermúdez Bausela (2005), Guzmán (2005), Biau and Pym (2006), Esselink (2006), Folaron (2006), O'Hagan (2006a) and Thelen, van de Staaij and Klarenbeek (2006).

literature relating to the training of game localizers, except for a few articles (i.e. Bernal-Merino 2008c; Granell 2011; Vela Valido 2011). Several factors can account for this, such as the relatively recent establishment of game localization as a streamlined industry practice. In addition, as has already been mentioned, training in game localization is still not widely available at university level, mainly due to the fact that universities cannot always adapt quickly enough to the demands of new specializations (Bernal-Merino 2008c). More precisely, Bernal-Merino (ibid.) identifies five main problematic areas hindering the introduction of game localization in translation curricula: (1) the lack of time and interest of staff; (2) the relatively small number of professionals working in the area; (3) the required investment in technology; (4) the difficulty in establishing industry-academia partnerships due to lack of time on both sides and the confidential nature of the game industry, and (5) the difficulty in obtaining authentic materials due to copyright issues (ibid., 144–145). In addition, the fact that some institutions hold a rather traditional view of translation – focusing on literary, scientific, technical, or legal translation in their courses – has probably also contributed to the slow introduction of game localization training in university translation programmes. However, the landscape is rapidly changing, and an increasing number of universities currently offer game localization courses.

Bernal-Merino (2008c) also makes several suggestions towards encouraging the introduction of more game localization courses, such as developing new programmes that meet market needs and inviting professionals to give talks and seminars to students on a regular basis. Furthermore, he argues that universities should arrange work placements for students, invest in technology (such as TM tools), and establish industry-university partnerships, by which the industry would provide some authentic materials and the universities would provide adequate training for students (ibid., 145–150). While some of these solutions, such as technology training with TM, have already been adopted in many translation degree programmes, others might prove difficult to put into practice at a time when many higher education institutions are rationalizing resources and reducing the number of courses and modules offered to students. Aware of this reality, Bernal-Merino (2008c) proposes a three-tiered approach to the introduction of game localization courses in existing translation programmes, consisting of:

1. *Introduction of different types of projects*
   Bernal-Merino proposes four types of projects, which he names according to the type of assets that need to be localized: (1) box and docs; (2) partial localization; (3) full localization, and (4) translating a multilingual game website. The first type of project, consisting of translating the manual and the text in

the game packaging, is the easiest to replicate in the classroom, as it is purely text-based.

2. *Introduction of text types and formats*
   Students are introduced to a variety of text types and genres using manuals, web resources, screenshots, and text files, all containing different text types, such as narration, instructions, technical specifications, promotional discourse and legal agreements. This allows students to familiarize themselves with the correct terminology, to apply documentation skills, and to ensure consistency across the different elements of a game.

3. *Introduction of workflow*
   The pedagogical use of workflow practices has been proposed by authors such as Gouadec (2007) to highlight the importance of simulating real work conditions in the classroom. Bernal-Merino also insists that industry practices should be simulated by using small game localization activities, arranging students in small groups and assigning them different roles, so that they can carry out a small multilingual project. The smaller teams could be made up of a translator and a language tester, and bigger teams could include other roles, such as a project manager.

Bernal-Merino's specific suggestions for how to set up game localization courses provide useful guidelines for departments considering introducing game localization training into their courses, as well as for lecturers developing modules on the topic. In the context of the Bologna framework,[78] we would further add to his recommendations that a clear distinction be drawn between designing undergraduate and postgraduate courses. In our view, this is important as there are different implications for course design at each level in terms of learning outcomes,[79] students' previous training and needs, and the type of syllabus, i.e., a core module, an elective, part of an AVT module, or a software localization module. In

---

78. The aim of the Bologna Framework is to provide a mechanism to relate different national qualification systems in order to provide international transparency, international recognition of qualifications, and international mobility of learners and graduates. For more information, see http://ec.europa.eu/education/higher-education/doc1290_en.htm.

79. We have adopted the following definition of learning outcomes (LOs) as "... verifiable statements of what learners who have obtained a particular qualification, or completed a programme or its components, are expected to know, understand and be able to do. As such they emphasize the link between teaching, learning and assessment" (*ECTS* [*European Credit Transfer System*] *User's Guide* 2009, 47). For another example of the design of translator training within the framework of the Bologna Process based on learning outcomes, see Dorothy Kelly's *A Handbook for Translator Trainers* (2005).

addition, postgraduate students may have some previous professional experience as translators working in other fields.

6.2.1 Game localizers' competence

The issue of competence has become a hotly debated topic in translator pedagogy (see Pym 2003 for an overview of different definitions of competence in Translation Studies). Kiraly (2000) proposes a distinction between "translation competence" and "translator competence". "Translation competence" encompasses the skills a translator requires to be able to "comprehend a text written in one language and produce an 'adequate' TT for speakers of a different language on the basis of that original text" (2000, 10). However, translation competence alone is not enough to guarantee a high level of professional service. It is also necessary to develop the ability to adapt to market demands, which quickly change as new media and technology become available to translators and shape their professional practice. For this reason, translators must also be able to:

> use the modern tools of the trade in a professional manner, to research new topics quickly and efficiently, to justify one's work when necessary, to negotiate and collaborate with other translators and subject matter experts to accomplish tasks at hand. (ibid., 13)

This is what Kiraly calls "translator competence", which he deems essential to being able to work successfully as a translator in the new digital era. In this book we use "competence" as a broad term that encompasses all those abilities and skills that translators should ideally have in order to perform their task successfully at any level, academic or professional, amalgamating Kiraly's translator and translation competences.

The competences required by game translators have been explored by several authors, including Mangiron (2006), Dietz (2007), and Chandler (2008a, 2008b), and they are also briefly mentioned by Ranyard and Wood (2009). All of these authors have professional experience in the game localization industry and, as a result, have insiders' perspectives on the skills required to become a good game localizer. As discussed in previous chapters, game localization has both its own unique aspects and features in common with other types of translation, such as software localization, technical translation, AVT, and literary translation. As outlined in Chapter 4, game localizers have to deal with different text types and text genres, depending on the kind of game they are translating, and they should be able to deal with the severe space restrictions and tight deadlines common to all software localization. In addition, they have to be lateral thinkers, ideally with creative writing skills, and be computer-literate to be able to use different tools and search efficiently for specialized information. For all these reasons, game localizers need to hone a number of specific skills that will now be explored in more detail.

Mangiron (2006, 311–316) focuses on seven core skills related to the knowledge and understanding game localizers should ideally have:

1. *Familiarity with software terminology and game platform terminology*
    As explained in Chapter 3, each first party publisher has its own official terminology and localization standards which must be strictly adhered to in order for approval to be gained to publish a game for a particular platform. Localizers must be familiar with the different platform terminology and use it correctly.
2. *Familiarity with audiovisual translation*
    Game localizers should be acquainted with the specific features of dubbing and subtitling. In relation to dubbing, they should ideally be aware of issues such as lip-synching and adjusting the time available for a character's intervention during a dialogue or a monologue. Regarding subtitling, localizers should be familiar with subtitling norms, such as condensing the message to allow players to be able to read it comfortably or segmenting subtitles so that they can be quickly and easily understood, paying special attention to the semantic unit.
3. *Mastering idiomatic language*
    Language in games must be natural, fluid, and idiomatic in order to facilitate smooth gameplay and the player's immersion in the game. Language used in RPG, adventure, and action games tends to be very colloquial, and it is important that this be reflected in the localized version to bring the game closer to the target audience.
4. *Creativity*
    Creativity is one of the pillars of game localization, crucial to producing an exciting and engaging game. Often humour and cultural references cannot be translated literally, so they need to be transcreated for the localized versions, while maintaining the appeal of the ST. For this reason, localizers are expected to be creative in their approach to translation.
5. *Cultural awareness*
    As discussed in Chapter 5, game localizers must have an enhanced cultural awareness of both source and target cultures to be able to detect all the cultural elements in the original game that could pose a comprehension problem or could be offensive in the target culture.

6. *Familiarity with game culture*

A game localizer should be familiar with game culture – that is, knowledge-able about video game genres, history, industry stakeholders, etc. – in order to be able to produce a good translation that can successfully transfer the game-play experience to the target audience. Game literacy is particularly impor-tant when translators are working virtually "blind-folded", without access to the original game, and have to infer the context from their experience. Most game genres have specific terminology that appears in different games. There may also be references to past instalments of the series or to other games. This self-referencing feature commonly found in games can provide humour (Mangiron 2010), and also serves a social function in that it allows players to feel part of the gaming community (even if not all players are able to detect and understand all these types of references). Thus localizers ideally should be able to identify such references and translate them following the estab-lished translation. Many job specifications for game localizers emphasize that applicants must be game literate, that is, they must be gamers, be familiar with game culture, and have a passion for games.

7. *Familiarity with global pop culture*

Familiarity with global pop culture is also desirable for game localizers, as games often contain intertextual allusions to popular books, comics, and movies. It is important to maintain consistency between different media and to follow the guidelines set by the licensing agreement, when applicable. Some developers/publishers, such as Square Enix, include a knowledge of Japanese and target pop culture as desirable for translators seeking employment with them, as will be further explored later in this chapter.

Dietz (2007, 2–4) proposes a set of skills for game translators that combines specific knowledge with practical and transferable skills. He outlines four basic skills, one of them game literacy, also mentioned by Mangiron (2006). The other three are:

1. *Computer skills*

This includes: (a) knowledge of the specific hardware and software terminol-ogy; (b) the ability to play the game; (c) the ability to deal with hardware and software conflicts, and (d) the ability to research quickly using electronic re-sources available on the Web.

2. *Subject matter expertise*

The thematic content of games can vary greatly, from the simple content typi-cally found in arcade games, to the very complex content in flight simulator games, with the required subject matter expertise ranging from literary to extremely technical translation.

3. *Virtual teamwork*
   Large projects are often divided between several translators who are not physically located in the same place. They should be able to communicate well, using e-mail or instant messaging, and they should be flexible, with a willingness to compromise on terminological and translation issues. Occasionally team members must take over some project management functions, such as acting as a TM manager updating and distributing appropriate TM, or being the query manager who collects questions and forwards them to the development team.

Chandler (2008a) presents an exhaustive list of qualities required of game localizers based on a combination of knowledge and practical skills. Similar to the other authors, she highlights creativity, knowledge of popular culture, a good knowledge of source and target cultures, and knowledge of the game industry, game genres and the development process. She also stresses the importance of dealing with strict text space restrictions and the ability to synthesize existing and new translations of game sequels, in order to preserve consistency within the game series. Chandler furthermore emphasizes the importance of technical skills for game localizers. She argues that localizers should be comfortable learning how to work with specialized hardware and software such as console test kits, high-end PCs, TM tools and PC troubleshooting. Translators should be able to manage different file formats and work with text containing variables (see Chapter 3). They are also expected to be flexible and be able to work under pressure to meet tight deadlines. In the "Ask the Experts" column of the *Game Career Guide* website, Chandler (2008b) also gives practical advice to translators interested in working in the game industry. She emphasizes the need to translate into the native language and the need to be well versed in the source culture and language, particularly the slang and idioms often used in game text. Chandler stresses the importance of being familiar with the game industry and of having a university degree in translation. She also advises interested translators to start developing a portfolio with their own, private translations of their favourite games, done for the sake of practising this type of translation, so that they can show their work to prospective employers. Finally, she recommends joining the Localization SIG of the IGDA to establish contacts in the industry. Chandler's practical advice is useful, especially the idea of developing a translation portfolio as a method of honing game translation skills and of becoming familiar with game genres as well as the kind of language and terminology used in them.

Finally, Vanessa Wood (Ranyard and Wood 2009), a localization services manager at Sony Computer Entertainment Eurpoe (SCEE), states that according to standard industry guidelines, game localizers are expected to translate 2,000 words per day and review up to 5,000 words per day. She highlights the fact that game localizers should above all be gamers, with a knowledge of the game industry, game terminology, and the branding issues related to the different platforms. She also mentions that due to the great variety of game genres, localizers are now tending to specialize in one or two genres. Wood remarks that game localizers must have good project management skills, be good communicators, and be able to work independently and under pressure.

Table 6.1 summarizes the main competencies a game localizer or any translator seeking to work for the game localization industry should have, based on the authors cited above. We group competence areas in four categories: (a) personal qualities and skills; (b) translation skills; (c) subject-specific knowledge (game literacy), and (d) transferable professional skills.

Furthermore, a survey of current vacancy advertisements for game translator positions confirms that those competences identified in the above table match the main skills sought by employers. For example, a job advertisement for a Japanese-Spanish translator from Nintendo of Europe[80] specifies the following skills:

- Thorough knowledge of European Spanish to a native level
- Proficiency in Japanese and English
- A degree in Japanese or translation, or previous experience in a similar role
- Familiarity with Microsoft Office
- Teamwork and flexibility
- Personal interest in video games is desirable but not essential

Interestingly, a similar ad by Nintendo of America[81] for an in-house contracted English-Spanish "localization translator" includes a number of different requirements:

- Ability to work with highly confidential information
- Ability to maintain a heavy workload on an ongoing basis
- Ability to produce high quality results under tight deadlines
- Excellent organizational skills
- Knowledge of industry trends and familiarity with Nintendo history and franchises helpful

---

80. Source: http://jobs.Nintendo.de. Accessed November 12, 2012.

81. Source: http://www.Nintendo.com/corp/jobs.jsp. Accessed July, 31, 2011.

Table 6.1 Key competence areas for game localizers

Personal qualities and skills	Translation skills			Subject specific knowledge (game literacy)		Transferable professional skills	
Motivation and commitment	General	Excellent knowledge of SL and TL: poetic, colloquial, technical language, etc.		Subject matter expertise	Game culture (recognizing different game genres, titles)	Computer skills	MS Office suite
							PC trouble-shooting
		Excellent knowledge of source and target cultures and intercultural awareness			Gameplay experience	Creativity	
					Game genres	Independent and team work (virtual and face to face)	
		Good writing skills			Branding issues and platform terminology	Project management (organizational skills)	
		Research skills			Game development process	Time management; ability to meet deadlines	
Flexibility	Working long hours	Specific	Familiarity with AVT	Dubbing	Good knowledge of global pop culture	Good communication skills	
				Subtitling			
	Availability to work on-site abroad		Familiarity with software localization	Space constraints		Good problem solving skills	
				Terminology			
				Variables		Ability to work in an international and intercultural environment	
				TM software			
			Familiarity with literary translation				
			Familiarity with technical translation (flight simulation, military, sports, etc.)				

- Excellent Spanish and English translation skills, including two to four years' specific translation experience
- Spanish and English interpreting skills, including experience interpreting business meetings and/or conference calls
- Familiarity with Latin American culture and customs
- Experience operating Microsoft Windows and Office software in Spanish.
- Native fluency in Spanish
- Undergraduate degree in Spanish or English or a related field equivalent

In this advertisement more emphasis is placed on the confidential nature of the job, as well as the heavy workload, tight deadlines and pressure sometimes experienced by game translators. In addition, as this is a job based in the USA, it focuses on Latin American culture and customs, as most localization will be for the Latin American market. Finally, the required Spanish and English interpreting skills are probably not directly related to game localization tasks per se, but rather to other associated tasks.

Another example of the skills and qualities required to work as a game translator can be found on the job vacancies page of Square Enix,[82] where they advertise positions as freelance translators for English or Japanese into FIGS. They distinguish between required and recommended skills, as detailed below:

Required
- Excellent native-level skills in both SLs and TLs
- High level of linguistic creativity
- Computer-literate, specifically with MS Office suite
- Excellent written, oral, and interpersonal communication skills in Japanese or English
- Excellent multi-tasking, time-management and problem-solving skills
- Excellent teamwork abilities

Recommended
- Previous experience in translation of video games, anime, manga, or literature
- Knowledge of Japanese and target-language pop culture

In their ad, Square Enix place a stronger emphasis on linguistic creativity than do Nintendo, as well as on multi-tasking and problem solving skills. In addition, more emphasis is placed on a knowledge of popular culture.

---

82. Source: http://www.Square Enix.com/eu/en/jobs/translators.html. Accessed July, 31, 2011.

US company Blizzard Entertainment, creators of the popular MMORPG *World of Warcraft* (*WoW*) (2004-), also list similar skill sets in their ad for a translator position[83] from English into Spanish:[84]

Responsibilities
- Coordinate the translation of Blizzard Entertainment games.
- Translate Blizzard Entertainment games from English to Spanish (Castellano)
- Create and maintain internal glossary
- Perform quality assurance for Blizzard Entertainment games and websites

Requirements
- Excellent English and Spanish (Castellano) language skills
- Higher education in language-related disciplines and/or work experience as a professional translator
- Excellent teamwork skills
- Ability to work independently
- Strong motivation and high level of commitment
- Passion for heroic fantasy world and science fiction
- Experience in website localization and technologies

Pluses
- Experience in game localization or game QA
- Experience with Blizzard Entertainment games

Blizzard Entertainment emphasize the ability to work independently, as well as a passion for science fiction and fantasy genres, and some experience in website localization and technologies (though the term "technologies" is used vaguely) probably due to the fact that *WoW* is an online game. In addition, they value experience in translating or testing games, as well as gameplay experience.

In surveying the competencies required from the industry's perspective, we wish to draw special attention to the importance of creativity and creative writing in games. For example, Square Enix requires applicants to submit a short piece of creative writing (800-1000 words) in the TL describing "an episode based on a character from a past Square Enix game who has been mysteriously transported

---

83. It must be highlighted that Blizzard uses the term "localization engineer" to refer to game translators, an unusual choice of vocabulary, as the term usually designates engineers in charge of the technical aspects of localization, such as the implementation of the different builds.

84. Source http://us.blizzard.com/en-us/company/careers/posting.html?id=1100057. Accessed November 12, 2012.

to Japan".[85] This type of test highlights creativity in game localization in addition to the candidate's subject knowledge relating to game literacy. It is a skill that often needs to be specifically developed, as is being recognized by some translation programmes[86] that incorporate elements of creative writing into translator training. The focus on creativity also goes hand in hand with the nature of game localization prioritizing the entertainment value of the end product in comparison to other types of translation which privilege fidelity to the original. For this reason, it is an aspect that should be addressed in game localization courses, especially to help certain students who have a fear of being "too creative" and of departing from the ST when translating.

6.2.2 Course design

In discussing game localization courses, Bernal-Merino (2008c) indicates that the first two or three sessions could be dedicated to working with text-based material that is easily available, such as "manuals, web resources, screenshots, and standard text files" (ibid., 152–153). Although he does not provide an overall structure or sample syllabus, he proposes a task-based approach, where students work in groups replicating the workflow of a game localization project, taking on different responsibilities, such as project manager, translator, and linguistic tester, and rotating these roles during the course (ibid., 153). He places considerable emphasis on workflow, project management skills, and the use of localization kits, which are useful in preparing students for their future careers. However, as was mentioned in the previous section, when designing a game localization course, it is crucial to map the course onto the bigger picture of a programme or award,[87] to be able to balance the specific learning outcomes of each module, and to avoid overlapping and over-assessment in specific areas. Such considerations are particularly relevant in scenarios where game localization components are introduced as part of localization or AVT programmes.

For example, if a translation programme also includes software localization in its curriculum, students are more likely to be familiar with the use of localization kits, the localization process and workflow, and with project management skills. If the degree incorporates translation technology, students will also be familiar with the use of TM software. This will allow the lecturer to spend less time on these

85. Source http://www.Square Enix.com/eu/en/jobs/translators.html. Accessed July, 31, 2011.

86. For example, see the translation programmes offered by the University of East Anglia and the University of Iowa.

87. This is the term coined to refer to a degree by the Bologna process.

transferable skills and to focus on other specific tasks relevant to game translation, such as translating and reviewing text types from different game genres, developing research and documentation skills (e.g. reporting bugs), gaining a familiarity with the terminology of different platforms, developing creative solutions, and translating humour. Likewise, if students are already familiar with AVT, less time will be needed to introduce dubbing and subtitling practices, which can simply be reviewed while drawing comparisons between general standard practices for the film industry and the type of dubbing and subtitling used in games. Mapping out game localization courses within the broader framework of the programmes in which they are included can help lecturers design courses on game localization while considering the alignment of the overall programme outcomes and those for each module.

As an example, in a Master's programme in localization or translation technology, game localization would be taught after covering software localization and CAT tools elements so that students would already be familiar with key areas within software localization, such as processes, agents, the localization kit, and the use of CAT tools. As a result, more emphasis could be placed on the traits which game translation shares with other translation modes such as AVT. On the other hand, in an AVT programme, students would have already covered the basics of dubbing and subtitling in a previous module. If students are not familiar with software localization, the use of TM and terminology management software, then part of the course should be devoted to these topics. This would leave fewer contact hours to focus on translation practice as such. In summary, the learning outcomes and the content of a game localization course should be carefully planned against the backdrop of the overall programme outcomes, so that the course provides students with the best possible set of skills needed to embark on a professional career as game translators.

Drawing on our teaching experience in this field, we now briefly present an indicative module descriptor for a postgraduate module on game localization as part of a Masters degree in AVT, in which the students are assumed to have already completed several modules of AVT (covering dubbing and subtitling, as well as theoretical issues). Following the current programme structures of the Master's courses on AVT taught at the Universitat Autònoma de Barcelona, we assume that students are already familiar with the basics of multimedia translation and localization, which are taught in different modules. If this is not the case in the curricula of other universities, then the learning outcomes and the indicative content should be modified accordingly in order to include some general principles of localization.

On the basis of contemporary educational ideals as envisaged by the Bologna Process and those of a social-constructivist perspective prevailing in translator training scholarship, we strongly believe in the relevance of learner-centred approaches to the training of video game translators and localizers. We are focusing on a postgraduate module because most undergraduate courses for translator training already include a great number of subjects and have little room for manoeuvre. In the current economic climate, the addition of new electives has become rather challenging, so offering game localization courses at postgraduate level, where courses are more specialized and it is easier to introduce new modules, seems the more realistic option. Having said that, despite the current difficulty, we believe it would be beneficial both for students and the game localization industry to consider training in game localization at undergraduate level. This could be included in the final year, as an elective or as part of an existing subject in AVT, so that students interested in this field could become acquainted with it and pursue further training at postgraduate level if so desired. Another option would consist of providing game localization as a possible option for students to investigate in the research component of their degree (e.g. an extended essay, or their final dissertation). In this way they can consider video game localization within the framework of Translation Studies which they have been taught elsewhere in their BA programme. It is worth noting that despite the fact that AVT has been present as an elective in the curriculum of several undergraduate translation degrees, for example in the Universitat Autònoma de Barcelona, training in software localization is still mainly provided at postgraduate level (Bermúdez Bausela 2005).

The module descriptor (Table 6.2) is only an indicative model to provide a starting point for lecturers and institutions wishing to introduce a course on game localization. The descriptor should be modified depending on the specific knowledge areas and learning outcomes students have achieved in previous modules in the overall programme, as well as the number of ECTS[88] credits the module is worth and the corresponding contact hours / independent learning time allocated by the institution. In relation to the language combinations, the model we propose is applicable to any language pair. As has already been mentioned, English and Japanese are the two dominant SLs in game localization. In the latter case, games may be translated first into English and subsequently into FIGS, or may be directly translated into FIGS. As English is the most commonly taught language in translation departments in European universities, it is also the most common

---

88. ECTS stands for European Credit Transfer and Accumulation System, deployed in Europe to guarantee smooth credit transfer between different European universities, as well as credit accumulation towards a degree. For more information, see http://ec.europa.eu/education/lifelong-learning-policy/doc48_en.htm.

Table 6.2 Indicative module descriptor[89] for game localization

Module title: Introduction to game localization	ECTS credits: 5

Description: This module provides an overview of the video game and the game localization industries. It presents the main features of this type of translation, focusing on aspects such as the game localization process, the agents involved, the main priorities and constraints, the competences to be acquired, the main similarities and differences between game localization and other types of translation, and research avenues in game localization.

Learning outcomes: On successful completion of this module, students will be able to:
1. Demonstrate an understanding of typical characteristics of video games as relevant to localization and translation
2. Identify linguistic and cultural issues involved in game localization
3. Identify different text typologies in a game and develop the skills necessary to translate them correctly
4. Compare game localization with other types of translation (software localization, AVT, literary translation, technical translation)
5. Critically discuss game localization research issues and conduct research on game localization from a Translation Studies perspective

Pre-requisite learning: The module assumes that students are already familiar with the following areas:
- Software localization   - Dubbing
- Terminology management tools   - Subtitling
- TM software

Indicative content:
- Introduction to video games in terms of history, the game industry, and game studies
- Video games and GILT (Globalization, Internationalization, Localization, and Translation)
- Video game localization process (pre-localization, localization, post-localization and quality assessment), participants, assets to translate, tools
- Video game localization models
- Game localizer competence and profile; characteristics of the job market; how to get started in this field
- Transmedia storytelling
- Creative writing
- Translation issues: translation strategies and techniques, text types, translation of humour, cultural adaptation in games
- Translation practice: in-game text, art, audio, and cinematic assets, printed materials
- Game localization as Translation Studies research

Assessment: 100% continuous assessment
              Portfolio: 60%
              Final project: 40%

Workload: 36 contact hours
              89 independent learning hours

Resources: This section should include the relevant bibliography as well as the games to be used and any other useful resources and materials, both in print and electronic form.

89. The format for the module descriptor is largely based on the descriptors used at Dublin City University, Ireland.

SL in training courses. However, if there are sufficient translation students with a good knowledge of Japanese classes geared for translating directly from Japanese could also be considered. Regarding the TL, it may also be possible to include several TLs in the one class if the lecturer has a good knowledge of those languages or if there is the possibility of bringing in instructors specializing in different languages. Again, this will depend on the resources available in each department as well as the profile of the students enrolled in the course.

From this basis we can develop a more detailed course outline, corresponding to a course with thirty-six contact hours (see Table 6.3). As is the case with any class plan, it can and should be adjusted to the group's progress and can vary over the course of a module. Ideally some practical sessions should take place in multimedia computer labs and, if possible, someone with practical experience in the game localization industry should be invited to deliver a seminar or workshop during the academic year, either within class hours or as an additional activity. This will add a degree of authenticity to the students' learning experience as well as promoting the link between academia and the industry, while enabling academic staff to keep up to date with the latest developments. Some of the in-class and at-home tasks should be performed individually and others in groups in order to replicate authentic professional conditions where possible. Emphasis should be placed on developing students' game literacy, and students would be required to play games from different genres – many demo versions are freely available online – to become acquainted with game genres, their main features and terminology, and the challenges they pose to translators. Translating a flight simulator game requires different domain knowledge and terminology to translating a golf game or an RPG game set in medieval times, where armour and weapons are described in detail. For this reason, it is important to select a wide array of texts to work with from different game genres, so that students become acquainted with the different genre features and terminology and develop the research skills.

Knowledge of popular culture, particularly that of entertainment media and the transmedia dimensions closely associated with games, should also be explored in the classroom. Students should become aware of the priorities and restrictions imposed when translating for each medium (e.g. comics, movies, animation, and games), as well as the importance of maintaining consistency across different media in terms of language, style, and terminology. Games based on other media, such as literary works and films, are subject to licensing agreements and must follow the original work very closely (Bernal-Merino 2009). For example, the licensing contract to develop a game based on Tolkien's *The Lord of the Rings: The Fellowship of the Ring* stipulated that all members of the development team should have read the novel and be able to pass a test on its contents, to ensure an

Table 6.3 Indicative course outline for a game localization module

Session (2 h)	Theoretical content	Examples of possible tasks and activities to do in class or at home
1	Introduction to video games in the context of game studies: definition, history, different platforms, game genres, main stakeholders in the industry, key terminology, sociological aspects, educational and therapeutic aspects, serious and casual games, etc.	– Present students' own experiences with games – Identify the different genres of games – Discuss issues related to the sociology of games: do games foster violence? Why do certain games attract a more male than female audience? What are the positive values of games?
2	– Video games and GILT: game localization from an industry perspective, internationalization, tie-ins with other entertainment sectors (notably film industry), popular culture genres (e.g. anime and comics), transmedia story telling – Video game localization process: participants, localization kit, assets to translate, tools, models, levels of localization	– Research AAA titles in the students' country and present findings – Discuss game industry tie-ins with other industries and the tendency towards transmedia storytelling – Ask students to research and present information about transmedia links: games that have become movies and vice versa; anime that have become games and vice versa, etc. – Discuss the main advantages and disadvantages of the different types of localization
3–4	– Game localizer competence and profile; job market – Creative writing	– Discuss the main similarities and differences between game localization and other types of translation – Creative writing practice
5–6	In-game text – I: features, typologies, translating with and without context ("blind-folded" model)	– Translation practice: localization of strings first without context ("blind-folded" localization) and then confirming the translation with the context (playing the games) – Translation practice: localization of system messages for different platforms – Translation practice: tutorials, menu lists, help messages
7–8	In-game text – II: priorities and constraints, translation strategies	– Translation practice: narrative and descriptive passages – Translation practice: not voiced-over, text-only dialogues

Table 6.3 (*continued*)

Session (2 h)	Theoretical content	Examples of possible tasks and activities to do in class or at home
9–10	In-game text – III: translation of variable and concatenated strings, the use of html and xml tags	– Translation practice: variable translation – Translation practice: translating text with xml tags
11–12	Audio and cinematic assets – I: audio localization, script translation for dubbing (priorities, constraints, translation of humour and cultural references, characterization)	– Translation practice: translating a fragment of a script to be dubbed
13–14	Audio and cinematic assets – II: subtitling for games (priorities, constraints, translation of humour and cultural references)	– Translation practice: translating a fragment of a script to be subtitled
15	Art assets (textual graphics) Printed materials – I: box, manual	– Translation practice: translation of textual graphics – Translation practice: manual excerpt
16	– Printed materials – II: promotional and legal materials, strategy guides – Online materials: official website, online help	– Translation practice: excerpt from strategy guide – Translation practice: excerpt from an official website
17	QA process and testing	– Practice in detecting errors and writing bug reports – Group project replicating game localization practices (project manager, localizer, tester)
18	– Game localization as Translation Studies research – Relevance of Game Studies	– Discussion about research avenues in game localization from a Translation Studies perspective with reference to Game Studies – Final discussion

accurate depiction of the original work and characters (Parson cited in Bernal-Merino 2009, 240).

Despite the constraints imposed by licensing agreements on game translators as described in previous chapters, game localization also requires translators to be highly creative in order to produce target versions that feel like an original to the players, where cultural references and humour are adapted and transcreated as necessary. For this reason, another area any course on game translation should incorporate is the development of creativity and creative writing skills, as this is one of the ways in which game localization stands out from other types of translation. From our experience, some students are reluctant to deviate from the original due to preconceived notions of fidelity, thus producing rather literal (and thus lacklustre) translations. Game localization is driven by the ultimate entertainment value of the end product, allowing the translator considerable freedom to attain this goal. Game developers and publishers therefore consider creativity a crucial attribute for game translators, which, as we have seen, is evident in recruitment tests requiring applicants to undertake a creative writing exercise. In order to develop their creative writing skills, students can be asked to do a similar exercise to the one required by Square Enix, taking a character from a given game and writing a short story involving that character. Students can also be asked to add an episode to an existing game and create the dialogue between the characters, or to create a different ending. Translating humour is also a good way to develop creative skills, as many jokes and plays-on-words are based on linguistic deviance and have to be created from scratch in the translations.

In addition, students could be required to read a range of articles, including industry reports and critical literature covering different aspects of game localization. Pairs or groups of three students, depending on numbers, could be assigned to give in-class presentations and critiques of articles they read, leading to class discussions on the key concepts. Such presentations can take place once a week and are a good way to accumulate domain knowledge as well as to encourage teamwork, critical, and analytical thinking, and presentation skills, which are transferable and applicable to other subjects and industry practices. Students usually benefit from this exercise, even if they find it daunting at the start. The only drawback of presentations is that they can be time-consuming, particularly in large groups, so they may impact on the amount of time left for in-class practice and discussions.

6.2.3 Assessment

The assessment of any type of course should be guided by the course learning outcomes and be aligned with the different tasks and activities undertaken by students. In addition, it should be clearly defined, authentic, and fair, so that students are aware of what is expected from them, can subsequently apply what they have learnt in the classroom to a professional situation, and are assessed in a balanced and objective way, taking into account the course objectives and expected learning outcomes.

Different institutions have different assessment requirements, and some may require a terminal examination at the end of the course. If that is the case, the assessment breakdown may include a percentage for continuous assessment and a percentage for performance in a final examination. We would strongly advise that the examination mirrors the typical procedure followed for translation tasks during the course, that is, using computers and allowing the use of dictionaries and Internet resources as opposed to approaches more geared towards testing language acquisition. The exam could reflect some of the standard translation tests performed in the industry for game localizers, such as the inclusion of different text types, a review, and variable translation, and could also adopt a similar time frame to that allocated to job applicants. If the regulations and assessment conditions permit, students could also be allowed to do the exam at home and have 24 hours to submit it, which also reflects more authentic professional practice. In relation to the breakdown between different elements of continuous assessment, this should vary depending on the learning outcomes and workload balance for the course.

For the course outlined in the previous section we propose an approach based on 100% continuous assessment, broken down as 60% for a portfolio (including all the tasks and translations carried out in the module) and 40% for a final project (as further explained in the next subsections). As already mentioned, this is only an indicative model that could and should be modified according to the specific aims and contexts in which the course is designed. We also recommend reviewing the assessment practices every year, taking into account students' performance and feedback as well as newer developments in the industry, and making the necessary adjustments to the course as required.

Portfolio
The portfolio would include all the tasks carried out by the students, both in class and at home, individually or as members of a team. It is advisable to include a number of group assignments, involving up to three students, so that students

gain experience in working in teams, reflecting industry practice, and have to ne-gotiate and agree on a final task. Depending on the time available and the number of students, it may be desirable to implement a formative assessment approach whereby students first submit a draft of their work, which can be broadly correct-ed by the lecturer, indicating errors and areas which could be improved, without revealing all the right answers, so that students can reflect on their own work in progress and make the appropriate corrections. This also makes it easier for the instructor, particularly when teaching large groups, as it minimizes the amount of correction in the final version and means that students get good practice at fol-lowing more recommended work procedures. The final mark would be awarded to the final submitted version, and it would also take into account the reflection and self-correction process undertaken by the student or group of students. As a variation, students can also be asked to peer-review and correct each other's work. In addition, the portfolio should be accompanied by a brief reflection on each of the performed tasks, outlining the main challenges faced by the students, how they overcame them, and a reflection on what they learned and achieved. This would be accompanied by an overall reflection on the course, their learn-ing curve, the activities they liked and why, how they found working in groups, any difficulties and challenges they encountered and how they solved them, as well as feedback about the course and suggestions for possible changes to the course design.

Final project

There are several possibilities for a final project in a game localization module, depending on the learning outcomes that are going to be assessed, the assessment policy of the institution, and the lecturer's preferences. There is also the possibility of alternating different types of projects in different academic years, to test which type of assessment best measures the learning outcomes achieved by students, as well as identifying assessments that students find more engaging and motivating.

a.   Essay
     One possibility is to ask students to write, individually or in pairs, a critical essay about game localization. The whole class could be allocated one single topic or they could be presented with a number of different topics from which they can choose. Students could also be given the option of finding their own topic, which should then be approved by the lecturer. Some possible topics might be:

1. Discuss the challenges involved in localizing video games, focusing on linguistic, cultural and/or technical issues.
2. Discuss the main similarities and differences between game localization and other types of translation.
3. Discuss the role of creativity in game localization, providing illustrative examples of localized games.
4. Discuss the process of cultural adaptation in games, providing a number of examples of games localized into your language.
5. Conduct a case study on a popular video game in your country that is localized from English or Japanese.

b. In-class presentation and essay

This is a variation of the previous project, which consists of presenting the research undertaken by students orally in the classroom, as well as submitting a written essay and the materials used for the presentation, such as Power-Point slides. In addition to presenting the topic, students should lead the class discussion and encourage other students to participate, either by asking them questions, or by devising small questionnaires and activities for them. As mentioned earlier, another possible topic for a presentation would consist of reading a few articles or sources on a given topic and then presenting the main ideas to the class, critiquing them and finding relevant examples of localized games covering one or several of the topics discussed in the articles. Students usually enjoy presentations and they are a good way to measure skills in organization, time management, communication and public speaking, and teamwork. In addition to presenting information, it is important that students critique the information and provide their own insights on the topic.

c. Translation with commentary

Another possible project that could be conducted either individually or in a team consists of the annotated translation of a lengthy excerpt of a script, an in-game tutorial, or a variety of text types, with students being asked to translate the passage and to reflect on the main challenges they faced and how they solved them. Students would also be asked to reflect on the main theoretical aspects studied during the course that are applicable to the practical translation work they have done. For example, how have space restrictions affected their translation? What subtitling strategies have they applied? How have they profiled the characters in a game in order to get across the image portrayed in the original game?

d. Wiki

The final project could consist of developing a game localization wiki, which is a collaborative authoring environment using an open source virtual learning platform such as Moodle. Different groups of students can be allocated different topics, one or two topics per group, and have to write about them, collaborating until they reach a final version they all agree on. Again, the topics should be formulated in a way that requires students to engage critically with them and that encourages them to present their own insights, rather than just paraphrasing somebody else's work.

e. Localization project

As Bernal-Merino (2008c) suggests, the final assignment could consist of the replication of a game localization project, in which a group of students cooperate to reproduce the workflow typically used in the industry. Bernal-Merino proposes that one of the students could take the role of the project manager, another the translator and a third could become the linguistic tester. In our proposed module descriptor, project management skills are not among the intended learning outcomes, and for this reason we have not suggested any assessment related to them. However, a localization project in which students have to compile a glossary, a style sheet and a game character guide, as well as to translate and to review the game, is a type of assessment that also reflects the professional reality. In addition, if it is possible for lecturers to work with a PC game developer – preferably an independent developer more willing to provide files with code – it will also be possible to work with files with xml tags and thus to be able to see the localized version of the game on a PC.[90] A relevant example is a case illustrated by the eCoLoMedia project (Merten et al. 2009).[91] The project was funded by the EU Leonardo da Vinci programme to create training materials in the area of multimedia localization, including game localization, that would be freely available online. In order to overcome the problem of not being able to persuade commercial game developers to make available a game or obtain permission to use any commercially available games, the project used a game developed by students at one of the project partner universities, Universitat Pompeu Fabra (Barcelona, Spain). The eCoLoMedia project will be described in more detail in the Section 6.3.

---

90. It is more difficult to make such arrangements with console game developers as they are usually subject to control by platform holders such as Nintendo, Sony, and Microsoft, and thus have less freedom in comparison with PC game developers.

91. More information may be found at the eCoLoMedia website available at http://ecolomedia.uni-saarland.de/project.html.

In this section we have detailed some assessment options as a guide to provide ideas for lecturers planning to incorporate the subject of game localization in their existing course or as a new course, although the list is not intended to be exhaustive and there are other alternative approaches. The key point is that the assessment must be credible, authentic, and fair, designed according to the defined learning outcomes and take into consideration the objectives and aims of the course.

6.3   Teaching materials and human resources

As is widely agreed by scholars and instructors, authentic materials should ideally be used on any translator training course in order to be able to prepare translators for the profession by mirroring the types of texts and challenges specific to the particular areas of translation (see, for example, Kiraly 2000; Nord 2005; Bernal-Merino 2008c; Gile 2009). However, copyright restrictions and the highly competitive and therefore confidential nature of the game industry make the task of using authentic materials in the game localization classroom a challenging, if not insurmountable, issue. When hired for a commercial project, translators must sign non-disclosure agreements (NDAs) (see Introduction) forbidding them from revealing information about the project for a given period of time, except for any information that may be already available in the public domain, such as trailers, reviews, press releases, and demos.

Due to the relative youth of game localization as an academic discipline, most lecturers in this field are practitioners or former practitioners, who tend to use in their classes materials they have translated. These materials are usually modified so that they do not contain any information on the game code, and the assets to be translated are presented in a text-only format, in tables or in spreadsheets. Another possibility may involve extracting text from games or game demo versions manually and introducing it in tables or Excel files. However, such uses would still require official permission from the copyright holders in order to avoid any potential legal issues. Materials may also be extracted from video game fan websites and discussion forums, where it is sometimes possible to find screenshots, as well as fully transcribed scripts, lists of objects, commands, and character descriptions. However, the use of such resources does not solve the copyright issues. Lecturers responsible for developing and preparing course materials are advised to check regulations on the legality of their educational use. Finally, another way of obtaining materials for the game localization classroom consists of using assets from free-to-use or open source games, as well as games developed as student projects, as in the case of a game used in the eCoLoMedia project (2007–2009) (see 6.3.1), although permission should always be sought from the source.

The difficulty of obtaining materials for game localization courses can become a deterrent to the introduction of this type of course, an issue also mentioned by Bernal-Merino (2008c). However, if more efforts are made to bridge the gap between academia and the industry by way of mutually beneficial collaboration, perhaps it will become possible to obtain small samples of the different localizable assets for educational purposes from game companies. These assets could be in text-only format, in order to protect the code, and they could belong to older games which are widely known and for which confidentiality is no longer an issue. The copyright issue can also be a hurdle in the teaching of AVT, although most universities only use short clips and include a subtitle in them, stating that the clip is being used for educational purposes. Some universities pay fees to gain permission to use films for courses and a similar system might also be introduced for games. In the long term, the establishment of a free-to-use database containing different excerpts of games, similar to the Internet Movie Script Database[92] (IMSDb) would help to solve the difficulty of accessing materials and would facilitate the training of future game localizers. However, the legal status of such resources is currently still unclear. For the game industry to continue to grow, a well-defined and pragmatic mechanism for an agreement between industry and academia, allowing lecturers and students to use games for educational purposes, would be beneficial for all parties concerned.

Another significant issue is finding suitably qualified trainers. The pool of experienced game translators who will be willing and able to teach is still relatively small, particularly from language combinations which feature Japanese and FIGS. Consequently, there are only a small number of trainers in game localization, most of whom also work (or have worked) as game translators. For this reason, even if an institution is willing to include game localization in their translation programmes, finding suitable trainers may be difficult, particularly if the fees paid by universities do not meet professional expectations. To overcome this problem, some courses are establishing links with the industry for the involvement of professional game localizers. For example, the Spanish game localization company GameLoc is formally involved in the teaching of several postgraduate courses, such as the Masters programme at the Universidad Europea de Madrid. A similar procedure could be followed to train translation lecturers who are interested in game localization, so that they can subsequently share with students the knowledge they have acquired. However, currently it seems that many universities in

---

92. For more information, see http://www.imsdb.com/.

continental Europe are not in a position to invest in developing the teaching skills of lecturers and translator trainers. Brief training courses could be developed, as well as workshops and short courses, for example as summer schools. On-line training courses are also a good option to train the trainers, giving them more flexibility in terms of location and time commitments. Lecturers with a background in AVT, software localization, and/or translation technology, who are familiar with what is involved in these types of translation, have a potential advantage of learning about game localization quite rapidly. However, this does not mean that other translation lecturers could not become specialized in game localization if there is a strong interest.

6.3.1   The eCoLoMedia game localization course

The eCoLoMedia[93] project is one of a series of projects funded by the Leonardo da Vinci Agency, following the earlier eCoLoRe and eCoLoTrain projects which were all designed to develop freely available training materials in the area of local-ization.[94] As noted earlier, the eCoLoMedia project focused on the development of shareable and customisable resources for training in multimedia e-content localization and involved academic institutions, industry professionals, and in-dependent experts from different countries. On the basis of an extensive survey of training needs both in the industry and in academic institutions conducted in 2008,[95] it produced four localization modules: audio, video, flash, and games. The modules are designed for a blended learning approach, combining the use of e-learning and face-to-face teaching. All courses cover theoretical and practi-cal issues associated with the translation of digital content for new media. The course on game localization has the following sections focused on theory and key concepts:

–   Introduction
–   Classification
–   Actors in the field
–   Process overview
–   Market overview

---

93. For more information, see http://ecolomedia.uni-saarland.de/project.html.

94. For more information on eCoLoRe, see http://ecolore.leeds.ac.uk/. For more information on eCoLoTrain, see http://ecolotrain.uni-saarland.de/index.php?id=717&L=1.

95. Available at http://ecolomedia.uni-saarland.de/en/project/overview/needs-analysis.html.

- Specific issues
  - Technical issues
  - Translation issues
  - Cultural issues

In addition, there are six practical exercises which involve working with different text types and file formats, as detailed below. This is an overview of the exercises included in the course:

- **Exercise 1** is an introductory activity designed to familiarize students with game localization. It involves the exploration of a game and the translation of a small fragment of the menu and an audio message.
- **Exercise 2** is designed to raise awareness about the difficulty of translating text strings in a spreadsheet without having access to the original game. Students have to translate a fragment of a monologue and a fragment of the menu with just the contextual information provided in the spreadsheet. They subsequently have to review it while playing the original game and they have to adjust their translation as necessary.
- **Exercise 3** consists of translating text strings in xml format using an xml editor and a translation memory system in order to experience the advantages and disadvantages of working with these two systems. Once they are finished, students can view the localized text in the game.
- **Exercise 4** focuses on subtitling for games, working with a very brief fragment of dialogue to be subtitled.
- **Exercise 5** is an audio localization exercise, consisting of translating two audio files and subsequently recording them with Audacity, a free-to-use sound recording and editing software package.
- **Exercise 6**: the final exercise focuses on cultural localization, asking students to reflect on the translations used in a free-to-play online game, as well as requiring them to translate a short passage containing some culturally-marked terminology.

The eCoLoMedia game localization course is a useful resource for translators wanting to know more about new localization practices, as well as for lecturers hoping to introduce some game localization content in their translation courses. The course can be used as a brief introduction to game localization, for example, in a module covering different types of localization. Due to its introductory nature, the course presents a general overview of game localization and the exercises are rather brief and do not include all text types or develop all the competences required to become a game localizer. It is also interesting to note the technical emphasis in the course – one activity, for example, involves working with tags, a tag editor, and another, an audio localization exercise.

While these are useful skills for a game translator, more emphasis could be devoted to distinguishing between dubbing and subtitling for games and developing a familiarity with different text typologies, such as those present in the UI of a game, as audio localization itself is a task typically the responsibility of localization engineers. Likewise, while sometimes a few xml tags are left in the files translators work with, in commercial environments they are usually removed and few translators actually have to work with them. However, when seen as a means of fostering understanding by students of potential technical problems, such exercises could still be useful. Given that the main objective of the eCoLoMedia course was to provide a complementary resource for trainers, these materials could indeed be usefully integrated with other existing materials and could be used for class exercises or to promote students' independent work rather than being treated as a fully fledged stand-alone module. That said, the approach taken by eCoLoMedia is productive and resonates with the collaborative and sharing spirit of the Internet, where interested users can further build on the resources.

6.4   Pedagogy in game localization: A vocational or an academic focus?

So far we have focused on the practical issues of designing university level courses in game localization. This leaves us finally to address the thorny question of the academic or the vocational nature of translator education as articulated by Kearns (2008), who maintains:

> The relationship between real-world vocational demands and the classical humanist traditions of academe has not always been an easy one. Nevertheless, it remains an issue which is central to translator training – a typically vocational activity which is often based in, and in other ways contingent on, academic settings. (184–185)

As we have stressed in this chapter, game localization is critically anchored in industry practices and no game localization programme can ignore the industrial settings under which both the key concept and the practice have evolved. Translation is not a scientific discipline where new innovations are clearly driven by research, but rather it is driven by practice from which theory develops. This is why translator training has to be firmly grounded in practical contexts and we maintain that trainers ideally should also be practitioners with experiential knowledge. And yet practical knowledge alone is not enough. The question of the need for theory in the practice of translation has been addressed by the profession and indeed has been taken up in academic discourse on translator training. Chesterman and Wagner (2002), in the form of a dialogue between the theoretician and the practitioner, illustrate the challenge in determining the relevance of translation theory to translation practice. Key arguments advocating the need for theory are to promote a more analytical and reflective approach to translation practices as well as to equip translators with general law or "norms" which they can make use of in solving real-world translation problems efficiently.

In considering the dynamic nature of the video game industry, above all we argue that a solely technique-based approach informed by experience alone will not be sufficient. A pedagogical approach without acknowledging general law behind the practice is not able to nurture the kind of agility translators need to work for the game industry. This is why we consider a broader approach drawing on insights from Game Studies as well as Translation Studies to be essential in designing university-level courses for game localization. Furthermore, creative thinking, which we have stressed as an essential requirement in translating games, can only be developed by following a wider educational scope than one that is narrowly focused and technique-based. This indeed links to the role of education to promote deeper conceptualization by learners beyond imparting to them procedural knowledge, so as to ultimately encourage them to be reflexive practitioners able to connect practical knowledge to theoretical knowledge and vice versa.

Given the popular perception of video games as frivolous pursuits, the domain of game localization is prone to being dismissed as lacking the depth worthy of academic attention; this may lead to game localization training being considered in exclusively vocational terms. The following response by the Dean of the School of Social Sciences at the University of California at Irvine to the faculty proposal to create a minor in computer games illustrates such a view:

> An academic program of study officially listed as focusing on Game Studies runs, I think, the strong risk of attracting people on the basis of prurient interest. I do not think we should send forth messages of this type if we wish to be a research university of the highest level of distinction.
>
> (Schonfeld, cited in Dean 2001)

In the context of the recent surge in interest in games in many disciplines beyond Game Studies, this kind of immediate dismissal once prevalent may no longer be common. Nevertheless one senses a residue of prejudice still apparent in academia about teaching video games and game localization in Translation Studies. This is a domain which seeks a unified approach of practice and theory, as argued by Kearns, who insists that enlightened educational practices result only from a synergy between academic and vocational impulses (2008, 210). We wish to stress the enormous benefit to Translation Studies of new insights which can be gained from the study of game localization. This in turn will depend on what approach we take in introducing this new field. Pedagogical issues are closely associated with research and a sure way of inhibiting the research potential in the field is to treat the subject as a mere technical activity requiring only procedural knowledge. The field naturally privileges practice, but by further providing a theoretical basis, the nurturing of a "reflective practitioner" (Schön 1987) can be encouraged. We strongly believe that both practitioners and trainers in game localization will be best rewarded by an approach that encourages theoretical and analytic reflection on the part of the learners. Practitioner-led initiatives such as by the Localization Special Interest Group at IGDA documenting game localization best practices (see Introduction) demonstrate evidence of the desire for deeper conceptualization by practitioners. It is now time for academia to embrace fully the new practices both to respond to the demand from the industry and also to expand the horizons of the current conceptualization of translation.

CHAPTER 7

Game localization research in Translation Studies

Introduction

Throughout this book we have shown that dimensions of game localization are distinct even from the closely associated practices of productivity software locali-zation and also from AVT. Given such unique characteristics, this sub-domain presents new research agenda. In this chapter we focus on research questions which arise from the inherent nature of games as interactive media, in turn high-lighting the significance of users. To this end, we propose a research direction which focuses on the end user of a translated product. In particular, moving away from product-oriented or process-oriented research paradigms well established in Translation Studies we explore a research impetus which is coming from user empowerment afforded by new communications environments, promoting col-laboration and sharing among users. Within this broad research framework we identify three specific areas of research which we believe can help situate game lo-calization in Translation Studies and further develop this emerging area of study.

First, we address today's heterogeneous media user groups, especially in terms of how their access to media is affected when they have various disabilities. This is one of the main concerns in the field of AVT, addressing the question of wider "media accessibility" through translation (Remael 2010, 14). Extending this line of enquiry to video games, we first address the research area of accessibility and also broader issues of game usability, which are currently under-developed, with few games designed for gamers with impairments. The topic provides ample scope for exploration both in academic and commercial contexts, further open-ing avenues to interdisciplinary and cross-sectoral research in the field of usability studies. We then shift our focus to another category of users broadly described as "fans". This group is deeply engaged in different aspects of games, forming the core of game culture. In some cases, they become co-creators, contributing to the emerging development of new media technologies as "co-creative media" (Morris 2003 cited in Dovey and Kennedy 2006, 123–143). This particular group of users is considered as "not simply consumers, but innovators in their own right", relating to the concept of "user-led innovation" (Flew 2008, 30). Of particular interest in translation contexts is fan translation, in some cases forming a highly innovative network of translation producers, albeit operating outside professional translation (Pérez-González 2006). This in turn is linked to the emerging and hotly debated topic of translation crowdsourcing, which is attracting considerable research interest in Translation Studies with potentially significant implications for the future of the translation profession (O'Hagan 2011b). The final section of this chapter addresses the research agenda on localization quality from a user perspective through research methodologies designed to collect physiological data from end users to gain an insight into the player experience (PX) of localized games. The chapter ends with some brief observations on the application of natural language processing (NLP) technologies in games for enhanced interaction between the user and the game system.

7.1   Game localization and accessibility research

Over the last decade, research on media accessibility from a Translation Studies perspective has gathered pace in Europe due to the implementation of legislation at European and local levels promoting a more inclusive society and ensuring universal access to culture and entertainment for all, regardless of users' capabilities. In particular, the switch from analogue to digital TV in Europe, completed during the course of 2012, has triggered a number of studies about how to ensure the universal accessibility of the media,[96] especially for audiences who are deaf and hard of hearing (DH) or blind. The main objective of media accessibility is to ensure that audiences with a sensory disability (hearing or visual) can enjoy and receive the full benefits of an audiovisual product that otherwise would not be available to them due to accessibility barriers (Díaz Cintas 2007, 19–20). The main barriers faced by DH viewers are absence or poor quality of subtitles. For blind audiences, the main stumbling block is the absence or poor quality of audio description (AD), that is, narration describing what is happening or what can be seen on the screen when there is no dialogue.

Accessibility to new technologies and digital media, such as software applications and websites, has also been extensively addressed both in academia (Paciello 2000; Thatcher et al. 2006) and by the industry, such as the Web Accessibility

---

96. See, for example, the DTV4ALL project, which brings together academics from different universities as well as broadcasters from several countries across Europe, at http://www.psp-dtv4all.org/. Also relevant are the edited volumes by Jiménez Hurtado (2007), Díaz Cintas et al. (2007), Matamala and Orero (2010), and Díaz Cintas et al. (2010).

Initiative (WAI).[97] This kind of accessibility differs considerably from accessibility to more traditional media, such as television and cinema, because new digital media involve a degree of interaction between the user and the product, while a cinema spectator adopts a more passive role as far as tangible user input is concerned. The accessibility of new media has been defined as "the matching of digital resources and services to the needs and preferences of the user" (Nevile 2005, 4), a broad definition that focuses not on disabled users, but rather on facilitating access to electronic media and services to all. IBM (n.d., online) also shares this broad view of accessibility and stresses the need to become aware of accessibility related issues:

> Understanding accessibility requires an awareness of the special needs of multiple user groups, including people with disabilities and mature users with age-related disabilities. A person with a disability may encounter one or more barriers that can be eliminated or minimized by the software or Web developer, the assistive technology, or the underlying operating system software and hardware platform.

As highlighted here, different groups of users have different needs and face different accessibility challenges, although accessibility barriers to electronic media can be minimised or even removed by means of appropriate software and hardware design, as well as the use of assistive technologies designed to enable disabled users to perform tasks that they would otherwise be unable to carry out or could perform only with great difficulty. For this reason, usability, defined by the ISO 9241-11 (1998) as "the degree to which products can be used by specified users to achieve specified goals with effectiveness, efficiency and satisfaction in a given context of use" is inextricably linked to accessibility. In order to be accessible, an electronic or software product must be user-friendly for the widest possible spectrum of users.

The other crucial feature required to make digital products and services accessible to a wider audience is to enhance their adaptability, both from a software and hardware perspective. Traditionally, the term "adaptability" in the field of computer science has been defined as "[a] measure of the extent to which a system (a) can continue to perform the functions it was designed to perform by making adjustments to compensate for environmental changes and (b) has the ability to adapt to its environment" (Weik 2000, 23). More recently, due to the proliferation of different media and platforms with which accessibility issues may arise, such as mobile phones, PDAs, and tablets, adaptability has been defined as "the transformation of digital resources and services for users as they change from

---

97. For more information, see http://www.w3.org/WAI/.

one access device to another, as is the case when one uses a telephone instead of a desktop computer screen to display an image" (Nevile 2005, 1). Adaptability combined with accessibility "involves more than device compatibility as it takes into account user's [sic] individual needs at the time of delivery of resources and services" (ibid.). An adaptable product allows for a high degree of customization and also supports the use of assistive technology, such as screen reading software for blind users or a keyboard with large keys for users with reduced mobility. Usability and adaptability are crucial to fostering accessibility to new media, and games are no exception, as will be explored in the next section.

7.1.1 Game accessibility and accessibility barriers in video games

While the accessibility of traditional media and software and web accessibility have been widely researched, there is still a paucity of studies focusing on game accessibility, despite the economic and cultural influence of the game industry. To date, interest in game accessibility has stemmed mainly from industry professionals and a handful of academics, mainly those with a computer science background, as we will explore in more detail in Section 7.1.3. The work of the Game Accessibility Special Interest Group (GA-SIG)[98] at the International Game Developers Association (IGDA) deserves a special mention. This group gathers game designers, producers, engineers, and academics who are interested in improving game accessibility, which they define as "the ability to play a game even when functioning under limiting conditions. Limiting conditions can be functional limitations, or disabilities – such as blindness, deafness, or mobility limitations" (IGDA Game Access SIG 2010). In their mission statement, the Game Accessibility SIG affirms that:

> Computer games are an important cultural and quality of life issue. By collaborating with the rest of the game development community the GA-SIG intends to develop methods of making all game genres universally accessible to all, regardless of disability. In order to do this we will promote education of game developers in accessibility design, tax incentives for accessible game developers, corporate sponsorship and accessibility ratings.   (ibid.)

The GA-SIG's view of accessibility is therefore a broad one, as their objective is to make video games playable for everyone, including younger, older, casual, and novice players, who may find playing a game challenging, although they pay special attention to gamers with disabilities. They also aim to promote an accessibility

---

98. For more information, see http://igda-gasig.org/.

ratings system, similar to the PEGI and the ESRB age ratings systems, providing information about how accessible a game is, i.e. whether it includes a tutorial mode, subtitles, whether it can be played with one hand, etc. The GA-SIG have published the white paper *Accessibility in Games: Motivations and Approaches* (IDGA Game Access SIG 2004), which provides information and guidelines for designing accessible games. It must be stressed that often in the game industry the term *accessibility* is used in this broader sense to refer to designing games that are intuitive and do not require a steep learning curve so that they can be played by all types of players, from different age groups and levels of ability. Many of the articles in the specialized industry journal *Gamasutra* use the term "accessibility" with this meaning.[99] Nintendo has always been one of the main advocates of this broad concept of "accessibility", developing intuitive and easy-to-learn hardware and software for all ages, including the Wii console and the games in the Touch Generation series, such as the *Brain Training* (2005–) franchise. Recently, Nintendo included a new accessibility feature in their well-known *New Super Mario Bros.* game (2009) for the Wii console that allows players who cannot progress past a difficult part of the game to switch to automatic mode. The game then completes the level for them and they can resume playing when they are ready. This accessibility feature is useful for novice and casual players, as well as players with cognitive and physical disabilities. Some hardcore gamers objected to it, claiming that this kind of built-in 'cheat' feature defeats the purpose of gaming, although it can also be argued that it is an optional feature that does not necessarily have to be used. Given that the difficulty levels are sometimes adjusted during the localization process in different locales (see Chapter 4), Nintendo's approach can be seen as handing over such decisions to the players themselves. At the same time, Nintendo also created an issue with left-handed players with its games requiring them to use their right hand for the stylus of DS/3DS and Wii U games (Tinnelly, personal communication, 15 February 2012), demonstrating that accessibility issues can be easily overlooked by developers and publishers, who tend to focus on mainstream users.

As mentioned earlier, one of the key differences between accessibility to traditional media and accessibility to new digital media lies in the interaction between the user and the medium. As electronic, interactive, and audiovisual media, the accessibility challenges posed by video games differ from those posed by other business-oriented applications or websites, as games' primary function is to entertain users. A video game player must complete several tasks and accomplish different missions in order to achieve a given goal, while enjoying the whole process.

---

99. See, for example, the articles by Alexander (2009), Graft (2010), Nutt (2010) and Saltsman (2010).

If a game is too difficult, this is likely to affect players' progress negatively, leading them to abandon the game without finishing it. In some cases a lack of accessibility may even make the game unplayable. For example, if a game containing voiced dialogue and cinematic scenes does not incorporate subtitles, an important part of the game may become inaccessible to DH players. Similarly if the colour patterns used in a puzzle game are difficult or impossible to distinguish for colour-blind players, they are likely to be left feeling frustrated. The great spectrum of potential users with different kinds of disabilities makes it extremely challenging to design a universally accessible mainstream game, as different users may face different accessibility barriers due to motor, sensory, or cognitive disabilities. Game design researchers Yuan et al. (2010) identify three main accessibility problems to games due to intrinsic interactivity:

– Not being able to receive visual, auditory, or tactile stimuli.
– Not being able to determine the adequate response to perform a given action required to advance in the game.
– Not being able to provide input to the game once the player has decided what action to take because they cannot use the interface device between themselves and the game, such as the mouse, the keyboard, or the controller.

DH players and blind players experience difficulties in overcoming the first barrier, as they do not receive the relevant sensory stimuli, while users with cognitive impairments may not always be able to determine the right response to the stimuli. On the other hand, gamers with reduced mobility can process and determine the answer to a given stimulus, but they may not be able to provide the required input to the game, especially within a given timeframe. After carrying out a study of several games that include a number of accessibility options, Yuan et al. (ibid.) reached the conclusion that different strategies must be applied to improve accessibility to different groups of users depending on their needs, and that some game genres are more suitable for certain groups of users than others. For example, while racing and rhythm games could be made accessible to blind players with relative ease, this is not the case for RPGs and strategy games.

Currently, players with hearing impairments face fewer and more clearly-defined barriers to games than players with visual or cognitive impairments. The main barrier for the former group is the loss of information that is presented only by means of the audio track, for example, voiced dialogue in the cinematic scenes or sound effects, such as approaching steps or the sound of a flying bullet as typically encountered in a **first-person shooter (FPS) game**. By comparison, cognitively impaired players are a very diverse group of users with varying needs. These players may experience difficulties related to the game speed and difficulty level, as well as reading and comprehension problems or memory deficiency. Players with reduced mobility face the challenge of having difficulties in providing the required input to the game in a timely manner, with the result that they cannot advance in the game. The speed of the game may be too fast for them to react and they may also experience some hand-eye coordination issues. Finally, players with visual impairments are also a heterogeneous group. Players with low vision may have trouble reading the text on the screen in small font or they may not be able to identify small icons. Colour-blind players are likely to experience difficulty when extracting information from elements that are based on colour. Blind or visually-impaired players cannot process information that is only provided visually. Given the wide spectrum of users and (dis)ability levels, the main challenge to the video game industry in terms of accessibility is to design mainstream games that are maximally optimised to address different limitations imposed on the users. Due to the primarily visual nature of the video game medium, accessibility for blind players remains the most difficult challenge and there seems to be widespread scepticism in the industry about the possibility of universally accessible games, in line with the findings of Yuan et al. (2010). However, some authors (e.g. Archambault et al. 2005; Savidis and Grammenos 2006; Glinert 2008) claim that in spite of the difficulty involved, it is possible to design universally accessible games. The topic of universally accessible video games will be further explored later when we describe the current research avenues in this field.

As described in Chapter 1, the evolution of game technology can, ironically, erect more accessibility barriers if players with disabilities are not taken into consideration. We highlighted how the evolutionary advances of audio technology eventually led to more common inclusions of recorded human voices into in-game dialogues, making the gameplay experience more realistic and cinematic. However, if the dialogues and sound effects in a game are not subtitled, this becomes an accessibility barrier for DH players – a barrier that did not exist when all text in games was provided in written form. The latest controller-free interface game technology Kinect, developed by Microsoft for Xbox 360, allows players to control the game with their body movements. No matter how revolutionary such a technology may be, it creates a new accessibility barrier for players with reduced mobility, excluding them from benefiting from the new innovation. While this may seem to be an insurmountable challenge, if accessibility issues are considered from the conceptual stage of development of game hardware and software, many of the barriers could be at least minimized with alternative solutions.

7.1.2 Benefits of game accessibility

The benefits of game accessibility are manifold as it enables the needs of a wide spectrum of users to be met. For Grammenos (2006, 1) accessibility not only benefits disabled players, but also any individual who may not be able to fully experience a game due to different circumstances, such as (a) noisy conditions in the environment where they operate, preventing them from hearing dialogue and sound effects; (b) the features of the hardware and software they use, for example, if they are using a portable device with a small screen, and (c) differences in gaming skills and preferences, such as different levels of hand-eye coordination in very young or elderly players. In addition, some accessibility features such as subtitles, are also beneficial for language learners, who can use them to hone their linguistic skills, or for any player who does not want to miss out on any of the dialogue of a fast-paced game. As already mentioned, the principle behind universal accessibility is to provide players with highly customizable games, where each player can adapt the game to their needs, for example, adjusting the speed of the game. Similar to the internationalization process applied in localization, the inclusion of accessibility considerations in the early design stage of game development could minimize the cost and be commercially viable by allowing the game to reach a wider target audience. Thus, accessibility can also be beneficial for the game industry, as it makes their products available to a wider cross-section of the population. According to a report by the AbleGamers Foundation (Robinson and Walker 2010, 11), there are almost 50 million gamers in the USA alone who suffer from an age-related disability. Among today's gamers 25% are over 50 years of age (ibid., 5) and as they become older, they will increasingly face accessibility barriers. It is therefore estimated that the game industry is losing 32.5 million potential customers and not realizing as much as USD3 billion of potential revenue every year by failing to include accessibility options in mainstream games (ibid., 11). Despite the fact that Robinson and Walker's figures are hypothetical and approximate, they highlight the fact that there is a solid economic argument in favour of addressing accessibility, particularly given the fact that approximately 10–12% of the world population have a disability, according to UN statistics (The World Bank 2009).

While there have been no universally accessible mainstream video games to date, there are some games with accessibility features. Individuals with a disability who wish to play games currently have three options: (a) playing non-commercial, tailor-made PC, web-based, and online games designed for a specific set of users with a given disability, usually freely available on the web; (b) playing a mainstream game with the support of assistive technology when available or the support of a family member or friend, and (c) modifying the game by means of patches or **mods** made by other users in order to enhance accessibility, such as the addition of subtitles. Some scholars, such as Savidis and Grammenos (2006), claim that there is a risk that games designed for specific groups of disabled users may encourage their segregation and social exclusion, rather than fostering their inclusion within the gaming community and wider society. However, as mentioned earlier, other authors, such as Yuan et al. (2010), opt for a more stratified approach and defend the need to adopt targeted accessibility strategies for different game genres and types of users. There is, however, consensus about the fact that making games accessible to different users inevitably involves altering the original gameplay to adjust it to the diverse abilities and skills of the players. This means that different types of players will enjoy the game differently, but the entertainment value will be preserved across the different groups.

In relation to games designed for specific groups of players, there are currently a number of games accessible to both sighted and blind players. The best known is the award winning *Terraformers* (2003), a 3D adventure game that can be played both in visual and audio modes by means of an audio interface and the use of sonars that provide players with approximate information about the distance between them and different objects. It was developed with the support of the Swedish Handicap Institute (Westin 2004). The rhythm game *AudiOdissey* (2007) was also purposely designed by the Singapore-MIT Gambit Game Lab[100] to be accessible for sighted as well as blind and visually impaired players. On the other hand, players with reduced hand mobility can play **one-switch games**, which allow them to advance in the game using just a single button.[101] There are also games aimed at players with specific cognitive disabilities, such as the games for autistic children, available at the WhizKid Games site.[102] Independent US Developer 7-128 also develops PC games which are easy to understand and play and are therefore accessible for cognitively impaired players.[103] As far as mainstream games are concerned, there are a number of games designed for disabled players, such as the PC games *My Football Game* (2009) and *My Golf Game* (2010). Both games include different difficulty levels and a tutorial mode. They are compatible with alternative input devices, unlike most games, which are currently not compatible with adapted digital controllers, such as controllers with bigger buttons or one-switch controllers (see Figure 7.1).

---

100. For more information, see http://gambit.mit.edu/loadgame/audiodyssey.php.

101. For examples of actual games, refer to the One Switch website at http://www.oneswitch. org.uk/2/switch-downloads.htm.

102. For more information, see http://www.whizkidgames.com/.

103. For more information, see http://www.7128.com/.

Games console switch interface   Switch

Figure 7.1 Adapted console controllers[104]

There are also a number of games featuring several accessibility options, often incorporated to make them more appealing and usable by a wider spectrum of users or to enhance the gameplay experience. Some games include subtitles for dialogue and sound effects, such as *Zork: Grand Inquisitor* (1997), *Half-Life 2* (2004), and *SiN Episodes: Emergence* (2006). Developers such as Square Enix include intralingual subtitles in their Japanese and English games, and since 2008 French developer and publisher Ubisoft also include intralingual subtitles for dialogues in all their in-house developed games, although sound effects are not captioned by any of these developers. There are also games that allow the player to adjust their difficulty level, such as *Everybody's Golf* (2000), which includes a tutorial mode, adjustable difficulty settings, and a game speed regulator so that players of different levels of skill can customise the game to their own requirements. The Able Gamers Foundation annually grants an award[105] to the most accessible mainstream game of the year; this was won in 2009 by the PC RPG game *Dragon Age: Origins* (2009) and by the racing game *Forza Motorsports 3* (2009) in 2010, in 2011 by *Star Wars: The Old Republic* (2011) and in 2012 by *FIFA 13* (2012). *Dragon Age: Origins* incorporates several accessibility options such as (a) viewing intralingual subtitles that include sound effects; (b) playing with the mouse or the keyboard (physical or on-screen); (c) easy to read, good sized font and icons; (d) different difficulty levels, and (e) pausing the game to process the information if more time is needed, even during battles. However, it should be highlighted that subtitles in the *Dragon Age* series do not conform to subtitling standards applied to TV, cinema, and DVDs, as they tend to be very long and use a white font

---

104. Source of game console switch interface http://www.oneswitch.org.uk/1shop.htm; source of switch: http://www.inclusive.co.uk/access-switch-p2297, copyrighted material of Inclusive Technology Ltd.

105. The Able Gamers Foundation looks at the October to October time-frame for eligible titles, as many games are released for the Christmas season.

Figure 7.2 Head mouse[106] and sip-and-puff switch[107]

directly onto the screen, which hinders legibility, depending on the background. For example, there are one-line subtitles with 57 and 90 characters that stay on screen for 6 seconds, above the recommended guideline based on two-line subtitles of 70–74 characters at a maximum for 6 seconds (Mangiron 2013, 48). *Forza Motorsports 3* (2009) allows gamers to play the whole game with just two buttons and it includes a "rewind mode" that allows players to do course corrections retrospectively as required without having to restart the race. To cite more recent examples, *Star Wars: The Old Republic* (2011) features several accessibility options, including full subtitles and the ability to control the game from the keyboard or with the mouse while *FIFA 13* (2012) is the first mainstream sports game that allows the user to control the game with only a mouse. Mainstream games can also be made more accessible by means of assistive technology, such as the use of one-switch or adapted controllers, head mice, sip-and-puff switches (that allow users to introduce commands with their mouth) (see Figures 7.1 and 7.2), voice recognition software, and screen readers.

In certain cases game software may be adapted by an independent developer or by means of mods by users with advanced programming skills, such as the close caption mod for the FPS *Doom 3* (2004). This mod includes subtitles for sound effects and a visual sound radar indicating the origin and the distance of different sounds (steps, shots, etc.) – information which is important in order to be able to play an FPS successfully.

Despite the fact that there are a number of games which include accessibility options available on the market, they are still very much in the minority in relation to the total number of games published. There is a long road ahead in terms of serving all types of users seeking enhanced accessibility to games. In general, there are more PC games designed with accessibility features than there are console counterparts, as many of the commercial and free games designed with

---

106. Source: http://depts.washington.edu/enables/myths/myths_at_people_independent.htm.

107. Source: http://www.orin.com/access/sip_puff/.

accessibility options are developed by small and independent developers for the PC platform. Designing for the latter does not entail a submission process imposed by the platform holders (see Chapter 3) nor the payment of high fees required to obtain a license to publish a game for a given platform. Furthermore, there are already many devices and software programmes designed to facilitate accessibility to computers and the web that can also be used for playing games on a PC, such as the above-mentioned screen reading software, adapted mice and keyboards and sip-and-puff devices. From a social perspective, video games provide disabled users with an alternative form of entertainment which can motivate them, improve their quality of life, and reinforce their sense of social inclusion. Guest (2007) reports how virtual environments in *Second Life* allowed a group of disabled users to chat, walk, dance, and fly, providing them with a freedom of movement and opportunities for social interactions which would not have been feasible in "real reality". These cases provide a powerful argument for increased awareness and implementation of enhanced accessibility features in both game hardware and software, contributing to a more inclusive and equitable society.

7.1.3 Research on game accessibility

So far most existing research on game accessibility has been conducted from a game engineering or game design perspective rather than a Translation Studies perspective. In addition, the interactive nature of games brings greater accessibility challenges as they need to be designed with consideration of players' input in response to the stimuli from the game. As a result, many accessibility solutions, particularly for players with mobility impairments, are related to game design or the development of assistive technologies that can be used with PCs and consoles. In terms of accessible game design, the pioneering research undertaken by the Universally Accessible Games group (UA-Games)[108] at the Human–Computer Interaction Laboratory of ICS-FORTH in Greece deserves a special mention. As their name indicates, the main objective of this group is to research how to design universally accessible games; they define a universally accessible game as "a game that can adapt its interface and content to best serve the requirements of a specific gamer under specific gaming conditions ... in order to render a fully customized, personalized, version of the game for each distinct player" (UA-Games 2007). According to Savidis and Grammenos (2006), both members of this group, the key consists of identifying accessibility barriers related to the game's interface, its content and rules, and developing design strategies to overcome them.

---

108. For more information, see http://www.ics.forth.gr/hci/ua-games/.

Universally accessible games should follow the principles of Design for All[109] so that they can be adapted to different gamer characteristics without the need for additional development. They can also be concurrently played among people with different abilities on various hardware and software platforms, and within alternative environments of use, interoperating with assistive technology add-ons when appropriate (ibid.).

UA-Games have developed three universally accessible games: *UA-Chess* (2004), *Access Invaders* (2005), and *Terrestrial Invaders* (2007), as well as the first "universally inaccessible" game, *Game Over!* (2007), which deliberately violates all the rules of accessible design. For example, to control the spaceship, the players must use awkward key combinations that they have to press at the same time, such as Shift + L + Left Arrow to go left. The main idea behind this game is to raise awareness about the importance of including accessibility features in games when they are designed. All these games were developed to be played on a PC and can be freely downloaded from the UA-Games website. The Game Accessibility project also focuses on improving game accessibility. It is funded by the NSGK (Dutch Foundation for the Disabled Child) and the SNS Bank, and involves partners such as the IGDA GA-SIG, the Technical University of Eindoven, and the Human–Computer Interaction Laboratory of ICS-FORTH. Its objective is to provide information about accessible games and to foster dialogue between academia and the industry while promoting research in the field.[110] In addition, currently most information about game accessibility is available on dedicated websites and blogs, such as AbleGamers,[111] Special Effect Accessible GameBase,[112] Deaf Gamers,[113] and One Switch.[114] The industry journal *Gamasutra*[115] also occasionally features accessibility-related articles. In the dynamic and rapidly evolving game industry, the lack of academic research means that websites and blogs other than

---

109. Stephanidis et al. (1998, 3) define *Design for All* as "the conscious and systematic effort to proactively apply principles, methods and tools, in order to develop IT&T [Information Technology and Telecommunications] products and services which are accessible and usable by all citizens, thus avoiding the need for a posteriori adaptations, or specialised design".

110. Their website contains articles, game reviews, etc. from an accessibility point of view. See http://www.game-accessibility.com/.

111. For more information, see http://www.ablegamers.com/.

112. For more information, see http://www.gamebase.info/.

113. For more information, see http://www.deafgamers.com/.

114. For more information, see http://www.oneswitch.org.uk/.

115. For more information, see http://www.gamasutra.com/.

specialised journals remain the main source of information about the current status and developments of accessibility practices.

Similarly, there is little existing research on game accessibility from a Translation Studies perspective. Mangiron's (2013) analysis of current subtitling practices in games highlights the lack of uniformity and the ad hoc subtitling approach in game localization and shows the need for standardization. In addition to the fact that many games still do not have subtitles, those which do include them display high levels of variation in the number of characters per line. There can be between 38 and 80, occasionally with more than three lines, and they sometimes do not remain long enough on screen to ensure that the player is able to read them and process the information. Little attention is given to the semantic unit and the subtitles are often fragmented. The font used is also often disproportionately small, making the subtitles poorly legible as illustrated in Figure 7.3. Furthermore, as most console games are currently being developed for high definition TVs, if the game is played on a standard definition television set, the font becomes almost illegible (also see 3.1). Some games that have been criticised for the small size of their subtitles include *Dead Rising* (2006),[116] *Mafia II* (2010),[117] and *Mass Effect 2* (2010).[118]

This lack of standardization is probably in part due to a low level of awareness, exacerbated by a general absence of AVT training among game localizers along with cost implications. As noted elsewhere in this book, the game industry

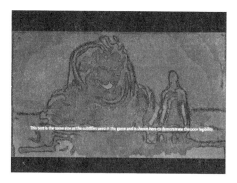

Figure 7.3 A mock-up illustrating the subtitle ratio in one example

---

116. For more information, see http://www.gamespot.com/forums/topic/27412400.

117. For more information, see http://forums.2kgames.com/showthread.php?79821-Subtitles-are-two-small-to-read.

118. For more information, see http://social.bioware.com/forum/1/topic/107/index/785123/1.

has pursued a solitary course independent of software localization and AVT, despite some obvious overlaps where cross-fertilization would have been beneficial. Mangiron (2013) highlights the need for further research into subtitling in game localization, including reception studies with users by means of interviews, questionnaires, and eye-tracking technology, in order to develop a subtitling standard for game localization that takes into account the interactive nature of the medium, thus factoring in the user's perspective. Such standards would provide a benchmark and become a useful tool for game developers, localizers, and game localization lecturers and students. They could contribute to the standardization of game localization practices, foster readability and accessibility, and ultimately lead to an enhanced gameplay experience across different locales. In addition to using good quality subtitles, game designer Richard Van Tol (2006) proposes several alternatives to traditional subtitles for displaying sound and information for deaf and hard of hearing (DH) players, such as using speaker portraits or speech balloons to identify the character who is speaking and displaying action captions, similar to those in comics. Van Tol also proposes using video clips displayed in a small part of the screen to indicate an action that is happening elsewhere and that players would normally identify by sound, such as the sound of a helicopter firing a rocket. In addition, danger meters can be used to indicate that danger is approaching and visual sound radar can indicate where a sound is coming from.

Other possibilities for depicting information for DH players could involve the use of icons to describe sound effects, e.g., the image of a phone to indicate that a phone is ringing, or the use of emoticons or small character portraits displaying the emotion of the character speaking (Mangiron 2013). Some of these methods have also been proposed for subtitles for the deaf and hard of hearing (SDH) for television and cinema, such as emoticons (Neves 2005) and icons to express sound effects (Civera and Orero 2010), although they are not yet widely applied. The more ludic nature of video games as a medium could arguably allow for greater variation in subtitling practices if they are conducive to enhancing the gameplay experience of the players. For this reason, it is worth exploring these alternative options for describing sounds and emotions in games.

Since 2008 the conference series Games for Health,[119] which focuses on the role of video games in health and healthcare, has been held annually in the USA. It brings together developers, academics, and health professionals who work with people suffering from various disabilities. The conference devotes one day – the Game Accessibility Day – to discussing the challenges of game accessibility, as well as the latest technological advances in the field, presenting case studies and

---

119. For more information, see http://www.gamesforhealth.org/.

discussing ways to use gaming to improve the quality of life for people with special needs. The International Conference on Translation and Accessibility in Video Games and Virtual Worlds series held in Barcelona (see the Introduction) focuses on game localization and accessibility. These conferences demonstrate an increasing awareness of the need for game accessibility, a socially rewarding topic for academic research and one with commercial implications. Contrary to the early biased view against video games (see Chapter 1), their wide ranging benefits to a large sector of the population because of their ludic, educational, therapeutic, and social value are now beginning to be recognized. Games can be a powerful educational tool, as is being increasingly recognized (e.g. Gee 2003), as most of them require attention and logical thinking, and they can contribute to the development of problem-solving skills and good hand-eye coordination, among other abilities. In turn, the Nintendo Wii platform is being used for therapeutic purposes in hospitals and care centres to improve coordination and balance, help weight loss, work on memory and attention, and alleviate depression (Miller 2007; Abrams 2008; Coslett 2010).

According to such authors as Bierre (2005), accessibility to video games and virtual worlds could in time become a matter of natural human rights. In the USA, the use of accessible technology in governmental agencies is a legal requirement according to section 508 of the Rehabilitation Act of 1973. In addition, the Americans with Disabilities Act provides for equal access for disabled citizens to many areas, which could easily be extended to video games and virtual environments over the coming years (ibid.). As mentioned in Chapter 4, in some countries such as Spain, video games have achieved the official status of "cultural products", and according to the Spanish Constitution all Spanish citizens are entitled to equal access to culture. As accessibility gains prominence in Spain, the possibility that the Government will eventually legislate in favour of equal access to video games will become more likely. To this end recent research initiatives have led to the formulation of key strategies that could be applied to promote game accessibility (Mangiron 2011a):

1. Raising awareness about the need to improve accessibility amongst different groups, such as game developers and publishers, gamers, and the wider society. Pressure could also be placed on governments to provide funding for research in this area, as well as legislation enforcing game accessibility, similar to the existing legislation granting access to digital TV in Europe. Information campaigns, events, conferences, press releases, more dedicated blogs and websites can contribute to promoting the importance of game accessibility.

2. Developing official game accessibility standards, such as ISO, that would provide game accessibility guidelines and become a point of reference for the industry.

3. Implementing an information and labelling system, similar to the PEGI rating system. This would provide potential players with information about the accessibility options included in games, such as the existence of a tutorial level or the inclusion of subtitles. Such information would be useful for all types of players, who could select games according to their accessibility options and avoid post-purchase disappointments due to the game being too difficult or inaccessible for them.

4. Promoting accessible game design from the early stages of the development process. As has been seen in the localization process in general, if accessibility options are included in game design from the outset, they need not become onerous or expensive.

5. Promoting the development and the use of assistive technology devices at an affordable price, as many of these solutions are currently rather expensive. For example, the development of a simplified controller compatible with all consoles and game types would be an important step forward in accessibility.

6. Fostering interdisciplinary research in the field of game accessibility. An interdisciplinary approach involving different fields, such as Communications, Audiovisual Translation, Psychology, and Health and Medical Studies would contribute to progress in this area.

To conclude this section we would like to highlight the importance of collaboration between the industry, users, and academia in order to overcome the accessibility barriers currently present in video games and pave the way towards a more inclusive society, where digital entertainment is available to different types of users, regardless of their (dis)abilities. Given how accessibility issues have become a major research focus in AVT, it is likely that they will form a part of key research agenda in game localization in the near future.

In the next section we remain focused on users, turning our attention to fans.

7.2   Game localization and fan studies: Fans as co-creators

Today, in the era of Web 2.0 and the proliferation of user-generated web content, users have become important players in the media ecosystem. In this section we provide an overview of a growing research area which is concerned with the role played by committed gamer fans who contribute to the unique fabric of game culture (Dovey and Kennedy 2006). The picture of game localization would not be complete without acknowledging the presence of fans, whose influence has been significant in shaping broader game culture. Newman (2008) provides a relevant discussion of the term "fan", which often carries negative connotations of enthusiastic amateurs within game cultures and communities. For example, the term "fanboys" is often used in reference to "gamers seen to offer overly partisan accounts, often displaying putatively excessive loyalty to a hardware platform…" (ibid., 18). By comparison, the term "fandom" communicates "a sense of community and coherence as an audience" and "qualities such as productivity, creativity and sociality" (ibid.).

Fan studies have been undertaken so far mainly by scholars in media and cultural studies, including early seminal works by Henry Jenkins such as *Textual Poachers: Television Fans and Participatory Cultures* (Jenkins 1992). Jenkins highlighted the active and participatory role played by fans as media consumers forming a "participatory culture", signifying their deep engagement with television media. Jenkins observed how *Star Trek* fans began creating their own media texts inspired by the series and sharing their creations among fan communities. A subsequent study on fandom by Matt Hills (2002) further built on the framework of media consumption, interpretation, and fan practices, with his view of fans as "creators". More recently the term "co-creation" has been used by media scholars. For example, Dovey and Kennedy (2006, 144) define the concept "co-creator" in the context of digital media as "the consumer of digital software products who uses them to make new artefacts and is thus said to be in a co-creative relationship with the original authors of the software". It is on this characteristic of the role of fans that we focus our discussion of game fans, whose activities have begun to embrace translation in modern gaming contexts.

7.2.1　Fan culture represented in the form of fan work

While it is beyond the scope of this section to cover exhaustively the entire spectrum of fan culture in games, we consider it relevant to discuss the background to fan activities, focusing on "fan work" (Burn 2006, 88), a manifestation of fan devotion to many aspects of gaming. Such fan work usually demonstrates a deeper level of fan engagement in games, which some authors see as forming a metaculture (Egenfeldt-Nielsen et al. 2008, 157). It evolves around serious players who are not satisfied with "just the game" and seek more "elaborate out-of-game" experiences in such forms as "fanart", "fanfic", "**walkthroughs** and FAQs", and "modding" that represent a considerable commitment in terms of time and effort. Their grouping and definitions differ somewhat from author to author (e.g. Burn ibid.; Dovey and Kennedy 2006, 123–143; Newman and Oram 2006, 80–87; Egenfeldt-Nielsen et al. ibid., 157–161; Newman 2008), but for our purposes we follow the descriptions provided by Newman and Oram (ibid., 82) for fanart, fanfic, walkthroughs, and FAQs, while drawing on Newman (2008, 151) for modding:

- fanart: "the production of visual art depicting or reinterpreting characters"
- fanfic (fan fiction):"the creation of narratives extending the existing storylines of games or bridging the storylines of games in a series"
- walkthroughs and FAQs: "formalised strategy guides that literally walk a player through every step of a game to success and demonstrate new and different ways of playing"
- modding (user modification): "commercial games … literally modified or even remade using software tools…creating different and sometimes wholly new playing experiences."

While walkthroughs, FAQs, and modding are specific to games; fanart and fanfic are not, and are shared across different media. It is generally agreed that modding requires the most complex technical skills, in particular an intimate familiarity with the given game system, and is therefore the rarest of fan activities (Newman and Oram ibid., 82). Newman (2008) further adds to the list what he calls "fan writing", through which fans may theorize aspects of different games often supported by extensive research of their own. Such work in turn circulates among the fan community for feedback and corrections, adding to its rich tapestry of knowledge shared and stored in the community's memory. Walkthroughs and FAQs designed for didactic purposes also illustrate other aspects of fans' desires, such as the yearning to claim a certain standing in the fan community by demonstrating their mastery and sophisticated knowledge of a particular game (Burn 2006; Newman 2008). For example, some of these guides may focus on exploiting the game's vulnerabilities and even some glitches found in the particular game, thereby verging on unethical behaviour. Given the global nature of the game culture, these guides are often translated by fans of different language groups, further spreading the influence of the particular fan work, and this in itself is considered by some authors of such guides as a sign of acknowledgement of their authority, thus adding to their recognized status (Burn ibid., 90). However, similar to other user-generated guides of various kinds which may be posted on the Internet, the fan-created walkthroughs and FAQs may betray their authors' mixed status as non-professional topic experts whose writing is described by Burn (ibid., 92) as "characterized by the excessive, excited language of the obsessive amateur on the one hand, and by the cool, detached tones of the professional on the other". These unofficial and often detailed guides are indeed constructed quite differently from their counterpart official strategy books. In particular, the notion of "cheating" is perceived differently by the authors and users of these guides and FAQs, who consider it more to be a "player's creative response to the limitations of the rule set imposed by the game" (Dovey and Kennedy ibid., 135). The same can be applied to the perception of fan translation work, which many fans consider legitimate, although it is not in the eyes of the law (Leonard 2005), even if some fan translations are voluntarily withdrawn as soon as the official translation comes out.

Modding in gaming represents the most illustrative example of deep user engagement. As such it can be treated as co-creation, closely linking a small cluster of highly skilled gamers to the original designer of a game. Although early modding can be traced back to the 1980s and the era of the Commodore 64 (see Table 1.1 for the historical development of game technologies), most sources consider the serious beginning of modding to be the mid-1990s (Egenfeldt-Nielsen et al. 2008, 160; Flew and Humphreys 2008, 134). The game *Doom* (1993) is often mentioned as the first case where the game developers started to formally grant some leeway to modders. While tending to focus on certain game genres such as FPS, real-time strategy games and more PC-based games, the practice now extends to console games (Newman 2008). The highly successful *Counter-Strike* (1999), which is a so-called "total conversion mod" of the commercial FPS title *Half-Life* (1998), showcased some significant raw talent, with some of these modders subsequently hired by Valve, the original developer of the game. While some consider mod practices to be typically "highly restricted" to a small group of extremely skilled gamers (Mactavish, cited in Dovey and Kennedy 2006, 134), Newman (2008, 167–168) maintains that mod culture is in fact supported by a wider community of gamers who work on different aspects of the game, including peer-review functionality. Modern video games are complex artefacts demanding different skill sets and some mods are only possible by effective teamwork, which reflects how games are produced in professional settings today (see Chapter 1). The importance of teamwork is also echoed in fan translation networks (O'Hagan 2008), which we discuss in the next section.

It may sound ironic that modding, which allows users substantial freedom to appropriate the original copyrighted product, is fully legal, whereas some other areas of fan engagement such as fan translation are not. This is due to an approach to intellectual property (IP) embodied in the **End User Licensing Agreements** (EULAs) which protects the interests of the industry by assigning the ownership of any modified game content to the original IP owner. For example, the EULAs make it necessary for mods to be only available locked into the code of the original commercial game, practically eliminating any possibility of modders gaining commercial advantage from their modified games. This allows the industry to encourage and support users' creative work by making tools and sometimes source code available to them without threatening the industry's own livelihood. The framework provided by the EULA can be seen as a way of coping with the shift to "co-creative media" (Dovey and Kennedy 2006), the modification and duplication of which can be afforded more readily and to a greater scale than non-electronic physical artefacts. In this way, while the practice of modding may seem to allow an infinite degree of freedom for user-fan co-creation, it is highly regulated. Nevertheless the EULA by no means solves all problems. For example, some radical modifications involving the unattributed use of copyrighted in-game characters and other visual representations from other media are far from unproblematic (Newman ibid., 171). This relates to the controversial and unclear boundary of "poaching", a term often used to describe some fan work practices where "fans creatively re-use content from other media" (Egenfeldt-Nielsen et al. 2008, 158).

In his case study of the fan work of the bestselling J-RPG *Final Fantasy VII* (1997), Burn (2006, 89) remarks on the complexities of modern digital games being multimedia and multimodal, usually limiting fans' attempts at "remaking and appropriation" reduced to "writing and drawing" in the form of fanfic or fanart. These are normally produced as a "tribute" to the original work of the game designer (Dovey and Kennedy ibid., 135) rather than as a deliberate act of subversion, even when so much liberty seems to be taken in the fan derivations. A case in point is "fan slash fiction" (the term derives from the slash used in the gender representation male/male), which typically elaborates on homosexual relationships which may not be explicit in the original. The example cited by Burn (2006) of *FFVII* fanfic depicted in YAOI[120] manga style produced in English illustrates an added layer of fusion of cultures and media forms.

In appropriating the representation of the game in this way, such practices indicate fans' acute awareness of the inherent cultural association of Japanese games in general with other popular culture genres such as manga. Furthermore, fanfic and fanart are circulated on the Internet not only among fan forums but also to wider audiences. These derivative works, considered to be "interpretive and discursive practice" by fans, seem to stimulate discussions which are otherwise not raised in the general popular account of video games (Newman and Oram ibid., 82). Furthermore, Newman and Oram (ibid., 83) point out the role of critical appraisal and rating by fans of their fellow fan work as geared towards "improving the quality of textual production with fans providing commentaries on each other's work". A similar tendency is also observed in the production of fan translation of manga and anime, where peer evaluation is valued by the fan creators and adds to their desire for high quality translation as a matter of pride (O'Hagan 2008). That said, the issue of translation quality – especially for fan

---

120. YAOI stands for *Yama-nashi, Ochi-nashi, Imi-nashi* in Japanese and roughly translates into English as "no climax, no point, no meaning" which, according to McLelland (cited in Burn ibid., 98), can broadly be equated with "American slash fiction of the PWP (Plot, What Plot?)" variety. See some FFVII Yaoi examples at http://www.fanfiction.net/community/Final-Fantasy-VII-Yaoi-Worth-Reading/3773/.

work – is never straightforward, as we noted in Chapter 4, even within the framework of a functionalist approach in which fans translate to serve the interest of the target (i.e. fellow fans). As we further elaborate below, this is especially the case when a sense of fun and playfulness impinges on the user reception and perception of localized games.

Evidence of the wider global media circulation of what would otherwise be local fan interests is demonstrated by the so-called "AYB wave", which occurred in 2000. As briefly touched on in Chapter 1, the now (in)famous line "All Your Base Are Belong to Us" taken from the extremely poor English translation of the Japanese game *Zero Wing* (1991) became an unexpected viral meme on the Internet. The whole sequence of the event is detailed by Dovey and Kennedy (2006, 136):

> The translation was...picked by a website specializing in weird game quotes which in turn inspired the Overclocked.org site to release a version of the cut scene with a parody voiceover using the original text. This version then spread through game related message boards, inspiring users to post their own 'All Your Base' images; this material was then collated with a remixed soundtrack and released online as a flash movie which rapidly spread outside the gamer communities throughout the web.... At this point...the mainstream media picked up on it with stories recounting the 'AYB' wave appearing in news media.

Dovey and Kennedy (ibid., 136) cite this incident as a case best illustrating "the divergent currents that flow through fan activity as it circulates in the unpredictable viral environment of the internet". Here fan work has become "play*ful* productivity" [emphasis in the original], (ibid.) leveraging (poor) translation which in fact worked to benefit the game's publisher in this case, rather than disadvantaging them as one might normally expect. The nature of games being primarily objects of entertainment seems to make user reactions to poorly translated games somewhat less straightforward, at least in some cases. Such a user response contrasts with other types of translation. The fact that Japanese games of earlier eras sold well internationally despite their often low quality translation suggests that there is an element of "playfulness" at work on the part of the receivers, which some might call "postmodern irony" in comparison to audience reception in domains such as literary translation or AVT in cinema. This in turn suggests that user expectations are complex and resist facile assumptions, and thus fan translations provide an interesting insight into user parameters as they purport to deliver translation by users for users (albeit for certain kinds of users).

7.2.2 Fan translation: Translation hacking and crowdsourcing

The fan work most directly relevant to our interest is fan translation, which has only relatively recently begun receiving scholarly attention in Translation Studies mainly through research on "fansubs" (Munday 2012, 279). The second revised edition of the *Routledge Encyclopedia of Translation Studies* (Baker and Saldanha [eds.] 2009) has references to fansubs and scanlation in the entries "Audiovisual Translation" and "Comics" respectively; fansubbing is introduced as a practice forming part of "amateur subtitling cultures" where "[a]mateur translators exploit traditional meaning-making codes in a creative manner" (Pérez González 2009, 19), while scanlation – a compound term from "scan" and "translation" – is considered as a manifestation of "the manga fan subculture in orienting translation practices" (Zanettin 2009, 40). Fansubs in their broadest sense may refer to any subtitles made by fans of foreign films, whereas their narrower definition points to fan subtitles specifically of anime (Leonard 2005). Scanlation in turn refers to "a streamlined manga fan translation practice" where officially published pages of manga are first scanned, translated, and distributed by fans (O'Hagan 2008, 162).

In these fields of popular culture (and particularly in the case of anime) such practices originated in the 1980s and have rapidly developed and flourished since the late 1990s as a result of the technological environments of more readily available media editing tools, the Internet and the advent of Web 2.0. These trends are explained by media studies scholars as being part of participatory culture, illustrating a deep engagement in media consumption by some fans (Jenkins 2006) as touched on earlier. Studies on fansub practices in Translation Studies have so far pointed to their variable quality and also their possible follow-on effect on AVT norms (Díaz Cintas and Muñoz Sánchez 2006). At the same time fans' search for authenticity is often provoked as a reaction to what they consider to be the excessive manipulation applied in the translation process, which in turn has been linked to an interventionist goal by such fans (Pérez González 2009). Nornes (2007) introduced the term "abusive subtitling", focusing on the often experimental and defiant approaches epitomized in some fansubs. Both practices have also been studied from the viewpoint of translation pedagogy and some of their elements have been found to fit well, somewhat paradoxically, within the framework of the social constructivist approach to translator training, where fans as translators-to-be learn how to translate in an authentic, social environment (O'Hagan 2008). There have also been discussions on fansubs from cultural and Asian studies perspectives often focusing on the cultural negotiations that fans engage in (Cubbison 2005; Leonard 2005; Levi 2006). One of the common observations made by scholars on these forms of translation is that fan translation is usually conducted in a team and fans are often savvy users of technology, making the maximum use of the Internet and various computer-based tools to facilitate production and distribution of fan work.

In contrast to the increasing attention given to the above forms of fan translation, there has been a lack of scholarly work in Translation Studies focusing on the fan translation phenomenon applied to video games. Among the few studies is one on "romhacking" by Muñoz Sánchez (2007, 2009) based on the author's own experience of game fan translation activities, thus providing first-hand insights into the actual processes involved. O'Hagan (2009b) in turn has examined the translation hacking of video games along with various other types of fan-based translation as a form of user-generated translation (UGT), linking it to the emerging practice of crowdsourcing. From an interest in game studies, Newman (2008, 156–160) discusses fan translation as part of a wide range of gamer activities, highlighting the "reconfiguration" of games undertaken outside the official industry framework. Fan translation of video games – commonly known as "translation hacking" – is another variety of "romhacking", i.e. hacking into data on the Read-only Memory (ROM) of a game program. As the name suggests, it is a breach of the Digital Millennium Copyright Act (DMCA), which prohibits manipulation of ROM content (Muñoz Sánchez 2009, 180). From a practitioner's perspective, Muñoz Sánchez (ibid., 170) provides a definition of ROM-hacking as "the process of modifying the ROM data of a video game to alter the games' graphics, dialogues, levels, gameplay…" which is carried out for the purpose of either "editing a game to create new levels or to change characters' attributes" or "translating it from one language into another". Translation hacking involves extracting the relevant text from the ROM and replacing it with a corresponding translated script. This process usually involves a hacker locating the game's font to produce what is known as a "table", which in turn allows text data to be identified and then to be copied ("dumped") in a file for translation. The resulting translation is released as a ROM patch to be applied to the original ROM to effect the translation and is played on a console emulator. Further details of the exact steps involved are available in Muñoz Sánchez (2009).

Given the highly specific technical skills required, the process of translation hacking is usually performed by a hacker and a fan translator working together (O'Hagan 2009b, 108). As can be discerned from this description, the work involved in game translation hacking is significantly more time-consuming and technically challenging than other types of fan translation (Newman 2008, 158). The above broad outline in turn can be compared to our description of the official game localization process explained in detail in Chapter 3, where localization engineers deal with the technical details required to prepare a localization kit as well as integration of the translated strings. The highly technical and laborious tasks involved in translation hacking raise the issue of what motivates fans to go to these lengths to produce a translation.

The literature points to two reasons why fans undertake the translation of games: while translations may occasionally be undertaken to compensate for poor official translations or localization, they are often carried out to compensate for a lack of availability of games in certain locales. As we demonstrated, the distribution of console games is tightly controlled by publishers' marketing strategies. These determine in which territories their games are to be released, with some territories inevitably missing out. For example, the limited availability of J-RPGs – which are generally known for their high volume of text – in the early days was considered to be related to "the potentially marginal profitability of the titles given the high costs of translating and localization" (Newman 2008, 156). As can also be noted with anime fan protests (Cubbison 2005), the first step taken to counter the lack of a translation seems to be for fans to collect signatures for a petition to bring the issue to the publisher's attention. If this fails, fans may then resort to fan translation by forming a project team. In the case of another J-RPG *Mother 3* (2006), published by Nintendo for Game Boy Advance, despite some 30,000 signatures on fan petitions asking for a localization (Miyamoto, cited in Newman 2008, 157), Nintendo decided not to localize the game, possibly due to poor US sales of the previous instalment, *Mother 2* (1994), known as *Earthbound* in the US (Newman ibid.). The resulting 2008 fan translation into English of *Mother 3* prompted over 100,000 downloads during its first week of release (Parkin 2008). Being aware of the precarious legal position of such undertakings, fan translation projects of games often declare, in a similar manner to fansubs, that they will stop their activities as soon as the publisher decides to release an official translation, as indicated in the following from the *Mother 3* Fan Translation website:[121]

> As we've mentioned throughout the history of the project, our team has agreed that this translation project will come to a full stop if/when we hear that Nintendo has chosen to pursue an official translation of the game. Our only goal is to get MOTHER 3 in the hands of the fans.

There are many cases where the IP owners turn a blind eye to such fan activities because fans normally pick for their projects old video games which do not affect sales, given that many of these titles are no longer marketed (Muñoz Sánchez 2009, 180). However, they do not always target obsolete games and fan translation groups occasionally receive legal warnings from the IP owner, as was the case with

---

121.   See http://mother3.fobby.net/blog/faqs/.

the highly popular Square Enix game *Chrono Trigger* (1995) (see Muñoz Sánchez 2009, 180–181). While modding, which comes under the scope of EULA, can be considered a legal way of enjoying fan co-creative activities, translation hacking is currently considered illegal, regardless of the fact that "romhacking projects are carried out by fans for fans with no profit motive in mind" (Muñoz Sánchez ibid., 181). From the point of view of the IP owners fan translation is far from innocent despite the typical fan manifesto that they do not seek commercial gain. In fact, even among fans there seem to be divergent views as to what constitutes ethically acceptable behaviour (Burn 2006, 102).

As may often be noted in examples of fan work, approaches seem to swing between reverence for the ST and the desire to remain faithful to it on the one hand, and, on the other, the impulse to "dramatically alter the original text, adapting it to express the particular interest of the fan or fan group" (Burn ibid., 88). We relate these fan desires to the different reasons why fans undertake their own translations. In addition to their main motivation to fill a gap in the games market as discussed above, fans may also undertake their own translations because they consider some official translations to be of poor quality. As such, unlike other kinds of fan work, fan translation generally seems to be motivated by a search for authenticity rather than the opportunity for embellishment. Newman (2008) argues that fans' dissatisfaction with official translations appears to relate to what has been deleted or altered in the localized versions from the original. Some fans accumulate a highly detailed knowledge of particular games, often through extensive research of their own, and some may develop various "theories" about certain aspects which are ambiguous or even do not make sense in localized games (Newman 2008, 155). Such theorizing is therefore often triggered by discrepancies which fans may spot between different regional releases (i.e. locales) of the game in relation to the original, in turn sometimes raising issues with localization and translation approaches. These gaps seem to lead to a certain scepticism among fans about the official localized versions. As Newman notes:

> This is indicative of a common complaint encountered in much of the discussion in gamer forums who tend [sic] to denigrate the official localizations and translations. There is a shared feeling that those involved with the official translations either take liberties with or are simply insufficiently well versed in the minute detail of the canon to produce a sensitive English language version. This dismissive distrust manifests itself in a number of ways and it is clear that the lack of care in preserving the continuity and integrity of the canon as envisioned by the originators aggravates these gamers. (Newman ibid., 61)

Seeking authenticity as a goal is also well recognized in other types of fan translation such as fansubs, with fans protesting that official translations represent what they consider to be undue alteration or sanitization of the original content (e.g. Cubbison 2005). As observed by Muñoz Sánchez (2009, 178), one of the traits of the fan translation of games is the deliberate ignoring of ratings requirements and restoring censored elements such as "foul language, sexual content or copyright issues with brand names". This illustrates how the subtraction of any elements from the original could be considered by fans to be a failure to meet their expectations. On the other hand, blatantly poor translations might well be accepted by fans, as happened in the early days of game localization, with little to no effect on sales (as discussed in Chapters 1 and 5). From the other side of the fence, some of these deficiencies are the direct result of the commercial pressures on official translators, including tight localization schedules, the less than optimal way in which they need to work without the full textual context or having to conform to censorship of sorts, be it age ratings for games or broadcasting codes by television networks in the case of TV anime. The empowered users and the commissioning "patrons" of translation, whose respective roles are not clear-cut in terms of internal and external knowledge perspectives (Pym 2004, 28), further challenge translators in terms of professional norms in relation to expectancy norms in delivering the final products.

Another form of translation which has recently emerged outside the official professional localization framework is the practice of volunteer translation known variously as "community translation", "collaborative translation" or "crowdsourcing". Coined by Howe (2008), the term "crowdsourcing" refers to the outsourcing of a task to an unspecified group of Internet users, the "crowd", generally on a voluntary basis. The wealth of user-generated content available on the Internet has shown that "users as both remediators and direct producers of new media content engage in new forms of large-scale participation in digital media spaces" (Flew 2008, 35–36). Facilitated by the general technological trends towards openness and sharing, such user-based solutions have spread to many different professional areas. Crowdsourcing has rapidly entered corporate discourse as a new and innovative way of tackling problems by soliciting help from the wider Internet community in the form of an open call (Howe 2006). The concept of "user-based task completion" has been pioneered by Wikipedia, where groups of people voluntarily contribute their domain knowledge and overwrite prior contributions by other people constantly improving the content, facilitated by the collaborative authoring platform *Wiki*. This draws on the power of Internet users, whose interest and knowledge in the given subject area drives them to perform a task voluntarily as a matter of pride and personal satisfaction, mostly without formal remuneration.

In the area of translation, similar participatory trends, leading to user-generated translation, have recently started to attract the attention of translation scholars (O'Hagan 2011b; Cronin 2013), while localization companies are looking to crowdsourcing as a viable business model applicable to for-profit enterprises (Ray 2009). Similar attempts by non-profit organizations often attract professional translators to volunteer alongside untrained translators. Highlighting the humanitarian orientation of some initiatives using crowdsourcing, Schäler (2009, 161) considers this concept to provide "emerging localization frameworks that are no longer predominantly focused on commercial concerns". The application of crowdsourcing in translation has become particularly well-known through its implementation by the social networking site Facebook. Facebook solicited its users to help meet its localization needs by involving them in the translation of short individual text fragments mainly for the UI of its website and by providing them with a dedicated translation platform (O'Hagan 2009b). This trend can thus be linked to the increasing influence of fans in the domain of video games, where they may freely localize games and distribute them online, in much the same manner as fansubbers create and distribute their own subtitles for their favourite anime or other types of audiovisual material (Pérez González 2006).

While crowdsourcing is an emerging topic in Translation Studies, there have been an increasing number of studies appearing from the commercial sector in the form of industry research reports, including those commissioned by CommonSense Advisory (DePalma and Kelly 2008), the Translation Automation Users Group (TAUS 2009) and LISA (Ray 2009). In the academic context, research initiatives have been ongoing to develop a computer-aided translation (CAT) platform especially to facilitate volunteer translator collaboration (e.g. Bey et al. 2006; Désilets 2007). Crowdsourcing is also discussed by García (2009) and O'Hagan (2009b) as having the potential to impact on the future working environment of professional translators and localizers. Perhaps the most notable and relevant aspect of this new Internet-based distributed problem-solving model is the change in our communications infrastructure and the move to open – as opposed to closed – networks demonstrated by social networking media. As we have observed, various types of fan work have been performed either individually or in groups, but all benefit from sharing the content and receiving feedback from peers interacting online. The formation of fan communities in turn exerts many different influences on the game industry by way of fan co-creation via modding or even through illegal translation hacking, often providing the industry with valuable user feedback on products (albeit through the back door). Crowdsourcing in turn tries to deploy the same energy and devotion of some users to facilitate organizations' needs, as demonstrated in the cases of Google, Microsoft, Intel, and Adobe, to name but a few global businesses. One of the key shifts from fan translation to crowdsourced translation is that the latter is usually a solicited practice normally organized by the IP owners of the text, and content is thus legal, whereas the former is a typically unsolicited illegal practice initiated by fans themselves. In the next section we further discuss these models from the viewpoint of academic study as well as the interests of the industry, especially with regard to the question of ethics in the case of user co-creation.

The translation journals *Linguistica Antverpiensia* (O'Hagan 2011b) and *The Translator* (Pérez-González and Susam-Saraeva 2012) have dedicated special issues to this topic, indicating the significance in Translation Studies of the phenomenon of translation undertaken by parties who fall outside the strictly professional community of translators. Among the lines of enquiry brought to light was the question of ethics arising from the fact that untrained translators are performing translation albeit without remuneration (McDonough Dolmaya 2011) and also the adequacy and relevance of existing professional codes of ethics in view of the newly emerging contexts of translation crowdsourcing (Drugan 2011). Conflict over the use of free "labour of love" for commercial benefit has arisen on a number of occasions. In 2009 the professional social networking site LinkedIn became embroiled in a debate among its translator members when their questionnaire asked the site's translator users about their willingness to translate for free, most likely intended in the same spirit of crowdsourcing translation implemented by Facebook. It led to the immediate formation of the group "Translators against Crowdsourcing for Commercial Business" with the then President of the American Translators Association (ATA) issuing a formal letter of complaint on the conduct of LinkedIn towards its professional translator members (Stejskal 2009). In her analysis of this reaction by the professional translator community, Kelly (2009), a subject specialist who had co-authored a report on the topic (DePalma and Kelly 2008), in turn commented that such a reaction suggests a lack of understanding by translation professionals of what crowdsourcing entails. Comparing it to negative reactions from freelance translators in the early days of CAT tools – tools which are now widespread in the translation industry – Kelly maintains that "it is simply another method of working in the digital age", implying a transformation in work environments.

Well before the emergence of the crowdsourcing phenomenon the movement from proprietary to open source approaches had already set the course for a certain change of mind-set, leading to volunteer collaboration and contributions for content creation and sharing. Berry (2008, 110–112) points out how the initial impetus towards the open source movement came from the practice in early computer science labs in the US where computer programmers worked in collaboration – rather than in competition – with fellow programmers, so they could avoid duplicating the laborious routine of programming. Such approaches form the backbone of the Internet, where users, including translators, are benefiting from free applications and information. Crowdsourcing could be understood as part of the same general tendency to shift from a proprietary and closed approach to one predicated on openness and collaboration. Based on a number of case studies of for-profit and non-profit crowdsourcing scenarios, McDonough Dolmaya (2011) in turn highlights what is at stake from a scholarly perspective on ethical issues. Her study identifies one problematic area as the way in which certain crowdsourcing initiatives are organized and presented to the public in a less than transparent manner. While such projects may serve to make translation work more visible in the eyes of the public, they can also devalue the perception of translation work as not requiring specialized skills (ibid., 106). She also points to a blurring of the boundaries between translation consumers and producers, as well as a shifting of some of the responsibilities for translation to users with future implications for the profession (ibid., 107). As implied by McDonough Dolmaya's nuanced comments, the question of ethics is rarely clear-cut, further adding to the "ethical dilemmas" encountered regularly in the context of translation and interpretation as substantiated by Baker (2011, 274–299).

Today's dynamic work environments increasingly require translators to adapt to new contexts, as is the case with game localization, sometimes leading to dilemmas of an ethical or moral nature.[122] One former student's recent interview experience for a localization position at an online game company further brought home the significance of the translator's response to such a dilemma. The interviewer asked the student how she would respond if a client called to say s/he intended to commit suicide as a result of playing a game that she (the student) had localized (Irwin, personal communication, January 5, 2012). As we mentioned before, moral questions are never far away when dealing with video games. Baker's suggestion to "approach every assignment not just as a technical but as a primarily ethical challenge" (2011, 290) may ring particularly true to those who work in the video game industry.

Returning to the increasing accommodation of user participation in content creation, the video game industry is something of a pioneer with its use of play testers and also permitting the practice of modding, where users are able to legally modify games. More recently many games promote user-generated content. Dovey and Kennedy (2006, 130) point out how today's game software production system understands "configurative practice" by users as their "brand loyalty". Salen and Zimmerman (2004, 539 cited in Dovey and Kennedy ibid.) in turn describe games which facilitate player creation as "open system games", relating them to the open source software movement. This relates to the concept of a game system facilitating **emergent gameplay**, thus working as a catalyst for such player

---

122. Baker (2011, 276) uses the terms "ethics" and "morality" interchangeably on purpose, despite accepting the commonly perceived distinction of "ethics" as more collective and "morality" as individualistic.

behaviours (Salen and Zimmerman ibid., cited in Dovey and Kennedy 2006, 131). Emergent gameplay refers to unexpected ways of playing the game, which may not have been intended by the game designer (Juul 2005, 76). Various fan work, including modding activities to edit the game, can indeed be viewed in this light, where games are increasingly designed to accommodate user customization. Some consider that modding under the control of the EULA provides the game industry with free R&D (Dovey and Kennedy ibid., 134) while avoiding any risk of modders gaining a financial advantage. The EULA is the game industry's way of plugging into such user creativity without adversely impacting their own business interests.

Cultural studies scholars such as Leonard (2005) point out how the generally lenient attitudes by Japanese IP owners of anime in the early days of their circulation permitted fans to appropriate content, in turn paving the way for the formation of a global fan-base for this initially esoteric Japanese sub-culture. A similar mutually beneficial relationship between the game industry and gamer-fans is demonstrated by the increasing presence and influence of elaborate fan work. Fan translation represents yet another new dimension arising from the significant impact of changing technologies in the development of co-creative media. When game publishers decide not to allocate resources for the localization of certain games for certain territories, they are leaving opportunities for translation hackers with highly sophisticated technical knowledge to bridge the gap, albeit not in an entirely legal manner. Given that the industry already has the precedence of legal modding, one could make a case for legalizing translation hacking and even providing certain tools to facilitate such activities, as in modding, to actively promote game localization crowdsourcing. Open source approaches are already applied to proprietary CAT tools originally designed for professional use, making such tools available to wider groups of general users who engage in various translation activities. We discuss the issue of translation technology in the last section of this chapter. The next section examines the issue of fan knowledge versus that of professional translators working in the field of game localization.

7.2.3 Fan translator expertise versus professional expertise

As already highlighted in previous chapters, game localizers should ideally be game literate and familiar with the games they translate. Yet this is not always the case due to various reasons and constraints. Prior studies (Mangiron 2006; Bernal-Merino 2007; Muñoz Sánchez 2009; O'Hagan 2009b) highlight factors less favourable to achieving high quality localization that are prevalent in commercial game localization, such as the constantly diminishing time to market in sim-ship contexts, which in turn squeezes the localization schedule to the bare minimum. These conditions more often than not deny translators the opportunity of carrying out sufficient research into their translation, including gaining a familiarity with the game or even being provided with sufficient context for the game they are being asked to work on. This contrasts with the increasing level of expertise accumulated especially by hardcore gamers, who are steadily improving their skills and knowledge of games, further facilitated by a collective knowledge-base that is readily available online mainly thanks to fan work. This widening gap in knowledge between non-gamer professional localizers and seasoned gamers has a number of implications for localization methods (Chapter 3) and also for translation pedagogy (Chapter 6) in relation to the question of professional translators' competence. As we discussed in Chapter 3, within the professional localization environment there is also a difference between the outsourcing model and the in-house model. In the outsourcing model, localizers tend to have limited access to the developer to seek information as well as to the game itself, while in the in-house model localizers are generally more likely to be given access to the full context of the game with opportunities to communicate directly with developers. In both cases, when fan translators criticize the shortcomings of some of the official translations, naturally they are unlikely to be fully aware of some of the conditions under which the work was carried out. Nevertheless from a consumer's point of view, final products should withstand the scrutiny of even the most knowledgeable of users. In this section we examine the increasingly visible presence of users, whose role is intersecting with that of professional localizers and translators, although there remain distinct differences.

In the context of the new generation of web technologies commonly referred to as Web 2.0, media studies scholars (Jenkins 2006; Flew 2008) and business commentators (Tapscott and Williams 2006) both highlight user empowerment. Supported by the powerful communication infrastructure provided by the Internet, and with a broad range of freely available tools at their disposal, various user activities or "co-creation" (Dovey and Kennedy 2006, 123–143) are being mainstreamed, albeit not always in entirely legal ways. Previously such activities may have been dismissed as marginal at best and verging on criminal at worst, but the situation is now changing. An example supporting this trend is the close link between fans and the game industry, evident in the fact that "most [game] developers are drawn from game fan communities" (Dovey and Kennedy 2006, 47). Similarly, studies on fan translation suggest a progressively broadening fan translation base, despite the question of legality. In the climate of increasingly deregulated open translation environments, as exemplified by crowdsourcing, user co-creation and user-led innovation are celebrated in certain areas of new media, although not always without controversy. Some authors (e.g. Keen 2007) question the merits of *Wikipedia* versus *Encyclopedia Britannica* or of fan work versus professional work, and caution against the hype to support "amateurs" over professionals. Taking both sides of the argument into consideration, we investigate the question of professional competence versus non-professional competence in the context of game localization practice. In addition to the debate on vocational training versus academic education raised in Chapter 6, we also consider the emerging requirements for preparing game translators in view of games as complex technological commercial products, on the one hand, and the broader view of games as co-creative media, on the other.

Returning to the motivation for fan translation of games, we note that one of the reasons why fans translate is linked to problems with the quality of officially translated games not meeting the expectations of certain gamers. The early days of game localization, when blatant and basic translation errors were rampant, seem to have largely gone, especially for mainstream console games. Yet there are still examples of fans claiming official localization to be of inferior quality, thus prompting fan translation as in the case of the Spanish version of the US RPG title *Oblivion IV: The Elder Scrolls* (2006) subsequently translated by the fan community Clan DLAN (Díaz Montón 2007). In turn the fan translation of Super Nintendo Entertainment System's (SNES) RPG title *Tales of Phantasia* (1996) is mentioned as an example of high quality fan translation work (Muñoz Sánchez 2009, 177–178) translated from Japanese into English by the fan group DeJap. In previous chapters we discussed the constraints associated with commercial game localization, stemming from a tight schedule, a lack of context for fragments of text to be translated and a model of game development which does not implement internationalization, all of which impose constraints that are detrimental to high quality localization.

Within the different areas of translation work, game localization probably has a less clear-cut division between professional and fan translators owing to the fact that the game industry values translators' game literacy, often prioritizing "experience as a gamer, and knowledge of the gaming world" (Mangiron 2006, 315). One such fan translator turned professional game translator, Clyde Mandelin, maintains that fan translation experience has been invaluable to his role as a professional translator (interview quoted in Parkin 2008, 2). To the extent that experience as a modder could count positively towards certain game development jobs, some industry professionals could legitimately come from a fan translator background. In an interview with the game developer magazine *Gamasutra* (Parkin 2008, 2), Mandelin is quoted as saying that "every pro translator [working in the game industry] I know is/was a fan translator". He himself is still engaged in fan translation, as exemplified in his work with the *Mother 3* fan translation project mentioned earlier. As a means of gaining "situated experience", fan translation can be considered to be advantageous in acquiring practical work experience, although there are obvious differences between working in fan and professional settings. In his comparative study on professional and fan game translation, Muñoz Sánchez (2009) highlights two areas as unique aspects of fan translation. Whereas professional localizers are bound by the age rating rules and censorship constraints imposed by different territories (see Chapters 4 and 5), fan translators are free to ignore any such constraints. He also points out a special injection of humour which may be added by fans, which was not present in the original (2009, 179–180). Similarly Mandelin (in Parkin ibid., 2) mentions the freedom fans enjoy in terms of being able to fix errors in the published official translation whereas professional translations will have to "go through tons of red tape to get things fixed" as he remarks:

> [W]ith a professional translation, you usually can't fix any mistakes. So if you make an error or a typo (perhaps due to a tight deadline), it'll be out there in the public forever for fans to pick apart. With fan translations, you can always make revisions and release new versions easily.   (Mandelin, cited in Parkin 2008, 2)

In some ways this can be seen as analogous to the comparison between *Wikipedia* and *Encyclopedia Britannica* – errors in the former can be quickly fixed, while the same is not true for the latter without having to go through the official hierarchy of the approval system.

As Dovey and Kennedy (2006, 134) point out, gamer feedback is already officially incorporated into the commercial production of games by way of gamer participation in **beta testing** and, in some instances, in more central game development work. A good example of this is the case of Lucas Arts, who hired fans as part of the design team for the online multiplayer game of *Star Wars* (*Star Wars: Republic Commando* 2005) (Jenkins 2003, cited in Dovey and Kennedy ibid.). In some cases, gamers with some linguistic knowledge and with a detailed understanding of games and game systems could complement the skills of professional translators whose knowledge of games may not match that of fans. O'Hagan (2008) suggests that translation skills may be picked up relatively quickly by highly motivated fan translators, owing to their experience in fan work being well "situated" in authentic contexts and also due to timely peer reviews and feedback. Nevertheless, in reality incorporating fan knowledge into time-pressured commercial localization practices in any formal way may not be easy. Similarly, linking the training of localizers in classrooms to fan communities by a formal arrangement will pose both pedagogical and administrative challenges. In an ideal scenario, collaboration between gamer-translators who lack formal translator training yet have substantial background knowledge of gaming and professional game translators/localizers who may not be game-literate should go some way towards filling the knowledge gap discussed earlier. To a certain extent, the game industry has already recognized the advantage of fan work experience and is acknowledging it in a positive light rather than treating it as evidence of a shady past which should be kept hidden.

These observations highlight the blurred boundary between "internal knowledge" and the "external knowledge" held by the localization insider and the outsider respectively, as we noted in Chapter 4. Seasoned hardcore gamers possess knowledge about a given game and this may be as great as, or sometimes greater than, that of game localizers, whose access to the game information may be severely curtailed due to the time pressure and the internal communication arrangements, for example, between the localizer and the game developer. At the same time various official constraints imposed on professional translators do not apply to their fan counterparts. This imbalance and overlap between internal and external knowledge could motivate a mass-scale collaboration model as a possible response to fully exploit the characteristics of new media, such as video games being more conducive to co-creation than other traditional media. A collaboration-based localization model between professional localizers and fans who reside outside the professional realm could combine external and internal knowledge in a fruitful way and might prove to be not only a productive solution, but the only solution in increasingly time-constrained localization scenarios, involving highly specialized game worlds. The way in which professional norms and expectancy norms influence each other can provide further clues to understanding the intricacies involved in translating games. That said, the actual implementation of such a collaborative model is undoubtedly challenging. Research in this direction could provide both a commercially productive and a worthwhile line of inquiry in Translation Studies by shedding light on the nature of the different types of knowledge needed in translation and their manifestation in the final product. Research into successful platform design which is purpose-built for translation crowdsourcing, such as Facebook Translations (Dombek 2011), may also provide insight into how collaboration takes place among disparate parties all involved in the same translation project.

The next section addresses a research avenue arising out of the impact of the technological changes affecting modern translation practices such as game localization, first with reference to physiological empirical research methodology and, second, relating to broader technological applications to video games with the potential to impact translation.

7.3   A new research direction in Translation Studies: User-focused empirical research

In this last section, keeping our focus on users, we discuss a research direction aimed at understanding how localized games are received by end users. We have stressed that game localization ultimately seeks to transfer player experience from the original to the end users in the target market. This makes game localization a function-oriented translation, often prompting the translator to transcreate, albeit within a set of strict constraints normally governed by the commissioning brief of game publishers. Given the skopos of game localization, focused on the user's satisfaction with the final product, we can argue that research addressing user reception is well justified. In particular, our main interest is about empirically-supported user studies which investigate players' physiological responses, in addition to collecting other subjective data through interviews and questionnaires. As mentioned in Chapter 4, game companies have recently started to collect "**game metrics**" to understand player behaviour and therefore player experience (PX). The section on PX studies is followed by some final brief observations on future developments in game technology and their potential impact on localization in the area of Natural Language Processing (NLP) applications aiming to enhance interaction between the player and the game system. This discussion is admittedly speculative and intended merely to point to some possible future implications for localization research.

7.3.1   Player experience studies

The importance of reception studies to understanding users' needs and the impact of AVT on users have been acknowledged by the AVT research community for some time now (e.g. Gambier 2003). Yet to date such research needs have not been fully met, as lamented by Gambier (2009, 52) who maintains: "[v]ery few studies have dealt with the issue of reception in AVT, and even fewer have looked at empirically [sic], even though we continually make references to readers, viewers, customers, users, etc." Part of the difficulty in operationalizing reception studies is due to a wide range of variables in relation to users as well as types of AV content. The inherent heterogeneity of the audience with varying preferences, ages and abilities, as well as that of AV content, all influence reception. At the same time, the meaning of "reception" itself lacks clarity, as Gambier points out (2009, 52–53). He proposes three types of reception on the basis of Kovačič (1995) and Chesterman (2007): response, reaction, and repercussion. "Response" is explained as "perceptual decoding" by the viewer, for example, relating to the "feeling" of the recipient, whereas "reaction" relates to "psycho-cognitive issues" in reference to the effects of translation such as subtitle readability, which may be influenced by such factors as the viewer's prior knowledge of the subject and inference process. "Repercussion" in turn arises from the viewer's "attitudinal issues", including preferences and habits, also relating to socio-cultural issues. Extended methodologies inspired by experimental psychology and eye-tracker-based user studies in AVT have recently been used to examine the notion of viewer "reaction", specifically captured as the objective physiological response to an AVT mode such as subtitles, often triangulated with other subjective perception data (e.g. Caffrey 2008; Künzli and Ehrensberger-Dow 2011). These studies aim to identify effective AVT strategies from users' perspectives and the same user-focus direction can be applied to game localization research.

To our knowledge, localized games are rarely tested systematically by authentic potential users prior to their release, other than through internal testing by assigned testers (see Chapter 3) during the localization process. We therefore assume that game localization is currently not directly informed by any formal user studies, despite the fact that such reception studies are ideally required for any software based systems which explicitly involve user interaction and thus are especially applicable to video games. Functional and linguistic testing has always been an integral part of the localization process to ensure that a given localized product works properly in the user environment. In the context of such testing, localizers in effect act as assumed end players in a given territory. However, as noted in Chapter 4, the distinction between internal and external knowledge can be significant, inherently limiting the ability of "insiders", such as localizers, to assume the role of the end users. Ideally, actual user tests of localized products, equivalent to play testing or beta testing commonly conducted during the game development phase (see Chapters 1 and 3), are desirable. However, anecdotal evidence from game localization testers suggests that the testing schedule is often extremely tight to the extent that it is not uncommon for testers to find their bug reports ignored unless they bring to light critical errors such as those contributing to the game crashing. Given the tight production schedule particularly in sim-ship scenarios, any extra testing session, if it can be fitted into the process, needs to be conducted in an efficient and focused manner.

As a subset of User Experience (UX), interest in capturing PX is gathering pace in the game industry as well as in game research. For example, the EU-funded research project "The Fun of Gaming: Measuring the Human Experience of Media Enjoyment (FUGA)" (2006–2009) was designed specifically to address the lack of established methods in measuring player experience in playing digital games. The objective of FUGA was to develop novel comprehensive methods to examine how the different aspects of player experience involving different emotions and cognitions can be assessed.[123] The FUGA project, as well as other recent game research aimed in a similar direction (Mandryk 2008; Drachen et al. 2009), suggest an increasing interest in more precisely identifying PX. In particular, there has been specific interest in the emotional and affective dimensions of PX (Nacke and Drachen 2011), which is justified by the fact that games are "affective media" (Juul 2005). Recent emotion-engineering approaches, also known as "affective computing" and applied in user-focused game research (e.g. Dormann and Biddle 2010; Orero et al. 2010) also illustrate the significance of user emotions in understanding PX. A point we have emphasized throughout this book is that there are marked differences between localizing productivity software and entertainment software such as games, and these can be attributed to the far more pronounced affective characteristic of the latter.

Researchers admit that PX is a complex concept for which current research has yet to identify precise variables (Nacke and Drachen 2011) and practically no research has been conducted in the context of localized games (O'Hagan 2010). For example, PX can be considered to encompass all of "response", "reaction" and "repercussion". This suggests significant scope for future empirical research in game localization focused on players as product users. Such research could also contribute to addressing the current paucity of empirically-robust reception studies in AVT, as mentioned above, while indicating a shift in interest from product-oriented or process-oriented research addressing translator behaviour to translation user experience which can be correlated to translation strategies. Furthermore, by implementing physiological data in the form of biometrics combined with subjective user perception data, a more holistic picture of PX can be expected to emerge. Such a research direction is in line with the interest which the game industry has been showing in PX, with companies such as Microsoft making a focused effort to obtain game metrics from players (see Kim et al. 2008). Nacke et al. (2009) define game metrics as numerical data obtained from game software about player behaviour which is useful for identifying what happens, when, and where during the gameplay. For example, game metrics could identify locations where and when "deaths" of the protagonist occur most frequently in a game. A summary and selected methods of their comparative analysis of different approaches in game metrics and biometrics to PX is shown in Table 7.1. On the basis of Nacke et al. (2009) the table indicates key advantages and disadvantages of more traditional approaches focused on play tester style and those of more recent approaches based on game metrics and biometrics. By condensing the original

---

123.   For more details, see the FUGA project site: http://fuga.aalto.fi/.

Table 7.1 Comparative observations of methods used in measuring player experience

Approach	Method	Advantages	Drawbacks
Play tester style	Direct observation	Get a feel for player interaction with game; importance of action (as opposed to what they say)	Presence of observers biasing results; behaviour requiring interpretation
Play tester style	Q & A: structured querying of play testers; validate play test goals; supplementary information	Answer specific design questions; determine specific player intent	Group biases; people don't know why they do what they do; potential for biased questions
Play tester style	Verbal reports: think aloud protocol	Glimpse into player thoughts, feelings, and motivations; bring up unnoticed details; effective for "why" questions	Interferes with gameplay; creates an artificial experience; inaccurate and biased
Play tester style	Surveys: set of standardized questions; forced choice responses; quantify feedback; player categorization	Less biased responses; response validation; forced choice revealing preferences; time-based comparisons	Nuance may be lost; difficulty converting ratings to meaningful decisions; limited solution space
Game metrics	Geographical information system (GIS): process information with spatial dimension	Flexible; off the shelf; cheaper; minimal customization	Overkill; not integrated into game engine; limited 3D representation
Biometrics	Galvanic skin response (GSR): measure sweat glands; measure electrical resistance (or conductance); correlate to psychological arousal	Easy to measure; inexpensive hardware; easy to interpret; non-intrusive	Noisy signal or signals add together; large individual variations in baseline and responsivity
Biometrics	Cardiovascular measures: heart rate (HR)	Easy to measure (HR); inexpensive hardware; salient established measures	Intrusive to measure accurately; affected by many factors
Biometrics	Eye-tracking: saccades (fast movement of the eyes); fixations (attention focus); pupil dilation/blink rate	Easy to use; objective; covert; continuous; quantifiable; replicable; advantage of empirical data	Expensive; time-consuming

Source: Adapted from Nacke et al. (2009).

information from Nacke et al. this is intended to be an at-a-glance guide for researchers hoping to conduct empirically-oriented game localization studies.

Rather than providing specific explanations of the information listed in the table, we will contextualise the information, relating it to our own research experience below. A previous small-scale preliminary study (O'Hagan 2009a) (also see Chapter 5) was based on a play tester style approach, using a video-captured gameplay trajectory (including recordings of any autonomous utterances by the player), and a structured player log kept by the subject. Designed to identify issues which could lead to less than optimum PX in a localized game, the experiment was set up in the subject's normal surroundings, as opposed to artificial lab conditions, and also without the presence of the researcher so as to remove any bias. This method relied on the self-reporting of the participant, which could raise the issue of data validity, but the setup allowed the player to play the game in a more natural authentic setting. The fact that a player log was made mandatory at each saving point to avoid a memory lapse made for fairly accurate reporting, and seemed to match the play trajectory (ibid.). The recordings of the subject proved valuable in considering the "what" question, while a retrospective player interview was able to address the "why" question to explain certain behaviours and actions taken which were shown in the play trajectory. Both data sets were used to identify potential problem areas, which may have lessened the PX of a localized version of a Japanese game. Interestingly in this experiment the participant rejected the use of real-time verbal reporting (i.e. Think Aloud Protocols or TAP) as too distracting, interfering with his gameplay and causing a reduced focus, and it therefore had to be abandoned (ibid.). Nevertheless, overall the experiment served to demonstrate the advantages of a detailed play tester-style user-study. As discussed in Chapter 5 under cross-cultural game design, the study (ibid.) highlighted particular aspects in the localized version of the Japanese game, indicating a need for specific areas of adjustment in the localized version which may have improved the PX. However, while this approach provided a pointer to allow a fine-grained qualitative analysis, it lacked more objective quantifiable data of the subject's response to the game, partly due to the study's limitation of relying on one subject and partly because no objective physiological data was collected.

Encouraged by this earlier study and taking into account the shortcomings identified, a further exploratory experiment was conducted to capture the PX of players playing the localized version of a game, this time focusing on biometric data, using eye-tracking, heart-rate and also galvanic skin response (GSR) measurements (O'Hagan 2010). This subsequent study focused on the specific emotional dimension of overt and covert humour as anchor points relating to one of the key entertainment values of the particular game *Plants vs. Zombies* (2009) in an attempt to define underlying factors affecting the PX of a localized game. This focus was based on the recognition that while games are localized for entertainment value and enjoyment, the concept of "entertainment" or "enjoyment" currently lacks a clear definition in the literature (Nacke and Drachen 2011). This pilot experiment showed some clearly quantifiable results similar to those reported by Nacke et al. (2009) while sharing the stated drawbacks relating to some of the measurements. For example, these included the lack of a standard baseline in GSR, making interpretations of the readings difficult, while increased heart rates (HR) can result from activities the subjects may have been engaged in just before the experiment. Furthermore, inaccurate HR measurements seem to have resulted from the incorrect positioning of the belt which needed to be worn by the experiment subject under their clothing. In turn, the eye-tracker generated a useful (though large) amount of data for analysis, though some missing data were found for certain subjects for no immediately obvious reasons. Beyond the more clear-cut factors such as the subject wearing heavy eye make-up or the processing speed of the computer on which the eye-tracker was installed, one possible explanation may have been that the particular type of eye-tracker employed was not optimized to be used for multimedia content with constantly moving high resolution graphics. We hope to gain further insights into the use of biometric approaches by collaborating with more experienced researchers familiar with these tools applied to games research.

Game publishers increasingly rely on localization to boost international sales of their games to cover the rising cost of game development (Chandler and Deming 2012, 3), yet there is little evidence of formal research being undertaken to refine game localization strategies. As we have demonstrated in this book, some games undergo elaborate transformations to appeal to the target market and yet it is not uncommon for the end player to feel as if localized games are inferior to the original (Chandler 2005, 4). Nevertheless, such claims are often made anecdotally and without empirical backing. While the level of awareness by game developers of the importance of localization is increasing (Chandler and Deming 2012), the common assumption in the industry is that any games which are expected to be successful in the home market will automatically succeed in their localized versions, leading to an approach to localization not based on evidence provided by the target user.

This demonstrates the need for practically-oriented empirical research to provide data for game companies, who are facing higher and higher stakes should their fully localized games fail to sell. Based on the assumption that the PX in the specific context of localized games could point to aspects of localization effectiveness and identify areas of failure, research in this direction should help to formulate game localization strategies as well as game design. So far these localization issues have been conspicuously neglected in PX research. The proposed area of research advocates a mixed methods approach with a view to developing a productive and more holistic framework to characterize the PX of localized games. This in turn could contribute to a broadening of Translation Studies by building links to the field of Human Computer Interaction (HCI) in which multilingual and multicultural dimensions currently appear to be seldom explored. This research direction also addresses the growing need for empirical research in Translation Studies to forge closer links between translation practice and theory, especially with emerging forms of translation. Furthermore, the proposed area of studies would open up a new approach based on biometrics to translation assessment by combining subjective user views and also objective user data drawn from users' physiological responses to translation, of which they themselves may not be aware. This will not only enrich Translation Studies with empirically-validated user research, but will also benefit other multi-disciplinary areas of research seeking to understand in a holistic manner user behaviours about a wide range of localized products. This direction towards biometrics begins to move translation research towards the rapidly developing field of neuroscience, as proposed by Tymoczko as "a frontier of research on translation" (2012, 84):

> Translation studies has explored many facets of the processes and products of translation and interpreting from the perspective of linguistics, textual studies, cultural studies, and cognitive science … but little is known about the production and reception of translation at the level of individual brain and the level of molecular biology… Moreover, translation studies has hardly even begun to inquire about the reception of translations at the cognitive or neurological level of the individual receiver.   (Tymoczko 2012, 83–84)

Such research directions will promote the much desired link between industry needs and translation research in game localization, moving towards the goal of knowledge consilience of previously separate areas of academic disciplines. The kind of interdisciplinary collaboration advocated by Chesterman (2005, 2007) will be key to achieving such aims, extending translation scholarship to such new areas as affective neuroscience.

7.3.2   Natural language interaction through AI, chatbot, and speech recognition

One of the relatively recent and significant game design innovations is the application of Artificial Intelligence (AI) technology to control certain game **avatars**. As noted by the game designer Ernest Adams (Edge Staff 2007), among the most sophisticated uses of AI in today's games is in the sports genre, where game characters driven by AI cooperate with the player's character to pursue a given goal.

Many games use AI to create autonomous game characters, but their capabilities usually do not extend to interaction through the use of natural language to respond spontaneously to non-scripted input. In fact, attempts have been made to ensure that such interaction does not occur between AI and the player character via natural language. The aforementioned J-RPG action game *ICO* (2001) which relies on co-operation between the player's character Ico and Yorda, a character driven by AI, is an example of this. Each character speaks a different language, both of which are non-existing invented languages. This design in turn led the game characters to rely on nonverbal communication. According to the game developer, this was a deliberate decision taken to avoid the AI-driven Yorda having to respond to Ico in a natural language to match the player input, which would likely have posed a major technical challenge (O'Hagan 2009a, 223). It can only be speculated that in future, when AI applications in games extend into the Natural Language Processing (NLP) sphere more extensively, AI-driven game avatars may be able to respond appropriately in a given language.

Interactions via written text have been well tried and tested in video games. One of the early game genres is known as "text adventure" (see Chapter 1), where the player types words to progress in a game. Despite the advances of game technologies in the intervening years, game-player interactions still mainly rely on button or motion-based commands input via the game controller, and the use of natural language, either written or spoken, in completely free form remains relatively rare. The most recent attempt is by Kinect, which uses the player's body gestures, language, and facial expressions as a game interface. However, this technology is still at an early stage of development and we have yet to see a full spectrum of games emerge to demonstrate the real impact of the innovations. NLP technology has been making steady progress and there is no question that it will increasingly permeate into the game sphere to allow the player to interact freely with game characters via unconstrained natural language, written or spoken, in future with such possibilities already being demonstrated in some games.

The 3D point-and-click adventure game *Starship Titanic* (1998), designed by Douglas Adams, is an early example of the use of a conversation engine, in this case, called "Spookitalk" to facilitate an interaction between the player and the robot through text. The typed user input is parsed and matched with an appropriate response from the pool of pre-recorded phrases, providing a response in written and spoken form. The parser technology behind Spookitalk was VelociText, developed by the Virtus Corporation of North Carolina.[124] Spookitalk is a type of what is today known as a "chatterbot" or "**chatbot**", which is a computer program

---

124. For VelociText see http://www.abenteuermedien.de/jabberwock/chatterbotfaq_en.html.

simulating a conversation with a human through text. *Façade* (2005) provides a subsequent relevant example of a game that draws heavily on NLP technology. The interactive conversation feature makes the game deeply engaging, in spite of its minimum level of visual sophistication, with cartoon-like graphics depicting the mood of the two game characters, Grace and Tripp. It maps a short sentence typed by the player (who is not represented graphically) to the so-called "discourse acts", where the input sentence is matched to a limited range of reactions – "agree, disagree, criticize or flirt" – by the game characters, expressed in voiced responses, without the system needing to always correctly interpret the meaning of the input (Wilcox 2011). An input sentence may map to a few discourse acts, but the system will link it to the most likely context, preferring a misinterpretation rather than being unable to respond and frustrating the player (ibid.). Designed as an interactive drama, the gameplay develops around the conversation between the three characters, triggered by a short sentence input by the player and the married couple Grace and Tripp who are going through marital problems. Depending on the conversation which develops between the player and the couple, the game's outcome is either their split or reconciliation. Interestingly this game has not been localized into other language versions, possibly because of the technical challenges entailed.

More recently, new chatbot technology has been used to generate sufficiently natural responses to the text input by the player. A case in point is the Sherlock Holmes game *221B* (2009),[125] which was developed to be played on Facebook in conjunction with the release of the Guy Richie film *Sherlock Holmes* (2009). Aside from serving as another example of a transmedia movie-game tie-in, the use of chatbot technology makes this online game a relevant example of an NLP application. The technology is used to allow the player – who can assume the role of either Holmes or Dr. Watson – to interrogate in written text witnesses or suspects. These characters are programmed with chatbot to keep the player on track by providing seemingly appropriate answers. Unlike the scripted dialogue often used in games (see Chapter 4), where the player cannot fashion his or her own line, chatbot allows the player to use a free form of questions in interaction, as in the case of *Façade*. In a BBC interview with the developer of the technology (Vallance 2009), the test sentences typed by the BBC interviewer playing Dr. Watson were responded to in the form of written text by the suspect/witness Gerald, whose speech is deliberately marked as substandard language through chatbot as shown in the following excerpt:

---

125. Further information on the game available at: http://www.guardian.co.uk/technology/ gamesblog/2009/dec/01/games-gameculture.

Example 1
Dr. Watson: Don't worry we are not going to hurt you.
Gerald: Ye're a copper at heart and ye're all bruits.

Example 2
Dr. Watson: Did you steal anything?
Gerald: I heard talk about a headpiece bein' stolen but honestly that's all
              I know.

Example 3
Dr. Watson: A headpiece?
Gerald: I really don't know why they would have chose to thieve that.
              Maybe it's really valuable or somethin'.
                                                        (Source: Vallance 2009)

The chatbot technology is able to keep the conversation in context and provides the game with varied modes of interface through which the player can interact with characters. The **sandbox** online adventure game *Bot Colony* under development by North Side Inc. at the time of writing is reportedly integrated with NLP technology, allowing a natural conversation in English between the player character and robots that are the game's **non-playable characters** (NPCs). The choice of robots as conversation partners is deliberate to avoid breaking the suspension of disbelief in case they fail to follow the conversation (Joseph 2012). Following an early prototype of the technology for natural language understanding shown at the Game Developers Conference (GDC) in San Francisco in 2009,[126] the game's dialogue functionality is now available as a beta version in which the player can carry on a fairly natural conversation with robots (Joseph 2012). The system incorporates the player input as text or speech via a speech recognition system (speech-to-text), then the English input is parsed by the system, involving disambiguation for polysemous words, co-reference resolution in a 3D environment (e.g. the player referring to an object in the shared space), Q&A reasoning and processing to understand the question and respond appropriately. It then finally leads to natural language generation in English, which needs to match the animation of the character. The game is also intended to be used as an English learning tool (ibid.). However, similar to *221B*, which is not localized into other languages, there seem to be no plans to make *Bot Colony* available in different languages. This raises the question of the scalability of such technologies to readily incorporate

---

126. See http://gdconf09.eventnewscenter.com/news/release/1030-north-side-unveils-bot-colony-the-worlds-first-conversation-video-game-at-gdc-in-san-francisco. Also several demo videos can be viewed in YouTube such as: http://www.youtube.com/watch?v=Jr5YrOJENPU.

different language versions. It also raises the next question of the application of MT technology, which some gamers may apply while playing the game, as such technology is becoming increasingly freely available.

MT is one of the prominent applications of NLP and has been researched and developed since the 1950s (Hutchins and Somers 1992). A recent paradigm shift in MT has seen the data-driven, as opposed to the classical rule-based, approach become the main focus, at least in research now mainly focused on statistical MT (SMT). Google Translate is one of the earliest commercial implementations of SMT seamlessly integrated into online platforms, enabling the translation of fragments of text, web pages or email messages and translating chat sessions which take place interactively via typed text. Google's NLP technologies also include automatic speech-to-text translation by combining speech recognition and MT, capable of generating interlingual subtitles (albeit not in a condensed form) for YouTube audiovisual clips. These technologies are designed with the goal of being fit-for-purpose and it is accepted that the translation quality will vary. Some users are likely to be satisfied if the alternative is no translation and when unpredictable less-than-perfect translation is of no serious consequence. NLP applications have progressed from text-to-text through text-to-speech or speech-to-text to speech-to-speech modalities, although they are still a long way from providing perfect translations as Fully Automatic High Quality Machine Translation (FAHQMT). With portable devices such as smart phones, voice-input may be preferred to text input under certain circumstances, and this may also apply to certain types of games. For example, Apple iPhone has incorporated a personal digital assistant (PDA) called Siri[127] with which the user can interact using voice commands in a number of different languages, while DoCoMo is testing a cloud-based on-demand translator phone.[128] While these attempts with PDA and interpreting phones are not entirely new and any overexpectations must be avoided, the rapid development of smart phones, cloud computing, and crowdsourcing mechanisms used to rapidly collect and integrate translation data into an MT engine may lead to new workable solutions in the not too distant future.

The game designer Ernest Adams (Edge Staff 2007) lists speech recognition as one of the technologies to impact game design, allowing players to interact via voice commands. In game cultures it is already a significant part of the game-play experience to use voice commands and also speech as a means of interaction among other players when playing MMOGs. This in turn creates an issue if

---

127. Further information is available on the Apple site: http://www.apple.com/iphone/features/siri-faq.html.

128. See http://en.akihabaranews.com/109387/phones/docomo-announces-cloud-based-translator-phone.

there are a number of languages spoken among players, as often happens in online game environments. For this very reason, in 1996 Electronic Arts (EA) licensed Systran's MT technology for integration into its MMORPG *Ultima Online: The Second Age* (1998). The application allowed speakers of English, German, and Japanese to be able to use automatic translation during the gameplay. Another early multiplayer online RPG title, *Phantasy Star Online* (2000), attempted to address the communication issue among players with use of symbols, which they called "Symbol Chat". In this system the speaker selects an intended emotion or simple instruction, which in turn appears in a speech bubble. The game also used a limited phrase book called "Word Select" which allowed the player to select a phrase to be automatically translated into a given language.[129] A similar approach based on a phrase-book was used in the Auto-Translate function[130] incorporated into another MMORPG title *Final Fantasy XI* (2002), enabling synchronous chat between Japanese- and English-speaking players. It is interesting to note that all these examples come from relatively early online games, indicating a clear awareness of the need to cater for communication needs among players who are likely to come from different parts of the world, speaking different languages. The application of MT in online games addresses real-time needs by gamers for interaction in multilingual environments and directly questions the limitations of today's approach to localization, which locks the user into a pre-determined language version. The need to interact in real time by gamers across languages challenges the assumption that localization is to serve the end user with products in a single fixed target locale. Some of these synchronous translation needs are increasingly being met, albeit informally, by users' own initiatives, accessing free translation services based on MT technologies integrated into different communications platforms. The technology's increased visibility, such as Google Translate, is likely affecting end users' perceptions about translation as an instantaneous service provided free of charge. Chapter 3 has discussed the use of translation technology by localizers to boost productivity of their translation work. Similarly, the players themselves may very likely "plug in" language tools as an increasing range of translation technologies become available in the public domain to fill the gap left in localization. Furthermore, the fan translator community will take advantage of any relevant tools to assist their translation effort, although such uses of technologies are not as yet reported in the literature.

As we have argued in this book, modern video games are first and foremost the products of technology applications, and game localization clearly needs to

---

129. http://en.wikipedia.org/wiki/Phantasy_Star_Online.

130. http://www.ffcompendium.com/h/interview2.shtml.

be able to keep up with the constantly unfolding technological landscape. What distinguishes localization in comparison with other forms of language transfer is that it manipulates language and culture on a dynamic digital platform. This is particularly evident in game localization, which demands that translation be part of game design and game development. It is this widened scope which makes game localization highly relevant to the concerns of Translation Studies, both in practice and in theory, giving rise to new research avenues.

Conclusion

Drawing our discussion to a close, in this final section of the book we highlight a number of key implications of game localization for translation. Game localization enables gamers to enjoy playing video games in their own language regardless of the original language of the product. Our main goal in this book has been to situate this still relatively under-explored practice in a Translation Studies context. Driven almost entirely by the needs of the game industry, from humble beginnings game localization has developed into an extremely specialized high stakes business. As we have demonstrated, modern video games are complex technological artefacts, while at the same time cultural products rich in cultural connotations which can stir players' emotions in ways that are somewhat different from other more traditional non-interactive media. Furthermore, the controversial nature of video games means that they are never far from causing moral panic, when connections are alleged between a crime and the culprit's game-playing habit or when game designers come up with bold new games that not only test the player's technical skills and emotional boundaries, but also society's tolerance of what is permissible. In this way, translating video games touches on a whole host of issues, including taboos and possible moral questions. While this is not the first time translation has come to be linked to such an agenda, the particular nature of games as interactive media, with gamers perceived as active agents, introduces a new context. Furthermore, the only way for such complex systems to be localized is to deconstruct them into constituent parts with each component operated on by a different party, and then to reassemble them. In this process contexts are often lost, while the original game keeps changing in the increasingly prevalent sim-ship mode. Will translators working in this manner be able to contribute to reconstructing the originally intended game world and player experience in the target version equivalent to that gained by the player of the original game?

Here we provide a brief summary of the key issues which have emerged from our exploration of this new topic in Translation Studies. They are not necessarily all tested ideas and indeed some of them are tentative positions based on our own experiences of translating games and researching and teaching game localization. Irrespective of whether readers will agree with our views, we hope to stimulate academic discussion on game localization and encourage the development of tangible collaboration efforts between the game industry and academia. We would also like to hear the opinions of gamers, whose observations are invaluable to researchers, game developers and publishers alike, be they elated or frustrated by translation when playing localized video games.

Game localization, game translation or game transcreation?

One of the fundamental questions we wanted to address in writing this book was how best to refer to the field under discussion: game localization or game translation? Having come to the end of our journey, our simple conclusion is that there is no clear-cut answer. We began by tracing the brief history of video games to underpin how translation practices within the game industry emerged largely in isolation, disconnected from other types of translation then in existence. The main reason for the disjunction lay in the new medium in which game text was couched, thus making it a "special case". As we explored in Chapter 2, the invention of the term "localization" in place of translation is significant and can be explained using the concept of "norms" (Toury 1995), where "the very use or avoidance of the label of translation and/or opting for a label such as adaptation or version instead...can tell us about the status of translation in society" (Schäffner 2010, 240). In the case of localization, as inherited in the term "game localization", the absence of the term "translation" indeed clearly signalled the perception, rightly or wrongly, among those in the industry that existing notions of translation did not fit their task at hand. In an attempt to provide some concrete evidence of why this practice was considered different, we noted in particular the technological dimensions of the medium of video games. We also stressed how culture is manifested in a specific manner in games, with significant implications for translation, including the impact of their historically less straightforward relationship with society at large (Chapter 5).

Having studied the phenomenon of video game localization extensively, we have come to confirm that any prescriptive approach is doomed to fail, given the sheer diversity of games and the new innovations constantly being applied to them. What is more, games are localized under many different operational conditions (see Chapter 3). Instead, we found it more useful to focus on the broader common picture based on contexts such as the particular structure of the game industry (Chapters 1 and 5), which significantly impact on translation decisions. This in turn directed our attention to the role of translation in social contexts, to translators' agency and, in particular, to their creativity, contributing to the continued growth and success of the digital entertainment industry as a global business. In game localization, professional norms and expectancy norms seem to

operate in a fascinating yet complex manner. Further exploration of game translators' behaviours will shed more light on their active contribution to "rewriting"
and on when, how and with what stimulus they transcreate. In his final analysis
scrutinizing "localization" and "translation" Mandiberg (2009, n.p.) concludes
that "localization renders them [games] leisurely legible but translation might
render them powerful". We suspect we are deliberating the same point at least to
a large extent while admitting the unresolved conceptual boundary between "localization" and "translation". We argue it is the recognition (visibility) of translators' agency which makes this practice indeed "powerful", whether termed "game
translation" or "game localization". Localization in its inherent link to the business
bottomline is inadvertently working to highlight translators' creativity under new
light when it is applied to this 21st century object of delectable and complex fun.
In many ways we feel that we have only touched the tip of the iceberg and we wish
to see more researchers take up this still largely unexplored subject and investigate further the full depth of the field.

Translation quality and users

As we charted the development of game localization over time, the lack of quality of early game translation became clear – a fact widely acknowledged within
the gamer community. The initial poor quality resulted from the fact that some
translations were literally done by a "programmer with a phrase book" at some
Japanese game development studios (Corliss 2007). Not engaging a professional
translator may well have been a legacy of the arcade game era, when very little
translation was required, thus not warranting the engagement of a full professional service (Edge Online 2006). For example, to date the highly successful Nintendo Entertainment System (NES) title *The Legend of Zelda* (1986) is one of the
most discussed games that created both gameplay difficulties and ambiguous and
contradictory timeline myths due to alleged translation errors and discrepancies
in different localized versions. Its English translations from Japanese generated
numerous discussions among fans, as summarized below in a dedicated online
discussion site:

> Especially in the *Legend of Zelda* series, the history of translating a game from its
> native Japanese language into the English language is a shaky one at best. Some
> of the biggest myths in our community were created because of such translation
> discrepancies over the years. While in the modern era of gaming, translation has
> become rather superb, the roots of the Zelda series haven't fully recovered from
> the days of yore.   (Damiani n.d.)

However, as we have pointed out, a rather ironic fact is that even poorly translated games have sold well, as Kohler notes: "...a better translation wouldn't necessarily equal more sales. So, many games that were written well enough in Japanese were rushed out the door in the US with English text that ranged from awkwardly stilted to embarrassingly poor" (2005, 210). Still today no clear correlation has been established between the quality of localization and the subsequent sales of a particular game (O'Hagan and Mangiron 2004), although there is a concern for the "image" of the publishers associated with poor translation (Darolle 2004). Even this point is debatable, given the fact that the recent popularity of online archiving by game fans and enthusiasts who collect erroneous translations has led to some game publishers capitalizing on their own vulnerability by deliberately retaining earlier errors in updated versions of the games. More interestingly from our point of view, the issue of poor translation has entered into the gamer community's consciousness and has become an ardent talking point (Newman 2008), prompting fan translation of games in some cases.

The question of quality remains an unresolved issue in terms of its direct relationship to sales. Equally ambiguous is how quality is perceived by different user groups. For example, while hardcore gamers may consider games that have been somewhat sanitized as not serving customers well by depriving them of the full original flavour, even a small trace of "foreignness" in a localized version may cause irritation to other gamers right at the onset of play, as is apparent in the comments of an American gamer when he set out to play *Resident Evil* (1996–).

> So it begins here...watching as a dateline title card – 1998 July – forcefully types itself across the television screen. "1998 July"? Why not "England, London"? Why not, "A time once upon"? ...Okay. This is a Japanese game.   (Bissell 2010, 17)

Translators soon discover that there are discerning gamers whose knowledge of a particular game series or game system could nearly equal that of the makers of the games, and are thus able to detect any fundamental lack of understanding of the game world on the part of the localization team. Regardless of the presence of critical end users, to translate a specialized domain in which translators have never been versed is challenging and likely to leave room for problems. We used the concept of "internal and external knowledge" (Pym 2004, 28), linking it to professional norms and expectancy norms in turn and also pointed out how the former may come in conflict with the latter. Furthermore, in the game industry translators are often challenged by the differences among "norm authorities" (Chesterman 1997), such as between the end users and the game publishers or developers. Users are normally not aware of the feat involved in localizing a large-scale RPG title with a massive amount of text to be translated, voiced, and simultaneously shipped in multiple languages. They are unlikely to know that some translations had to be completed without context and without screenshots. At the same time, linguistic testers who submit their bug reports are told that the errors they spotted are not serious enough to delay the whole shipment schedule – only to discover subsequently that fan forum discussions are pointing out the very issues they had flagged in their reports which were ignored. Nevertheless the game sells well and the same process is repeated in the next project. The question of quality in game localization is never straightforward. This is also due to the fact that what affects the sense of enjoyment from the user's perspective is not easily definable, especially in relation to the impact of translation or localization as a whole. This indeterminate nature of quality in video games as assessed by the user's sense of "fun" has extended to that of localized games.

Localization directionality and regional variations of language

Unlike productivity software, a significant proportion of game software is currently produced in Japanese. Despite attempts by foreign game publishers, non-Japanese games have largely remained less popular in the Japanese market. However, newer genres such as social and casual games on social networks and playable on mobile devices are lowering the entry barriers to game production and games may be produced by independent programmers and game designers anywhere and in any language, not just English or Japanese. This has clear implications for localization language directionality. At the same time, the growth of online games produced in countries such as Korea and China suggests that these other Asian languages may become major SLs in the near future in addition to Japanese. In the meantime, while English retains its key status as the major SL, it poses the issue of regional differences. Games for the US and the UK markets are typically localized separately due to the NTSC/PAL conversions (see Chapter 3) and also to address regional language differences. Some languages have regional variations, including English, Spanish, French, and Portuguese, and localizers need to be acutely aware of such differences in order cater to them by distinguishing the language associated with the region. While such differentiations are also made with other media, as in the case of the US versions of *Harry Potter* books and films such as *Trainspotting* and *Billy Elliot*, video games can further pose extra challenges due to their generally frequent and deliberate use of colloquial language, involving slang and profane expressions. Certain slang expressions may be received in a more or less similar manner across different regions, but others have markedly different regional connotations, as with some examples discussed earlier (see Chapter 5). Video games have today become a pervasive form of entertainment as never before, reaching such a wide range of age groups and types of users, and are thus open to more traps, keeping the translator on his/her toes.

Differences in accents are also leveraged by the game medium, which is increasingly becoming more cinematic in routinely incorporating voiced dialogues, highlighting audio localization as both a major challenge and an opportunity. In order to characterise certain game protagonists in a locale, regional accents are increasingly exploited, even when the original characters do not have any particular accent. Such a strategy is less frequent in other types of translation and is an expensive option, yet is often considered effective in instantly creating a certain image of the character in the player's mind (see Chapter 4). This means that a high level of awareness of the reception of language in the target territories and for certain age groups is required, and this brings home the fundamental message in localization that language matters.

International game design and internationalization

With the game industry having developed into a global business, game developers and publishers are increasingly conscious of international audiences, regardless of the origin of the game. As we mentioned in Chapter 4, the flagship RPG title by Square Enix *Final Fantasy XIII* (2009) was developed not only with input from an international team but also involved focus groups in Japan and the US. In the past, some Japanese publishers tried to develop games directly in English as a way of overcoming translation difficulties. *Secret of Evermore* (1995), a game for Super Nintendo Entertainment System (SNES), was developed by the Japanese game developer/publisher Square (before the merger with Enix) via their US development studio. However, this pseudo-sequel to a previously well received Japanese game in the US did not go down well with US fans, despite its well-written English script and fantastic graphics. Ted Woolsey, who later worked and translated games at Square, is quoted as saying that the North American fans felt "it just didn't feel like a Square game. It had none of the magic of J-RPGs" and that "everyone concerned underestimated the unique product coming out of the Japanese development studios" (Kohler 2005, 227–228). Such comments stress the complexity of producing a successful game which appeals to foreign markets and they highlight the fact that producing a game in the TL alone (thus bypassing the translation process) is no guarantee of international success.

While game localization generally tends to seek domestication strategies, we have found that certain overseas fans of J-RPGs, for example, actively welcome foreign – i.e. Japanese – elements (O'Hagan and Mangiron 2004; Mangiron and O'Hagan 2006). As we noted before, the key to successful game localization is not always a matter of adhering to an approach by uprooting all foreign elements – what Iwabuchi (2002) calls "odourless". In some instances in which the foreign and the familiar are co-present, an approach termed as "fragrant" (Iwabuchi ibid.), can prove to be a successful globalization strategy, constituting "hybridization" (Consalvo 2006; Di Marco 2007). This is indeed a complex issue which cannot be readily resolved by thinking in binary terms of foreignization and domestication and it touches on something fundamental about producing a product with a universal appeal to end users who judge the game from multiple dimensions. With the internationalization process increasingly embedded in the initial design of many digital products, the issue of the clash of cultures is being recognized by game developers and publishers. Translation scholars have long acknowledged that the object of their study goes far beyond language per se into the question of culture at large, as highlighted in the cultural turn in Translation Studies (Snell-Hornby 1990). Esselink (2000) once described localization as where language meets technology. We now suggest that game localization is where language, technology, and culture meet and collide in a major way, with transcreation widening the scope of translator's creativity.

Technology applications and the future of game localization

One of the most uncertain influences on the future of game localization is how game technology will develop. Observing how word processors and spreadsheets have remained largely the same during the last fifteen years, the internationally acclaimed game designer Sir Peter Molyneux points out in an interview that "there is not another form of technology on this planet that has kept up with games" (cited in Bissell 2010, 201). In this book we have attempted to show how the practice of game localization has been significantly affected by game technology. During the last few years the market has seen the development of new game user interfaces from Nintendo's Wii remote to Sony's Move, to Microsoft's Kinect, which uses the player's own body as the interface. These technologies interpret the player's physical movements, exploiting his or her nonverbal communication cues, which are both universal and distinct across cultures, in turn raising the question of how localization will address the differences. Similarly, the next big innovations may come from the rapidly growing casual and social games, using mobile devices such as smart phones and tablet computers. On these platforms interfaces using voice or other nonverbal means such as graphic images are likely to be sought owing to the more confined space available for translated text. Added to this trend is the growth in massively multiplayer online games (MMOGs) in which gamers interact among themselves in real time, needing a means to efficiently overcome communication barriers across languages. Any of these developments can profoundly affect the direction and the focus of game localization in the future.

In these technical developments, "patrons" of console games such as Nintendo, Sony, and Microsoft, as well as other large international game publishers such as Square Enix, Electronic Arts (EA), Activision, and Ubisoft, will continue to play a pivotal role. Their globalization strategies, though they may not always be obvious, are shaping how games are "rewritten" in relation to dominant ideologies and the "poetics" of game texts, which can be exposed to tens of millions of players the world over. Furthermore, it is inevitable that natural language processing (NLP) technology and AI will feature more prominently not only in games systems but also in the localization process, thus affecting the role of human translation. Having resisted computer-aided translation (CAT) for long, game localization is now rapidly becoming CAT-friendly and developing its own tailored tools. Given the game industry's inherent affinity with technology the next innovation for translation technology may very well emerge from this sector. Regardless of the technology scenario, game translators will continue to have to negotiate between forces applied from the patrons above, on the one hand, and from grassroots gamers, on the other, who are increasingly knowledgeable about game systems and at times act as co-creators by adding value to the original product.

In a macro-perspective, one of the outcomes of advances in digital technologies in an increasing range of devices has been a blurring of the boundary between work and play. Distributed computer technologies are making the concept of "desktop computers" as the default designated workspace obsolete, while social networking platforms are increasingly blending business into leisure pursuits and vice versa. This blurring of boundaries is also characterized by translation becoming more of a social rather than a purely professional activity in certain situations, illustrated most acutely by Facebook Translation launching translation crowdsourcing in 2008. The increasingly visible user-generated translation produced by a highly motivated Internet crowd who are situated strictly outside the translation profession is perhaps one of the least anticipated consequences of the technological developments for translation. Controversial though it may be among translation professionals, it serves to highlight the current limitations and drawbacks of the dominant professional translation modus operandi (O'Hagan 2011b). In this book we have highlighted some such problems in the context of game localization, where technological innovation has led to new translation challenges. The game industry has been nurturing a partnership of sorts with gamers and in this sense may be well-positioned to pursue the further involvement of users as domain-experts to help deliver higher quality localization in a timely fashion. Such an approach may see a positive cross-fertilization between professional norms and expectancy norms. A more open approach involving collaboration with a diverse group of talented and knowledgeable users, inviting them to participate in the game localization process, could be the 21st-century response needed to resolve some of the intractable localization problems, not only of a linguistic and a cultural nature but also relating to accessibility. In the meantime the concept of "games" is rapidly permeating the public consciousness, not only through casual and social games, but also through the way in which everyday tools are being designed. The concept of "gamification" (Bartle 2011) is gaining currency and being applied to enhance user engagement with a product or service. While general consumer products such as electric tooth brushes are incorporating new and fun ways of engaging users, gamification is now increasingly being discussed by educators who seek to apply a ludic dimension to education for more effective teaching and learning (The Future of Teaching 2012). In this sense, the game concept seems set to spread beyond the successful yet currently confined domain of entertainment.

The unknown but expanding potential of the world of games as modern technological and cultural artefacts presents both the practice and academic study of translation with significant food for thought, making game localization a wholly worthwhile topic to ponder. In her exploration of theories of translation, Jenny Williams (2013, 119) paints a picture of "the prevalence of translation in a globalized world and the complexity of the phenomenon", proposing a new mission of Translation Studies to ensure that anyone who engages with the varied practices of translation is well-informed of the true nature of their undertaking and also to encourage them in theorizing what they do. In the same spirit as Williams who calls on translators, trained or untrained, to grab their paintbrushes and make their contributions it is our hope that this book will promote further research and continued discourse about this fascinating and dynamic field.

References

Aarseth, Espen. 1997. *Cybertext: Perspectives on Ergodic Literature*. Maryland: Johns Hopkins University Press.

Aarseth, Espen. 2001. "Computer Game Studies, Year One." *Game Studies* 1(1). Accessed May 3, 2011. http://www.gamestudies.org/0101/editorial.html.

Abrams, Megan. 2008. "Wii-hab: Video Games are Becoming the New Trend in Rehabilitation Hospitals." *Suite101*, March 19. Accessed March 14, 2011. http://www.suite101.com/content/wiihab-a48195#ixzz1GbpRuMBQ.

ActiveGaming Media. n.d. "History of Game Localization." Accessed December 12, 2010. http://www.activegamingmedia.com/news/hitory-of-game-localization.

Alexander, Leigh. 2009. "Opinion: If You're Not Having Fun, Play Something Else." *Gamasutra*, October 8. Accessed January 25, 2011. http://www.gamasutra.com/view/news/25040/Opinion_If_Youre_Not_Having_Fun_Play_Something_Else.php.

Altanero, Tim. 2002. "Localization: Deep in the Heart of Texas." *Localization Ireland* 1(1): 16–19.

Altanero, Tim. 2006. "The Localization Job Market in Academe." In *Translation Technology and Its Teaching (With Much Mention of Localization)*, Anthony Pym, Alexander Perekrestenko and Bram Starink (eds), 31–36. Tarragona: Intercultural Studies Group, Universitat Rovira i Virgili.

Apperley, Thomas H. 2008. "Video Games in Australia." In *The Video Games Explosion: A History from Pong to PlayStation* and Beyond*, Mark J. P. Wolf (ed.), 223–227. Westport, Connecticut and London: Greenwood Press.

Archambault, Dominique, Damien Olivier, and Harry Svensson. 2005. "Computer Games that Work for Visually Impaired Children." In *Proceedings of HCI International 2005 Conference*, Constantine Stephanidis (ed.). Las Vegas, Nevada. CD-Rom.

Arsenault, Dominic. 2008. "System Profile: The Nintendo Entertainment System (NES)." In *The Video Game Explosion: A History from Pong to Playstation and Beyond*, Mark J. P. Wolf (ed.), 109–114. Westport, Connecticut and London: Greenwood Press.

Arthur, K. A., Brandt, B., Fedane, A. and Hannan, D. 2010. "Automated Text Generation for the Localization of an Online Game." *The International Journal of Localization* 9(1): 36–45.

Ashcraft, Brian. 2008a. "How to Bring the West to Japan." *Kotaku*, April 30. Accessed July 31, 2011. http://kotaku.com/385604/how-to-bring-the-west-to-japan.

Ashcraft, Brian. 2008b. "Bethesda Censors Fallout 3 for Japan." *Kotaku*, November 11. Accessed July 11, 2011. http://kotaku.com/5082637/bethesda-censors-fallout-3-for-japan.

Ashcraft, Brian. 2009. "Rape Games Officially Banned in Japan." *Kotaku*, June 2. Accessed July 21, 2011. http://kotaku.com/5275409/rape-games-officially-banned-in-japan.

Ashcraft, Brian. 2012. "How Square Enix Screwed Up Black Ops II for Japan." *Kotaku*, November 3. Accessed December 3, 2012. http://kotaku.com/5962753/how-square-enix-screwed-up-black-ops-ii-for-japan.

Baer, Brian James and Geoffrey S. Koby (eds). 2003. *Beyond the Ivory Tower: Rethinking Translation Pedagogy*. Amsterdam and Philadelphia: John Benjamins.

Bailey, Kat. 2009. "Nier Gestalt Only Version Coming West", 15 December. Accessed January 16, 2013. http://www.1up.com/news/nier-gestalt-version-coming-west.

Baker, Liana B. 2011. "Analysis: Sony's Breach a Hiccup to Online Game Phenomenon." *Reuters*, May 23. Accessed December 9, 2011. http://www.reuters.com/article/2011/05/23/us-onlinegaming-idUSTRE74M66D20110523.

Baker, Mona. 2011. *In Other Words: A Coursebook on Translation* (2nd ed.). London and New York: Routledge.

Baker, Mona (ed.). 1998. *Routledge Encyclopedia of Translation Studies*. London: Routledge.

Baker, Mona and Gabriela Saldanha (eds). 2009. *Routledge Encyclopedia of Translation Studies* (2nd revised ed.). London: Routledge.

Bartle, A. Richard. 2011. "Games or Gaming? How Social Games Become Games." A keynote lecture given at *Gamelab 2011 Conference*, 29 June – 1 July 2011, Barcelona, Spain.

Bartelt-Krantz, Michaela. 2011. "Game Localization Management: Balancing linguistic quality and financial efficiency." *TRANS: Revista de Traductología*, 15: 83–88. Accessed December 13, 2011.

Bassnett, Susan and André Lefevere (eds). 1990. *Translation, History and Culture*. London and New York: Pinter.

Bassnett, Susan and Harish Trivedi. 1999. *Post-Colonial Translation: Theory and Practice*. London and New York: Routledge.

Bastin, George. 2009. "Adaptation." In *Routledge Encyclopedia of Translation Studies* (2nd revised ed.), Mona Baker and Gabriela Saldanha (eds), 3–6. London and New York: Routledge.

Bateman, Chris. 2006. *Game Writing: Narrative Skills for Videogames*. Boston, MA: Charles River Media.

BBC News Technology. 2012. "Game sales surpassed video in UK, says report", 22 March. Accessed November 11, 2012. http://www.bbc.co.uk/news/technology-17458205.

Behrmann, Malte. 2010. "Computer Games and Culture." *Developer Front*, March 4. Accessed May 16, 2011. http://developerfront.com/tag/games-culture-neeli-kroes-cultural-diversity-cultural-industry-dg-competition-state-aid-c-4706.

Bermúdez Bausela, Montserrat. 2005. "Teaching Localization in Spanish Universities." *Localization Focus: The International Journal of Localization,* September 2005.

Bernal-Merino, Miguel. 2006. "On the Translation of Video Games." *Jostrans: The Journal of Specialised Translation* 6: 22–36. Accessed December 11, 2011. http://www.jostrans.org/issue06/art_bernal.php.

Bernal-Merino, Miguel. 2007. "Challenges in the Translation of Video Games." *Revista Tradumàtica. Núm. 5: La localització de videojocs*: 1–7. Accessed December 11, 2011 http://www.fti.uab.es/tradumatica/revista/num5/articles/02/02art.htm.

Bernal-Merino, Miguel. 2008a. "Where Terminology Meets Literature." *Multilingual* 19 (5): 42–46.

Bernal-Merino, Miguel. 2008b. "What's in a Game?" *Localization Focus: The International Journal of Localization* 6 (1): 29–38.

Bernal-Merino, Miguel. 2008c. "Training Translators for the Video Game Industry." In *The Didactics of Audiovisual Translation,* Jorge Díaz-Cintas (ed.), 141–155. Amsterdam and Philadelphia: John Benjamins.

Bernal-Merino, Miguel. 2008d. "Creativity in the Translation of Video Games." *Quaderns de Filologia. Estudis literaris XIII*: 71–84.

Bernal-Merino, Miguel. 2009. "Video Games and Children's Books in Translation." *Jostrans: Journal of Specialised Translation* 11: 234–247. Accessed December 9, 2011. http://www.jostrans.org/issue11/art_bernal.pdf.

Bernal-Merino, Miguel (ed.). 2011. *TRANS. Revista de Traductología* 15. Special issue on games localization. Accessed December 9, 2011. http://www.trans.uma.es/trans_15.html.

Berry, David M. 2008. *Copy, Rip, Burn: The Politics of Copyleft and Open Source.* London: Pluto Press.

Bey, Youcef, Christian Boitet, and Kyo Kageura. 2006. "The TRANSBey Prototype: An Online Collaborative Wiki-based CAT Environment for Volunteer Translators." In *Proceedings of the Third International Workshop on Language Resources for Translation Work, Research & Training (LR4Trans-III)*, Elia Yuste (ed.), 49–54.

Biau, José R. B. and Anthony Pym. 2006. "Technology and Translation (A Pedagogical Overview)." In *Translation Technology and Its Teaching (With Much Mention of Localization)*, Anthony Pym, Alexander Perekrestenko, and Bram Starink (eds), 5–19. Tarragona: Intercultural Studies Group. http://isg.urv.es/library/papers/BiauPym_Technology.pdf

Bierre, Kevin. 2005. "Improving game accessibility." *Gamasutra.* Accessed November 2, 2012. http://www.gamasutra.com/features/20050706/bierre_01.shtml.

Billiani, Francesca. 2009. "Censorship." In *The Routledge Encyclopaedia of Translation Studies* (2nd revised edition), Mona Baker and Gabriela Saldanha (eds.), 28–31. London and New York: Routledge.

Bissell, Tom. 2010. *Extra Lives: Why Video Games Matter.* New York: Pantheon Books.

Bogost, Ian. 2006. *Unit Operations: An Approach to Videogame Criticism.* Cambridge and London: MIT Press.

Bramwell, Tim. 2008. "Qur'an References Force Worldwide LittleBigPlanetRecall". Accessed February 18, 2012. http://www.eurogamer.net/articles/quran-references-force-worldwide-littlebigplanet-recall.

Brink, Julie. 2012. "Planning Game-based Learning." *Multilingual* 23 (4): 35–38.

Brinster. 2009. "Faith Connors: Inclusive Character Design." Accessed September 28, 2012. http://borderhouseblog.com/?p=645.

Brøndsted, Katrine and Cay Dollerup. 2004. "Names in Harry Potter." *Perspectives: Studies in Translatology* 12 (1): 56–72.

Brooks, David. 2000. "What Price Globalization? Managing Costs at Microsoft." In *Translating Into Success: Cutting-edge Strategies for Going Multilingual in a Global Age*, Robert C. Sprung (ed.), 43–57. Amsterdam and Philadelphia: John Benjamins.

Brownlie, Siobhan. 2007. "Examining Self-censorship: Zola's Nana in English Translation." In *Modes of Censorship and Translation: National Contexts and Diverse Media*, Francesca Billiani (ed.), 205–234. Manchester: St. Jerome.

Bryce, Jo and Jason Rutter. 2006. "An Introduction to Understanding Digital Games." In *Understanding Digital Games*, Jason Rutter and Jo Bryce (eds), 1–17. Thousand Oaks, CA: Sage Publications.

Buckingham, David. 2006. "Studying Computer Games: Text, Narrative and Play." In *Computer Games: Text, Narrative and Play*, Diane Carr, David Buckingham, Andrew Burn and Gareth Schott (eds), 1–13. Cambridge: Polity Press.

Burn, Andrew. 2006. "Reworking the Text: Online Fandom." In *Computer Games: Text, Narrative and Play*, Diane Carr, David Buckingham, Andrew Burn and Gareth Schott (eds), 88–102. Cambridge/Malden, MA: Polity Press.

Caffrey, Colm. 2008. "Using Pupillometric, Fixation-Based and Subjective Measures to Measure the Processing Effort Experienced when Viewing Subtitled TV Anime with Pop-Up Gloss". In *Looking at Eyes: Eye-tracking Studies of Reading and Translation Processing*, Susanne Göpferich, Arnt Lykke Jakobsen and Inger M. Mees (eds), 125–144. Copenhagen: Samfundslitteratur.

Caillois, Roger. 1958/2001. *Man, Play and Games*. Urbana: University of Illinois Press.

Carless, Simon. 2004. "Lost in Translation: Japanese and American Gaming's Culture Clash". *Gamasutra*, January 21. Accessed August 1, 2011. http://www.gamasutra.com/view/feature/2024/lost_in_translationjapanese_and_.php?page=2.

Carlson, Rebecca and Jonathan Corliss. 2011. "Imagined Commodities: Video Game Localization and Mythologies of Cultural Difference". *Games and Culture* 6 (1): 61–82.

Carter, Christopher S. 2012. "Gamification is Serious Business". *Multilingual* 23 (4): 24–27.

CESA. See under Computer Entertainment Suppliers Association.

Chakraborty, Joyram and Anthony F. Norcio. 2009. "Cross Cultural Computing Gaming. In *Internationalization, Design and Global Development,* Nuray Aykin (ed.), 13–18. Berlin and Heidelberg: Springer-Verlag.

Chandler, Heather M. 2005. *The Game Localization Handbook*. Massachusetts: Charles River Media.

Chandler, Heather M. 2008a. "Practical Skills for Video Game Translators". *Multilingual* 19 (5): 34–37.

Chandler, Heather M. 2008b. "Ask the Experts: Translating Video Games". *Game Career Guide*, July 28. Accessed August 5, 2011. http://www.gamecareerguide.com/features/574/ask_the_experts_translating_video_.php.

Chandler, Heather M. 2008c. "Localization as a Core Game Development". Presentation given at the Localization Summit at the International Game Developers Conference 2008, San Francisco, February 20, 2008.

Chandler, Heather M. and Stephanie O'Malley Deming. 2012. *The Game Localization Handbook* (2nd ed.). Sudbury, MA; Ontario and London: Jones & Bartlett Learning.

Chatfield, Tom. 2010. *Fun Inc.: Why Games Are the 21st Century's Most Serious Business* (updated ed.). London: Virgin Books.

Chesterman, Andrew. 1997. *Memes of Translation*. Amsterdam and Philadelphia: John Benjamins.

Chesterman, Andrew. 2005. "Consilience and Translation Studies". *Revista Canaria de Estudios Ingleses* 51: 19–32. Accessed December 2, 2011 from http://www.helsinki.fi/~chesterm/2005l.Consilience.html.

Chesterman, Andrew. 2007. "Bridge Concepts in Translation Sociology". In *Constructing a Sociology of Translation*, Michaela Wolf and Alexandra Fukari (eds), 171–183. Amsterdam and Philadelphia: John Benjamins.

Chesterman, Andrew and Emma Wagner. 2002. *Can Theory Help Translators? A Dialogue Between the Ivory Tower and the Wordface*. Manchester: St. Jerome.

Cheung, Martha (ed). 2006. *An Anthology of Chinese Discourse on Translation 1: From Earliest Times to the Buddhist Project*. Manchester: St. Jerome.

Chiaro, Delia. 2009. "Issues in Audiovisual Translation". In *The Routledge Companion to Translation Studies,* Jeremy Munday (ed.), 141–165. London and New York: Routledge.

Chiaro, Delia. (ed.). 2010. *Translation, Humour and the Media: Translation and Humour*, Volume 2. London and New York: Continuum.

Christou, Chris, Jenny McKearney, and Ryan Warden. 2011. "Enabling the Localization of Large Role-Playing Games." *Trans: Revista de Traductología* 15: 39–51. Accessed December 1, 2011 from http://www.trans.uma.es/pdf/Trans_15/39-51.pdf.

Christensen, Tina Paulsen. 2011. "Studies on the Mental Processes in Translation Memory-assisted Translation: The State of the Art". *trans-kom* 4 (2): 137–160. Accessed February 19, 2012 from http://www.trans-kom.eu/bd04nr02/trans-kom_04_02_02_Christensen_Translation_Memory.20111205.pdf.

Civera, Clara and Pilar Orero. 2010. "Introducing Icons in Subtitles for the Deaf and Hard of Hearing: Optimising Reception." In *Listening to Subtitles. Subtitles for the Deaf and Hard of Hearing*, Anna Matamala and Pilar Orero (eds), 49–162. Vienna: Peter Lang.

Computer Entertainment Suppliers Association (CESA 2010). 2010. CESA Games White Paper. CESA: Tokyo.

Computer Entertainment Suppliers Association (CESA 2012). 2012. CESA Games White Paper. CESA: Tokyo.

Consalvo, Mia. 2006. "Console Video Games and Global Corporations: Creating a Hybrid Culture." *New Media & Society* 8 (1): 117–137.

Cooke, Tim. 2010. *Border Lands: Fractured Identity and the Body in Game Localization and Cyberspace*. Unpublished MA thesis, Dublin City University.

Corliss, Jon. 2007. "All Your Base are Belong to Us! Videogame Localization and Thing Theory." Accessed July 15, 2012. http://www.columbia.edu/~sf2220/TT2007/web-content/Pages/jon1.html.

Coslett, Calli. 2010. "How Wii is Used for Rehab." *eHow*. Accessed March 14, 2012. http://www.ehow.com/about_6331525_wii-used-rehab.html.

Crash Mania. 2008. "Crash Mania Interview with Josh Mancel". *Crash Mania*, March 4. Accessed August 1, 2011. http://crashmania.net/interviewjosh.php.

Crawford, Chris. 1982. *The Art of Computer Game Design*. Berkeley: McGrath Hill/Osborne Media.

Crawford, Garry and Jason Rutter. 2006. "Cultural Studies and Digital Games." In *Understanding Digital Games*, Jason Rutter and Jo Bryce (eds), 148–204. London: Sage.

Cronin, Michael. 2003. *Translation and Globalization*. London and New York: Routledge.

Cronin, Michael. 2013. *Translation in the Digital Age*. London and New York: Routledge.

Crosignani, Simone, Andrea Ballista and Fabio Minazzi. 2008. "Preserving the Spell in Games Localization." *Multilingual* 19 (5): 38–41.

Crosignani, Simone and Fabio Ravetto. 2011. "Localizing the Buzz! Game Series", *Trans: Revista de Traductología*, 15: 29–38. Retrieved November 20, 2011 from http://www.trans.uma.es/pdf/Trans_15/29-38.pdf.

Cubbison, Laurie. 2005. "Anime Fans, DVDs, and the Authentic Text." *The Velvet Light Trap* 56: 45–57.

Cunningham, A. Michael. 2012. "Inside Gaming: Interview with Former Square Enix Translator Tom Slattery." April 23, *RPGamer*. Accessed September 23, 2012. http://www.rpgamer.com/features/insidegaming/tslatteryint.html.

Damiani, Mike. (n.d.). "Lost in Translation". *The Hylia*. Accessed January 22, 2013. http://www.thehylia.com/lost_in_translation.shtml.

Darolle, Katrin. 2004. "Challenges in Videogames Localization." In *LISA Newsletter Global Insider XIII* 3.3.

Davies, Marsh. 2012. "Is the Japanese Game Industry Dead?" *Edge*. Accessed December 2, 2012. http://www.edge-online.com/features/japanese-game-industry-dead/.

Deaf Gamers. 2011. "The Lord of the Rings: The Battle for Middle Earth II." Accessed August 2, 2010. http://www.deafgamers.com/06reviews/lotr_bfme2_pc.html.

Dean, Katie. 2001. "Gaming: Too Cool for School?" *Wired*, January 15. Accessed July 13, 2011. http://www.wired.com/culture/lifestyle/news/2001/01/40967?currentPage=all.

DeLaHunt, Jim. 2004. *Go West, Young Bandicoot: Changes in the Japanese version of "Crash Bandicoot" for Playstation*. Accessed August 28, 2012. http://www.stanford.edu/group/htgg/cgi-bin/drupal/sites/default/files2/jdelahunt_2004_1.pdf.

DePalma, Donald A. 2006. "Quantifying the Return on Localization Investment." In *Perspectives in Localization*, Keiran Dunne (ed.), 15–36. Amsterdam and Philadelphia: John Benjamins.

DePalma, Donald and Nataly Kelly. 2008. "Translation Of, For, and By the People." Lowell, MA: Common Sense Advisory, Inc.

Désilets, Alain. 2007. "Translation Wikified: How will Massive Online Collaboration Impact the World of Translation?" *ASLIB Translating and the Computer 29 Conference Proceedings*. London: ASLIB.

Di Giovanni, Elena. 2008. "Translations, Transcreations and Transrepresentations of India in the Italian Media." *Meta* 53 (1): 26–43.

Di Marco, Francesca. 2006. "From Translation to Localization: Videogames Between Organizations, Cultures and Communities." Presentation given at the round table on game localization part of the *E-Week*, held at the Universitat de Vic, Barcelona, Spain, November 10, 2006.

Di Marco, Francesca. 2007 . "Cultural Localization: Orientation and Disorientation in Japanese Video Games." *Revista Tradumàtica*. 5: "La localització de videojocs." Accessed December 10, 2011. http://www.fti.uab.es/tradumatica/revista/num5/articles/06/06art.htm.

Díaz-Cintas, Jorge. 2003. *Teoría y práctica de la subtitulación inglés/español* [Theory and Practice of English/Spanish Subtitling]. Barcelona: Ariel.

Díaz-Cintas, Jorge. 2007. "Traducción audiovisual y accesibilidad" [AVT and Accessibility]. In *Traducción y accesibilidad: Subtitulación para sordos y audiodescripción para ciegos* [Translation and Accessibility: New Modalities of AVT], Catalina Jiménez Hurtado (ed.), 9–23. Frankfurt: Peter Lang.

Díaz-Cintas, Jorge (ed.). 2008. *The Didactics of Audiovisual Translation*. Amsterdam and Philadelphia: John Benjamins.

Díaz-Cintas, Jorge and Pablo Muñoz Sánchez. 2006. "Fansubs: Audiovisual Translation in an Amateur Environment." *Jostrans: The Journal of Specialised Translation* 6. Accessed July 12, 2011. http://www.jostrans.org/issue06/art_diaz_munoz.pdf.

Díaz-Cintas, Jorge, Pilar Orero and Aline Remael (eds). 2007. *Subtitling for the Deaf, Audiodescription and Sign Language*. Amsterdam and New York: Rodopi.

Díaz-Cintas, Jorge and Aline Remael. 2007. *Audiovisual Translation: Subtitling*. Manchester: St. Jerome.

Díaz-Cintas, Jorge, Anna Matamala and Josélia Neves (eds). 2010. *New Insights into Audiovisual Translation and Media Accessibility: Media for All 2*. Amsterdam and New York: Rodopi.

Díaz Montón, Diana. 2007. "It's a Funny Game." *The Linguist* 46 (3). Accessed July 12, 2011 http://www.wordlabtranslations.com/download/its_a_funny_game_EN.pdf.

Díaz Montón, Diana. 2011. "La traducción amateur de videojuegos al español [Amateur Videogame Translation into Spanish]." *TRANS: Revista de Traductología* 15: 69–82. Accessed December 15, 2011. http://www.trans.uma.es/pdf/Trans_15/69-82.pdf.

Dietz, Frank. 1999. "Beyond PacMan: Translating for the Computer Game Industry." *ATA Chronicle* 28 (9): 57.

Dietz, Frank. 2006. "Issues in Localizing Computer Games." In *Perspectives in Localization*, Keiran J. Dunne (ed.), 121–134. Amsterdam and Philadelphia: John Benjamins.

Dietz, Frank. 2007. "How Difficult Can That Be? The Work of Computer and Video Game Localization." *Revista Tradumàtica* 5: "La localització de videojocs." Accessed July 12, 2011. http://www.fti.uab.es/tradumatica/revista/num5/articles/04/04art.htm/.

Dietz, Frank. 2008. "More than Beeps and Blasts: Computer Game Localization and Literary Translation." *ATA Source – ATA Newsletter of the Literary Division* 43: 7–10.

Dollerup, Cay, and Vibeke Appel (eds). 1996. *Teaching Translation and Interpreting 3: New Horizons*. Amsterdam and Philadelphia: John Benjamins.

Dollerup, Cay, and Anne Loddegaard (eds). 1992. *Teaching Translation and Interpreting. Training Talent and Experience*. Amsterdam and Philadelphia: John Benjamins.

Dollerup, Cay, and Annette Lindegaard (eds). 1994. *Teaching Translation and Interpreting 2: Insights, Aims and Visions*. Amsterdam and Philadelphia: John Benjamins.

Dombek, Magdalena. 2011. "Translation Crowdsourcing: The Facebook Way – In Search of Crowd Motivation". Paper presented at *the School of Applied Language and Intercultural Studies Postgraduate Showcase*. November 9, 2011. Dublin City University, Dublin, Ireland. Accessed December 1, 2012. http://issuu.com/dublincityuniversity/docs/magdalenadombek/1.

Donovan, Tristan. 2010. *Replay: The History of Video Games*. East Sussex: Yellow Ant Media.

Dormann, Claire, and Robert Biddle. 2010. "Supporting Affective Learning in the Design of Serious Games." In *Proceedings of the Kansei Engineering and Emotion Research international Conference 2010*, 1694–1704. JSKE and A&M ParisTech.

Dovey, John and Helen W. Kennedy. 2006. *Game Cultures: Computer Games as New Media*. Berkshire: Open University Press.

Drachen, Anders, Lennart E. Nacke, Georgios Yannakakis and Anja Lee Pedersen. 2009. "Correlation Between Heart Rate, Electrodermal Activity and Player Experience in First-Person Shooter Games". In *Proceedings of the 5th ACM SIGGRAPH*, 49–54. ACM-SIGGRAPH Publishers.

Drugan, Joanna. 2011. "Translation Ethics Wikified: How Do Professional Codes of Ethics Apply to Non-Professionally Produced Translation?" *Linguistica Antverpiensia* 10: 111–127.

Dunham, Jeremy. 2005. "Dragon Quest VIII: Journey of the Cursed King. Now THIS is What Role-playing is All About". Accessed July 31, 2011. http://uk.ps2.ign.com/articles/666/666876p1.html.

Dunne, Keiran (ed.). 2006. *Perspectives in Localization*. Amsterdam and Philadelphia: John Benjamins.

ECTS Users' Guide. 2009. Luxembourg: Office for Official Publications of the European Communities. Accessed June 6, 2011. http://ec.europa.eu/education/lifelong-learning-policy/doc/ects/guide_en.pdf.

Edge Online. 2006. "Q&A – Square Enix's Richard Honeywood." *Square Haven*, February 1. Accessed July 8, 2010. http://squarehaven.com/people/Richard-Mark-Honeywood/?interview=41.

Edge Online. 2007. "The Games People Buy 2007". Accessed April 9, 2013. http://www.edge-online.com/features/games-people-buy-2007/.

Edge Staff. 2007. "50 Greatest Game Design Innovations." *Edge*. Accessed November 1, 2011. http://www.next-gen.biz/features/50-greatest-game-design-innovations/.

Edge Staff. 2011. "Localized Culture." *Edge*, July 26. Accessed August 8, 2011. http://www.next-gen.biz/features/localized-culture.

Edwards, Kate. 2007. "Sensitive Content Issues in Japan." *Multilingual* 18 (4): 29–31.

Edwards, Kate. 2008. "Reaching the Global Gamer." *Multilingual* 19 (7): 26–27.

Edwards, Kate. 2011. "Culturalization: The Geopolitical and Cultural Dimension of Game Content." *TRANS: Revista de Traductología* 15: 19–28. Accessed December 15, 2011. http://www.trans.uma.es/pdf/Trans_15/19-28.pdf.

Edwards, Kate. 2012. "Culturalization of Game Content." In *The Game Localization Handbook* (2nd ed.), Heather Chandler and Stephanie O'Malley Deming, 19–34. Sudbury, MA; Ontario and London: Jones & Bartlett Learning.

Egenfeldt-Nielsen, Simon, Jonas H. Smith and Susana P. Tosca. 2008. *Understanding Video Games*. New York and London: Routledge.

Ellison, Blake. 2009. "Fallout 3 Censorship Goes Global." *Shacknews*, September 9. Accessed August 1, 2011. http://www.shacknews.com/onearticle.x/54651.

Ensslin, Astrid. 2012. *The Language of Gaming*. New York: Palgrave MacMillan.

Entertainment Software Association (ESA). 2012. "2012 Sales, Demographic and Usage Data: Essential Facts about the Computer and Video Game Industry." Accessed September 2, 2012. http://www.theesa.com/facts/pdfs/ESA_EF_2012.pdf.

Esselink, Bert. 2000. *A Practical Guide to Software Localization* (Rev. ed.). Amsterdam and Philadelphia: John Benjamins.

Esselink, Bert. 2006. "The Evolution of Localization." In *Translation Technology and Its Teaching (With Much Mention of Localization)*, Anthony Pym, Alexander Perekrestenko, and Bram Starink (eds), 21–29. Tarragona: Intercultural Studies Group.

Ether Saga Online Forum; Suggestion Box-Keyboard Mapping. 2009. Accessed August 28, 2011. http://eso-forum.perfectworld.com/showthread.php?t=140951.

Famitsu. 2012. Audio Localization Secret for Square Enix with Moomle. Accessed September 28, 2012. http://www.famitsu.com/news/201203/07011098.html.

Feeser, Jeff. 2009. "Nemesis – The Games that Haunt Us: Ninja Gaiden". Accessed December 2, 2012. http://www.spectaclerock.com/2009/02/07/nemesis-the-games-that-haunt-us-ninja-gaiden/.

Fenlon, Wesley. 2011. "The Rise of Squaresoft Localization." *1up.com*, April 28. Accessed July 12, 2011. http://www.1up.com/features/squaresoft-localization.

Fernández, Anna. 2007. "Anàlisi de la localització de Code name: Kids next door. Operation V.I.D.E.O.G.A.M.E.". *Revista Tradumàtica* 5: "La localització de videojocs". Accessed November 15, 2011. http://www.fti.uab.es/tradumatica/revista/num5/articles/08/08art.htm.

Fernández-Costales, Alberto. 2011. "Adapting Humor in Video Game Localization." *Multilingual* 22 (6): 33–35.

Fernández-Costales, Alberto. 2012. "Exploring Translation Strategies in Video Game Localization." *Monographs in Translation and Interpreting (MONTI)* 4: 385–408.

FF Archives & FF 20th Anniversary DVD. 2007. Tokyo: Square Enix.

Flatley, Helen and Michael French. 2003. *Videogaming*. London: Pocket Essentials.

Flew, Terry. 2008. "Twenty Key New Media Concepts." In *New Media: An Introduction* (3rd ed.), Terry Flew (ed.), 21–36. Oxford: Oxford University Press.

Flew, Terry and Sal Humphreys. 2008. "Games: Technology, Industry, Culture." In *New Media: An Introduction* (3rd ed.), Terry Flew (ed.), 126–142. Oxford: Oxford University Press.

Folaron, Debbie. 2006. "A Discipline Coming of Age in the Digital Age." In *Perspectives in Localization*, Keiran Dunne (ed.), 195–222. Amsterdam and Philadelphia: John Benjamins.

Folaron, Debbie and Gregory Shreve. 2012. "Introduction". *Translation Spaces* 1: 1–4.

Frasca, Gonzalo. 2001. "Rethinking Agency and Immersion: Video Games as a Means of Consciousness-Raising." Essay presented at SIGGRAPH 2001. Accessed July 15, 2011 http://siggraph.org/artdesign/gallery/S01/essays/0378.pdf.

Freigang, Karl-Heinz. 2001. "Teaching Theory and Tools: Translation Technology and Software Localization at the University of the Saarland." *Language International* 13 (4): 20–23.

Fry, Deborah. 2003. *The Localization Primer* (2nd ed. revised by Arle Lommel). Accessed July, 15, 2012. http://www2.ilch.uminho.pt/falves/documentos/LISAprimer.pdf.

The Future of Teaching: Difference engine: Let the Game Begin, The Economist, January 27, 2012. Accessed February 4, 2012. http://www.economist.com/blogs/babbage/2012/01/future-teaching?page=1.

Gadget Boy. 2009. "Online Petition Stalls Plan to Ban Violent Videogames in Germany". *Kijo*, July 28. Accessed July 14, 2011 http://www.kijo.co.uk/games/online-petition-stalls-plan-to-ban-violent-videogames-in-germany.

Gallant, Mathew. 2008. "A Brief History of A & B." *The Quixotic Engineer*, September 16. Accessed August 22, 2011. http://gangles.ca/2008/09/16/a-brief-history-of-a-b/.

Gamasutra Podcast. 2006. "Gamasutra Podcast: Game Localization Panel, Part 1 Facilitated by Simon Carless." *Gamasutra*, September 13. Accessed July 11, 2011. http://www.gamasutra.com/php-bin/news_index.php?story=10859.

Gambier, Yves. 2003. "Screen Transadaptation: Perception and Reception." *The Translator* 9 (2): 171–190.

Gambier, Yves. 2009. "Reception and Perception of Audiovisual Translation: Implications and Challenges." In *The Sustainability of the Translation Fields*, Hasuria Ch. Omar, Haslina Haroon and Aniswal A. Ghani (eds), 40–57. Kuala Lumpur: Malaysian Translators Association.

Gambier, Yves, and Luc van Doorslaer (eds). 2010. *Handbook of Translation Studies*. Amsterdam and Philadelphia: John Benjamins.

Gamefreaks. 2011. "EA Dumps Printed Manuals for Digital." *Gamefreaks*, March 23. Accessed August 22, 2011. http://www.gamefreaks.co.nz/2011/03/23/ea-dumps-printed-manuals-digital.

Games Localization Round Table. 2008. Accessed August 30, 2009 http://gamecareerguide.com/thesis/080721_localization_roundtable.pdf.

GameVision. 2010. *Video Gamers in Europe 2010*. Accessed July 13, 2011. http://www.isfe-eu.org/index.php?oidit=T001:662b16536388a7260921599321365911.

Game Watch. 2010. An interview with Game Watch conducted at Square Enix May 19, 2010. Accessed September 23, 2012. http://game.watch.impress.co.jp/docs/interview/20100531_370231.html.

García, Ignacio. 2009. "Beyond Translation Memory: Computers and the Professional Translator." *Jostrans: Journal of Specialised Translation* 12.Accessed December 9, 2011 http://www.jostrans.org/issue12/art_garcia.pdf.

Gee, James P. 2003. *What Video Games Have to Teach us about Learning and Literacy*. Basingstoke: Palgrave Macmillan.

Gee, James P. 2006. "Why Game Studies Now? Video Games: A New Art Form." *Games and Culture* 1 (1): 58–61.

Gee, James P. and Elisabeth R. Hayes. 2011. *Language and Learning in the Digital Age*. London and New York: Routledge.

Gentzler, Edwin. 2001. *Contemporary Translation Theories* (2nd revised ed.). Clevedon: Multilingual Matters.

Giantbomb. n.d. "Piston Hondo". Accessed August 1, 2011. http://www.giantbomb.com/piston-hondo/94-158.

Gibson, James. 1979. *The Ecological Approach to Visual Perception*. Boston: Houghton Mifflin.

Giddings, Seth and Helen W. Kennedy. 2006. "Digital Game as New Media." In *Understanding Digital Games*, Jason Rutter and Jo Bryce (eds), 129–147. London, Thousand Oaks, New Delhi: Sage Publications.

Gile, Daniel. 2009. *Basic Concepts and Models for Interpreter and Translator Training* (2nd ed.). Amsterdam and Philadelphia: John Benjamins.

Glinert, Eitan. 2008. "Designing Games that Are Accessible to Everyone". *Gamasutra*. Accessed March 24, 2013. http://www.gamasutra.com/view/feature/3538/designing_games_that_are_.php/.

González Davies, Maria. 2004. *Multiple Voices in the Translation Classroom: Activities, Tasks, and Projects*. Amsterdam and Philadelphia: John Benjamins.

Gottlieb, Henrik. 2004. "Language Political Implications of Subtitling." In *Topics in Audiovisual Translation*, Pilar Orero (ed.), 83–100. Amsterdam and Philadelphia: John Benjamins.

Gouadec, Daniel. 2007. *Translation as a Profession*. Amsterdam and Philadelphia: John Benjamins.

Graft, Kris. 2010. "Playdom Dev: 'Difficult' Does Not Equal 'Hardcore.'" *Gamasutra*, September 21. Accessed July 31, 2011. http://www.gamasutra.com/view/news/30526/Playdom_Dev_Difficult_Does_Not_Equal_Hardcore.php/.

Grammenos, Dimitris. 2006. "The Theory of Parallel Game Universes: A Paradigm Shift in Multiplayer Gaming and Game Accessibility". *Gamasutra*. Accessed November 9, 2012. http://www.gamasutra.com/view/feature/130260/the_theory_of_parallel_game_.php?print=1.

Granell, Ximo. 2011. "Teaching Video Game Localization in Audiovisual Translation Courses at University." *Jostrans: The Journal of Specialised Translation* 16: 185–202. Accessed December 1, 2012. http://www.jostrans.org/issue16/art_granell.pdf.

Greenfield, Patricia M. 1996. "Video Games as Cultural Artifacts." In *Interacting with Video*, Patricia M. Greenfield and Rodney R. Cocking (eds), 85–94. New Jersey: Ablex Publishing Corporation.

Greenwood, Timothy G. 1993. "International Cultural Differences in Software". *Digital Technical Journal* 5 (3): 8–20. Accessed August 3, 2011. http://www.1000bit.it/ad/bro/digital/djt/dtj_v05-03_1993.pdf.

Guest, Tim. 2007. *Second Lives: A Journey Through Virtual Worlds*. London: Hutchinson.

Guldin, Rainer. 2008. "Devouring the Other: Cannibalism, Translation and the Construction of Cultural Identity." In *Translating Selves: Experience and Identity Between Languages and Literatures*, Paschalis Nikolaou and Maria-Venetia Kyritsi (eds), 109–122. London: Continuum.

Guzmán, Rafael. 2005. "E-learning for Localization Tools Training." *Translating Today* 2: 14–16.

Hartley, Tony. 2009. "Technology and Translation." In *The Routledge Companion to Translation Studies*, Jeremy Munday (ed.), 106-127. London and New York:: Routledge.

Hasegawa, Ryoichi. 2009. "ゲームローカライズの歴史とこれから [Game Localization History and Future]". In デジタルコンテンツ制作の先端技術応用に関する調査研究報告書 [*Study Report on Advanced Technology Applications for Developing Digital Content*], 121–132. Tokyo: JKA. Accessed August 5, 2011. http://www.dcaj.org/report/2009/data/dc_09_03.pdf.

Hatim, Basil. 2001. *Teaching and Researching Translation*. Essex: Pearson Education.

Heimburg, Eric. 2006. "Localizing MMORPGs." In *Perspectives in Localization*, Keiran Dunne (ed.), 135–154. Amsterdam and Philadelphia: John Benjamins.

Hermans, Theo (ed.). 2006. *Translating Others*. Manchester: St. Jerome.

Herz, Jessie Cameron. 1997. *Joystick Nation: How Videogames Ate Our Quarters, Won Our Hearts, and Rewired Our Minds*. London: Abacus.

Hills, Matt. 2002. *Fan Cultures*. London: Routledge.

Holmes, James S. 1988/2000. "The Name and Nature of Translation Studies." In *The Translation Studies Reader*, Lawrence Venuti (ed.), 175–185. London and New York: Routledge.

Holson, Laura M. 2005. "'King Kong' Blurs Line between Films and Games." *New York Times*, October 24. Accessed July 20, 2011. http://www.nytimes.com/2005/10/24/technology/24kong.html?pagewanted=all.

Honeywood, Richard. 2007. "The Square-Enix Approach to Localization." Presentation at the *Game Developers Conference*, San Francisco, March 5–9.

Honeywood, Richard and Jon Fung. 2012. *Best Practices for Game Localization*. Accessed November 7, 2012. http://englobe.com/wp-content/uploads/2012/05/Best-Practices-for-Game-Localization-v21.pdf.

Howe, Jeff. 2006. "The Rise of Crowdsourcing." *Wired* 14 (6). Accessed December 1, 2011. http://www.wired.com/wired/archive/14.06/crowds.html.

Howe, Jeff. 2008. *Crowdsourcing: How the Power of the Crowd is Driving the Future of Business*. London: Random House.

Huizinga, Johan. 1938/2000. *Homo Ludens: A Study of the Play-Element in Culture*. London: Routledge.

Hung, Eva. 2002. *Teaching Translation and Interpreting 4: Building Bridges*. Amsterdam and Philadelphia: John Benjamins.

Hung, Eva and Judy Wakabayashi (eds). 2005. *Asian Translation Traditions*. Manchester: St Jerome.

Hurtado Albir, Amparo (ed.). 1999. *Enseñar a traducir: Metodología en la formación de traductores e intérpretes* [Teaching how to Translate: Methodology for Training Translators and Interpreters]. Madrid: Edelsa.

Hutchins, John W. and Harold L. Somers. 1992. *An Introduction to Machine Translation*. London: Academic Press Limited.

IBM. n.d. "Understanding Accessibility." *Human Ability and Accessibility Center*. Accessed August 6, 2011. http://www-03.ibm.com/able/access_ibm/disability.html.

IGDA Game Access SIG. 2004. *Accessibility in Games: Motivations and Approaches*. Accessed July 20, 2011. http://archives.igda.org/accessibility/IGDA_Accessibility_WhitePaper.pdf.

IGDA Game Access SIG. 2010. Accessed August 7, 2011. http://igda-gasig.org.

IGDA Localization SIG. Accessed July 4, 2011. http://www.igda.org/wiki/Localization_SIG.

Irwin, Sarah. 2012. Personal communication, January 5.

Ishaan. 2011. "Acting Out A Slice Of Life: An Interview With The Voice Director Of Catherine." Accessed July 20, 2011 http://www.siliconera.com/2011/07/25/acting-out-a-slice-of-life-an-interview-with-the-voice-director-of-catherine.

ISO 9241-11. 1998. *Ergonomics requirements for office work with visual display terminals (VDTs) – Part 11: Guidance on usability*. Accessed January 22, 2013. http://www.it.uu.se/edu/course/homepage/acsd/vt09/ISO9241part11.pdf.

Iwabuchi, Koichi. 2002. *Recentering Globalization*. Durham, NC: Durham University Press.

Jayemanne, Darshana. 2009. "Generations and Game Localization." An Interview with Alexander O. Smith, Steven Anderson and Matthew Alt. *The Journal for Computer Game Culture* 3 (2): 135–147.

Jenkins, Henry. 1992. *Textual Poachers: Television Fans and Participatory Cultures*. London: Routledge.

Jenkins, Henry. 2003a. "Transmedia Storytelling: Moving Characters from Books to Films to Video Games Can Make Them Stronger and More Compelling." *Technology Review*. Accessed July 13, 2011. http://www.technologyreview.com/biomedicine/13052/page1.

Jenkins, Henry. 2003b. *Rethinking Media Change: The Aesthetics of Transition*. Cambridge, MA: MIT Press.

Jenkins, Henry. 2005. "Games, the New Lively Art." In *Handbook of Computer Game Studies*, Joost Raessens and Jeffrey Goldstein (eds), 175–192. Cambridge, MA: MIT Press.

Jenkins, Henry. 2006. *Convergence Culture: Where Old and New Media Collide*. New York: NYU Press.

Jenkins, Henry. 2007. "Transmedia Storytelling 101." Accessed July 14, 2011. http://www.henryjenkins.org/2007/03/.

Jiménez-Crespo, Miguel Ángel. 2009. "The Effect of Translation Memory Tools in Translated Web Texts: Evidence From a Comparative Product-Based Study." In *Linguistica Antverpiensia New Series* 8/2009, Walter Daelemans and Veronique Hoste (eds), 213–232.

Jiménez Hurtado, Catalina. 2007. *Traducción y accesibilidad: Subtitulación para sordos y audiodescripción para ciegos: nuevas modalidades de traducción audiovisual* [Translation and Accessibility: Subtitling for the Deaf and Hard of Hearing and Audiodescription for the Blind: New Modalities of AVT]. Frankfurt: Peter Lang.

Joseph, Eugene. 2012. "Bot Colony: A Video Game Featuring Intelligent Language-Based Interaction with the Characters." Paper given at *the first Workshop of Games and NLP (GAM-NLP-12)*, Kanazawa, Japan. Accessed October 15, 2012. http://lang.cs.tut.ac.jp/japtal2012/special_sessions/GAMNLP-12/papers/gamnlp12_submission_3.pdf.

Jones, Derek (ed.). 2001. *Censorship: A World Encyclopedia*. Chicago: Fitzroy Dearborn.

Joyce, Julian. 2007. "Halo 3 Central to Microsoft's Strategy". *BBC News*. Accessed July 15, 2011. http://news.bbc.co.uk/2/hi/business/7014292.stm.

Juul, Jesper. 2005. *Half-real: Video Games Between Real Rules and Fictional Worlds*. Cambridge, MA and London: MIT Press.

Kafai, Yasmin B., Heeter, Carrie, Denner, Jill and Jennifer Y. Sun. 2008. *Beyond Barbie & Mortal Kombat: New Perspectives on Gender and Gaming*. Cambridge, MA: MIT Press.

Kalata, Kurt. 2007. "Clash of the Cultures: The Differences between Western and Japanese Game Design Philosophies." *1Up.Com*, January 18. Accessed July 28, 2011. http://www.1up.com/do/feature?pager.offset=0&cId=3155815.

Kearns, John (ed.). 2006. *New Vistas in Translation and Interpreting Training: A Special Issue of Translation Ireland* 17 (1).

Kearns, John. 2008. "The Academic and the Vocational in Translator Education." In *Translator and Interpreter Training: Issues, Methods and Debates*, John Kearns (ed.), 184–214. London: Continuum.

Keen, Andrew. 2007. *The Cult of the Amateur*. New York: Doubleday.

Kehoe, Barry and David Hickey. 2006. "Games Localization." *Localization Focus* 5: 27–29.

Keller, Mathew. 2004. *PALGN's Guide to 60 Hz Games*. Accessed July 29, 2012. http://palgn.com.au/1060/palgns-guide-to-60-hz-games/.

Kelly, Dorothy. 2005. *A Handbook for Translator Trainers*. Manchester: St. Jerome.

Kelly, Nataly. 2009. "Freelance Translators Clash with LinkedIn over Crowdsourced Translation." Accessed November 4, 2011. http://www.commonsenseadvisory.com/Default.aspx?Contenttype=ArticleDetAD&tabID=63&Aid=591&moduleId=391.

Kenny, Dorothy. 2007. "Translation Memories and Parallel Corpora: Challenges for the Translation Trainer". In *Across Boundaries: International Perspectives on Translation*, Dorothy Kenny and Kyongjoo Ryou (eds), 192–208. Newcastle-upon-Tyne: Cambridge Scholars Publishing.

Kent, Steve L. 2001. *The Ultimate History of Video Games: From Pong to Pokémon and Beyond: The Story Behind the Craze that Touched our Lives and Changed the World*. New York: Three Rivers Press.

Kent, Steve L. 2004. "Video Games that Get Lost in Translation: Why Most U.S. Titles Don't Fare Well in Japan (and Vice Versa)." *Msnbc*, April 28. Accessed July 28, 2011. http://www.msnbc.msn.com/id/4780423.

Kerr, Aphra. 2006a. *The Business and Culture of Digital Games: Gamework and Gameplay*. London, Thousand Oaks, New Deli: Sage publications.

Kerr, Aphra. 2006b. "The Business of Making Digital Games." In *Understanding Digital Games*, Jason Rutter and Jo Bryce (eds), 36–57. London, Thousand Oaks, New Delhi: Sage Publications.

Kietzmann, Ludwig. 2010. "Final Fantasy XIII Launches on Japanese Xbox 360 to Tepid Sales." *Joystiq.com*, December 23. Accessed July 25, 2011. http://www.joystiq.com/2010/12/23/final-fantasy-xiii-launches-on-japanese-xbox-360-to-tepid-sales.

kilgray.com. 2012. Accessed December 1, 2012. http://kilgray.com/webinars/introducing-memoq-gamesloc-1700-cest-1800-gmt.

Kim, Jun H., David V. Gunn, Eric Schuh, Bruce Phillips, Randy J. Pagulayan and Dennis Wixon. 2008. "Tracking Real-time User Experience (TRUE): A Comprehensive Instrumentation Solution for Complex Systems." In *Proceedings SIGCHI*, 443–452. Toronto: ACM Publishers.

Kiraly, Don. 2000. *A Social Constructivist Approach to Translator Education. Empowerment from Theory to Practice*. Manchester: St. Jerome.

Kohler, Chris. 2005. *Power-up: How Japanese Video Games Gave the World an Extra Life*. Indianapolis: Brady Games.

Kohler, Chris. 2010. "In Japan, Gamemakers Struggle to Instill Taste for Western Shooters", *Wired*. Accessed December 1, 2012. http://www.wired.com/gamelife/2010/09/western-games-japan.

Kohler, Chris. 2012. "World of Warcraft Has Lost Its Cool." *Wired*. Accessed September 24, 2012. http://www.wired.com/gamelife/2012/09/mists-of-pandaria/.

Kohlmeier, Bernhard. 2000. "Microsoft Encarta Goes Multilingual." In *Translating Into Success: Cutting-edge Strategies for Going Multilingual in a Global Age*, Robert C. Sprung (ed.), 1–12. Amsterdam and Philadelphia: John Benjamins.

Kosaka, Takashi and Masaki Itagaki. 2003. "Building a Curriculum for Japanese Localization Translators: Revisiting Translation Issues in the Era of New Technologies." In *Beyond the Ivory Tower: Rethinking Translation Pedagogy*, Brian J. Baer and Geoffrey S. Koby (eds), 229–249. American Translators Association Scholarly Monograph Series, XII. Amsterdam and Philadelphia: John Benjamins.

Kovačič, Irena. 1995. "Reception of Subtitles: The Non-existent Ideal Viewer." *Translatio* (Nouvelles de la FIT/FIT Newsletter) 14 (3–4): 376–383. Audiovisual Communication and Language Transfer, International Forum, Strasbourg. 22–24 June, 1995.

Kroes, Neelie. 2008. "Commission Decision of 11 December 2007 on State Aid C 47/06 (ex N 648/05) Tax Credit Introduced by France for the Creation of Video Games." *Official Journal of the European Union*, 6.5.2008: 16–29. Accessed July 30, 2011. http://developerfront. com/wp-content/uploads/2010/03/LexUriServ.pdf/.

Künzli, Alexander and Maureen Ehrensberger-Dow. 2011. "Innovative subtitling: A reception study." In *Methods and Strategies of Process Research*, Cecilia Alvstad, Adelina Hild and Elisabet Tiselius (eds), 187–200. Amsterdam and Philadelphia: John Benjamins Publishing Company.

Kussmaul, Paul. 1995. *Training the Translator*. Amsterdam: John Benjamins.

Lagoudaki, Elina. 2008. *Expanding the Possibilities of Translation Memory Systems: From the Translator's Wishlist to the Developer's Design*. PhD Thesis. Imperial College London.

Lal, P. 1996. *Transcreations: Seven Essays on the Art of Transcreation*. Calcutta: Workers' Workshop.

Langdell, Tim. 2006. "Beware of the Localization." In *Game Writing: Narrative Skills For Videogames*, Chris Bateman (ed.), 201–208. Boston, MA: Charles River Media.

Leary, Liesl. n.d. *Fundamentals of Multilingual Game Design*. Accessed November 25, 2011. http://www.slideshare.net/Enlaso/games-l10n.

Lefevere, André. 1992. *Translation, Rewriting and the Manipulation of Literary Frame*. London and New York: Routledge.

Leonard, Sean. 2005. "Progress Against the Law: Anime and Fandom, with the Key to the Globalization of Culture". *International Journal of Cultural Studies* 8 (3): 281–305.

Leppihalme, Ritva. 1997. *Culture Bumps: An Empirical Approach to the Translation of Allusions*. Clevedon: Multilingual Matters.

Levi, Antonia. 2006. "Americanization of Anime and Manga: Negotiating Popular Culture." In *Cinema Anime*, Steven T. Brown (ed.), 43–63. New York: Palgrave MacMillan.

Lewinski, John Scott. 2010. "The Mass Effect 2: The Future of Gaming." Accessed February 19, 2012. http://www.popsci.com/entertainment-amp-gaming/gallery/2010-01/gallery-mass-effect-2.

Lin, Ying-Chia H. 2006. *Culture, Technology, Market and Transnational Circulation of Cultural Products: The Glocalization of EA Digital Games in Chinese Taiwan*. PhD Thesis, University of Washington.

Lommel, Arle. 2006. "Localization Standards, Knowledge- and Information-Centric Business Models, and Commoditization of Linguistic Information." In *Perspectives in Localization*, Keiran Dunne (ed.), 223–240. Amsterdam and Philadelphia: John Benjamins.

Los Angeles Times (20 January 2012). "Star Wars: The Old Republic – The Story Behind a Galactic Gamble." Accessed February 17, 2010. http://herocomplex.latimes.com/2012/01/20/star-wars-the-old-republic-the-story-behind-a-galactic-gamble/#/0.

Loureiro, Maria. 2007. "Un paseo por la localización" [A Tour of Localization]. *Revista Tradumàtica* 5: "La localització de videojocs" [Game Localization]. Accessed December 10, 2011. http://www.fti.uab.es/tradumatica/revista/num5/articles/03/03art.htm.

Lovell, Nicholas. 2009. "Ghostbusters: Different Age Ratings for Different Platforms." *GAMESbrief: The Business of Games*. Accessed August, 1, 2011. http://www.gamesbrief. com/2009/03/ghostbusters-different-age-ratings-for-different-platforms/.

Lundin, Therese. 2009. *Game Localization and the Game: How Localising Accents and Dialects Affects the Game Experience* (Unpublished BA thesis). Dublin City University, Ireland.

Lundin, Therese. 2012. Personal communication, January 27.

MacDonald, Kenza. 2012. *Xenoblade Chronicles Review*. Accessed December 5, 2012. http:// www.ign.com/articles/2012/04/03/xenoblade-chronicles-review?page=2.

Malmkjær, Kirsten, (ed.). 1998. *Translation and Language Teaching. Language Teaching and Translation*. Manchester: St. Jerome.

Malmkjær, Kirsten (ed.). 2004. *Translation in Undergraduate Degree Programmes*. Amsterdam and Philadelphia: John Benjamins.

Mandiberg, Stephen. 2009. "Localization (is) Not Translation: Language in Gaming." Paper presented at the 8th Digital Arts and Culture Conference After Media: Embodiment and Context. University of California, Irvine. 12–15 December, 2009. Accessed November 15, 2010. http://escholarship.org/uc/item/6jq2f8kw;jsessionid=9F954A203A3FAF9 DC0D00A047E9A7A1F.

Mandiberg, Stephen. 2012. "Money isn't Everything: On the Problems of Transcreating Video Games". A paper presented at the International Conference on Video Game and Virtual Worlds Translation and Accessibility Fun for All: II. 22–23 March, 2012. TransMedia Catalonia Group at the Universitat Autònoma de Barcelona.

Mandryk, Regan L. 2008. "Physiological Measures for Game Evaluation." In *Game Usability: Advice from the Experts for Advancing the Player Experience*, Katherine Isbister and Noah Schaffer (eds), 207–235. New York: Morgan Kaufman.

Mangiron, Carmen. 2004. "Localizing Final Fantasy: Bringing Fantasy to Reality." *LISA Newsletter* 13, 1.3. Accessed July 11, 2011. http://www.lisa.org/globalizationinsider/2004/03/ bringing_fantas.html.

Mangiron, Carmen. 2006. "Video Game Localization: Posing New Challenges to the Translator." *Perspectives* 14 (4): 306–317.

Mangiron, Carmen (ed.). 2007. *Tradumàtica 05: Localització de videojocs*. Accessed July 10, 2011. http://www.fti.uab.es/tradumatica/revista/num5/sumari.htm.

Mangiron, Carmen. 2008. "Cultural Localization in Games." Paper given at the Languages and the Media conference, Intercontinental Hotel, Berlin, October 31.

Mangiron, Carmen. 2010. "The Importance of *Not* Being Earnest: Translating Humour in Video Games." In *Translation, Humour and the Media*, Delia Chiaro (ed.), 89–107. London: Continuum.

Mangiron, Carmen. 2011a. "Accesibilidad a los videojuegos: estado actual y perspectivas futuras" [Video Game Accessibility: Current Situation and Future Perspectives]. *Trans: Revista de Traductología* 15: 53–67. Accessed December 2, 2011. http://www.trans.uma. es/pdf/Trans_15/53-67.pdf.

Mangiron, Carmen. 2011b. "La localización de videojuegos japoneses: Traducir para divertir" [The Localization of Japanese Games: Translating for Entertaining]. In *Japón y la Península Ibérica: cinco siglos de encuentros [Japan and the Iberian Peninsula: Five Centuries of Contact]*, Fernando Cid Lucas (ed.), 311–330. Oviedo: Satori.

Mangiron, Carmen. 2012. "Exploring New Paths towards Game Accessibility." In *Audiovisual Translation and Media Accessibility at the Crossroads: Media for All 3*, Aline Remael, Pilar Orero and Mary Carroll (eds), 43–59. Amsterdam and New York: Rodopi.

Mangiron, Carmen. 2013. "Subtitling in Game Localization: A Descriptive Study". *Perspectives: Studies in Translatology* 21 (1): 42–56.

Mangiron, Carmen and Minako O'Hagan. 2006. "Game Localization: Unleashing Imagination with 'Restricted' Translation." *Jostrans: The Journal of Specialised Translation* 6: 10–21. Accessed February 11, 2011. http://www.jostrans.org/issue06/art_ohagan.php.

Manovich, Lev. 2001. *The Language of New Media*. Cambridge, MA: MIT Press.

Maragos, Nich. 2005. "Dragon Quest VIII Review." *1up*, November 14. Accessed June 15, 2011. http://www.1up.com/do/reviewPage?cId=3145697&p=2.

Marazzato, Romina L. 2005. "Globalising Localization Training: Academic Curricular Review." *Localization Focus* 4 (3): 22–24.

Mata, Manuel. 2004. "Optimum-Cost-Ware in Translator Training for the Localization Market." *Localization Focus* 3, (4).

Matamala, Anna and Pilar Orero (eds). 2010. *Listening to Subtitles: Subtitles for the Deaf and Hard of Hearing*. Frankfurt am Main: Peter Lang.

Mäyrä, Frans. 2006. "Welcome to Mapping the Global Game Cultures: Issues For a Socio-Cultural Study of Games and Players." Accessed July 19, 2011. http://www.uta.fi/~tlilma/mapping_global_game_cultures.pdf/.

Mazur, Iwona. 2007. "The Metalanguage of Localization: Theory and Practice." *Target* 19 (2): 337–357.

McAllister, Ken S. 2004. *Game Work: Language, Power and Computer Game Culture*. Tuscaloosa: The University of Alabama Press.

McCarthy, David, Stephen Curran, and Simon Byron. 2005. *The Complete Guide to Game Development, Art, and Design*. Lewes, East Sussex: ILEX Press Ltd.

McDonough Dolmaya, Julie. 2011. "The Ethics of Crowdsourcing." *Linguistica Antverpiensia* 10: 97–110.

McDougall, Julian and Wayne O'Brien. 2008. *Studying Videogames*. Leighton Buzzard: Auteur.

McLuhan, Marshall. 1967. *The Medium is the Message*. London: Penguin Books.

Melby, Alan. 1995. *The Possibility of Language: A Discussion of the Nature of Language, with Implications for Human and Machine Translation*. Amsterdam: John Benjamins.

Melnick, Lloyd and Dimitri Kirin. 2008. "Localization: A Key Element in Successful Casual Games." *Casual Connect Magazine*, Winter 2008. Accessed July 15, 2011. http://www.casualconnect.org/content/Amsterdam/MelnickWinter08.html.

Merino, Raquel and Rosa Rabadán. 2002. "Censored Translations in Franco's Spain: The TRACE Project – Theatre and Fiction (English-Spanish)." *TTR : Traduction, terminologie, rédaction* 15 (2): 125–152.

Merten, Pascaline, Yamile Ramirez, and Alina Secara. 2009. "eCoLoMedia Helping You Respond to Multimedia Training." Proceedings of the 3rd International Conference *Media for all: Quality Made to Measure*, Antwerp, Belgium, 137.

Miller, Joe. 2007. "Wii Speeds Up the Rehab Process." *USA Today*, July 24. Accessed July 31, 2011. http://www.usatoday.com/tech/gaming/2007-07-24-wii-therapy_N.htm.

Milton, John. 2009. "Translation Studies and Adaptation Studies." In *Translation Research Projects 2*, Anthony Pym and Alexander Perekrestenko (eds), 51–58. Tarragona: Intercultural Studies Group.

Milton, John and Paul Bandia. 2008. "Introduction: Agents of Translation and Translation Studies." In *Agents of Translation,* John Milton and Paul Bandia (eds), 1–18. Amsterdam and Philadelphia: John Benjamins.

Miyabe, Miyuki. 2004. *ICO – 霧の城 [Ico: The Castle in the Mist]*. Tokyo: Kodansha.

Morris, Sue. 2003. "Wads, Bots and Mods: Multiplayer FPS Games as Co-creative Media." In *Level Up: Digital Games Research Conference Proceedings,* Marinka Copier and Joost Raessens (eds), 338–349. University of Utrecht. CD-Rom.

Mosco, Vincent. 1996. *The Political Economy of Communication. Rethinking and Renewal*. London: Sage.

Munday, Jeremy. 2001. *Introducing Translation Studies: Theories and Applications*. London and New York: Routledge.

Munday, Jeremy. 2008. *Introducing Translation Studies: Theories and Applications* (2nd ed.). London and New York: Routledge.

Munday, Jeremy (ed.). 2009. *The Routledge Companion to Translation Studies*. London and New York: Routledge.

Munday, Jeremy. 2012. *Introducing Translation Studies: Theories and Applications* (3rd ed.). London and New York: Routledge.

Muñoz-Sánchez, Pablo. 2007. "Romhacking: localización de videojuegos clásicos en un contexto de aficionados" [Romhacking: the Localization of Classic Video Games in an Amateur Context]. *Tradumàtica 05: Localització de videojocs* [Game Localization]. Accessed August 10, 2011. http://www.fti.uab.es/tradumatica/revista/num5/sumari.htm.

Muñoz-Sánchez, Pablo. 2008. "En torno a la localización de videojuegos clásicos mediante técnicas de romhacking: particularidades, calidad y aspectos legales" [The Localization of Classic Video Games by Means of Romhacking: Characteristics, Quality and Legal Issues]. *Jostrans: The Journal of Specialised Translation* 9: 80–95. Accessed July 11, 2011 http://www.jostrans.org/issue09/art_munoz_sanchez.php.

Muñoz-Sánchez, Pablo. 2009. "Video Game Localization for Fans by Fans: The Case of Rom Hacking." *The Journal of Internationalization and Localization* 1 (1): 168–185. Accessed December 10, 2011. http://www.lessius.eu/jial.

Muzii, Luigi. 2005. "Gruppo L10N's Experience of Teaching Localization in Italy." *Localization Focus* 4 (3): 10–11.

Nacke, Lennart, Mike Ambinder, Alexander Cannosa, Regan Mandryk and Tadeusz Stach. 2009. "Game Metrics and Biometrics: The Future of Player Experience Research." Panel at Future Play, Canadian Game Developers Conference, Algoma University, Vancouver.

Nacke, Lennart and Anders Drachen. 2011. "Towards a Framework of Player Experience Research." In *Proceedings of the 2011 Foundations of Digital Games Conference*, Bordeaux, France. EPEX 11 Workshop. Toronto: ACM Publishers. Accessed July 10, 2012. http://andersdrachen.files.wordpress.com/2011/01/submission16_camready.pdf.

Nae. 2009. "El videojuego ya es cultura en España" [Video Games are now Culture in Spain]. *Anait*, March 26. Accessed July 31, 2011. http://www.anaitgames.com/noticias/videojuego-cultura-en-espana.

Neves, Josélia. 2005. *Audiovisual Translation: Subtitling for the Deaf and the Hard-of-Hearing*. PhD dissertation, Roehampton University.

Nevile, Liddy. 2005. "Adaptability and Accessibility: A New Framework." In *Proceedings of OZCHI 2005*, 1–10. CD-Rom.

Newman, James. 2004. *Videogames*. London and New York: Routledge.

Newman, James. 2008. *Playing Videogames*. London and New York: Routledge.

Newman, James and Barney Oram. 2006. *Teaching Videogames*. London: British Film Institute.

Newman, Rich. 2009. *Cinematic Game Secrets for Creative Directors and Producers*. Burlington: MA: Elsevier.

Ng, Benjamin Wai-ming. 2006. "Street Fighter and The King of Fighters in Hong Kong: A Study of Cultural Consumption and Localization of Japanese Games in an Asian Context." *Game Studies* 6 (1). Accessed August 31, 2009. http://gamestudies.org/0601/articles/ng.

Ng, Benjamin Wai-ming. 2008. "Video Games in Asia." In *The Video Games Explosion: A History from Pong to PlayStation* and Beyond*, Mark J. P. Wolf (ed.), 211–222. Westport, Connecticut and London: Greenwood Press.

Ní Chuilleanáin, Eiléan, Cormac Ó Cuilleanáin, and David Parris (eds). 2009. *Translation and Censorship: Patterns of communication and inference*. Dublin: Four Courts.

Nida, Eugene and Charles R. Taber. 1969. *The Theory and Practice of Translation*. Leiden: E. J. Brill.

Nielsen. 2009. *The State of the Video Gamer: PC Game and Video Game Console Usage. Fourth Quarter 2008*. Accessed July 11, 2011. http://blog.nielsen.com/nielsenwire/wp-content/uploads/2009/04/stateofvgamer_040609_fnl1.pdf.

Nintendo's Censorship. (n.d.). Accessed August 1, 2011. http://www.filibustercartoons.com/Nintendo.php.

Nintendo President Interview Series. 2013. Accessed June 23, 2013. http://www.nintendo.co.jp/wii/interview/sl2j/vol1/index3.html.

Nord, Christiane. 1997. *Translation as a Purposeful Activity: Functionalist Approaches Explained*. Manchester: St. Jerome.

Nord, Christiane. 2005. *Text Analysis in Translation: Theory, Methodology, and Didactic Application of a Model for Translation-Oriented Text Analysis* (2nd ed.). Amsterdam and New York: Rodopi.

Nornes, Abé M. 2007. *Cinema Babel: Translating Global Cinema*. Minneapolis and London: University of Minnesota Press.

Nutt, Christian. 2008. "Interview: Nintendo, Advance Wars, & The Art Of Localization." *Gamasutra*, January 23. Accessed August 1, 2011. http://www.gamasutra.com/php-bin/news_index.php?story=17079#.UHGuLk3Ad_U.

Nutt, Christian. 2010. "Opinion: Love, It's Working – Meaning and Action in Games." *Gamasutra*, August 27. Accessed August 1, 2011. http://www.gamasutra.com/view/news/30120/Opinion_Love_Its_Working_Meaning_And_Action_In_Games.php.

O'Hagan, Minako. 2005. "Multidimensional Translation: A Game Plan for Audiovisual Translation in the Age of GILT." In *Proceedings of EU High Level Scientific Conferences: Multidimensional Translation (MuTra) 2006*. Accessed May 15, 2010. http://www.euroconferences.info/proceedings/2005_Proceedings/2005_O'Hagan_Minako.pdf.

O'Hagan, Minako. 2006a. "Training for Localization (Replies to a Questionnaire)." In *Translation Technology and Its Teaching (With Much Mention of Localization)*, Anthony Pym, Alexander Perekrestenko and Bram Starink (eds), 39–43. Tarragona: Intercultural Studies Group.

O'Hagan, Minako. 2006b. "Manga, Anime and Video Games: Globalizing Japanese Cultural Production." *Perspectives* 14 (4): 242–247.

O'Hagan, Minako. 2007. "In Pursuit of Japanese Cool: Globalizing Anime, Manga and Videogames." In *Proceedings of the EU High Level Scientific Conference Series MuTra 2007: LSP Translation Scenarios*. Vienna: University of Vienna.

O'Hagan, Minako. 2008. "Fan Translation Networks: An Accidental Translator Training Environment?" In *Translator and Interpreter Training: Issues, Methods and Debates*, John Kearns (ed.), 158–183. London: Continuum.

O'Hagan, Minako. 2009a. "Towards a Cross-cultural Game Design: An Explorative Study in Understanding the Player Experience of a Localized Japanese Video Game." *Jostrans: The Journal of Specialised Translation* 11: 211–233. Accessed August 3, 2011. http://www.jostrans.org/issue11/art_ohagan.pdf.

O'Hagan, Minako. 2009b. "Evolution of User-generated Translation: Fansubs, Translation Hacking and Crowdsourcing." *The Journal of Internationalization and Localization* 1 (1): 94–121. Accessed July 31, 2011. http://www.lessius.eu/jial.

O'Hagan, Minako. 2009c. "Putting Pleasure First: Localizing Japanese Video Games." *TTR – Traduction, Terminologie, Rédaction: Special issue: La Traduction au Japon / Translation in Japan* 22 (1): 147–165.

O'Hagan, Minako. 2010. "Engineering Emotion? Translators' New Role in Serving the Digital Entertainment Industry." Invited keynote presented at the *International Conference on Translation and Accessibility in Video Games and Virtual Worlds*, Universitat Autònoma de Barcelona, Barcelona, Spain.

O'Hagan, Minako. 2011a. 日本のテレビゲームの創造翻訳 [Transcreation of Japanese Video Games]. In トランスレーション・スタディーズ [Translation Studies], Nana Sato-Rossberg (ed.), 179–197. Tokyo: Misuzu.

O'Hagan, Minako. 2011b. "Community Translation: Translation as a Social Activity and Its Possible Consequences in the Advent of Web 2.0 and Beyond." *Linguistica Antverpiensia* 10: 11–23.

O'Hagan, Minako. 2012a. "Transcreating Japanese Video Games: Exploring a Future Direction for Translation Studies in Japan." *Translation Studies in Japanese Contexts*, Nana Sato-Rossberg and Judy Wakabayashi (eds), 183–201. London: Continuum.

O'Hagan, Minako. 2012b. "The Impact of New Technologies on Translation Studies: A Technological Turn?" In *Routledge Handbook of Translation Studies*, Carmen Millán-Varela and Francesca Bartrina (eds), 503–518. London and New York: Routledge.

O'Hagan, Minako. 2012c. "Entertainment and Translation in the Digital Era". *Translation Spaces* 1: 123–141.

O'Hagan, Minako and David Ashworth. 2002. *Translation Mediated Communication in a Digital World: Facing the challenges of globalization and localization*. Clevedon, UK: Multilingual Matters.

O'Hagan, Minako and Carmen Mangiron. 2004. "Games Localization: When 'Arigato Gets Lost in Translation." In *Proceedings of New Zealand Game Developers Conference Fuse 2004*, 57–62. Dunedin: University of Otago.

Onyett, Charles. 2005. "E3 2005: Interview with Yuji Horii." *IGN* May 19. Accessed December 6, 2011. http://ie.ps2.ign.com/articles/617/617479p1.html.

Orero, Joseph O., Florent Levillain, Marc Damez-Fontainea, Maria Rifqia and Bernadette Bouchon-Meuniera. 2010. "Assessing Gameplay Emotions From Physiological Signals: A Fuzzy Decision Trees Based Model." In *Proceedings of the International Conference Kansei Engineering and Emotion Research (KEER) 2010*, 1684–1693.

Orero, Pilar. 2004. "Audiovisual Translation: A New Dynamic Umbrella." In *Topics in Audiovisual Translation*, Pilar Orero (ed.), vii–xiii. Amsterdam and Philadelphia: John Benjamins.

Ortiz-Sotomayor, Jesús M. 2007. "Multiple Dimensions of International Advertising: An Analysis of the Praxis in Global Marketing Industry From a Translation Studies Perspective." In *Proceedings of the EU-High-Level Scientific Conference Series MuTra 2007: LSP Translation Scenarios*. Vienna: University of Vienna.

Paciello, Michael G. 2000. *Web Accessibility for People with Disabilities*. Kansas: CMP Books.

Parish, Jeremy. 2007. "GDC 2007: The Square-Enix Approach to Localization: How Final Fantasy Went From Spoony to Sublime." *1Up.com*, March 11. Accessed July 31, 2011. http://www.1up.com/do/newsStory?cId=3157937.

Parish, Jeremy. 2012. "Square Enix Localization Looks to the Future." *1Up.com*, June 3. Accessed July 31, 2012. http://www.1up.com/news/square-enix-localization-future.

Parker, Seb. 2011. "Modern Warfare 3 Day One Sales." *VGChartz*, November 9. Accessed December 3, 2012. http://www.vgchartz.com/article/88431/modern-warfare-3-day-one-sales/.

Parkin, Simon. 2008. "You Say Tomato: A Pro on Fan-translating Nintendo's Mother 3. *Gamasutra*, December 26. Accessed April 3, 2011. http://www.gamasutra.com/view/feature/3891/you_say_tomato_a_pro_on_.php.

Pérez-González, Luis. 2006. "Fansubbing Anime: Insights Into the Butterfly Effect of Globalisation on Audiovisual Translation." *Perspectives: Studies in Translatology* 14 (4): 260–277.

Pérez-González, Luis. 2009. "Audiovisual Translation." In *Routledge Encyclopedia of Translation Studies* (2nd revised ed.), Mona Baker and Gabriela Saldanha (eds), 13–20. London: Routledge.

Pérez-González, Luis and Şebnem Susam-Saraeva. 2012. "Non-professionals Translating and Interpreting: Participatory and Engaged Perspectives." *The Translator* 18 (2): 149–165.

Perrino, Saverio. 2009. "User-generated Translation: The Future of Translation in a Web 2.0 Environment." *Jostrans: The Journal of Specialised Translation* 12: 55–78. Accessed August 6, 2011. http://www.jostrans.org/issue12/art_perrino.php.

Pesquet, Claude Henri. 1993. "Foreword." *Digital Technical Journal* 5 (3): 6–7. Accessed July 28, 2011. http://www.1000bit.it/ad/bro/digital/djt/dtj_v05-03_1993.pdf.

Picard, Martin. 2009. "Haunting Backgrounds: Transnationality and Intermediality in Japanese Survival Horror Video Games." *Horror Video Games: Essays on the Fusion of Fear and Play*, Bernard Perron and Clive Baker (eds), 95–120. Jefferson: McFarland & Company.

Plunkett, Luke. 2007a. "*No More Heroes* Violence Toned Down For Japanese Market." *Kotaku*, September 22. Accessed July 14, 2011. http://kotaku.com/gaming/tgs07/no-more-heroes-violence-toned-down-for-japanese-market-302724.php.

Plunkett, Luke. 2007b. "*No More Heroes Censored For Europe*". *Kotaku*. December 10. Accessed November 11, 2012. http://kotaku.com/331787/no-more-heroes-censored-for-europe.

Plunkett, Luke. 2010. "A Ratings System just for Islam." Kotaku, November 20. Accessed July 1, 2011. http://kotaku.com/5702099/a-ratings-system-just-for-islam.

Poole, Steven. 2000. *Trigger Happy: The Inner Life of Video Games*. London: Fourth Estate.

Prakash, Navneet. 2008. "Fallout 3: Not coming to India". *Techtree*. Accessed March 24, 2013. http://www.techtree.com/India/News/Fallout_3_Not_Coming_to_India/551-94432-585.html.

Pruett, Chris. 2005. "The Role of Culture In Video Game Characters." *Interface: The Journal of Education, Communities and Values* 5 (1). Accessed July 14, 2011. http://bcis.pacificu.edu/journal/2005/01/pruett.php.

Pym, Anthony. 1999. "Localization in Translator Training Curricula." *Linguistica Antverpiensa* 33: 127–137. http://www.fut.es/~apym/on-line/localization.html.

Pym, Anthony. 2002. "Localization and the Dehumanization of Discourse". Accessed November 2, 2012. http://usuaris.tinet.cat/apym/on-line/translation/localization.html.

Pym, Anthony. 2003. "Redefining Translation Competence in an Electronic Age: In Defence of a Minimalist Approach." *Meta* 48 (4): 481–497. Accessed July 11, 2011. http://www.erudit.org/revue/meta/2003/v48/n4/008533ar.html.

Pym, Anthony. 2004. *The Moving Text: Localization, Translation, and Distribution*. Amsterdam and Philadelphia: John Benjamins.

Pym, Anthony. 2005. "Explaining Explicitation". In *New Trends in Translation Studies. In Honour of Kinga Klaudy*, Krisztina Károly and Ágota Fóris (eds), 29–34. Budapest: Akadémia Kiadó.

Pym, Anthony. 2006. "Asymmetries in the Teaching of Translation Technology." In *Translation Technology and Its Teaching (With Much Mention of Localization)*, Anthony Pym, Alexander Perekrestenko and Bram Starink (eds), 113–124. Tarragona: Intercultural Studies Group, Universitat Rovira i Virgili.

Pym, Anthony. 2009. "Translator Training." Pre-print text written for the *Oxford Companion to Translation Studies*. Accessed May 11, 2010. http://www.tinet.cat/~apym/on-line/training/2009_translator_training.pdf.

Pym, Anthony. 2010. *Exploring Translation Theories*. London and New York: Routledge.

Raessens, Joost and Jeffrey Goldstein (eds). 2005. *Handbook of Computer Game Studies*. Cambridge, MA: MIT Press.

Ranyard, Dave and Vanessa Wood. 2009. Interview with Miguel Bernal-Merino. *Jostrans: The Journal of Specialised Translation* 11. Accessed July 27, 2011. http://www.jostrans.org/issue11/int_sony_ent.php.

Ray, Rebecca. 2009. *Crowdsourcing: The Crowd Wants to Help You Reach New Markets*. Romainmôtier: Localization Industry Standards Association (LISA).

Rehak, Bob. 2008. "Genre Profile: First-Person Shooting Games." In *The Video Games Explosion: A History from Pong to PlayStation® and Beyond*, Mark J. P. Wolf (ed.), 187–193. Westport, Connecticut and London: Greenwood Press.

Reinecke, Leonard. 2009. "Games and Recovery: The Use of Video and Computer Games to Recuperate From Stress and Strain." *Journal of Media Psychology: Theories, Methods, and Applications* 21 (3): 126–142.

Reineke, Detlef (ed.). 2005. *Traducción y localización. Mercado, gestión y tecnologías* [Translation and Localization: Market, Management and Technologies]. Las Palmas: Anroart Ediciones.

Reiss, Katharina. 1971/2000. *Translation Criticism: The Potentials & Limitations: Categories and Criteria for Translation Quality Assessment*. Manchester: St. Jerome.

Relentless Software. 2009. "*Buzz! Brain of...*" Accessed July 17, 2011. http://www.relentless.co.U.K./news/?id=68.

Remael, Aline. 2010. "Audiovisual Translation." In *Handbook of Translation Studied*, Yves Gambier and Luc van Doorslaer (eds), 13–17. Amsterdam and Philadelphia. John Benjamins.

Richards, Jonathan. 2007. "Nintendo Withdraws Game that Taunts 'Spastics'." *The Times*. July 17, 2007. Accessed December 16, 2011. http://www.thetimes.co.uk/tto/technology/article1861508.ece.

Robinson, Douglas. 2003. *Becoming a Translator*. London and New York: Routledge.

Robinson, Eleanor and Stephanie M. Walker. 2010. *Gaming on a Collision Course: Averting Significant Revenue Loss by Making Games Accessible to Older Americans*. Accessed December 10, 2011. http://ablegamers.org/publications/Gaming_on_a_Collision_Course-AGF-7128.pdf.

Rundle, Christopher. 2000. "The Censorship of Translation in Fascist Italy." *The Translator* 6 (1): 67–86. Manchester: St. Jerome.

Rutter, Jason and Jo Bryce. 2006. *Understanding Digital Games*. London, Thousand Oaks, New Delhi: Sage Publications.

Salen, Katie and Eric Zimmerman. 2004. *Rules of Play: Game Design Fundamentals*. Cambridge, MA and London: MIT Press.

Saltsman, Adam. 2010. "Analysis: Game Design Accessibility Matters." *Gamasutra*, January 6. Accessed August 4, 2011. http://www.gamasutra.com/view/news/26386/Analysis_Game_Design_Accessibility_Matters.php.

Sato-Rossberg, Nana (ed.). 2011. トランスレーション・スタディーズ [Translation Studies]. Tokyo: Misuzu Shobo.

Sato-Rossberg, Nana and Judy Wakabayashi (eds). 2012. *Translation Studies in Japanese Contexts*. London: Continuum.

Savidis, Anthony and Dimitris Grammenos. 2006. "Unified Design of Universally Accessible Games (Say What?)". *Gamasutra*. Accessed November 9, 2012. http://www.gamasutra.com/features/20061207/grammenos_01.shtml.

Schäffner, Christina. 2001. *Annotated Texts for Translation: English-German: Functionalist Approaches Illustrated*. Clevedon: Multilingual Matters.

Schäffner, Christina. 2010. "Norms of Translation." In *Handbook of Translation Studied*, Yves Gambier and Luc van Doorslaer (eds), 235–244. Amsterdam and Philadelphia. John Benjamins.

Schäffner, Christina and Beverly Adab (eds). 2000. *Developing Translation Competence*. Amsterdam and Philadelphia: John Benjamins.

Schäler, Reinhard. 2009. "Localization." In *Routledge Encyclopedia of Translation Studies* (2nd revised ed.), Mona Baker and Gabriela Saldanha (eds), 157–161. London and New York: Routledge.

Schäler, Reinhard. 2010. "Localization and Translation." In *Handbook of Translation Studies*, Yves Gambier and Luc van Doorslaer (eds), 209–214. Amsterdam and Philadelphia: John Benjamins.

Schliem, Aaron. 2012. "GDC 2012 [March 5–9] Increases Localization Focus", *Multilingual* 23 (4): 8–9.

Schodt, Frederik. 1996. *Manga! Manga! The World of Japanese Comics*. Tokyo: Kodansha International.

Scholand, Michael. 2002. "Localización de videojuegos" [Game Localization]. *Revista Tradumàtica 1*. Accessed December 5, 2011. http://www.fti.uab.es/tradumatica/revista/articles/mscholand/mscholand.PDF.

Schön, Donald. 1987. *Educating the Reflective Practitioner*. San Francisco: Jossey-Bass.

Schules, Doublas. 2012. "When Language Goes Bad: Localization's Effect on the Gameplay of Japanese RPGs." In *Dungeons, Dragons, and Digital Denizens: Digital Role-Playing game*, Gerald A. Voorhees, Joshua Call and Katie Whitlock (eds), 88–112. New York and London: Continuum.

Sheff, David. 1993. *Game Over: Nintendo's Battle to Dominate an Industry*. London: Hodder & Stoughton.

Sheffield, Brandon. 2011. "Gamelab 2011: Molyneux Addresses Concerns About Fable: The Journey." *Gamasutra*, June 30. Accessed August 22, 2011. http://gamasutra.com/view/news/35552/Gamelab_2011_Molyneux_Addresses_Concerns_About_Fable_The_Journey.php.

Shintaku, Junjiro. and Fusahiko Ikuine. 2001.アメリカにおける家庭用ゲームソフトの市場と企業戦略—現状報告と日米比較 [US Console Game Markets and Corporate Strategies: Current Situation and US-Japan Comparisons]. *ITME Discussion Paper* 47. University of Tokyo.

Shuttleworth, Mark and Moira Cowie (eds). 1997. *Dictionary of Translation Studies*. Manchester: St. Jerome.

Simeoni, Daniel. 1998. "The Pivotal Status of the Translator's Habitus." *Target* 10 (1): 1–39.

Simon, Sherry. 1996. *Gender in Translation: Cultural Identity and the Politics of Transmission*. London and New York: Routledge.

Sinclair, Brendan. 2008. "Sony Buzz-ed with Trademark Suit." *Gamespot*, January 28. Accessed August 1, 2011. http://www.gamespot.com/news/6185211.html.

Sioli, Fulvio, Fabio Minazzi and Andrea Ballista. 2007. "Audio Localization for Language Service Providers." *Multilingual Localization: Getting Started Guide*, October–November 2007, 18–23. Accessed December 8, 2011. http://www.multilingual.com/downloads/screen-Supp91.pdf.

Smith, O. Alexander. 2001. "The Last Word." すばる [*Subaru*] 12: 36–37.

Smith, O. Alexander. 2009. E-mail message to O'Hagan, February 17.

Smith, O. Alexander. 2011. *Ico-Castle in the Mist*. Trans. San Francisco: Viz Media.

Smuts, Aaron. 2005. "Are Video Games Art?" *Contemporary Aesthetics* 3. Accessed August 1, 2011. http://www.contempaesthetics.org/newvolume/pages/article.php?articleID=299.

Snell-Hornby, Mary. 1990. "Linguistic Transcoding or Cultural Transfer? A Critique of Translation Theory in Germany." In *Translation, History and Culture*, Susan Bassnett and André Lefevere (eds), 79–86. London and New York: Pinter Publishers.

Snow, Jean. 2008. "Fallout 3 Pulls Nuke References for Japan." *Wired*, November 11. Accessed July 14 2011. http://www.wired.com/gamelife/2008/11/japanese-fallou.

Sony Computer Entertainment. 2002. *ICO Official Guidebook*. Tokyo: Softbank.

Square Enix. 2004. *Final Fantasy X-2 International+Last Mission Ultimania*. Tokyo: Square Enix.

Square Enix Responds To Modern Warfare 2 English Voice Acting Criticism. 2009. Accessed August 23, 2012. http://www.siliconera.com/2009/12/04/square-enix-responds-to-modern-warfare-2-english-voice-acting-criticism/.

Steinkuehler, Constance A. 2006. "Why Game (Culture) Studies Now?" *Games and Culture* 1: 97–102.

Stejskal, Jiri. 2009. Letter to Jeff Weiner, dated 30 June 2009. Accessed February 15, 2011. http://www.atanet.org/pressroom/linkedIn_2009.pdf.

Stephanidis, Constantine, Gavriel Salvendy, Demosthenes Akoumianakis, Nigel Bevan, Judy Brewer, Pier Luigi Emiliani, Anthony Galetsas, Seppo Haataja, Ilias Iakovidis, Julie A. Jacko, Phil Jenkins, Arthur I. Karshmer, Peter Korn, Aaron Marcus, Harry J. Murphy, Christian Stary, Gregg Vanderheiden, Gerhard Weber and Juergen Ziegler. 1998. "Toward an Information Society for All: An International R&D Agenda." *International Journal of Human-Computer Interaction* 10 (2): 107–134. Accessed March 7, 2011. http://www.ics.forth.gr/proj/at-hci/files/white_paper_1998.pdf.

Steussy, Edwin. 2010a. "GDC Localization 2010: Bioware Presentation at GDC." Accessed December 3, 2011. http://www.apogeecommunications.com/blog/2010/03/15/gdc-localization-2010-bioware-presentation.

Steussy, Edwin. 2010b. "Market for Games Localization in China and the Rest of the World. Presentation at the LISA Localization Forum in Suzou." Accessed December 4, 2011. http://www.apogeecommunications.com/blog/2010/07/09/successful-presentations-at-lisa-suzhou/.

Stevens Heath, Nora. 2010. "Text-Based Adventure: The Art of Translating Video Games." *The ATA Chronicle*, August 2010, 16–19.

Takahashi, Dean. 2011. "Even with Half the Users, Zynga's FarmVille Made More Money than Ever Before in Q1". *Venture Beat*, July 5. Accessed July 11, 2011. http://venturebeat.com/2011/07/05/even-with-half-the-users-zyngas-farmville-made-more-money-than-ever-before-in-q1.

Tang, Li. 2009. "Preparing your Product for the Chinese Market." *Multilingual* 102: 32–35.

Tapscott, Don and Anthony Williams. 2006. *Wikinomics: How Mass Collaboration Changes Everything*. New York: Portfolio.

TAUS (Translation Automation User Society). 2009. *Increasing Leveraging From Shared Industry Data*. Translation Automation User Society. Accessed December 1, 2012. http://www.translationautomation.com/articles/increasing-leveraging-from-shared-industry-data.

Tennent, Martha (ed.). 2005. *Training for the New Millennium: Pedagogies for Translation and Interpreting*. Amsterdam and Philadelphia: John Benjamins.

Thatcher, Jim, Michael R. Burks, Christian Heilmann, Shawn Lawton Henry, Andrew Kirkpatrick, Patrick H. Lauke, Bruce Lawson, Bob Regan, Richard Rutter, Mark Urban and Cynthia Waddell. 2006. *Web Accessibility: Web Standards and Regulatory Compliance*. New York: Apress.

Thayer, Aexander and Beth E. Kolko. 2004. "Localization of Digital Games: The Process of Blending for the Global Games Market." *Technical Communication* 51 (4): 477–488.

Thelen, Marcel, Han van de Staaij and Anne Klarenbeek. 2006. "Localization in the Netherlands: Training and Career Opportunities." *Localization Focus* 5 (3): 15–18.

Thomson-Wohlgemuth, Gaby. 2007. "On the Other Side of the Wall: Book Production, Censorship and Translation in East Germany." In *Modes of Censorship and Translation: National Contexts and Diverse Media*, Francesca Billiani (ed.), 93–116. Manchester: St. Jerome.

TIGA. 2011. *Investing in the Future: A Tax Relief for the UK Video Games Developing Sector*. Accessed July 17, 2011. http://www.tiga.org/Documents/TIGA_TaxRelief_Summary.pdf.

Timiani Grant, Flavia. 2001. "A Leisure Industry but a Serious Business". *Language International* 13 (5): 16–19.

Tinnelly, Brendan. 2007. "Videogames and the Translator: Exploring the Impact of Ever-Advancing Technology on the Translator" (Unpublished BA thesis). Dublin City University, Ireland.

Tinnelly, Brendan. 2012. Personal communication, February 15.

Totilo, Stephen. 2008. "'Mirror's Edge' Producer Found Sexed-Up Fan Version of Heroine Depressing." Accessed September 23, 2008. http://multiplayerblog.mtv.com/2008/11/25/mirrors-edge-producer-depressed-by-sexy-fan-verision-of-faith/.

Toury, Gideon. 1995. *Descriptive Translation Studies and Beyond*. Amsterdam and Philadelphia: John Benjamins.

Trainor, Helen. 2003. "Games Localization: Production and Testing." *Multilingual* 14 (5): 17–20.

Translating EverQuest II. 2006. 翻訳事典 *2007* [Dictionary of Translation 2007], 36–37. Tokyo: Alc.

Tymoczko, Maria. 2006. "Reconceptualizing Western Translation Theory." In *Translating Others*, Theo Hermans (ed.), 1: 13–22. Manchester: St. Jerome.

Tymoczko, Maria. 2009. "Censorship and Self-Censorship in Translation: Ethics and Ideology, Resistance and Collusion". In *Translation and Censorship: Patterns of Communication and Interference*, Eiléan Ní Chuilleanáin, Cormac Ó Cuilleanain and David Parris (eds), 24–45. Dublin: Four Courts Press.

Tymoczko, Maria. 2012. "The Neuroscience of Translation." *Target* 24 (1): 83–102.

UA-Games. 2007. "What are UA Games?" Accessed November 2, 2012. http://www.ics.forth.gr/hci/ua-games/.

Uemura, Masayuki. 2012. Personal communication, January 19.

UNESCO Institute for Statistics. 2005. *International Flows of Selected Cultural Goods and Services, 1994–2003: Defining and Capturing the Flows of Global Cultural Trade.* Montreal: UNESCO Institute for Statistics. Accessed July 23, 2011. http://unesdoc.unesco.org/images/0014/001428/142812e.pdf.

Vallance, Chris. 2009. "AI Aims to Solve In-game Chatter." BBC Radio 4 Interview. Accessed July 23, 2011. http://news.bbc.co.uk/2/hi/technology/8426523.stm.

Vandaele, Jeroen. 2007. "Take Three: The National-Catholic Versions of Billy Wilder's Broadway Adaptations". In *Modes of Censorship and Translation: National Contexts and Diverse Media*, Francesca Billiani (ed.), 279–310. Manchester: St. Jerome.

Vandepitte, Sonia. 2008. "Remapping Translation Studies: Towards a Translation Studies Ontology." *Meta* 53 (3): 569–588.

Van Genabith, Josef. 2009. "Next Generation Localization." *The International Journal of Localization* 8 (1): 4–10. Accessed July 14, 2011. http://www.localization.ie/resources/locfocus/LF_Vol_8_Issue_1.pdf.

Van Tol, Richard. 2006. "The Sound Alternative". *Game Accessibility*. Accessed December 10, 2011. http://www.accessibility.nl/games/index.php?pagefile=soundalternative.

Vela Valido, Jennifer. 2011. "La formación académica de los traductores de videojuegos en España: retos y propuestas para docentes e investigadores" [Video game translators academic training in Spain: Challenges and proposals for lecturers and researchers]. *Trans: Revista de Traductología*, 15: 89–102. Accessed December 9, 2011. http://www.trans.uma.es/pdf/Trans_15/89-102.pdf.

Venuti, Lawrence. 1995. *The Translator's Invisibility: A History of Translation.* London and New York: Routledge.

Vermeer, Hans. 1989/2000. "Skopos and Commission in Translational Action." In *Translation Studies Reader*, Laurence Venuti (ed.), 221–232. London and New York: Routledge.

Vieira, Elise Ribeiro Pires. 1999. "Liberating Calibans: Readings of Antropofagia and Haroldo de Campos' Poetics of Transcreation." In *Postcolonial Translation: Theory and Practice*, Susan Bassnett and Harish Trivedi (eds), 95–113. London and New York: Routledge.

Vinay, Jean Paul and Jean Darbelnet. 1958/1995. *Comparative Stylistics of French and English: A Methodology for Translation*, transl. by Juan C. Sager and Marie-Josée Hamel. Amsterdam and Philadelphia: John Benjamins.

Wallop, Harry. 2009. "Video Games Bigger than Film". *The Telegraph*, December 26. Accessed July 31, 2011. http://www.telegraph.co.uk/technology/video-games/6852383/Video-games-bigger-than-film.html.

Warren, Ben. 2012. "Tips on Audio Localization: Synthetic vs. Real Voices". *Multilingual* 23 (4): 28–31.

Watanabe, Kazuya. 2010. "Establishment of the Age-based Rating System for Household Games in Japan". In *2010 CESA Games White Papers*, 1–15. Tokyo: CESA.

Watssman, Jeremy. 2012. "Ludonarrative Theory: An Introduction." Accessed October 30, 2012. http://forums.penny-arcade.com/discussion/167680/essay-ludonarrative-dissonance-explained-and-expanded.

Way, Andy. 2009. "A Critique of Statistical Machine Translation." *Linguistica Antverpiensia* 8: 17–42.

Weik, Martin. 2000. *Computer Science and Communications Dictionary*. Vol. I. Norwell: Kluwer Academic Publishers.

Westin, Thomas. 2004. "Game Accessibility Case Study: Terraformers – A Real-time 3D Graphic Game." In *Proceedings of the 5th International Conference of Disability, Virtual Reality & Associated Technology*, 95–100. Oxford.

Wilcox, Bruce. 2011. "Beyond Façade: Pattern Matching for Natural Language Applications." *Gamasutra*, March 15. Accessed August 2, 2011. http://www.gamasutra.com/view/feature/6305/beyond_fa%C3%A7ade_pattern_matching_.php.

Williams, Dmitri. 2002. "Structure and Competition in the US Home Video Market Industry." *The International Journal on Media Management* 4 (1): 41–54.

Williams, Jenny. 2013. *Theories of Translation*. London: Palgrave MacMillan.

Wilson, O. Edward. 1998. *Consilience: The Unity of Knowledge*. New York: Alfred A Knopf.

Winterhalter, Ryan. 2011. "Why Japanese Games are Breaking Up With the West." *1Up.com*. Accessed December 2, 2012. http://www.1up.com/features/japanese-games-breaking-west.

Wolf, Mark J. P. and Bernard Perron (eds). 2003. *The Video Game Theory Reader*. New York: Routledge.

Wolf, Mark J. P. (ed.). 2008. *The Video Games Explosion: A History from Pong to PlayStation® and Beyond*. Westport, Connecticut and London: Greenwood Press.

Wood, Vanessa, Sophie Krauss and Fabio Ravetto. 2010. "Behind the Curtains of *Buzz*." Presentation given at the Localization Summit at the International Game Developers Conference 2010, San Francisco, March, 10, 2010.

The World Bank. 2009. "How Many Disabled People are There World-Wide?" *Disability and Development*. Accessed December 10, 2011. http://web.worldbank.org/WBSITE/EXTERNAL/TOPICS/EXTSOCIALPROTECTION/EXTDISABILITY/0,,contentMDK:21150847~menuPK:420476~pagePK:210058~piPK:210062~theSitePK:282699,00.html#HowMany.

Xloc.com. n.d. Accessed December 5, 2011. http://www.xloc.com.

Yahiro, Shigeki. 2005. テレビゲーム解説論序説：アセンブラージ [Towards a General Theory of Video Games: Assemblage]. Tokyo: Gendaishokan.

Yoshida, Takeshi. 2008. シネマゲーム完全読本: ゲームになった映画たち [Comprehensive guide to movie licensed games: Movies that became games]. Tokyo: Sansai Books.

Yuan, Bei, Eelke Folmer and Frederick Jr. Harris. 2010. "Game Accessibility: A Survey." *Universal Access in the Information Society* 10: 1–10. Accessed July 26, 2011. http://www.cse.unr.edu/~fredh/papers/journal/29-gaas/paper.pdf.

Yunker, John. 2003. *Beyond Borders: Web Globalization Strategies*. Indianapolis, IN: New Riders.

Zabalbeascoa, Patrick. 2008. "The Nature of the Audiovisual Text and its Parameters." In *The Didactics of Audiovisual Translation*, Jorge Diaz Cintas (ed.), 21–38. Amsterdam and Philadelphia: John Benjamins.

Zanettin, Federico. 2009. "Comics." In *Routledge Encyclopedia of Translation Studies* (2nd revised ed.), Mona Baker and Gabriela Saldanha (eds), 37–40. London and New York: Routledge.

Zatlin, Phyllis. 2005. *Theatrical Translation and Film Adaptation: A Practitioner's View*. Clevedon: Multilingual Matters.

Zervaki, Thei. 2002. *Globalize, Localize, Translate: Tips and Resources for Success*. Bloomington, IN: 1st Books Library.

Zhang, Xiaochun. 2008. "'Harmonious' Games Localization for China." *Multilingual* 19 (7): 47–50.

Zhang, Xiaochun. 2009. "China Localizes Online Games for Global Players." *Multilingual* 20 (7): 40–45.

Zhang, Xiaochun. 2010. "Challenges of Internet Slang in Game Localization in China." *Multilingual* 21 (7): 40–44.

Zhang, Xiaochun. 2011. "Games in China: Virtual Assets and Localization". *Multilingual* 22 (2): 35–39.

Zhou, Ping. 2011. "Managing the Challenges of Game Localization." In *Translation and Localization Project Management: The Art of the Possible*, Keiran Dunne and Elina Dunne (eds), 349–378. Amsterdam and Philadelphia: John Benjamins.

Gameography

Game title (publisher, year of first release)

221B (SoupDog 2009)
688(I) Hunter/Killer (Electronic Arts 1997)
Access Invaders (UA-Games 2005)
Advance Wars: Days of Ruin (Nintendo 2008)
Adventure (Atari 1976)
America's Army (US Army 2002)
Age of Empires (Microsoft Game Studio 1997)
Angry Birds (Rovio Mobile 2009)
Animal Crossing (Nintendo 2001)
Animal Crossing E- Plus (Nintendo 2003)
Animal Crossing: New Leaf (Nintendo 2012)
Assassin's Creed III (Ubisoft 2012)
Asteroids (Atari 1979)
AudiOdissey (Gambit 2007)
Baldur's Gate (Interplay 1998)
Batman: Arkham City (Warner Bros. Interactive Entertainment 2011)
Batman Begins (Electronic Arts, Warner Bros. Interactive Entertainment 2005)
Bot Colony (North Side Inc. forthcoming)
Bouncer (Square 2000)
Brain Training series (Nintendo 2005–)
Buzz! series (Sony Computer Entertainment 2005–)
Buzz!: The Music Quiz (Sony Computer Entertainment Europe 2005)
Buzz!: Brain of the U.K. (Sony Computer Entertainment 2009)
Call of Duty 4: Modern Warfare (Activision 2007)
Call of Duty: Modern Warfare 2 (Activision, Square Enix (Japan) 2009)
Call of Duty: Black Ops (Activision, Square Enix (Japan) 2010)
Call of Duty: Modern Warfare 3 (Activision, Square Enix (Japan) 2011)
Call of Duty: Black Ops II (Activision, Square Enix (Japan) 2012)
Catherine (Atlus 2011)
Child of Eden (Ubisoft 2011)
Chocobo Racing (Square 1999)
Chrono Trigger (Square 1995)
Civilization (2K Games 1991)
Codename: Kids Next Door – Operation: V.I.D.E.O.G.A.M.E. (Global Star Software 2005)
Command and Conquer (Electronic Arts 1996)
Computer Space (1971)
Conflict Zone (Ubisoft 2001)

Counter-Strike (Valve [mod version] 1999/ [retail version] 2000)
Crackdown (Microsoft Game Studio 2007)
Crash Bandicoot series (Sony Computer Entertainment 1996–)
Dance Dance Revolution (Konami 1998)
Dead Rising (Capcom Production Studio 1 – Capcom 2006)
Donkey Kong (Nintendo 1981)
Doom (Activision 1993)
Doom 3 (id Software – Activision 2004)
Dragon Age: Origins (Bioware – Electronic Arts 2009)
Dragon Quest VIII (Square Enix 2004)
Dragon Quest IX: Sentinels of the Starry Skies (Square Enix 2009)
Dragon Quest Monsters: Terry's Wonderland 3D (Square Enix 2012)
Ducktales (Capcom 1990)
Earthbound (Nintendo 1994)
Enter the Matrix (Atari 2003)
Escape from Woomera (Escape from Woomera Project Team 2004)
Ether Saga Online (Perfect World Entertainment 2008)
EverQuest (Sony Online Entertainment 1999)
EverQuest II (Sony Online Entertainment 2004–)
Everybody's Golf (Clap Hanz – SCE 2000)
Fable (Lionhead Studios/Microsoft Studios 2004)
Fable II (Lionhead Studios/Microsoft Developer Studios 2008)
Façade (Procedural Arts LLC 2005)
Facebreaker (EA Sports 2008)
Fallout 3 (Bethesda Softworks 2008)
FarmVille (Zynga 2009)
Far Cry 3 (Ubisoft 2012)
FIFA series (Electronic Arts 1993–)
FIFA Soccer 13 (Electronic Arts 2012)
Final Fantasy (Square 1987)
Final Fantasy VI (Square 1994)
Final Fantasy VII (Square 1997)
Final Fantasy VIII (Square 1999)
Final Fantasy IX (Square 2000)
Final Fantasy X (Square Enix 2001)
Final Fantasy XI (Square Enix 2002)
Final Fantasy X-2 (Square Enix 2003)
Final Fantasy XII (Square Enix 2006)
Final Fantasy XIII (Square Enix 2009)
Final Fantasy XIII Ultimate Hits International (Square Enix 2010)
Final Fantasy XIV (Square Enix 2010)
Final Fantasy XIII-2 (Square Enix 2011)
Food Force (United Nations World Food Programme 2005)
Football Manager (Sega 2005)
Forza Motorsports 3 (Turn 1o Studios – Microsoft Game Studios 2009)
Game Over (UA-Games 2007)

Ghostbusters (Atari 2009)

Ghost Recon 2 (Ubisoft 2004)

Gran Turismo (Sony Computer Entertainment 1998)

Grand Theft Auto series (Rockstar Games 1997–)

Grand Theft Auto III (Rockstar Games 2001)

Grand Theft Auto: Vice City (Rockstar Games 2002)

Grand Theft Auto IV (Rockstar Games 2008)

Guitar Hero series (Activision 2005–)

Habitat (Fujitsu 1985)

Half-Life (Sierra Entertainment 1998)

Half-Life 2 (Valve Corporation – Electronic Arts 2004)

Halo (Microsoft Studios 2002)

Halo 2 (Microsoft Studios 2004)

Halo 3 (Microsoft Studios 2007)

Halo 4 (Microsoft Studios 2012)

Harry Potter and the Deathly Hallows: Part 2 (Electronic Arts 2011)

Hearts of Iron (Paradox Interactive 2002)

Heavenly Sword (Ninja Theory/Sony Computer Entertainment Europe 2007)

Heavy Rain (Sony Computer Entertainment 2010)

Homefront (THQ 2011)

Ico (Sony Computer Entertainment 2001)

InFAMOUS (Sony Computer Entertainment 2009)

InFAMOUS 2 (Sony Computer Entertainment 2011)

Just Dance 4 (Ubisoft 2012)

Kakuto Chojin (Dream Publishing 2002)

Kinect Adventures! (Microsoft Studio 2010)

Kingdom Hearts (Square Enix 2002–)

L.A. Noire (Rockstar 2011)

Lineage II: The Chaotic Chronicle (NCsoft 2004)

LittleBigPlanet (Sony Computer Entertainment 2008)

Lost: Via Domus (Unisoft 2008)

Lux-Pain (Marvelous Entertainment 2008)

Madden NFL 13 (EA Sports 2012)

Mafia II (2kCzech/Massive Bear Studios – 2KGame/1C Company 2010)

Manhunt 2 (Rockstar Games 2007)

Manic Miner (Bug-Byte 1983)

Marc Eckō's Getting Up: Contents Under Pressure (Atari 2006)

Mario Bros. (Nintendo 1983)

Mario Kart Wii (Nintendo 2008)

Mario Kart 7 (Nintendo 2011)

Mario Party 8 (Nintendo 2007)

Mario Party 9 (Nintendo 2012)

Mass Effect (Electronic Arts 2007)

Mass Effect 2 (Bioware – Electronic Arts 2010)

Metal Gear series (Konami 1987–)

Metal Gear Solid (Konami 1998)

Metal Gear Solid 2: Sons of Liberty (Konami 2001)
Microsoft Flight Simulator series (Microsoft Game Studios 1982–)
Mike Tyson's Punch-Out!! (Nintendo 1987)
MindQuiz (Ubisoft 2007)
Mirror's Edge (Electronic Arts 2008)
Monster Hunter Tri (Capcom 2009–)
Mortal Kombat (Midway Games 1993)
Mother 2 (Nintendo 1994)
Mother 3 (Nintendo 2006)
My Football Game (VTree LLC and EA Sports 2009)
My Golf Game (VTree LLC and EA Sports 2010)
Myst (Brøderbund, Ubisoft 1994)
New Super Mario Bros. (Nintendo 2009)
New Super Mario Bros. 2 (Nintendo 2012)
NierReplicant (Square Enix 2010)
NierGestalt (Square Enix 2010)
Ninja Ryukenden (Tecmo 1988)
Nintendo Land (Nintendo 2012)
No More Heroes (Ubisoft 2007)
Oblivion IV: The Elder Scrolls (2K Games, Bethesda Softworks 2006)
Ōkami (Capcom 2006)
One Piece: Pirate Musou (Namco Bandai 2012)
Pac-Man (Namco 1980)
Paper Mario: The Thousand Year Door (Nintendo 2004)
Pet Society (PlayFish/Electronic Arts 2008)
Peter Jackson's King Kong (Ubisoft 2005)
Phantasy Star Online (Sega 2000)
Plants vs. Zombies (PopCap 2009–)
Pocket Monster (Nintendo 1996)
Pokémon Black / White Version 2 (Nintendo 2012)
Pong (Atari 1972)
Populous (Electronic Arts 1989)
Prince of Persia: The Sands of Time (Ubisoft 2003)
Pro Evolution Soccer series (Konami 2001–)
Punch-Out! (Nintendo 1987)
Quake (GT Interactive (PC), PXL computers (Amiga), MacSoft (Macintosh), Midway Games (N64), Sega (SS), Pulse Interactive (mobile), Macmillan Digital Publishing USA (Linux), Activision/Valve, Corporation (Steam1996))
RapeLay (Illusion Soft 2006)
Resident Evil series (Capcom 1996–)
Resident Evil 5 (Capcom 2009)
Resident Evil 6 (Capcom 2012)
Resistance: Fall of Man (Sony Computer Entertainment 2006)
Restaurant City (PlayFish/Electronic Arts 2008)
Riot Act (Microsoft Game Studio 2008)
Seaman (Sega 1999)

Secret of Evermore (Square Soft 1995)

September 12th (Newsgaming 2003)

Saints Row the third (THQ 2011)

SimCity (Brøderbund, Maxis, Nintendo, Electronic Arts, Superior Software/Acornsoft and Infogrames Entertainment, SA (first European release) 1989)

SiN Episodes: Emergence (Ritual Entertainment – Valve Corporation and EA, 2006)

SingStar series (Sony Computer Entertainment 2004–)

SingStar Rocks (Sony Computer Entertainment 2006)

Sonic the Hedgehog (Sega 1991)

Space Invaders (Taito 1978)

Spacewar! (developed and released by Steve Russell et al. 1962)

Starship Titanic (Simon and Schuster Interactive 1998)

StarTropics (Nintendo 1990)

Star Wars: Force Unleashed (Lucas Art 2008)

Star Wars: The Old Republic (Electronic Arts 2011)

Star Wars: Republic Commando (Lucas Arts (US) / Activision (EU) 2005)

Story of Thor (Sega 1994)

Street Fighter IV (Capcom 2008)

Super Castlevania 4 (Konami 1991)

Super Mario Bros. (Nintendo 1985)

Super Mario Bros. 3 (Nintendo 1988)

Super Mario 3D Land (Nintendo 2011)

Tales of Phantasia (Namco, Nintendo 1996)

Team Fortress 2 (Valve 2007)

Tennis for Two (William Higinbotham 1958)

Terraformers (Pin Interactive 2003)

Terrestrial Invaders (UA-Games 2007)

Tetris (Nintendo 1985)

The Legend of the Condor Heroes (Sony Computer Entertainment 2000)

The Legend of Zelda (Nintendo 1986–)

The Legend of Zelda: Ocarina of Time (Nintendo 1997)

The Lost Experience (ABC 2006)

The Simpsons: Hit and Run (Vivendi Universal Games 2003)

The Sims (Electronic Arts 2000)

Tokyo Xtreme Racer (Genki (Japan), Crave Entertainment (NA/EU), Ubisoft (EU) 1999)

Tomb Raider (Eidos Interactive 1996–2009; Square Enix 2010–)

Toy Story 2 (1999 Disney Interactive studios)

UA-Chess (UA-Games 2004)

Ultima Online (Electronic Arts 1997)

Ultima Online: The Second Age (Electronic Arts 1998)

Uncharted series (Sony Computer Entertainment 2007–)

Watchmen: The End is Nigh (Warner Bros. Games 2009)

Wii Sports (Nintendo 2006)

Wolfenstein (Activision 2009)

World of Warcraft (Blizzard 2004–)

Xenoblade (Nintendo 2010)

零 *Zero* (Japan) / *Fatal Frame* (Europe and Australia) / *Project Zero* (North America) (Tecmo 2001)
Zero Wing (Sega 1991)
Zork (Infocom 1980–)
Zork: Grand Inquisitor (Activision 1997)

Postgraduate courses in game localization in Spain

In this Appendix we present a brief overview of Masters courses that include some component of game localization currently offered in Spain where we have had either direct involvement or where we were able to gather reliable information available at the time of writing. Detailed analyses of each course are beyond the scope of this book, but this overview suggests that such courses are becoming increasingly popular. We indicate the name of the providing institution and the title of the programme with information on the content and the delivery mode (online or face-to-face). The readers are advised to check the latest information as new courses are constantly being created while the existing ones listed here may be revised.

Providing institution and programme title	Overview of the programme
Universitat Autònoma de Barcelona (UAB, Spain) and the Università degli Studi di Parma (Italy) *European Masters Degree in Audiovisual Translation*	A joint online Masters degree offered by the Universitat Autònoma de Barcelona (UAB, Spain) and the Università degli Studi di Parma (Italy). Each university offers the same modules in their respective language (Spanish and Italian) and there are also two modules offered in English to students from both universities. Students are awarded a double degree by the UAB and the Università degli Studi di Parma. There is an elective module on game localization through Spanish only for the time being.
Universidad Alfonso X El Sabio *Experto en Tradumática, Localización y Traducción Audiovisual [Postgraduate Course in Translation Technologies, Localization and Audiovisual Translation]*	A face-to-face course including a module on localization that incorporates a 20-hour course on game localization.
Universitat Autònoma de Barcelona *Masters in Audiovisual Translation*	A face-to-face Masters programme with a compulsory module on video game localization, the first to be offered in Spain since the academic year 2003–2004.
Universitat Autònoma de Barcelona *Online Masters in Audiovisual Translation*	See entry under European Masters Degree in Audiovisual Translation.

Providing institution and programme title	Overview of the programme
Universitat Autònoma de Barcelona *Tradumática* [*Masters in Translation Technology*]	A face-to-face module on Web, multimedia and game localization.
Universidad de las Palmas de Gran Canarias *Masters in Audiovisual Translation, Subtitling for Deaf and Hard of Hearing and Audiodescription*	A face-to-face Masters programme with a module dedicated to game localization.
Universidad Europea de Madrid *Masters in Dubbing, Translation and Subtitling*	A face-to-face course offering a module on audiovisual translation including a course in game localization.
Universidad Europea de Madrid *Masters in Video Game Design*	A face-to-face course in game design, including a module on game localization, focusing on the technical aspects of localization engineering.
Universitat Jaume I *Masters in Translation Technologies and Localization*	A face-to-face course, including a module on video game localization.
Universitat de València, Universitat d'Alacant i Universitat Jaume I *Masters in Creative and Humanistic Translation*	A face-to-face course, including an elective module on video game and comic translation. Interestingly, game translation is paired with comic translation, with which it shares some features, such as the use of humour. Emphasis is placed on the creative nature of this type of translation.
Universitat de Vic *Online Masters in Specialised Translation*	A module on audiovisual and multimedia translation, made of four units, one of them on video game localization.
Universidad Internacional Menéndez Pelayo *Masters in Translation and New Technologies: Software and Multimedia Localisation*	A module on software and game localization.

Index